Business BASICS

A study guide for degree students

HUMAN RESOURCE MANAGEMENT

BPP PUBLISHING

First edition May 1995

Second edition June 1997

ISBN 0 7517 2122 0 (previous edition 0 7517 2076 3)

British Library Cataloguing-in-Publication Data

A catalogue record for this book
is available from the British Library

Published by
BPP Publishing Limited
Aldine House, Aldine Place
London W12 8AW

Printed and bound by Progressive Printing (U.K.) Limited, Leigh-on-Sea, Essex.

This book was written for BPP by Claire Wright.

All our rights reserved. No part of this publication may be reproduced, stored in a retrieval system or transmitted, in any form or by any means, electronic, mechanical, photocopying, recording or otherwise, without the prior permission of BPP Publishing Limited.

Our thanks are due to:

Mark Holloway for assistance in developing the open learning aspects of the text.

Genesys Editorial for additional editorial and production work.

We are grateful to the Institute of Chartered Secretaries and Administrators for permission to reproduce past examination questions, the answers to which have been prepared by BPP Publishing Ltd

©

BPP Publishing Limited

1997

	Page
Preface	(v)
How to use this Study Guide	(vi)

1 Human resource management — 1
Personnel Management or Human Resource Management?
Who is the 'client' of HRM?
HRM within the organisation structure
HRM in the European Union

2 Human resource planning and flexibility — 18
The need for human resource planning
The process of human resource planning
Labour turnover
Management succession and promotion
Labour flexibility

3 Recruitment — 44
The external labour market
A systematic approach to recruitment
Job analysis and description
Personnel specification
Job advertisement
The evaluation of recruitment procedures

4 Selection — 63
The selection process
Interviews
Selection testing
The offer and contract of employment

5 Discrimination and equal opportunity — 82
Discrimination at work
The legislative framework
The practical implications
Sexual harassment

6 Training and development — 96
The role of training in the organisation
Training needs and objectives
Learning theory
Training methods and media
Validation and evaluation of training schemes
Management development

7 Performance appraisal — 121
The purposes of performance appraisal
Appraisal procedures
Problems with appraisal
Performance management and other trends
The identification of potential

8 Motivation and rewards — 140
Motivation and performance
Need theories
Two-factor theory
Expectancy theory
Non-monetary rewards
Pay as a motivator

9 Pay and benefits — 159
Job evaluation
Other factors in setting remuneration levels
Payment systems
Incentive schemes
Benefits
Payroll

10 Welfare, health and safety — 188
Welfare
Health and safety
Accidents
Occupational health
Counselling
Time off work

11 Industrial relations — 214
The parties in industrial relations
The ideological framework: conflict and co-operation
The power of the unions
Collective bargaining and negotiation
Participation and consultation
HRM as a change agent

12 Discipline and grievance handling — 237
Discipline
Grievance procedures

13 Termination of employment — 246
Retirement and resignation
Dismissal
Redundancy

14 Personnel records — 258
Information requirements
Design of the information system
Computers in HRM
Confidentiality

Glossary — 273

Multiple choice questions — 279

Exam style questions — 303

Answers to multiple choice questions — 307

Answers to exam style questions — 309

Index — 329

Order form — 337

Review form — 339

PREFACE

BUSINESS BASICS are targeted specifically at the needs of:

- students taking business studies degrees;
- students taking business-related modules of other degrees;
- students on courses at a comparable level;
- others requiring business information at this level.

This *Human Resource Management* text has been written with two key goals in mind.

- To present a substantial and useful body of knowledge on human resource management at degree level. This is not just a set of revision notes - it explains the subject in detail and does not assume prior knowledge.
- To make learning and revision as easy as possible. Each chapter:
    - starts with an introductory signpost and clear objectives;
    - contains numerous activities;
    - includes a chapter roundup summarising the points made; and
    - ends with a quick quiz

  and at the back of the book you will find
    - multiple choice questions. and solutions
    - exam style questions and solutions
    - a glossary and index

The philosophy of the series is thus to combine techniques which actively promote learning with a no-nonsense, systematic approach to the necessary factual content of the course.

BPP Publishing have for many years been the leading providers of targeted texts for professional qualifications. We know that our customers need to study effectively in order to pass their exams, and that they cannot afford to waste time. They expect clear, concise and highly-focused study material. As university and college education becomes more market driven, students rightly demand the same high standards of efficiency in their learning material. The BUSINESS BASICS series meets those demands.

BPP Publishing

June 1997

Titles in this series

Accounting

Quantitative Methods

Law

Information Technology

Economics

Marketing

Organisational Behaviour

Human Resource Management

You may order other titles in the series using the form at the end of this text. If you would like to send in your comments on this book, please turn to the review form following the order form.

HOW TO USE THIS STUDY GUIDE

This book can simply be read straight through from beginning to end, but you will get far more out of it if you keep a pen and paper to hand. The most effective form of learning is active learning, and we have therefore filled the text with activities for you to try as you go along. We have also provided objectives, a chapter roundup and a quick quiz for each chapter. Here is a suggested approach to enable you to get the most out of this book.

(a) Select a chapter to study, and read the introduction and objectives at the start of the chapter.

(b) Next read the chapter roundup at the end of the chapter (before the quick quiz and the solutions to activities). Do not expect this brief summary to mean too much at this stage, but see whether you can relate some of the points made in it to some of the objectives.

(c) Next read the chapter itself. Do attempt each activity as you come to it. You will derive the greatest benefit from the activities if you write down your solutions before checking them against the solutions at the end of the chapter.

(d) As you read, make use of the 'notes' column to add your own comments, references to other material and so on. Do try to formulate your own views. In business, many things are matters of interpretation and there is often scope for alternative views. The more you engage in a dialogue with the book, the more you will get out of your study.

(e) When you reach the end of the chapter, read the chapter roundup again. Then go back to the objectives at the start of the chapter, and ask yourself whether you have achieved them.

(f) Finally, consolidate your knowledge by writing down your answers to the quick quiz. You can check your answers by going back to the text. The very act of going back and searching the text for relevant details will further improve your grasp of the subject.

(g) You can then try the multiple choice questions at the end of the book, and the exam style questions, to which you are referred at the end of the chapter. Alternatively, you could wait to do these until you have started your revision - it's up to you.

Further reading

While we are confident that the BUSINESS BASICS books offer excellent range and depth of subject coverage, we are aware that you will be encouraged to follow up particular points in books other than your main textbook, in order to get alternative points of view and more detail on key topics. We recommend the following books as a starting point for your further reading on Human Resource Management.

This bibliography includes the most important references (some other references are given in the body of the text) and a variety of suggestions for further reading both on human resource management generally and on specific topics.

In addition to the books listed below it is recommended that students regularly read a quality newspaper (for example the *Financial Times* carries a column on human resource issues on Wednesdays), and the magazine of the Institute of Personnel and Development, *People Management*, published every fortnight.

NOTES

Anderson, A H, *Effective Personnel Management: A Skills and Activity-Based Approach*, 1994, Blackwell

Armstrong, M, *Employee Reward,* 1996, IPD (London)

Armstrong, M, *Performance Management*, 1994, Kogan Page

Beardwell, I and Holden, L, *Human Resource Management A Contemporary Perspective* (2nd ed), 1997, Pitman (London)

Beaumont, P B, *Human Resource Management: Key Concepts and Skills*, 1993, Sage Publications

Bennett, R, *Dictionary of Personnel and Human Resources Management*, 1992, Pitman

Bowers, J, *Bowers on Employment Law,* 4th edn, 1995, Blackstone Press

Buchanan, D and Huczynski, A, *Organizational Behaviour,* 2nd edn, 1991, Prentice Hall

Clutterbuck, D, *The Power of Empowerment,* 1994, Kogan Page

Cole, G A, *Personnel Management: Theory and Practice*, 4th edn, 1997, Letts Educational

Connock, S, HR Vision: *Managing A Quality Workforce*, 1991, IPM

Drucker, P, *The Practice of Management*, 1954, Harper and Row (and many other books by this author)

Gennard, J and Judge, G, *Employee Relations,* 1997, IPD (London)

Handy, Charles, *The Empty Raincoat*, 1994, Century Hutchinson

Handy, Charles, *Understanding Organizations*, 1993, Penguin

Harrison, R, *Employee Development,* 1997, IPD (London)

Hendry, C, *Human Resource Management: A Strategic Approach to Employment,* 1995, Butterworth Heinneman (Oxford)

Hyman, J and Mason B, *Managing Employee Involvement and Participation*, 1995, Sage (London)

Marchington, M and Wilkinson, A, *Core Personnel and Development*, 1995, IPD (London)

Oram, M and Johns T, *Employee Resourcing*, 1997, IPD (London)

Storey, J (ed), *Human Resource Management: A Critical Text*, 1995, Routledge (London)

NOTES

Chapter 1

HUMAN RESOURCE MANAGEMENT

Introduction

In this chapter we introduce the 'personnel' function of organisations. Organisations are made up of people and at the very least it is commonly recognised that someone in every organisation will need to be responsible for the many matters which arise in connection with the recruitment, selection, training, motivation and payment of staff, and compliance with the various laws relating to employment.

However, as the pace of social and technological change has quickened, there has been a growing recognition that people are an essential resource of any organisation, and that thought must be given to this resource at an earlier stage and a higher level of organisational planning, than has so far been the case. This has encouraged the long-term, proactive approach to people management known as 'Human Resource Management (HRM)'.

In this chapter we also explore the nature of the HR manager's effective authority in the organisation. Many managers in 'line' departments like Sales and Production regard personnel managers as pure administrators, rule-makers or 'fire-fighters' when labour turnover, shortages or unrest become a problem. HRM can seem pseudo-scientific or simply 'airy fairy' to managers who deal in 'hard', quantifiable information and performance targets. As specialists in an area which all managers see as their job - people management - HR managers are frequently operating in others' 'territory': we will also look at the politics of organisations.

Your objectives

After completing this chapter you should:

(a) be able to outline the role and tasks of the 'personnel' function;
(b) understand the shift in approach which has led to the term 'HRM';
(c) understand the implications of the term 'HRM';
(d) understand the need for a specialised 'personnel' function;
(e) be able to distinguish between 'line' and 'staff' authority and
(f) appreciate the political constraints on the HR manager's authority.

1 PERSONNEL MANAGEMENT OR HUMAN RESOURCE MANAGEMENT?

1.1 The personnel function

The personnel function *may* consist of a specialist department or departments under the control of a personnel manager (or director, where the function is represented on the Board) - but may, in a smaller organisation, be the owner, manager, company secretary or other officers undertaking the necessary tasks.

Indeed, it has been suggested that a separate personnel function need not exist at all: *all* line managers need to achieve results through the efforts of other people, and must therefore take an interest in personnel policy and practice as the basis of both employee relations and task performance.

The leading body representing personnel managers is the Institute of Personnel and Development (IPD). The IPD has said that:

> *Personnel Management is that part of management concerned with people at work and with their relationships within an enterprise. It applies not only to industry and commerce but to all fields of employment. Personnel management aims to achieve both efficiency and justice, neither of which can be pursued effectively without the other.*
>
> *It seeks to bring together and develop into an effective organisation the men and women who make up an enterprise, enabling each to make his or her own best contribution to its success both as an individual and as a member of a working group. It seeks to provide fair terms and conditions of employment, and satisfying work for those employed ... Personnel management must also be concerned with the human and social implications of change in internal organisation and methods of working, and of economic and social changes in the community.*

Note that the emphasis is both on people/relationships/justice etc and on the development of effective organisation, and contribution to success.

1.2 Personnel management: the traditional view

Traditional views of personnel management have been essentially task-, activity- or technique-based.

Dr Dale Yoder of the Graduate School of Business, Stamford University, defines the personnel management function as follows.

Definition

(a) Setting general and specific management policy for employment relationships and establishing and maintaining a suitable organisation for leadership and co-operation.

(b) Collective bargaining (negotiations between employer and employee representatives to reach agreement on terms and conditions of work.

(c) Staffing and organisation: finding, getting and holding prescribed types and numbers of workers.

(d) Aiding and self-development of employees at all levels, providing opportunities for personal development and growth as well as requisite skills and experience.

(e) 'Incentivating': developing and maintaining *the* motivation work.

> (f) Reviewing and auditing human resource and management in the organisation.
>
> (g) Industrial relations research, carrying out studies designed to explain employment behaviour, and thereby improve human resource management.

In 1968, Crichton (Personnel Management in Context) complained that personnel management was often a matter of 'collecting together such odd jobs from management as they are prepared to give up.'

Other writers have shared this view, notably Peter Drucker, who - while recognising the importance of human resources in the organisation - saw the personnel function of the time as 'a collection of incidental techniques without much internal cohesion'. According to Drucker, the personnel manager saw his role as 'partly a file clerk's job, partly a housekeeping job, partly a social worker's job and partly 'fire fighting' to head off union trouble or to settle it.'
(The Practice of Management, 1955).

Activity 1

For each of Drucker's categories (listed below) give three examples of commonly perceived 'Personnel' tasks.

(a) File clerk;

(b) Housekeeping;

(c) Social work;

(d) 'Fire-fighting.'

Note that 'housekeeping' is not just to do with the organisation's premises, but 'maintenance' tasks in general.

A more imaginative set of job titles for personnel managers - albeit just as depressing, insofar as they reflect a purely administrative and reactive role for Personnel - was suggested by Nick Georgiades (*Personnel Management*, February 1990).

Definition

> (a) 'The administrative handmaiden' - writing job descriptions, visiting the sick, and so on.
>
> (b) 'The policeman' - ensuring that both management and staff obey the rules and do not abuse the job evaluation scheme, and keeping a watchful eye on absenteeism, sickness and punctuality.
>
> (c) 'The toilet flusher' - administering 'downsizing' policies (cutting staff numbers).
>
> (d) 'The sanitary engineer' - ensuring that there is an awareness of the unsanitary psychological conditions under which many people work.

The status and contribution of the personnel function is still often limited by the image of 'fire-fighting', an essentially reactive and defensive role. The personnel manager is judged according to his effectiveness in avoiding or settling industrial disputes, preventing accidents and ill-health (and their associated costs), filling vacancies and so on.

'People may be regarded as a vital resource - at least plenty of lip service is paid to this concept by company chairmen in their annual statements - but many managers find it difficult to appreciate where the personnel department fits in, except in the simplest terms as a procurement and fire-fighting function.'
Armstrong, *A Handbook of Personnel Management Practice*

This is a vicious circle. As long as personnel policy and practice is divorced from the strategy of the business, and fails to be proactive and constructive, it will be perceived by line management to have little to do with the 'real' world of business management, or the 'bottom line' (profitability): personnel specialists therefore command scant respect as business managers, and their activities continue to be limited to areas of little strategic impact.

The situation has, however, been changing, and a new approach emerged in the 1980s which has been labelled *Human Resource Management*.

'The real requirement is proactive and constructive rather than defensive and reactive. To discharge their true role, personnel managers must anticipate the needs of the organisation in the short and the long term. They must develop the policies to produce solutions to anticipated problems resulting from the external and internal environment, whilst influencing and creating the attitudes amongst employees needed for the enterprise's survival and success.'
Livy, *Corporate Personnel Management*

1.3 Human Resource Management (HRM)

A precise and positive interpretation of HRM centres on the following notions.

(a) Personnel management has been changing in various ways in recent years. Many of its activities have become more complex and sophisticated and, particularly with the accelerating pace of change in the business environment, less narrowly concerned with areas previously thought of as personnel's sole preserve (hiring and firing, training, industrial relations and human resource planning). HRM implies a shift of emphasis in personnel management from the peripheral 'staff' role of the past to mainstream business management. Michael Armstrong has suggested that 'twenty years ago people in equivalent positions would have been more likely to talk about [personnel activities] as if these were techniques or areas of knowledge which had intrinsic value and did not need to be considered in terms of fit with business strategies or impact on business results.' The personnel function has become centrally concerned with *issues of broader relevance to the business and its objectives*, such as:

(i) change management;
(ii) the development of organisation 'culture' or 'identity' to support employee motivation and foster commitment to core values such as quality or innovation; or
(iii) the implications of falling birthrates, ageing workforces and skill shortages for the resourcing of the business.

Activity 2

List five 'changes' in an organisation or its environment that would have an impact on its employees or potential labour source.

(b) Personnel management can and should be integrated with the *strategic planning* of the business, that is, with management at the broadest and highest level. The objectives of the personnel function can and should be directly related to achieving the organisation's goals for growth, competitive gain and

Chapter 1: Human resource management

improvement of 'bottom line' performance. *All* business planning should recognise that the ultimate source of 'value' is people, and should appreciate the human resource implications and potential constraints associated with any long-term strategies evolved.

(c) Personnel managers can and should be businessmen or women - even *entrepreneurs*.

Definition

> Entrepreneurship is the 'shifting of economic resources out of the area of lower and into an area of higher productivity and greater yield' (JB Say).
>
> Say's description is essentially what HRM embodies, in terms of finding, obtaining and developing - getting the best out of - the human resources of the business.

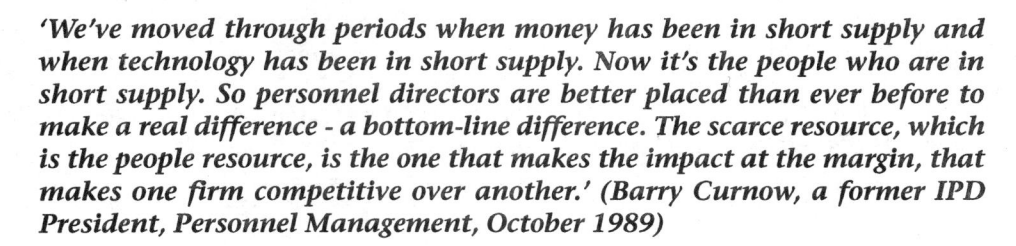

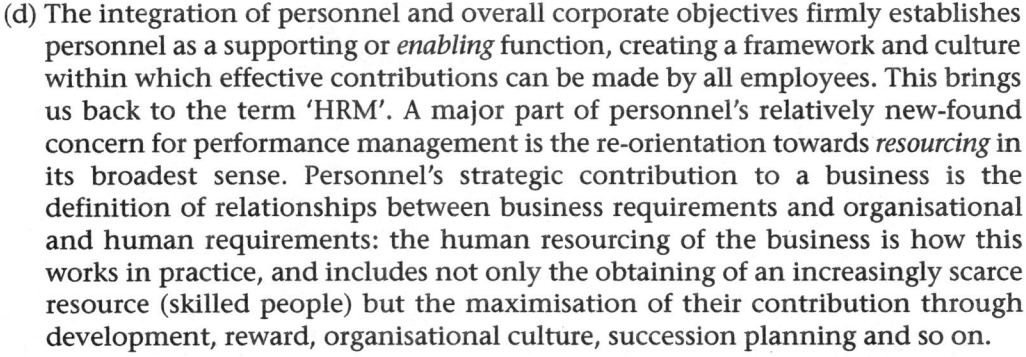

'We've moved through periods when money has been in short supply and when technology has been in short supply. Now it's the people who are in short supply. So personnel directors are better placed than ever before to make a real difference - a bottom-line difference. The scarce resource, which is the people resource, is the one that makes the impact at the margin, that makes one firm competitive over another.' (Barry Curnow, a former IPD President, Personnel Management, October 1989)

(d) The integration of personnel and overall corporate objectives firmly establishes personnel as a supporting or *enabling* function, creating a framework and culture within which effective contributions can be made by all employees. This brings us back to the term 'HRM'. A major part of personnel's relatively new-found concern for performance management is the re-orientation towards *resourcing* in its broadest sense. Personnel's strategic contribution to a business is the definition of relationships between business requirements and organisational and human requirements: the human resourcing of the business is how this works in practice, and includes not only the obtaining of an increasingly scarce resource (skilled people) but the maximisation of their contribution through development, reward, organisational culture, succession planning and so on.

S Tyson and A Fell (*Evaluating the Personnel Function*) suggest four major *roles* for personnel/human resource management which illustrate the shift in emphasis from the 'odd job' to the 'strategic' viewpoint.

(a) To represent the organisation's central value system (or 'culture').

(b) To maintain the boundaries of the organisation (its identity and the flow of people 'in' and 'out' of it).

(c) To provide stability and continuity (through planned succession, flexibility and so on).

(d) To adapt the organisation to change.

Don Beattie, personnel director of STC, has defined the job of personnel directors as follows.

'To know what business they are in, to know where it is going, and to ensure that the input to get there is available from a human resourcing and organisational capability point of view.'

In June 1993 *Personnel Management* magazine (subtitled 'The magazine for human resource professionals') published an article entitled 'The mystery of the missing human resource manager', reporting on a survey whose results suggested, among other things, that:

(a) only 17% of establishments in the UK employing more than 25 people have a personnel specialist;

(b) only 44 out of the 2,061 respondents used the 'HRM' title;

(c) there was, however, some evidence to support the possibility that HRM is found at head offices, 'a strategic phenomenon at the strategic apex of the organisation'.

Activity 3

'Perhaps predictably, the title (of the 'personnel' function) does not necessarily reflect practice. IBM, for example, has retained the personnel title despite being frequently held up in the past as an exemplar of human resource management. Even in the United States, where it has been estimated that over half of the top 50 corporations now use the human resource title, IBM has kept the personnel label. One explanation is that it only makes sense to change if it provides some competitive advantage. Maybe establishments in the UK have taken that message on board. Certainly, we can refute the 'old wine in new bottles' argument that some of us promulgated. There may be some good wine around - some good human resource policy and practice - but it is still marketed in the old bottles.' *(Personnel Management,* June 1993)

Why might the name of the function matter to the people who perform it, to the employees of the organisation, and to the organisation as a whole?

2 WHO IS THE 'CLIENT' OF HRM?

An ambiguity may exist for the personnel function in determining whose interests to serve: who is its 'client'?

According to the IPD's Code of Professional Practice in Personnel Management, the personnel manager has three principal areas of responsibility. [Italics ours.]

(a) 'A personnel manager's primary responsibility is to his *employer.*'

(b) He will 'resolve the conflict which must sometimes exist between his position as a member of the management team and his special relationship with the *workforce* in general and with individual *employees.*'

(c) He will 'use his best endeavours to enhance the standing ... of his *profession*', in dealings with other bodies.

Personnel managers may have to occupy the middle ground between employee and employer on some occasions. In a sense both employers/management and employees are their clients. Yet the personnel manager is not in any formal sense the 'representative' of the workforce, and is paid to be part of the organisation's management team, as both representative and adviser. The 'diplomatic' role of personnel may thus pose a dilemma of dual allegiance - particularly where there is conflict in the relationship between the personnel function and other (line) members of the management team, as we go on to discuss in section 3 below.

2.1 'Customer care' and the personnel function

Values to do with the *customer* ('the customer is king, 'know your customer') and his needs have been a major feature of the perception of quality, and the achievement of success, in the 1980s and 1990s. Strategically, there has been a move away from a technical or production orientation, to a marketing orientation: the objectives of a business can best be met by identifying the market, its needs and wants, and by fulfilling those needs and wants in the most efficient and effective way possible.

'Customer care' initiatives have been a feature of this orientation, since it has been recognised that:

(a) customers have an ever-widening choice of products and services available to them; and

(b) service (including sales service, delivery, after-sales service and, in general, communication and contact between the customer and the organisation) is of major importance in winning and retaining customers.

One consequence of a customer orientation for the *personnel* function is that it must identify with the organisation's objectives of winning and retaining *external customers,* in order to achieve business success. So, for example, if the organisation establishes a service improvement or customer care policy, the personnel department's objectives will be to staff the organisation (and particularly those units which deal directly with customers) with people who have a strong service ethic, good communication skills and so on - whether through recruitment and transfer, training or retraining.

One conspicuous example might be in banks, which were once regarded as non-responsive bureaucratic organisations. They have made particular efforts to establish a customer-friendly culture at branch level. Staff are being trained in complaint handling, face-to-face transactions ('personal banking'), explaining bank procedures and technology and so on. Quality/service surveys are being used to find out what customers think of the service they get from staff.

2.2 Internal customers

An equally important concept for the personnel function is that of the *internal customer.*

Market forces can be a useful way of compelling departments or functions in an organisation to reappraise their performance, and their relationship to each other. Personnel - like any other unit - may focus on its activity for its own sake, as if it had no objective or purpose outside the department. It may take for granted its relationship to other units, having a 'take it or leave it' attitude to the service it provides, being complacent about quality because it appears to have an effective monopoly on that service or task ('if we don't do it - it doesn't get done'). The concept of the internal customer aims to change all that.

As the term suggests, the internal customer concept implies the following.

(a) Any unit of the organisation whose task contributes to the task of other units (whether as part of a process, or in a 'staff' or 'service' relationship) can be regarded as a supplier of services like any other supplier used by the organisation. The receiving units are thus *customers* of that unit.

(b) The concept of *customer choice* operates within the organisation as well as in the external market environment. If an internal service unit fails to provide the right service at the right time and cost, it cannot expect customer loyalty: it is in *competition* with other internal and external providers of the service. Although there are logistical and control advantages to retaining the provision of services within the organisation, there is no room for complacency.

(c) The service unit's objective thus becomes the efficient and effective *identification of* and *satisfaction of customer needs* - as much within the organisation as outside it. This has the effect of integrating the objectives of service and customer units throughout the organisation. (It also makes units look at the *costs* of providing their services and what *added value* they are able to offer.)

The internal customers of personnel include:

(a) line managers, who expect the right quality and quantity of labour resources to meet their own objectives;

(b) senior management and shareholders, who expect the strategic objectives of the organisation to be met through human resource management; and

(c) employees, who expect their contract of employment to be fulfilled, and to have their interests preserved (insofar as they do not conflict with those of the other internal customers).

Personnel must find out what the needs and wants of these customers are (yet another reason why personnel managers need to be closely involved in objective-setting at all levels of the organisation). These needs and wants must then be satisfied as far and as efficiently as possible. The personnel department, in its various activities, may be in competition with:

(a) external service providers (say, training companies, recruitment consultancies, industrial relations services like ACAS (Advisory, Conciliation and Arbitration Service), or computer bureaux for record-keeping and modelling); and/or

(b) internal service providers - notably, line managers who might wish to decentralise many personnel functions and perform them themselves.

Activity 4

Peter, who works in the word processing department, types a letter drafted by Sarah, the human resource manager.

Who is the 'internal customer' in this transaction?

3 HRM WITHIN THE ORGANISATION STRUCTURE

Personnel managers can, operate in different areas and at different levels - from crisis handling and routine administration on the one hand, to policy-making and innovation on the other.

3.1 Personnel as a specialist function

Whatever the size of the organisation, the finding and keeping of high-quality staff will necessitate the existence of the personnel function. In a small organisation, this may be a non-specialist function, the responsibility of any appropriate manager or administrator.

In larger organisations, more time is likely to be taken up with organisational and personnel problems. It may then be felt that a specialist member of staff is required to take on full-time responsibility for:

(a) advising management on personnel matters; and
(b) implementing well-defined policies.

This is not a situation in which management simply 'hives off' its responsibility for 'people management': it is an acknowledgement that line managers need to have available (and listen to) a specialist because:

(a) there are areas developing in personnel management in which expertise is increasingly required; and

(b) there is a need for consistency in the design and application of personnel management practice.

Heads of departments basically have technical responsibilities; the personnel specialist's job is to explain to them reasons for social behaviour which may not be obvious. Why, for example, are decisions that are technically and economically sound sometimes met by seemingly irrational resistance by subordinates? What emotional factors are at play when this sort of thing happens? Offering advice to clarify such situations is a task that demands an expert who has been trained to perceive the ways in which individuals and groups interact within an organisation, and who can convey his understanding in practical terms to departmental heads who are too pre-occupied with their technical activities to have time to consider the social system of the workplace as a whole. M W Cuming, *The Theory and Practice of Personnel Management*

Several factors have contributed to the perceived need for a specialised personnel function.

(a) The need to comply with increasing regulation and legislation means that expert attention must be given to such matters as recruitment and selection (to avoid racial or sexual discrimination), termination of the employment contract (especially, for example, in circumstances involving trade union membership, or maternity), and health and safety at work.

(b) High staffing costs, and the changing workforce (as technology becomes widespread, skill requirements change, women enter or re-enter the market, temporary and home working increases and so on) also require that recruitment and staffing policies are designed and implemented by individuals with current knowledge of the labour market.

(c) There is continuing pressure for social responsibility towards employees, with information to be provided, schemes for worker participation and rulings on working conditions - from the European Commission among others.

(d) Behavioural sciences (chiefly psychology, sociology and social psychology) have become highly developed in organisational contexts, and are gaining currency as important elements in managers' mental equipment. Up-to-date research on such matters as motivation, stress, resistance to change, industrial fatigue and response to leadership style should be monitored.

(e) Trade unions and their officials, Industrial Tribunals, ACAS and others have a continuing role in industrial relations: familiarity with legislation, rulings and practice, liaison and information will be required.

Managers, if one listens to the psychologists, will have to have insights into all kinds of people. They will have to be in command of all kinds of psychological techniques. They will have to understand an infinity of individual personality structures, individual psychological needs, and individual psychological problems... But most managers find it hard enough to know all they need to know about their own immediate area of expertise, be it heat-treating or cost accounting or scheduling. Drucker: *Management*

The personnel manager sees the overall effect of personnel policies and practices in the organisation. At organisational level, his role is that of specialist adviser, and interpreter/executor of personnel policy - in consultation and co-operation with line managers. At departmental level, the personnel manager is still likely to be concerned mainly with the broader effects of personnel policy on staff, such as:

(a) human resource planning and problems of turnover;

(b) recruitment and selection systems; training and development systems;

(c) consultations and negotiations with trade union representatives and outside bodies, like ACAS, professional associations, wages councils;

(d) compliance with employment legislation; and

(e) maintenance of records.

3.2 Line and staff relationships

There are two ways of looking at the distinction between line and staff management.

(a) Line and staff can be used to describe *functions* in the organisation. Line management consists of those managers directly involved in achieving the objectives of an organisation (for example production and sales managers in a manufacturing company). Every other manager is staff (including accounting, research and development and personnel).

(b) Line and staff can be used to denote *relationships* of authority. A line manager is any manager who has been given (delegated) authority over a subordinate down the chain of command. Thus in personnel (a 'staff' department), the personnel director will have line authority over the managers in charge of recruitment and training. In other words, the 'line' represents the chain of command through the management hierarchy. Staff authority, on the other hand, resides not in official position, but influence - by means of special knowledge or expertise, resources or other desirable qualities. The legal expert would thus have staff authority in the personnel department - whatever his official 'rank'.

Staff functions and relationships exist in many organisations where there is a need for specialisation of management: accountants, personnel administrators, economists, data processing experts and so on. Where this expertise is 'siphoned off' into a separate department, the problem naturally arises as to whether the experts:

(a) exist to *advise* line managers, who may accept or reject the advice given; or

(b) can step in to *direct* the line managers on what to do - in other words, to assume authority themselves. This is usually defined as 'functional' authority, based on the recognition of expertise in areas which are vital to the achievement of line objectives: a personnel manager might have such authority over industrial relations decisions throughout the organisation, for example.

Definitions

Line management is *both* managers involved in achieving the objectives of the organisation *and* any manager within a hierarchy.

Staff management is *both* managers other than line managers *and* those with special skills.

Functional authority is where specialist staff managers exercise authority over all levels of managers.

The ambiguities of line/staff relationships create a potential for conflict, where staff managers are, or are perceived to be, merely interfacing in areas of the business for which they have no real responsibility.

Activity 5

Give five examples of situations where conflict may arise from the actions of staff managers or the perception of them by line managers.

The solutions to these problems are easily stated, but not easy to implement in practice.

(a) Authority must be clearly defined, and distinctions between line authority and staff advice clearly set out (for example, in job descriptions).

(b) Senior management must encourage line managers to make positive efforts to discuss work problems with staff advisers, and to be prepared to accept their advice. The use of experts should become an organisational way of life, part of the culture.

(c) Staff managers must be fully informed about the aspects of the business in which, as functional experts, they will become involved. They should then be less likely to offer impractical advice.

(d) When staff advisers are used to plan and implement changes in the running of the business, they must be kept involved during the implementation, monitoring and review of the project. Staff managers must be prepared to accept responsibility for their failures, and this is only really possible if they advise during the implementation and monitoring stages.

3.3 'Personnel' as a staff function

In an article in *The Administrator* entitled 'The Personnel Function - A shared responsibility', Laurie Mullins wrote:

It is the job of the personnel manager to provide specialist knowledge and services to line managers, and to support them in the performance of their jobs. It is not the job of the personnel manager to manage people, other than direct subordinates. The personnel manager has no direct control over other staff except where a specific responsibility is delegated directly by top management, for example, if nominated as safety officer under the Health and Safety at Work Act 1974. The personnel manager has executive authority for such delegated responsibility and for the management of the personnel department and its staff ... In all other respects the personnel manager's relationship with other managers, supervisors and staff of the organisation is indirect, that is an advisory or 'functional' relationship.

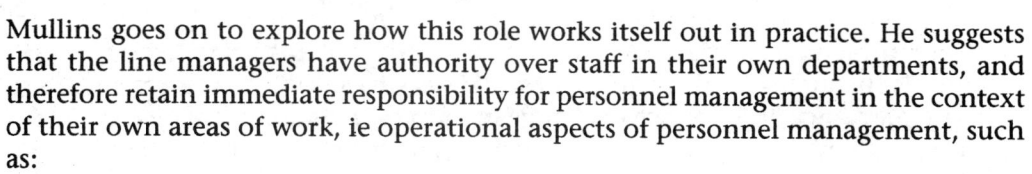

Mullins goes on to explore how this role works itself out in practice. He suggests that the line managers have authority over staff in their own departments, and therefore retain immediate responsibility for personnel management in the context of their own areas of work, ie operational aspects of personnel management, such as:

(a) the organisation and allocation of work;
(b) minor disciplinary matters and staff grievances;
(c) standards of performance;
(d) on-the-job training and induction;
(e) communication; and
(f) safe working practices and maintenance of a tidy, healthy work environment.

Line managers 'have both the right and the duty to be concerned with the effective operation of their own department, including the management and well-being of their staff'. After all, it is the line managers who are directly affected by the symptoms of poor personnel management: lateness, low morale, hostility, absenteeism, incapacity to perform to standard or whatever.

Personnel managers will, however, act as advisers and arbitrators where necessary, even in this 'front-line' territory, where legislation and other areas of expertise are involved.

3.4 Organisational politics

The topic of 'political' behaviour in organisations is not about left- or right-wing ideologies, nor the national party-political scene: it is broadly concerned with competition, conflict, rivalry and power relationships in organisations. Organisations are political systems in the sense that they comprise individuals and groups who have their own interests, priorities and goals: there is competition for finite resources, power and influence; there are cliques, alliances, pressure groups and blocking groups, centred around values, opinions and objectives which may be opposed by others.

Aspects of politics in organisations include:

(a) *self-interest*. Individuals wish to experience 'victory' and avoid 'defeat'. They have their own objectives which are not always reconcilable with those of the organisation - from 'an easy life' to job security. These will have to be overcome, or harmonised with the organisation's objectives if possible;

(b) *power plays*. There are inevitable disparities of power and influence in hierarchical organisations - and despite rational organisation design, events are in reality decided by dominant individuals or coalitions within and/or outside the organisation. Other individuals tend to want to influence, join or overthrow the dominant coalition. HR managers have to 'win' power and influence;

(c) *persuasion/negotiation*. Organisations are constantly involved in compromise, reconciling or controlling differences, and settling for the 'real' rather than the 'ideal'. Expectations of imposing plans and changes without modification or resistance are likely to prove unrealistic. HR managers must in general avoid theoretical or 'utopian' solutions to problems; and

(d) *interdepartmental conflict*. 'Territory' is a useful analogy for the jealousies and rivalries over boundaries of authority, specialisms, spheres of influence etc. The HR manager is often perceived as an 'outsider' and interloper in line departments, as we noted above.

Politics is most obvious in its impact on change management. Change threatens the status quo, the established order, security - and particularly the security of those who have power and resources. Change is most likely to be resisted by those who have something to lose, arousing instincts of self-interest and self-preservation (if 'survival' is threatened - say, by job losses). This is why middle managers are often the principle source of resistance to change in most organisations: their position, in the face of widespread delayering of management structures, is most precarious, and they are perceived to have more to lose than either low-level or high-level employees.

3.5 The authority of the human resources manager

In effect, the HR manager's authority depends on several means of *influence*.

According to Michael Armstrong (*A Handbook of Personnel Management Practice*): 'What in effect the personnel manager says is that "this is the personnel policy of the company, ignore it at your peril". He can seldom forbid anyone to do anything, except where it contravenes a law or negotiated procedure, but he can refuse to authorise something - say, a pay increase - if it is in his power to do so. And he can refer a matter to higher authority (the joint superior of the two managers concerned) and request that the action be delayed until a ruling is made.'

The personnel specialist may lack 'positional' or 'legal power' in the organisation, in relation to line departments, but may possess:

(a) 'resource' power - through control over human resource and pay; and
(b) 'expert' power - where his specialist knowledge is recognised.

In addition, he can 'influence' (direct and modify the behaviour of others) through:

(a) establishing rules and procedures;
(b) bargaining and negotiation;
(c) persuasion; and
(d) 'ecology' or environmental control.

The design of work, the work, the structure of reward and control systems, the structure of the organisation, the management of groups and the control of conflict are all ways of managing the environment in order to influence behaviour. Let us never forget that although the environment is all around us, it is not unalterable, that to change it is to influence people, that ecology is potent, the more so because it is often unnoticed.   **Handy**

The establishment of policy and procedure is a particularly potent source of influence for the personnel function, although it can have adverse effects if it causes resentment and/or inefficiencies. Formal policies are helpful in terms of consistency, standardisation throughout the organisation, impartiality and clarity. But as Armstrong (*Handbook of Personnel Management Practice*) notes, they 'may be inflexible, or platitudinous, or both, and therefore useless or dangerous.' If the policy is couched in purely abstract terms, it may lack credibility: if it is fixed, it may become a stranglehold on the organisation's flexibility and power in negotiation (if a pay policy specifies a certain salary level, for example). Fixed policies may also inhibit initiative and creative problem-solving, and may not allow junior managers, in particular, to develop if their activities are closely prescribed.

Activity 6

Find out about the jobs of three people you know. Are their jobs 'line' or 'staff' in the nature of their authority? What kinds of authority or power do they have personally in their jobs (whether or not formal authority is involved)? How do they influence other people, when they need them to do something for them at work?

Does the personnel function in their organisations have power, and if so what kind? What tactics does the personnel department use to 'get its way' in the organisation?

Whatever the range of the personnel function's formal responsibilities, it is important to remember that it operates largely by *consent,* and the *perception of its authority* by line management. Personnel managers frequently suffer from lack of credibility related to:

(a) lack of definition of the personnel function and its contribution to business objectives;
(b) the perceived idealistic and/or theoretical basis of people-oriented activity;
(c) the perceived ambiguity in personnel's 'clientele', whereby its loyalty to the management position may be seen as suspect; and
(d) the traditionally administrative role of personnel, lacking the creativity and pro-activity expected of a management function.

'Sometimes it seems as though a great many very talented personnel specialists are wasting an awful lot of time. They carefully watch developments in the industrial relations, political and labour market environments; they develop sensible, well thought-out personnel policies that would make their company one of the most progressive and highly respected of employers. And then they see their efforts continually frustrated and subverted by a management team that seems determined to ignore most of what the personnel department does.'
Brewster and Richbell, *Getting Managers to Implement Personnel Policies*

3.6 The structure of the HR function

Charles Handy (*Understanding Organisations*) suggested that the effectiveness of the 'traditional' personnel department is reduced by ambiguity about the role of the department, or conflict between different roles of the department. Personnel managers are expected to act in a variety of ways.

(a) As line managers - for example, in negotiating and implementing industrial agreements with trade unions; perhaps also enforcing safety procedures.
(b) As advisers - for example, in welfare work, or in helping with problems of human attitudes and behaviour in various departments.

(c) As a service department - for example, in recruitment, training and education.

(d) As 'auditors' - for example, in checking on the effectiveness of appraisal schemes, or the training structure, or perhaps in reporting on the effectiveness of the management of the organisation (ie carrying out a management audit).

(e) As co-ordinators and planners - for example, in human resource planning.

Handy suggested that this ambiguity leads to inefficiency and loss of authority for the personnel function, which attempts to bolster its influence by expansion, and by proliferating rules and procedures as a form of control over line management. In other words, the personnel department develops into a bureaucratic institution, regardless of the type of organisation it serves. One solution, put forward by Handy, was to split the personnel function, within the organisation structure, into separate 'executive', 'advisory', 'service', 'auditing' and 'planning and co-ordinating' functions.

Karen Legge suggested a *matrix* structure with the key *functions* of personnel (such as human resource planning, selection, training and welfare) on one axis of the grid, set against key *process* activities (such as policy-making, innovation, the establishing of routines and crisis handling) on the other. Key personnel roles can then be allocated in a more rational manner.

Activity 7

'New Forest District Council has adopted a comprehensive programme of empowering line managers. They now carry out their own recruitment, maintain personnel records and deal with disciplinary procedures, including dismissal. Line managers also issue their own employment contracts using a standard computerised system that protects the council's core values and service conditions, while giving managers maximum discretion in other matters. They also have substantial flexibility in determining patterns of work and other organisational arrangements.' (*People Management*, 23 March 1995)

New Forest still has personnel specialists. Do you think they are necessary?

4 HRM IN THE EUROPEAN UNION

4.1 European issues

The implications of European human resource management are still being worked out, and questions about the 'subsidiarity' of European Community (now 'European Union') legislation are still to be answered, but personnel specialists will clearly need to be aware of the following.

(a) European Commission directives with regard to health and safety, recruitment, worker participation, and other matters. (These are discussed, where appropriate, in relevant chapters of this text.) In particular, the Social Charter could have wide-ranging effects on HRM. The Introduction to the Charter says that economic competitiveness and the development of employment must be priorities for the EU, as well as the harmonisation of living and working conditions. The IPD has supported the general thrust of many of the directives, notably to give part-timers equal treatment, increase the accessibility of maternity leave, improve health and safety, and increase of the provision of information to employees. However: 'Many of these detailed proposals seem to go beyond the basic principle they intent to implement and would, in the IPD's view, add to employers' costs or introduce restrictions and rigidities, without adding to managerial effectiveness.' (*Personnel Management*, June 1991)

(b) Recognition and comparison of qualifications in member states, for the purposes of recruitment. The directive on recognition of vocational qualifications between member states, for example, was adopted by the EU and implemented in national law but the situation is still quite complex.

(c) Differences in employment law and practice in other countries, where the organisation may intend to recruit and/or employ a labour force. 'Harmonisation' is by no means complete, as yet.

(d) The need for staff training in the languages and cultures of other states, in order to be able to compete in the foreign marketplace.

(e) The increased mobility of the labour pool, affecting human resource planning through fluctuations of labour supply and demand.

Chapter roundup

- People may be regarded as a vital resource ... but many managers find it difficult to appreciate where the personnel department fits in, except in the simplest terms as a procurement and fire-fighting function.' (Armstrong)
- Personnel is a 'staff' rather than a 'line' function, and so must exploit to the full its resource, expert and ecological power and influence, rather than the rational/legal power possessed by line managers.
- This view is changing, with the concept of human resource management, or HRM, which basically views the personnel specialists' job as a strategic one: 'To know what business they are in, to know where it is going, and to ensure that the input to get there is available from a human resourcing and organisational capability point of view.' (Beattie)
- Organisations are political systems in the sense that they are composed of individuals and groups who have their own interests, priorities and goals: competition, conflict, rivalry and power relationships have to be taken into account by the HR manager.

Quick quiz

1. List seven traditional functions of personnel management.
2. What is 'human resource management'?
3. List four strategic roles for personnel/human resource management.
4. What is the 'internal customer concept'? Who is the customer of the personnel function?
5. Distinguish between 'line' and 'staff' management.
6. What (a) enhances and (b) undermines the authority of the personnel specialist?
7. List four aspects of 'politics' in organisations.
8. List four issues raised by the European marketplace for labour.

Solutions to activities

1 Your examples may be different, but suggestions include these.

(a) Keeping and updating personnel records (eg on employee training, pay, disciplinary records etc); retrieving information on employees and the workforce as a whole for managers (eg when appraisal or pay negotiations are imminent); ensuring that the organisation has up-to-date information on relevant legislation/regulation relating to employment.

(b) Gathering and disseminating statistics on the workforce, as required for various personnel 'returns' to government departments and their regulatory bodies; hiring and firing on request; co-ordinating training programmes.

(c) Employee counselling; handling disciplinary action; co-ordinating benefits, welfare programmes and so on.

(d) Conflict-resolution meetings with employee representatives; grievance handling; pay negotiations.

2 Again, there is a wide variety to choose from, but suggestions include:

(a) relocation of the organisation's premises;

(b) restructuring of departments or levels of management;

(c) the introduction of new technology in the workplace;

(d) the introduction of new work methods such as shift-working or teamworking;

(e) the entry into the market of a competitor offering higher rates of pay.

3 It clearly matters to some of the people who perform the function, for their own sense of self-esteem. An important consideration is whether the employees - the humans whom the function manages - view the idea of themselves as 'resources' positively or negatively and whether practice justifies the more 'enlightened' sounding title or is indeed viewed cynically as the same 'old wine' in a fancy 'new bottle'. Adoption of the title may be a sign of conflict and power struggles within the organisation or it may enhance the organisation's reputation as an employer.

4 Arguably, if you identified only one of the parties involved you have missed the point. Sarah supplies Peter with work to do; but she is wasting Peter's time if she provides a bad draft that has to be altered extensively. Peter supplies Sarah with the finished product and he will waste Sarah's time if it is badly typed and needs extensive correction. Thus they are both customers. If both individuals perform well, the organisation as a whole is the beneficiary.

5 (a) Staff managers *are* held in low regard as overheads who contribute nothing to the bottom line but have considerable nuisance power in imposing rules and policies.

(b) Staff managers are in fact divorced from the business objectives of line management, but impose rules and procedures in the interests of their profession or speciality, or to enhance their power.

(c) Staff managers undermine - intentionally or otherwise - the authority of line managers.

(d) Staff managers report over the heads of line managers, as advisers to senior management.

(e) Staff managers are not held accountable for the results of their advice - or *are* held accountable for the results of their advice, without having the authority to get it properly implemented.

7 The article makes it clear that they are.

'This process has allowed the council's personnel specialists to focus on more strategic issues and on major projects such as the local government review, as well as providing back-up to the line. "Empowerment has significantly increased line managers' responsibilities." The director of personnel and management development says, "but it has also increased their confidence. Efficiency and productivity have improved and paybills have fallen. And as the managers get more confident, they become more adventurous and they innovate more, so they expect higher expertise from us, not just answers to routine questions. In the early days some managers thought, 'That's it, now we can ignore the centre', but they soon understood what it was all abo

Further question practice

Now try the following questions at the end of this text.

Multiple choice questions	**1 to 7**
Exam style questions	**1**

Chapter 2

HUMAN RESOURCE PLANNING AND FLEXIBILITY

Introduction

'Manpower' is a general term for people at work, or 'labour', or 'human resources': people are one of the resources of an organisation which management must control. They are a relatively difficult resource to control because they are not only subject to environmental factors which cause fluctuations in supply and demand, but also to the complexities of human behaviour at individual and group level.

Thus, for example, a shortage of a particular skill which affects the performance of an organisation may be caused by: long-term declines in education and training, or in population (nationally or in the local area); the immediate effects of a competitor entering the market or area and employing some of the pool of skilled labour; increases in demand for the product or service for which the skill is required; or the relocation, resignation or demotivation of key skilled people - for all sorts of personal and circumstantial reasons.

It is arguable that as control over the labour resource becomes more difficult - because of increasing uncertainty and rate of change - it also becomes more necessary, because the risks of 'getting it wrong' are correspondingly greater. Human resource planning is thus a form of risk management. It involves realistically appraising the present and anticipating the future (as far as possible) in order to get the right people into the right jobs at the right time.

Your objectives

After completing this chapter you should:

(a) appreciate the need for human resource planning;
(b) be able to outline the process of human resource planning;
(c) appreciate the advantages and disadvantages of labour turnover;
(d) appreciate the role of management succession and promotion planning;
(e) understand the increasing need for labour flexibility, and how it can be achieved.

1 THE NEED FOR HUMAN RESOURCE PLANNING

Definition

Human resource planning is a form of supply and demand management, aiming to minimise the risk of either surplus (and therefore inefficiency) or shortage (and therefore ineffectiveness) of relevant kinds of labour.

This management process may be broadly outlined as follows.

(a) Forecast demand for each grade and/or skill of employee.

(b) Forecast supply of each grade and/or skill of employee, both within and outside the organisation.

(c) Plan to remove any discrepancy between demand and supply. If there is a shortage of labour, for example, you would need to reduce demand (say, through improved productivity), or improve supply (through training and retention of current staff, or recruitment from outside, for example).

1.1 Proactive or reactive?

The risk management approach assumes that human resource planning is about anticipating and preventing problems (as far as possible) before they occur: a proactive and forward-looking process. However, it may seem to you (perhaps on the basis of your past experience in an organisation) that this is impractical - and not really necessary - for most small to medium-sized concerns. If you are short of staff, you hire some, or train or promote one of your existing employees. If your activities decline, on the other hand, and you have superfluous staff, you make some redundancies, or 'downsize' your staff.

Things are not, in fact, so simple. An attempt to look beyond the present and short-term future, and to prepare for contingencies, is increasingly important.

(a) Jobs often require experience and skills which cannot easily be bought in the marketplace, and the more complex the organisation, the more difficult it will be to supply or replace highly specialised staff quickly. It takes time to train and develop technical or specialist personnel so there will be a lead time to fill any vacancy: the need will have to be anticipated in time to initiate the required development programmes.

Activity 1

Give three examples of jobs for which specialist training is likely to be required, lengthening the lead time for filling a vacancy and obtaining performance at the required level.

(b) Employment protection legislation and general expectations of 'social responsibility' in organisations make staff-shedding a slower and more costly process. Attempted redundancies in the coal mining industry in October 1992 indicated the extent to which the general public - recession-hardened as it might be - still responds to job losses with a sense of outrage.

(c) Rapid technological change is leading to a requirement for human resource which is both more highly skilled and more adaptable. This follows the replacement of human labour by technology in routine areas of activity, and changes in work practices. Labour flexibility, in particular, is a major issue, and means that the career and retraining *potential* of staff are at least as important as their actual qualifications and skills - and need to be assessed in advance of requirements. (In fact, multi-skilling and 'trainability' as major criteria for selection, are some of the most popular innovations of the HRM era of personnel management.)

(d) Recessionary pressures highlight problems of productivity and human resource costs, and the need to make efficient use of labour. Meanwhile, with contraction rather than expansion the order of the day, the organisation will need to rethink its policies on job security, promotion and other means previously developed to *retain* staff. Attempts to 'prune' staff levels can have adverse effects on the ratio of indirect to direct labour, on the age distribution of the workforce (through early retirement policies) and so on.

(e) The UK continues to suffer from specific skill shortages (with wide local variations), despite high unemployment levels. This is exaggerated by demographic trends, discussed later. Skill shortages also create a tendency to greater career mobility, which complicates the human resource planners' assumptions about labour wastage rates (the number of people leaving the organisation for any reason).

(f) The amount and variety of markets, competition and labour is being increased by political and economic moves such as the opening of Eastern Europe and the continuing progress towards European Union.

(g) Computer technology has made available techniques which facilitate the monitoring and planning of human resource over fairly long time spans: manipulation of human resource statistics, trend analysis, 'modelling' and so on.

Human resource planning has maintained its imperatives for several reasons: (i) a growing awareness of the need to look into the future, (ii) a desire to exercise control over as many variables as possible which influence business success or failure, (iii) the development of techniques which make such planning possible.   Bryan Livy, *Corporate Personnel Management*

2 THE PROCESS OF HUMAN RESOURCE PLANNING

The complexity of the supply and demand equation with regard to the vital human resource of an organisation necessitates an integrated, systematic approach to each of the following.

(a) Forecasting *human resource requirements*, by grades and skills, to meet the long- and short-term needs of the organisation (the human resource strategy). The forecast will be based on the objectives of the organisation (and any likely changes), present (and anticipated future) human resource utilisation - including productivity - and any external factors which will influence demand for labour (such as new technology, market expansion or recession, or employee demands for longer holidays).

(b) Forecasting the *human resource supply* available to meet these needs, taking into account labour turnover, the potential production capacity of the existing labour force, and the accessible pool of labour in the environment.

(c) Acquiring or shedding human resource where necessary and controlling the rate and direction of its *flow* through the organisation (through conditions of employment, pay, job enrichment, career development, redeployment, employee relations, termination of employment and other succession and retention strategies).

(d) Developing required *skills and abilities* within the organisation, to enhance the workforce's capacity, and providing the conditions and resources necessary to enhance or maintain productivity.

Human resource planning is an interdisciplinary activity. It requires the combined technical skills of statisticians, economists and behavioural scientists together with the practical knowledge of managers and planners ...

Chapter 2: Human resource planning and flexibility

At the level of the firm, human resource planning deals with problems of recruitment, wastage, retention, promotion and transfer of people within the firm and in relation to its environment.'
(Bartholomew)

2.1 Forecasting labour demand and supply

The *demand* for labour must be forecast by considering the following variables.

(a) The *objectives* of the organisation, and the long- and short-term plans in operation to achieve those objectives. Where plans are changed, the effect of the changes must be estimated: proposed expansion, contraction or diversification of the organisation's activities will obviously affect the demand for labour in general or particular skills, and may be estimated by market research, competitive analysis, trends in technological advances and so on (although sudden changes in market conditions complicate the process: the effect of the collapse of the Soviet Union on defence spending, for example).

(b) *Human resource utilisation* - how much labour will be required, given the expected productivity or work rate of different types of employee and the expected volume of business activity. Note that productivity will depend on capital expenditure, technology, work organisation, employee motivation and skills, negotiated productivity deals and a number of other factors.

(c) The *cost* of labour - including overtime, training, benefits and so on - and therefore what financial constraints there are on the organisation's human resource levels.

(d) *Environmental factors* and trends in technology and markets that will require organisational change, because of threats or opportunities. Economic recession has created conditions in which expectations of labour demand in the short term are low: downsizing of staff and delayering of organisation structures are the current trend.

The financial services sector, in particular, has undergone huge job losses, especially the banking industry. Lloyds Bank, for example, cut more than 15,000 jobs between 1990 and 1996.

Activity 2

Pick any organisation you are familiar with: one of which you have been an employee, member or informed customer. Is the need for human resource in the organisation growing, shrinking or simply 'moving' into new skill areas? What, if anything, is the organisation doing about this?

The available *supply* of labour will be forecast by considering:

(a) wastage (turnover through resignations and retirements), promotions and transfers, absenteeism and other staff movements. This will require information on:
   (i) the age structure of staff (forthcoming retirement or family start-up);
   (ii) labour turnover for a comparable period; and
   (iii) the promotion potential and ambitions of staff;

(b) the production level and potential of the existing work force, and its structure (age distribution, grades, location, sex, skills, hours of work and rates of pay); and

(c) the potential supply of new labour with the relevant skills from the environment - the external labour market. This is the area expected to be hardest hit by the so-called 'demographic time bomb'.

2.2 UK demographic trends

Demography is the study of statistics to do with births, deaths, population distribution and so on. In the late 1980s, its major concern was the projected decline in the number of school-leavers entering the job market, due to falling birthrates after the post-war 'baby boom'. This 'demographic timebomb' or (less sensationally) 'demographic downturn' became a major HR issue. It has lost some of its importance with recessionary falls in the demand for labour: redundancies, rather than labour shortages, have been the story of the 1990s. However, the downturn is still having knock-on effects in specific skills and areas, and may re-emerge as a major problem once it is no longer masked by the recession.

The changes currently facing the UK appear to be twofold. The number of young people (16-19 year olds) entering the labour market has been falling since the mid 1980s and fell to a minimum in 1994. At the same time, improved health and improved opportunities for women and racial minorities have created an expanding adult workforce, including significantly higher numbers of women and older workers (say, over 45). European law has contributed to this expansion, with decisions in the European Court of Justice and further provisions for minority groups, pregnant workers and part-time workers. This means that:

(a) employers who previously recruited large numbers of school leavers will need to alter their strategies;

(b) the need to employ more women will require consideration of equal pay and opportunities, discrimination and sexual harassment in the workplace, cover for maternity leave and facilities for workers with children;

(c) the need to employ older workers may mean higher entry grades of pay, consideration of retraining and possibly adapted working conditions and environments; and

(d) similar pressures (and anti-discrimination provisions) may necessitate added facilities for the disabled, policies on racial abuse or sexual orientation and so on.

Activity 3

Give an example of:

(a) a major traditional recruiter of school leavers; and

(b) provisions required to attract and retain women to the workforce.

Consider the people you are studying with: what is the composition of your study group in terms of age, race and sex. What does this say about:

(a) the aspirations; and

(b) the prospects of these groups, in business?

2.3 Closing the gap between demand and supply

Shortages or surpluses of labour which emerge in the process of formulating the human resource position survey may be dealt with in various ways.

A *deficiency* of labour may be met through:

(a) internal transfers and promotions, training and development;

(b) external recruitment;

(c) the extension of temporary contracts, or the contracts of those about to retire;

(d) reducing labour turnover, by reviewing possible causes, including pay and conditions;

(e) the use of freelance/temporary/agency staff;

(f) encouraging overtime working;
(g) productivity bargaining (to increase the productivity of existing staff levels); or
(h) automation (thereby increasing productivity, and/or encouraging the elimination of jobs).

A *surplus* of labour may be met by:

(a) running down manning levels by natural wastage (or 'accelerated wastage' - encouraging labour turnover by reducing job satisfaction, pay or other incentives to stay);
(b) restricting or 'freezing' recruitment;
(c) redundancies (voluntary and/or compulsory);
(d) early retirement;
(e) a tougher stance on discipline, enabling more dismissals;
(f) part-time working or job sharing;
(g) eliminating overtime; or
(h) redeployment of staff to areas of labour shortage. This may necessitate diversification by the organisation, to find new work for its labour force.

Human resource strategy thus requires the integration of policies for:

(a) pay and conditions of employment;
(b) promotion;
(c) recruitment;
(d) training; and
(e) industrial relations.

Tactical plans can then be made, within this integrated framework, for pay and productivity bargaining; management and career development; organisation and job specifications, recruitment, downsizing and so on.

2.4 The human resource plan

The human resource plan is prepared on the basis of the analysis of human resource requirements, and the implications for productivity and costs. The plan may consist of various elements, according to the circumstances.

(a) *The recruitment plan*: numbers and types of people, and when required; the recruitment programme.
(b) *The training plan*: numbers of trainees required and/or existing staff needing training; training programme.
(c) *The redevelopment plan*: programmes for transferring or retraining employees.
(d) The *productivity plan*: programmes for improving productivity, or reducing human resource costs; setting productivity targets.
(e) *The redundancy plan*: where and when redundancies are to occur; policies for selection and declaration of redundancies; redevelopment, retraining or relocation of redundant employees; policy on redundancy payments, union consultation and so on.
(f) *The retention plan*: actions to reduce avoidable labour wastage.

The plan should include budgets, targets and standards. It should allocate responsibilities for implementation and control (reporting, monitoring achievement against the plan and making adjustments as necessary).

2.5 How 'scientific' is human resource planning?

Human resource planning is regarded as a scientific, statistical exercise, but it is important to remember that:

(a) statistics are not the only element of the planning process, and are subject to interpretation and managerial judgements (about future growth, say, or the potential for innovation) that are largely qualitative and even highly speculative;

(b) trends in statistics are the product of social processes, which are not readily quantifiable or predictable: staff leave for various social reasons in (unpredictable) individual cases, to get married, relocate or whatever. The growth of the temporary and freelance workforce is a social trend, as are the buying patterns which dictate demand for goods and services.

Forecasting is not an exact science. Few exponents of even the most sophisticated techniques would claim that they are wholly accurate, although:

(a) the element of guesswork has been substantially reduced by the use of computer and other models to test various assumptions, and to indicate trends; and

(b) the general principles can still be applied, to indicate problems and stimulate control action.

The uncertainty of the future is the main problem for human resource planning of any long-range nature. This is not to say that the exercise is in itself futile (indeed it will be even more necessary, in order to assess and control the risk of manpower resourcing problems in the future) but a measure of flexibility should be built into the plan, so that it can be adapted to suit likely or even unforeseen contingencies. Above all, it should not be seen and communicated as an inflexible plan, as if it were based on certainty.

Activity 4

What are the particular difficulties of human resource planning in the following organisations?

(a) A company designing, manufacturing and selling personal computers.

(b) An international airline, or publicly owned international airline.

Statistical methods are varied in their approach and degree of sophistication. Computerisation has greatly enhanced the speed, ease and accuracy with which they can be applied. Simple extrapolation, regression analysis and sensitivity analysis can be used to create a more accurate model of the future than simple subjective estimates. Even so, there are a number of assumptions involved.

Moreover, the results are limited in value: they are *quantitative* - for example, numbers of staff required - where *qualitative* information may be required as well: the effects of change, restaffing, or management style on the culture of the organisation and individual/group behaviour and so on.

Work study methods aim to set standards of man-hours per unit of output in order to achieve maximum productivity. Where end-products are measurable, work-study techniques can offer a reasonably accurate forecast of human resource requirements, for direct workers at least. In service sectors and 'knowledge work', however, end products and output may not be easily subject to standard-setting: the numbers of telephone calls, interviews, customers served, or ideas generated are likely to fluctuate widely with the flow of business and the nature of particular transactions.

Managerial estimates form the simplest and cheapest method of assessment: as such, they may be the most appropriate - and are the most common - method for small organisations. At the best of times, however, this method has the disadvantage of a high degree of subjectivity, and although this can, to an extent, be controlled (by requiring managers to support their estimates with reasons and to reconcile their estimates with those of senior management), it is a source of potential risk.

Clearly, the more precise the information available, the greater the probability that human resource plans will be accurate. But, in practice, they are subject to many imponderable factors, some completely outside an organisation's control ... international trade, general technological advances, population movements, the human acceptance of or resistance to change, and the quality of leadership and its impact on morale. The environment, then, is uncertain, and so are the people whose activities are being planned. Human resource plans must therefore be accepted as being continuous, under constant review, and ever-changing. Since they concern people, they must also be negotiable.

Cuming, *Personnel Management*

2.6 The human resource audit

Many large organisations have instituted human resource planning systems to meet their staffing requirements. It is important to ensure that such systems work as they are intended to do and that the plans they incorporate are properly implemented. This is the purpose of a *human resource audit*.

Regular headcount summaries should be produced to ensure that the human resource trend is in line with forecasts. The summaries should show breakdowns of actual human resource against flexed budgets for the organisation as a whole and for divisions and departments within it.

Another common feature of the human resource audit is checking through a batch of personnel records to see whether each change (promotion, transfer, redundancy, recruitment, etc) has been properly approved. This process may uncover:

(a) inadequate authorisation of particular types of change. For example, it may be common to transfer employees within the same department without proper approval or reference to the overall human resource plan; and

(b) unauthorised or unnecessary use of agency or temporary personnel.

Actual manning levels should be checked against manning standards. There are various ways in which actual manning may become out of line with agreed standards.

(a) If the standards were originally agreed on the basis that manning levels would gradually decrease through natural wastage, it is important to ensure that such wastage is allowed to happen. It is a natural tendency for managers to seek replacements for any staff losses, even those which have been budgeted for.

(b) The standards themselves may be (or have become) inappropriate. The human resource plan is constantly evolving and it is necessary to review and revise human resource standards as a regular process.

A further step is the audit of human resource utilisation. Organisations need to review how well they use their employees in the skill categories concerned. It may be that this process will uncover a need for some fundamental change (such as a complete restructuring of work practices). This might become evident, for example, from instances of employees leaving because they feel under-employed. Apart from the satisfaction and development of employees, it should be clear that under-utilisation of a skill category is an inefficient use of the organisation's resources. Paying a shorthand typist a shorthand typist's wage to perform copy-typing duties is one obvious example of wastage.

2.7 The labour market

Do not forget that labour supply is potentially located both inside and outside the organisation. The market for labour, within which organisations compete for skills and experience and individuals compete for jobs, is likewise both internal and external.

Business Basics: Human Resource Management

The external labour pool will be covered in the following chapter on recruitment.

Three aspects of the *internal* labour pool, which we will discuss here, are:

(a) labour turnover, or wastage - in other words, people leaving the organisation;

(b) management succession and promotion - the flow of people 'upwards' within the organisation; and

(c) labour flexibility - ways of adapting the workforce to fluctuating labour demand.

3 LABOUR TURNOVER

3.1 How do you measure labour turnover?

There are different ways of measuring labour turnover. Most simply, actual gross numbers of people leaving may provide a basis for identifying recruitment numbers - but the statistic does not say anything about whether or not these people *need* replacing. To measure labour turnover in a more systematic and useful way, an index may be used, allowing managers to make comparisons between, for example, different organisations in the same industry, or different departments in the same organisation: the *significance* of the wastage figures then emerges.

Here are some examples.

(a) *Crude labour turnover rate* (the BIM Index, British Institute of Management, 1949). Here we express turnover as a percentage of the number of people employed.

$$\frac{\text{Number of leavers in a period}}{\text{Average number of people employed in the period}} \times 100 = \% \text{ turnover}$$

This is normally quoted as an annual rate and may be used to measure turnover per organisation, department or group of employees. The disadvantage of this index is that it does not indicate the length of service of leavers, which makes it impossible to identify long-term employees and therefore the size of the stable workforce. (In fact, most wastage occurs among young people and those in the early stages of their employment in an organisation: stability tends to increase with length of service.)

(b) *Labour stability*

Here we try to eliminate short-term employees from our analysis, thus obtaining a better picture of the significant movements in the workforce.

$$\frac{\text{Number of employees with one or more years' service}}{\text{Number of employees employed at the beginning of the year}} \times 100 = \% \text{ turnover}$$

Particularly in times of rapid expansion, organisations should keep an eye on stability, as a meaningful measure.

Activity 5

Suppose a company has 20 employees at the beginning of 19X5, and 100 at the end of the year. Disliking the expansion, 18 of the original experienced labour force resign. At the end of 19X5, the company works out that it has:

BIM Index: $\dfrac{18 \text{ leavers}}{60 \text{ (average) employees}} \times 100 = \%$ turnover

This is not uncommon, and would cause no undue worries. Work out the stability index for the company for 19X5, and comment on your findings.

(c) The labour stability index ignores new starts during the year but does not consider actual length of service, which may be added to the measurement via *length of service analysis*, or *survival rate analysis*. Here, the organisation calculates the proportion of employees who are engaged within a certain period who are still with the firm after various periods of time. There may be a survival rate of 70% after two years, for example, but only 50% in year three: the distribution of losses might be plotted on a survival curve to indicate trends.

3.2 Advantages and disadvantages of labour turnover

It would be wrong to think of labour turnover as purely disadvantageous to every organisation. Potential *advantages* include:

(a) opportunities to inject 'new blood' into the organisation: new people bringing new ideas and outlooks, new skills and experience in different situations. Absence of labour turnover would simply create an increasingly old workforce;

(b) the creation of opportunities for promotion and succession. If there were no labour turnover, junior staff and management would face a long career without development, waiting for someone higher up the ladder to retire, with no incentives or encouragement to ambition; and

(c) the ability to cope with labour surpluses, in some grades of job, without having to make redundancies. Natural wastage can save industrial relations problems in this way.

However, *disadvantages* of labour turnover include the following.

(a) It breaks the continuity of operations, culture and career development. It is generally recognised by employers that continuity offers stability and predictability, which is beneficial to efficiency. When people leave, there is bound to be a hiatus while a replacement is found and - through induction, training and experience - brought 'on line' to the same level of accustomed expertise of the previous jobholder.

(b) It may be perceived by other employees as a symptom of job dissatisfaction, causing the problem to escalate. High labour turnover can foster a culture low in morale and loyalty.

(c) The costs of turnover can be high, including:

   (i) *replacement costs*: the cost of recruiting, selecting and training replacements; loss of output or efficiency during this process; possible wastage, spoilage and inefficiencies because of inexperience in new staff; and also

   (ii) *preventative costs*: the cost of retaining staff, through pay, benefits and welfare provisions, maintaining working conditions or whatever.

It is common to hear that staff turnover is bad when it is high - but this cannot be assessed in isolation. What is an acceptable rate of turnover and what is excessive? There is no fixed percentage rate of turnover which is the borderline between acceptable and unacceptable. Labour turnover rates will be a signal that something is possibly wrong when:

(a) they are higher than the turnover rates in another similar department of the organisation. For example, if the labour turnover rate is higher at branch A than at branches B, C and D in the same area, something might be wrong at branch A;

(b) they are higher than they were in previous years or months. In other words, the situation might be deteriorating; and

(c) the costs of labour turnover are estimated and are considered too high - although they will be relative to the costs of *preventing* high turnover by offering employees rewards, facilities and services that will keep them in the organisation.

Otherwise, the organisation may live with high rates because they are the norm for a particular industry or job, because the organisation culture accepts constant

Business Basics: Human Resource Management

turnover, or because the cost of keeping employees is greater than the cost of replacing them.

3.3 Causes of labour turnover

A systematic investigation into the causes of undesirable turnover will have to be made, using some or all of the following methods.

(a) Information given in *exit interviews* with leaving staff, which should be the first step after an employee announces his intention to leave. It must be recognised, however, that the reasons given for leaving may not be complete, true, or those that would be most useful to the organisation. People may say that they are 'going to a better job', while the real *reason* for the move is dissatisfaction with the level of interest in the current job. The interviewer should be trained in interview techniques, and should be perceived to be 'safe' to talk to and objective in his appraisal of the situation (and therefore probably not the supervisor against whom the resigning employee has a complaint or the manager who is going to write a reference).

(b) Information gleaned from interviews with leavers, in their homes, shortly after they have gone. This practice is occasionally used, intended to encourage greater objectivity and frankness, but one which requires tact and diplomacy if it is not to be resented by the subject.

(c) Attitude surveys, to gauge the general climate of the organisation, and the response of the workforce as a whole to working conditions, management style and so on. Such surveys are notoriously unreliable, however.

(d) Information gathered on a number of (interrelated) variables which can be assumed to correlate with labour turnover. Some of these are listed below.

Labour turnover might be influenced by any of the following factors.

(a) *The economic climate and the state of the jobs market*. When unemployment is high and jobs outside the organisation are hard to find, labour turnover will be much lower.

(b) *The age structure and length of service of the work force*. An ageing workforce will have many people approaching retirement. However, it has been found in most companies that labour turnover is highest amongst:

   (i) young people, especially unmarried people with no family responsibilities;
   (ii) people who have been in the employment of the company for only a short time.

   The employment life cycle usually shows a decision-point shortly after joining, when things are still new and perhaps difficult: this is called the 'first induction crisis'. There is then a period of mutual accommodation and adjustment between employer and employee (called the 'differential transit' period): in the settling of areas of conflict, there may be further turnover. A second (less significant) induction crisis occurs as both parties come to terms with the new status quo. Finally, the period of 'settled connection' begins, and the likelihood of leaving is much less.

(c) *The organisation climate or culture*, and its style of leadership. An organisation might be formal and bureaucratic, where employees are expected to work according to prescribed rules and procedures. Other organisations are more flexible, and allow more scope for individual expression and creativity. Individuals will prefer - and stay with - one system or the other.

(d) *Pay and conditions of employment*. If these are not good enough, people will leave to find better terms elsewhere, or will use this as a focus for their discontent in other areas.

(e) *Physical working conditions*. If working conditions are uncomfortable, unclean, unsafe, or noisy, say, people will be more inclined to leave.

(f) *Career prospects and training*. If the chances of reaching a senior position before a certain age are low, an ambitious employee is likely to consider leaving to find a job where promotion may come more quickly. The same may be true where an employee wants training for qualification or skill development, and opportunities are limited in his current job.

Activity 6

List the factors that might have prompted you to leave an organisation where you worked (or where you are now studying). What (if anything) could or should your employers (or tutors) have done (or do now) to keep you?

3.4 Control of labour turnover

Some reasons for leaving will be genuine and largely unavoidable, or unforeseeable, such as:

(a) illness or accident (although transfer to lighter duties, excusing the employee from shiftwork or other accommodations might be possible);

(b) a move from the locality for domestic reasons, transport or housing difficulties;

(c) marriage or pregnancy. Many women still give up working when their family situation changes, although the opportunity to return is now provided for in law;

(d) retirement; and

(e) career change.

However, where factors in the work environment - like leadership, pay and conditions - are identified as sources of employee dissatisfaction and departure, problems can be addressed, if it is considered worthwhile to do so. Selection systems may be revised to ensure that future recruits are more compatible with the culture and leadership of the organisation, and with the demands of their jobs (since some people will be able to handle monotony, pressure, responsibility or lack of it better than others). Alternatively, the organisation itself may be adapted to the needs of the 'type' of people it wishes to employ.

4 MANAGEMENT SUCCESSION AND PROMOTION

Although organisations have typically downsized and delayered to the extent that, according to Herriot, there are often only five or six levels between junior supervisor and chief executive, promotion and succession policies are still a vital part of the human resource plan, as a form of risk management associated with the internal supply of labour. The planned development of staff (not just skills training, but experience and growth in responsibility) is essential to ensure the *continuity* of performance in the organisation. This is particularly so for *management* planning. The departure of a senior manager with no planned or 'groomed' successor could leave a gap in the organisation structure: the lead time for training and developing a suitable replacement may be very long.

Promotion is useful from the firm's point of view, in establishing a management succession, filling more senior positions with proven, experienced and loyal employees. It is also one of the main forms of *reward* the organisation can offer to its employees, especially where, in the pursuit of equity or fairness, employees are paid a rate for the job rather than for their performance in the job: pay ceases to be a prime incentive. In order to be a motivator, promotion must be seen to be both available (to give employees a focus for their ambition), and fair (so that they can see the link between merit - or seniority, or whatever - and promotion, and work towards it on that basis). Unplanned promotions can cause political and structural problems in the organisation, with gaps or overlaps in managerial responsibilities, jealousies and rivalries.

4.1 Promotion policy

A coherent policy for promotion is needed. This may vary to include provisions such as the following.

(a) All promotions, as far as possible, and all things being equal, are to be made from within the firm. This is particularly important with reference to senior positions if junior ranks are not to be discouraged and de-motivated. Although the organisation will from time to time require new blood if it is not to stagnate, it will be an encouragement to staff to see that promotion is open to them, and that the best jobs do not always go to outsiders.

(b) Merit and ability (systematically appraised) should be the principal basis of promotion, rather than seniority (age or years of service). Loyalty and experience will obviously be considered but should not be the sole criterion. Younger staff may grow impatient if they feel that they are simply waiting to grow old before their prospects improve. Promotion on ability is more likely to have a motivating effect. Management will have to demonstrate to staff and/or employee representatives, however, that their system of appraisal and merit rating is fair and fairly applied, if the bases for promotion are to be trusted and accepted. Appraisal should be conducted on the basis of potential for the future, as well as (if not instead of) past performance.

(c) Vacancies should be advertised and open to all employees of the organisation.

(d) There should be full opportunities for all employees to be promoted to the highest grades.

(e) Personnel and appraisal records should be kept and up-dated regularly.

(f) Training should be offered to encourage and develop employees of ability and ambition in advance of promotion.

(g) Scales of pay, areas of responsibility, duties and privileges of each post and so on should be clearly communicated so that employees know what promotion means - in other words, what they are being promoted *to*.

4.2 Promote or recruit?

The decision of whether to promote from within or fill a position from outside will hinge on many factors. If there is simply no one available on the current staff with the expertise or ability required (say, if the organisation is venturing into new areas of activity, or changing its methods by computerisation), the recruitment manager will obviously have to seek qualified people outside the organisation. If there is time, a person of particular potential within the organisation could be trained in the necessary skills, but that will require an analysis of the costs of training and development (including time and reduced productivity), as compared to the possible (and probably less quantifiable) benefits.

Where the organisation has the choice, it should consider the following points.

(a) Management will be familiar with an internal promotee: there will be detailed appraisal information available from employee records. The outside recruit will to a greater extent be an unknown quantity - and the organisation will be taking a greater risk of an unacceptable personality or performance emerging later.

(b) A promotee has already worked within the organisation and will be familiar with its:

(i) culture, or philosophy; informal rules and norms about dress and behaviour, as well as stated policy;

(ii) politics; power-structures and relationships;

(iii) systems and procedures;

(iv) objectives; and

(v) other personnel (who will likewise be familiar with him or her).

(c) Promotion of insiders is visible proof of the organisation's willingness to develop people's careers. This may well have an encouraging and motivating effect. Outsiders may well invite resentment or a feeling that extra effort is pointless, because it is unrewarded.

(d) Internal advertisement of vacancies might contribute to the implementation of equal opportunities policies depending on the current makeup of the workforce. Many women are employed in secretarial and clerical jobs from which promotion is unlikely - and relatively few are in higher-graded roles. Internal advertising could become a route for opening up opportunities for women at junior levels.

(e) On the other hand, an organisation must retain its ability to adapt, grow and change, and this may well require new blood, wider views, fresh ideas. Insiders may be too socialised into the prevailing culture to see faults or be willing to 'upset the apple cart' where necessary for the organisation's health.

Activity 7

What factors might make you either hire or promote for the following vacancies?

(a) A senior management vacancy in Kentucky Donalds, a fast food chain with a very strong cultural identity and uniformity of style/practice across its (global) branch structure.

(b) A junior management position in Barcloyd's Bank, a highly structured, bureaucratic organisation which invests heavily in in-house training.

(c) A senior management position in a family-owned, highly traditional textile manufacturer, which has retained its manufacturing methods and product portfolio for many years, but is now steadily losing market share.

4.3 The promotion programme

A comprehensive *promotion programme*, as part of the overall human resource plan (for getting the right people into jobs at the right time) will include:

(a) establishment of the relative significance of jobs, by job analysis, job description and job classification, so that the line (and consequences) of promotion are made clear;

(b) establishment of methods of assessment of staff and their potential for fulfilling the requirements of more senior positions;

(c) planning in advance for training where necessary to enhance potential and develop specific skills; and

(d) policy with regard to internal promotion or external recruitment and training.

The human resources manager will have to use the utmost sensitivity in applying any policies formulated. It is often difficult to persuade departmental managers to agree to the promotion of a subordinate out of a department, especially if he has been selected as having particular ability: the department will be losing an able member, and will have to find, induct and train a replacement. Additional interpersonal problems may be created if 'fast track' promotions (say, of graduates) create a 'leapfrog' effect, where junior staff outstrip their seniors. Moreover, if the promotion does not take place, and the manager's resistance were made known, there would be a motivational problem to contend with. The human resource manager will have to be able to back his recommendation with sound policies for providing and training a replacement with as little loss of the department's efficiency as possible.

5 LABOUR FLEXIBILITY

Flexibility is an area of current interest in human resource management, as economic pressures require more efficient use of human resource.

Definition

Labour flexibility involves the development of *versatility* or 'multi-skilling' in the labour resource, and the management of that versatility through the complex human relations problems which commonly surround the application of flexibility in many of its forms.

For the *organisation*, flexibility offers a cost effective, efficient way of utilising the labour resource. Under competitive pressure, technological innovation, and a variety of other changes, organisations need a versatile, 'lean' workforce for efficiency, control and predictability: the stability of the organisation in a volatile environment depends on its ability to adapt swiftly to meet changes, without incurring cost penalties or suffering waste. If employee flexibility can be achieved with the co-operation of the employees and their representatives, there may be an end to demarcation disputes, costly redundancy packages and other consequences of apparently rational organisation design.

From the point of view of the *employee*, the erosion of rigid specialisation, the micro-division of labour and the inflexible working week can also offer:

(a) a higher quality of working life;
(b) an accommodation with non-work interests and demands;
(c) greater job satisfaction through variety of work; and perhaps
(d) job security and material benefits, since a versatile, mobile, flexible employee is likely to be more attractive to employers and have a higher value in the current labour market climate.

5.1 Ways of developing flexibility

Organisational and cultural mechanisms for developing flexibility include the following.

(a) *The erosion of demarcations between job areas.* Workers can be encouraged, trained and organised to work across the boundaries of their job or craft. This has, historically, been difficult to achieve because craft and occupational groups have supported demarcation in order to protect jobs and maintain skills, standards and differentials. With the need for adaptability, however, rigid job descriptions and specialisation have gone out of fashion and 'multi-skilled' labour is much prized on the market.

(b) *Flexibility in the deployment of the workforce in terms of man hours.* With the shrinking demand for some categories of labour, ideas about full employment, full-time employment and 'one man, one job' have had to be revised. There are various ways in which individuals can be given a flexible job in terms of working hours, and organisations can avoid overmanning and idle time.

   (i) Fixed-term contracts, job sharing and splitting, or annual hours contracts are ways of countering various problems of seasonal or task-oriented fluctuations in the demand for labour, avoiding redundancies and lay-offs. Raines Dairy Foods, for example, announced in 1995 that it was using its profit related pay scheme to persuade its 1,000 employees to move gradually from a standard 40-hour week plus overtime to an annual hours system.

(ii) The employment of non-permanent, non-career labour creates flexibility. Part-time work, casual labour, temporary working (the 'temping' boom, not only, as traditionally, in secretarial work but in accounting, nursing and teaching, for example) and consultancy are popular options, both for the workers and for the organisations who benefit from their services without long-term contractual obligations.

(iii) Flexitime is another area in which conventional rules and boundaries are increasingly bent or broken: '9 to 5' is no longer the most effective scheme of working in large city areas where commuting is a problem, and in a workforce where parents and home makers are having to reconcile the requirements of family, household and work.

(c) *Cultural flexibility.* All of the above methods will require cultural change - or will involve cultural upheaval - in the organisation and in society as a whole. Ideas about specialism, about career, about the relationship between work, leisure and self-identity are threatened.

Quite apart from the initial change of attitude required to smooth the way for these methods, there is an important role for HRM in the development and maintenance of an organisation culture which accepts and applauds flexibility generally: this will be the key to task- and customer-orientation, adaptability to environmental changes, innovation and entrepreneurship which - according to many current theories - is the basis of survival in the modern business environment.

The human resource function has a role to play in designing flexible systems for recruitment and deployment of labour (permanent and non-permanent, full-time and part-time) within employment legislation. It must organise and administer these systems. It must be responsible for the communication, consultation and negotiation that will be required not only to avoid industrial relations problems but to sell the ideas and values that will become a flexible organisation culture. There may be welfare considerations, counselling and so on as a side effect of major change. So the issue of employee flexibility will impact on much of the human resource function's activity in the organisation.

Activity 8

Pick an organisation that you have worked for, or are familiar with, or can find out about. How flexible is the workforce in this organisation? Is it versatile, multi-skilled and happy to work unorthodox hours or without a strict job description? What does the human resource department in this organisation do to encourage, or to discourage, flexibility of labour? (Think about job descriptions, training and development, working hours and so on.)

5.2 Flexible working methods

G A Cole (*Personnel Management: Theory and Practice*) sums up the pressures on managerial decisions about the size and nature of the workforce as follows.

Business Basics: Human Resource Management

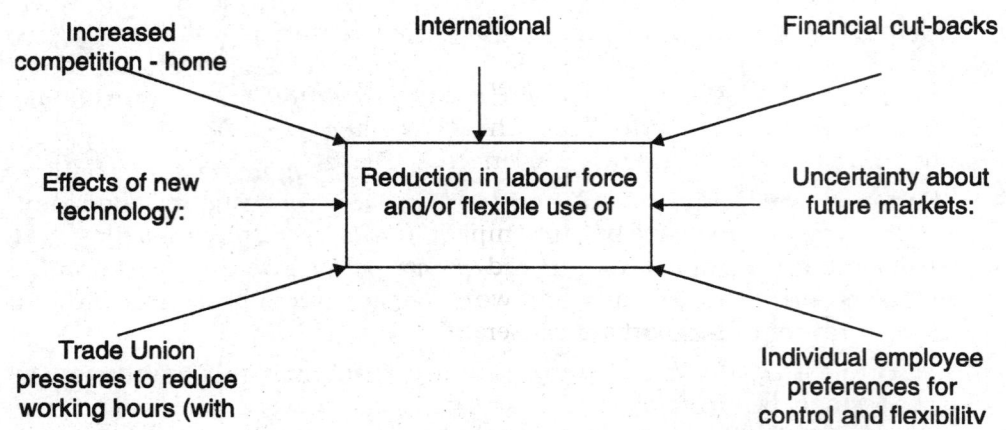

```
Increased              International           Financial cut-backs
competition - home
         ↘                  ↓                       ↙
Effects of new    →  Reduction in labour force  ←  Uncertainty about
technology:          and/or flexible use of        future markets:
         ↗                  ↑                       ↖
Trade Union                                      Individual employee
pressures to reduce                              preferences for
working hours (with                              control and flexibility
```

Figure 2.1 Cole's summary of workforce decisions

Torn between the need to downsize (or at least not expand) their workforce and the desire to offer a measure of security of employment, many organisations build themselves a 'buffer' by increasing the proportion of non-permanent labour in their workforce. Categories which generally supplement the permanent (full- or part-time) workforce include trainees, student or agency 'temps' (temporary workers), and subcontract workers. Alternatively, *job sharing* may be used: an existing job is split in two, so that two people can share it, paid pro-rata (much like ordinary part-time working).

Atkinson, in a paper written in 1984 but still extremely influential (*Flexible Manning: the way ahead*), suggested that the workforce be divided into:

(a) a *core* group: permanent, functionally flexible or 'multi-skilled', (and trained and rewarded accordingly), and representing the lowest number of employees required by work activity at any time throughout the year; and

(b) a *peripheral* group, which can be taken on at any season when staff requirements rise above the minimal. The periphery may consist of:

   (i) *top-up* staff, recruited as short-contract, casual or part-time staff; or
   (ii) *permanent* employees in areas where there is traditionally a high level of mobility and therefore wastage/turnover: clerical, secretarial and so on.

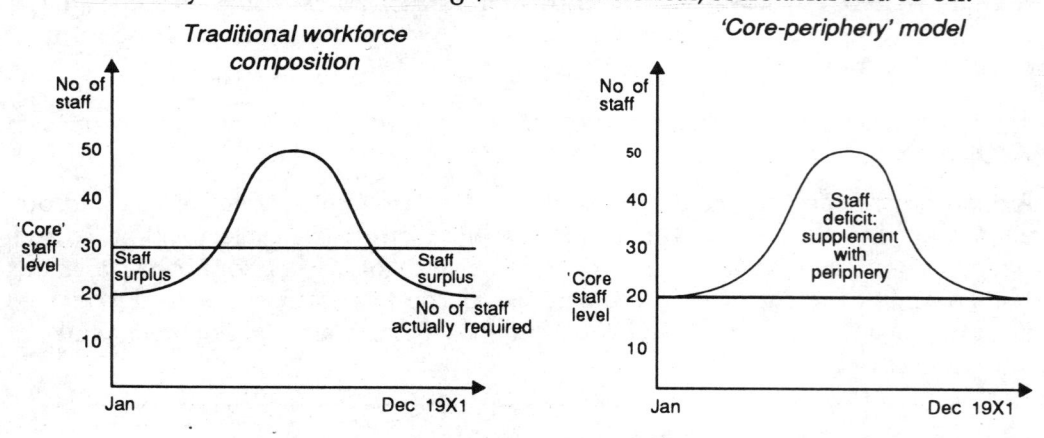

Figure 2.2 Traditional v 'core-periphery' model

The question, touched on above, of *rewarding* functionally versatile employees is an important one. A *single status* policy, or the provision of common salary and benefit systems, facilitates redeployment of staff. Breaking down artificial status and reward barriers not only helps to secure greater transferability of skills and labour, but may have advantages of morale and the broadening of staff loyalty and commitment to embrace organisational, rather than sectional, goals. However, according to the Employment in Britain Survey (1993), organisations must develop part-timers and temporary workers in the same way as full-timers, or else risk underperformance and an inclination to avoid responsibility.

EXAMPLE: CALOR GAS

In *Personnel Management Plus* (September 1992) it was reported that:

'Calor Gas has replaced more than a third of its hourly paid workers with temporary staff on lower rates of pay, after terminating the contracts of the entire manual workforce.

Two-thirds of the group have been re-employed on new contracts, including 500 drivers, and 100 skilled workers and supervisors, whose pay levels have been maintained. But they are now working more flexibly under a new agreement with the Transport and General Workers Union.

The temporary workers... have replaced full-time operatives who cleaned and filled gas bottles at nine depots around the country.

John Harris, operations and personnel director, said the company needed to cut costs, increase productivity and change its culture. The market was seasonal and Calor Gas had always used temporary workers in the winter. The difference now was that there was a core of temps, many of whom he expected would work for the company on a long-term basis, as well as a fluctuating periphery.

The company had also replaced its single national pay rate with varying regional rates for the contract workers. "We have fewer people, paid less and they are very much more productive," said Harris.'

EXAMPLE: SMITHKLINE BEECHAM

SmithKline Beecham has introduced multi-skilling at its factory in Irvine (*People Management 9 February 1995*). This was accomplished across a great 'divide' of strict demarcation between *operators* (belonging to the Transport and General Workers' Union, TGWU) and *craftsmen* (represented by the Amalgamated Electrical and Engineering Union, AEEU). Further problems were posed by deeply-entrenched working practices, and the strong trade union traditions of western Scotland.

In the past, process operators faced with a blockage in the pipes (carrying materials from one stage of the process to another) have had to tell their supervisor, who would tell the engineering foreman, who would send a fitter to deal with it: meanwhile, production would grind to a halt. After multi-skilling, the job could be done by whoever was best placed to do it: craftsman or - more often - operator).

Analysis of such situations by working parties resulted in the concept of the 'best person': instead of jobs being 'owned' by particular groups, the most appropriate individual to do a particular job should be trained and skilled to do it.

'The intention was to increase efficiency across the whole site by cross-skilling electrical, mechanical and instrument engineers, while at the same time equipping operators with basic engineering, materials movement and analytical skills'.

Agreement was achieved after three years' consultation and negotiation with the unions. Support was added by a grant from the European Commission, under the 'Force' programme (since superseded by the Leonardo de Vinci programme). Force aimed to promote employee development by encouraging the sharing of information about good practice and successful initiatives like multi-skilling at SmithKline Beecham.

5.3 Flexible working hours

There are various techniques for flexibility of working hours, including the following.

Overtime working

Overtime working involves offering above-standard rates of pay for hours worked in excess of standard. This is highly flexible, but can be expensive, and may encourage slower working during standard hours. However, a great deal of overtime goes unseen and unpaid: according to the Institute of Management evening work is frequently undertaken by more than half of British managers and more than a third regularly work at weekends.

Shift working

Increasing numbers of workers are employed on a shift basis. The advantage to the organisation is that overhead costs can be spread over a longer productive 'day', and equipment and labour can be used more efficiently.

There are three main systems in operation.

(a) *Double-day system* - ie two standard working day (eight hour) shifts, say from 6am to 2pm, and 2pm to 10pm. The physical and social problems of such a system are much less acute than where night-work is required - although the hours may seem somewhat 'anti-social' and hard on the evening social life.

(b) *Three-shift system* - ie three eight-hour shifts covering the twenty-four hour 'day' (say 6am to 2pm, 2pm to 10pm, 10pm to 6am). The main problem here is the 'unnaturalness' of night-time work on the third shift. There are physiological, psychological and social effects - which we will discuss below. Most complaints are directed at the so-called 'dead fortnight', when the pattern of afternoon and night shifts interfere most with normal social life.

(c) *Continental or 3-2-2 system.* This entails more frequent changes than the traditional system, enabling employees to have 'normal' leisure time at least two or three times per week. Over a four-week cycle, shifts rotate so that workers do 3 mornings, 2 afternoons, 2 nights, 3 rest days, 2 mornings, 2 afternoon etc (see table below). This gets away from the 'dead fortnight', but it may cause confusion initially, and also means that there are no entirely free weekends - which may be important to families.

3-2-2 system						
Week	Mon	Tue	Wed	Thur	Fri	Sat	Sun
1	6-14	6-14	14-22	14-22	22-6	22-6	
2	-	-	6-14	6-14	14-22	14-22	22-6
3	22-6	22-6	-	-	6-14	6-14	14-22
4	14-22	14-22	22-6	22-6	-	-	6-14

Average 42 hours per week

The 3-2-2 system is becoming increasingly popular - and is already established in the chemical, iron and steel industries. ICI operate it in two factories, and surveys show 80% of the workforce in favour because:

(a) shorter, though more frequent, spells on each shift were found to be less fatiguing than longer periods on, say, the night shift;

(b) the variety was more enjoyable;

(c) employees felt that they had more time off for social and family life; and

(d) senior staff found it easier to keep in touch with the shiftworkers.

A study by Folkard and Monk suggests that the best way of adapting to hours which are not normal for the human body is to work permanently on one shift, allowing the body to develop a 'revised schedule'. This is, however, unlikely to be widely implemented because of the anti-social nature of evening and night work.

Activity 9

What do you think the effects of shift-working would be on an employee's life? Think about:

(a) physiological/medical effects;
(b) psychological effects;
(c) social effects; and
(d) economic effects.

Flexitime

There are many 'flexitime' systems in operation providing freedom from the restriction of a '9 to 5' work-hours routine.

Definition

Flexitime is when predetermined fixed times of arrival and departure from work are replaced by a working day split into two different time zones.

(a) The main part of the day is called 'core time' and is the only period when employees *must* be at their job (this is commonly 10.00 to 16.00 hours).

(b) The flexible time is at the beginning and the end of each day and during this time it is up to the individual to choose when he arrives and leaves. Arrival and departure times would be recorded by some form of 'clocking in' system. The total working week or month for each employee must add up to the prescribed number of hours, though he may go into 'debit' or 'credit' for hours from day to day, in some systems.

A flexitime system can be as flexible as the company wishes.

(a) The most basic version involves flexibility only within the day, with no possibility of carrying forward debit or credit hours into other days, so if you arrive late, you work late. This type of system is used in some factories where transport difficulties make arrivals and departures difficult.

(b) Another system is flexible hours within the span of the week. Hours can be carried forward to the next day. This enables an employee to cope with a fluctuating work load without overtime and gives him some control over his work and leisure time.

(c) Finally, flexitime may be operated by the month. Each employee will have a coded key which can also serve as an identity card, and this will be used on arrival and departure by insertion into a key acceptor, which records hours worked on a 24 hour clock.

(d) An even more flexible option is *annual hours contracts*, compensating for seasonal patterns of demand by agreeing yearly (rather than weekly) hours of work. Some or all of these hours may be committed to a rota schedule, while some additional 'bank hours' may be held in reserve for unforeseen fluctuations (such as the need to cover for absences), plus 'reserve hours' designated for specific purposes other than normal working (such as training). During the intensive work period, longer working days, or more intensive shifts may be used - without incurring 'overtime' costs, since the extra hours are compensated for by leisure time (from 'shift-free' days to long blocks of time) in a slack period.

Flexitime enables workers to plan their lives on a more personal basis, as long as they work their contracted hours in the period. Where the employee works longer hours than necessary, he is usually able to save these hours for holiday or days off.

> *Flexible working hours not only bring order into this disorder [peak hour travel, traffic strikes etc]; within limits that are clearly defined and acceptable to management, it gives staff a new facility deliberately to vary arrival and departure times for personal reasons, and to do so with candour and dignity.*
>
> M W Cuming, *Personnel Management*

Activity 10

Suggest three advantages to the organisation of implementing a flexitime system.

Part-time working

The 1980s saw a 'boom' in part-time working. The number of part-time employees as a proportion of all employees in the UK grew from 19.1% in 1978 to 24.2% in December 1989. According to the 1993 Income Data Services Survey, this figure had risen to 26%. Of these, 80% are women. Stephen Connock (*HR Vision*) gives seven main reasons for the increase in part-time working.

(a) Employers can match working hours to operational requirements better.

(b) The personal circumstances of key staff can be accommodated through part-time working. This will be particularly relevant to female returners.

(c) The productivity of part-timers is generally higher than that of full-timers (hardly surprising, since work is undertaken in more concentrated time periods).

(d) The absence levels of part-timers are generally lower: domestic requirements can be more easily fitted into the free periods in the part-time schedule.

(e) A pool of trained employees is available for switching to full-time work, or extending working time temporarily.

(f) Difficulties in recruiting full-time staff have prompted organisations to recruit and train part-time staff. Female returners are more likely to be attracted to an organisation if the hours of work are suitable, which will generally mean working part-time.

(g) Part-time working can cut overtime costs, since it is possible to avoid paying premium rates.

There has for some years been concern about equal treatment for part-time workers in regard to terms and conditions - especially since, with a higher percentage of part-time workers being women, less favourable terms can be construed as indirect discrimination on the grounds of sex. This was judged to be the case (*Equal Opportunities Commission v Secretary of State for Employment* March 1994) in the House of Lords. The EOC claimed that the UK provisions restricting part-timers' access to redundancy payments and unfair dismissal remedies were in breach of European Union Laws on equal opportunities. As a result, employment law has been amended to provide the same protection for part-time and full-time staff.

Temporary work is more regulated in most other member states of the EU than it is in the UK. Many EU employers have a legal obligation to justify temporary work, provide a contract, limit the duration of the contract and provide comparable or similar pay and conditions. Fixed-term contracts automatically become permanent in most states, if they over-run.

Three European Commission directives cover the employment of part-time and temporary staff, as part of the Social Charter.

(a) The first directive deals with equal treatment of part-time, temporary and full-time permanent staff. (The introduction welcomes the positive effects on flexibility and job creation of the increase in part-time and temporary employment, but notes that the treatment of such employees is not always on a par with others, in terms of employment and working conditions.)

(b) The second directive deals with the legal rights of part-time and temporary workers. It welcomes flexible work patterns, but warns that the different treatment of these contracts across the member states creates dangers of distorted competition due to differences in indirect wage costs.

(c) The third directive deals with the health and safety protection of temporary workers. It says that 'in general temporary workers are more exposed to the risk of accidents at work and occupational diseases than other workers'. In particular, night-work and shift-work are causes for concern, and the establishment of minimum rest periods is considered essential.

The directives, upheld by decisions in the European Court of Justice (ECJ) and the UK House of Lords mean some changes to UK legislation.

(a) Following the decision of the House of Lords in favour of the Equal Opportunities Commission, all employment rights currently available to 'full timers' (those working 16 hours or more) should be extended to 'part-timers' (those working eight hours or more). The rights include, for example, an itemised pay statement and a statement of terms and conditions after 13 weeks; a minimum period of notice and sickness benefit after one month; unfair dismissal protection, redundancy, maternity leave and right to return after two years.

(b) Occupational benefits such as access to pension scheme membership should be given to all those working more than eight hours: this has been upheld by recent ECJ decisions. Occupational sick pay and holidays should also be given on an equal pro-rata basis.

(c) Most of the regulations on temporary staff would be new. However, apart from the requirement for a more detailed contract, most of the health and safety provisions for temporary staff would be covered by existing legislation.

The UK government is concerned that the proposals will add to costs, make it harder to compete internationally, and in the long term, damage job creation.

5.4 Teleworking and homeworking

According to a survey by the Henley Centre, reported in *The Times* on 5 September 1996, the number of employees working from home increased by 50% between 1992 and 1995. Off-site or out-of-office working may be available to employers, with the availability of telecommunications and computer networking.

Definition

'Telecommuting' (The Administrator, August 1992) 'describes the process of working from home, or from a satellite office close to home, with the aid of computers, facsimile machines, modems or other forms of telecommunication equipment'.

Telecommuting offers:

(a) savings on overheads, particularly premises costs, in view of rising rents in many of the major cities in the UK;

(b) the opportunity to bring into employment skilled and experienced people for whom traditional working practices have hitherto been impracticable: single parents, mothers, the handicapped, carers and so on. (The greatest impact of this may be increased opportunities for the handicapped, according to the article in *The Administrator);*

(c) elimination of the need to commute - with consequent reductions in traffic congestion, fuel consumption, travel costs, pollution etc;

(d) potential reduction in stress, since there is less conflict with non-work goals and needs, and a more congenial environment (with no commuting to undergo).

In addition to 'telecommuters', home workers may be:

(a) traditional *outworkers,* such as home typists or wordprocessors and envelope-fillers (for mailshots), writers and editors, tele-canvassers and market-researchers. These may be employed by the firm or subcontracted (freelance);

(b) *itinerants* such as salesmen, who do not have a permanent presence in the office, and use their home (and even car) for working on the move. These people may be employed by the firm, or self-employed; or

(c) those in personal services, like ironing and mending of clothes, out-of-salon hairdressing, music teaching and so on.

Activity 11

What problems can you anticipate for both management and workers, from homeworking?

EXAMPLE: RANK XEROX

Rank Xerox launched a successful networking scheme as long ago as 1981. They closed down a central London office costing them £300,000 a year, 'fired' the staff and then re-engaged them on networking contracts: each became a separate company working from home, linked direct to HQ, and guaranteed income if they supplied work on time.

The advantages were reported to be that:

(a) as 'self-employed' workers, the networkers developed the discipline and motivation to work conscientiously;

(b) the more they did, the more they earned, and the firm encouraged them to use their spare time to take on contracts outside Rank Xerox itself;

(c) networkers travelled in to Head Office only one day per week;

(d) some banded together to form multiple units, or shared office premises near their homes, thus overcoming any sense of isolation.

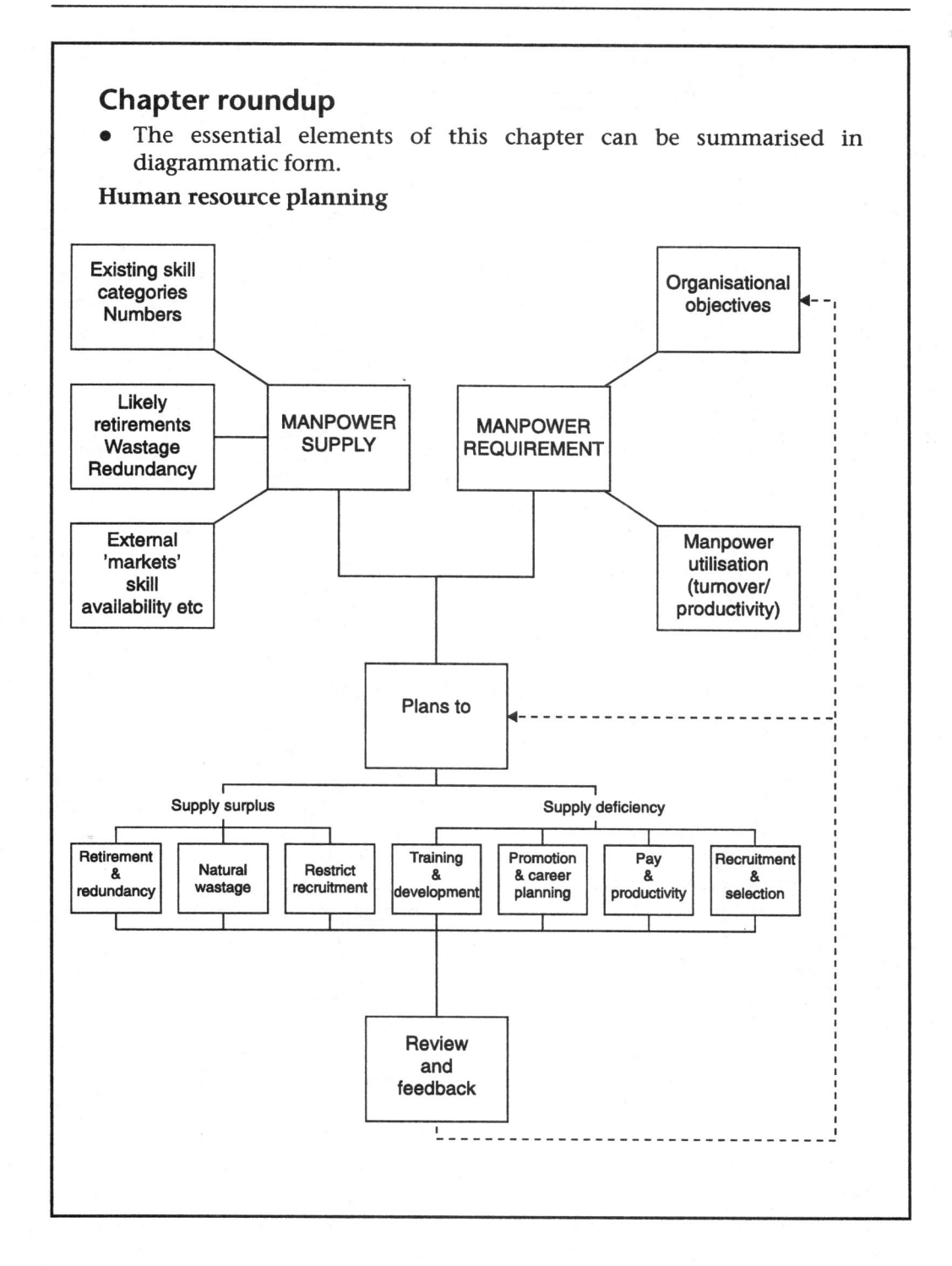

Chapter 2: Human resource planning and flexibility

Chapter roundup

- The essential elements of this chapter can be summarised in diagrammatic form.

Human resource planning

```
[Existing skill categories / Numbers]
[Likely retirements / Wastage / Redundancy]    →  MANPOWER SUPPLY
[External 'markets' skill availability etc]

[Organisational objectives]
[Manpower utilisation (turnover/ productivity)]  →  MANPOWER REQUIREMENT

                    ↓
                [Plans to]
                    ↓
    Supply surplus          Supply deficiency
    - Retirement & redundancy
    - Natural wastage
    - Restrict recruitment
                            - Training & development
                            - Promotion & career planning
                            - Pay & productivity
                            - Recruitment & selection
                    ↓
            [Review and feedback]
```

Quick quiz

1. Outline a systematic approach to human resource planning.
2. List three types of method used in human resource forecasting. Indicate to what degree each is a 'scientific' method.
3. When is labour turnover to be regarded as a bad thing?
4. List four reasons why an organisation might wish to promote an existing employee rather than recruit someone from outside to fill the post. What might make this a less desirable option from the firm's point of view?
5. What three broad 'types' of flexibility may be developed by an organisation? List some examples of each.

Business Basics: Human Resource Management

Solutions to activities

1 There is a huge variety to choose from, but you may have used such examples as air traffic controllers or airline pilots, computer programmers in a specialist field or language, or - more common - doctors, veterinary surgeons, lawyers.

3 Suggestions include:

   (a) banks

   (b) career breaks, crèches, flexible working hours or annual hours contracts.

4 The computer company is in an extremely volatile and changing market, which will present planning difficulties. It is also a highly skilled business, however, with long training times and skill shortages - so despite the difficulties, human resource planning will be important, especially since the company is likely to have a flexible structure in order to be able to respond quickly to change.

   The international airline is a business which is potentially volatile (transatlantic price wars, political/terrorist action, closely protected airspace, crashes affecting popularity etc) and which is critically dependent on scarce employees with long training cycles.

5 Stability index: Those with two or more years' service × 100 = 10% *stability*

   Only 10% of the labour force is stable (and therefore offering the benefits of experience and acclimatisation to the work and culture of the organisation)! The crude turnover rate has disguised the significance of what has happened.

7 (a) Kentucky Donalds probably has a highly motivational approach to the development of staff (above the high-turnover 'casual' levels) which would suit promotion from within. This would also help to ensure consistency and continuity of management style, culture and work practices, which might be disrupted by an outsider.

   (b) Highly-structured organisations tend to encourage a clear career progression through the ranks, in order to maintain stability and retain staff: again, this would encourage promotion from within. Although redundancies in the financial services sector have made available a pool of experienced/trained labour, which might be a 'ready-made' alternative to developing an existing staff member, Barcloyds' investment in in-house training suggests that they have their own ways of doing things, which would make an internal employee, again, more suitable.

   (c) The textile manufacturer seems to be stuck in a rut, failing to adapt to competition, new manufacturing technology and/or fashion trends. It needs new product ideas, perhaps new marketing ideas, perhaps a new - or reorganised - plant. The problem may well be in the narrow viewpoint and inertia of the existing management team and organisation culture. Since this is a senior management position (a junior manager could not hope to influence the culture and decisions sufficiently), new blood should be sought outside

9 (a) *Physiological or medical effects* - a disruption of body-temperature, disturbance of digestion, inability to sleep during the day resulting from the disorientation of the body's 'clock', its regular cycle of meals, sleep and energy expenditure. Shiftwork tends to conflict with the body's 'circadian rhythms', or 24-hour body cycles. Stress-related ill-health may also be caused. Some people suffer more from the physical disruption than others: in particular, diabetics, epileptics and those prone to digestive disorders should be screened by management, and excluded from shiftwork for health reasons.

   (b) *Psychological effects*. The experience of variety can be stimulating. On the other hand, the fatigue and sense of physical disorientation can be stressful. Those with strong security or structure needs may feel threatened by a lack of 'rhythm' in working life. A sense of isolation and lack of variety arising from the social problems of shiftwork may also be threatening - particularly if strain is being put on non-work relationships and roles.

(c) *Social effects.* Some forms of shiftwork involve high social costs, though others - in particular double-day working - very little. In some systems, the normal hours of socialising - afternoon and evening - are taken up at work, which may isolate the individual from his non-work social circle. Family problems may be acute - especially where weekends are lost: not only is the worker absent, leaving a role gap in the family, but the routine of the whole family will be disrupted by his sleeping and eating patterns.

(d) *Economic effects.* Overtime is not necessarily eliminated by shiftwork: premiums for double-shift and Sundays are common in practice. Shiftworking itself is inherently unpopular, and its appeal will largely depend on financial incentives.

10 Morale is improved by allowing staff to arrange their days to fit particular needs, leisure pursuits, available transport and so on. Stress (related to frustration, monotony, isolation, fears associated with being 'late for work') is reduced. The temptation to take time off is also reduced: pioneer schemes showed that absenteeism dropped, because trips to the dentist, social visits and so on were allowed for, and the idea that 'I'm late for work; I may as well not go in at all' were discounted.

11 (a) *Control.* Supervision of the work process on a day-to-day basis is impossible, so there needs to be a shift towards monitoring and controlling work output or results. Hours of work will also need to be monitored.

(b) *Communication.* Out-stationed workers may feel isolated from the culture and work-flow of the organisation. Communication for planning, control and co-ordination - as well as morale, motivation and team-building - will need to be constantly pursued.

(c) *Co-ordination.* Employing outworkers increases the project management aspects of a task. Integrated plans, communication and control will be required to ensure that the outworkers' output fits into the overall operation in which they are involved.

(d) *Employee appraisal and development.* Performance assessment, analysis of training needs, training and career planning must be given attention, especially as the worker is inaccessible most of the time. The basis of assessment may need to be adjusted, given that working conditions will be different and certain skills and attributes (such as teamworking) irrelevant.

(e) *Risks associated with 'networking'* (a method by which remote computer terminals can be linked to a central computer at the office). Computer viruses, industrial espionage or 'hacking' and hardware/software incompatibility remain technical problems to be resolved.

(f) *Health and safety.* Housing is not always well adapted to work: there may be problems with electrical wiring, fire precautions and other matters which can be more closely controlled at a central office.

Further question practice

Now try the following practice questions at the end of this text

Multiple choice questions	8 to 15
Exam style question	2

Chapter 3

RECRUITMENT

Introduction

The overall aim of the recruitment process is to obtain the quantity and quality of employees the organisation requires to fulfil its objectives. This process can be broken down into three main stages.

Defining the organisation's general and specific labour requirements (in other words, deciding the categories and 'kinds' of people the organisation wants to employ for various positions or tasks, and for specific vacancies, as they arise).

Attracting potential employees: choosing and using various methods of reaching sources of job applicants, which may be inside as well as outside the organisation.

Selecting the appropriate people for the job or the appropriate job for the people.

Note that there is a distinction between recruitment and selection.

Definition

Recruitment is the part of the human resourcing process concerned with finding the applicants: it is a positive action by management, going into the labour market (internal and/or external), communicating opportunities and information, and hopefully generating interest. *Selection* is the part of the process which involves choosing between applicants for jobs: it is largely a negative process, weeding out people who are unsuitable for the job or the organisation (and for whom the job or organisation might be unsuitable).

Your objectives

After completing this chapter you should:

(a) appreciate the impact on recruitment policy of changes in the external labour market;

(b) be able to outline a systematic approach to recruitment;

(c) understand the role and processes of job analysis and description;

(d) understand the role of a personnel specification;

(e) be aware of a range of media and criteria for successful job advertisement;

(f) be able to suggest how recruitment procedures can be evaluated.

1 THE EXTERNAL LABOUR MARKET

A systematic approach to recruitment should be closely related to the human resource planning activity of the organisation.

A recruiter operates at the interface between an organisation's demand for manpower and the supply of people as may be available on the open market.
Livy, *Corporate Personnel Management*

The labour market is variously defined by economists, but for the recruitment officer, it consists of the group of potential employees, internal, local or otherwise, with the types of skill, knowledge and experience that the employer requires at a given time. It thus consists of people within the organisation, people who are out of work at that time, and also people in other organisations who may wish to change jobs or employers.

The size and composition of the *external* market for labour depends on factors such as:

(a) Government policies (on matters such as benefits, taxation or employment protection);

(b) the level of activity in the economy (with associated unemployment levels);

(c) education/training standards and opportunities, and occupational choice trends among school leavers;

(d) wage and salary levels;

(e) competition between organisations for particular skills;

(f) trade union attitudes and the expectations of existing and potential employees (with regard to wages, the role of technology, the adoption of flexible working methods and so on);

(g) the extent to which new technology replaces human skills in a given area; and

(h) population changes affecting the number of people in an area, the age or sex distribution of the population and other demographic factors.

The labour market has changed dramatically in the last couple of decades. Writers on human resource planning in the 1970s suggested that a 'seller's market' had been established, as technology increased the skills and therefore scarcity value of employees in certain jobs, and the scale of state benefits blunted the fear of unemployment. The initiative seemed to be with the employee, or with organised groups of employees. The 'demographic downturn' (discussed in Chapter 2) was anticipated to worsen labour shortages, as the number of young people entering the market fell. Economic recession, equal opportunities initiatives, and the more general application of technology, among other factors, have changed that situation: a 'buyer's market' for labour now gives employers considerable power, with a large pool of available (and often trained and experienced) labour created by redundancy and unemployment. Some organisations still face massive difficulties, however, in finding the right number of the right people. As reported in *People Management* (March 1997), the Samaritans has launched the biggest ever recruitment drive by a UK charity in the hope of attracting 10,000 new volunteers, in the face of stiff competition and a general decline in the number of people who are willing, or able, to donate their time.

This shift in the market changed the purpose and practice of recruitment. In times of low unemployment, employers have to compete to attract desirable categories of labour (and may also have to downgrade their selection requirements if the competition is too 'stiff'). In times of high unemployment, and therefore plentiful supply, 'the problem is not so much of attracting candidates, but in deciding how best to select them' (Cole, *Personnel Management: Theory and Practice*). In times of low demand for labour, however, socially responsible employers may have the additional policy of using existing staff (internal recruitment) rather than recruiting from outside, in order to downsize staff levels through natural wastage and redeployment.

Even in conditions of high overall employment, particular skill shortages still exist and may indeed be more acute because of recessionary pressures on education and training. Engineers and software designers, among other specialist and highly trained groups, are the target of fierce competition among employers, forcing a revaluation of recruitment and retention policies.

Activity 1

What are the main features of the labour market in your geographical areas and education/skill areas? Identify any changes or trends. How do these elements affect your perception of your own value in the labour market?

What are you doing (if anything) to enhance your value in this market?

Market intelligence will clearly have to be gathered, as part of the human resource planning process, in order to monitor fluctuations in the local, regional and national labour supply for the variety of skills the organisation requires.

2 A SYSTEMATIC APPROACH TO RECRUITMENT

A systematic approach to recruitment will involve the following stages.

(a) Detailed *human resource planning* defining what resources the organisation needs to meet its objectives.

(b) *Job analysis*, so that for any given job there is:

   (i) a *job description*: a statement of the component tasks, duties, objectives and standards;

   (ii) a *job specification*: a specification of the skills, knowledge and qualities required to perform the job; and

   (iii) a *personnel specification*: a reworking of the job specification in terms of the kind of person needed to perform the job.

(c) An identification of vacancies, from the requirements of the human resource plan or by a *job requisition* from a department, branch or office in which a vacancy has opened (reviewed to ensure that the vacancy really needs filling, with reference to the human resource plan).

(d) Evaluation of the *sources of labour*, which again should be forecast and included in the human resource plan. Internal and external sources, and media for reaching both, will be considered.

(e) Preparation and publication of *information,* which will:

   (i) attract the attention and interest of potentially suitable candidates;

   (ii) give a favourable (but accurate) impression of the job and the organisation; and

   (iii) equip those interested to make an attractive and relevant application (how and to whom to apply, desired skills, qualifications and so on).

(f) *Processing applications* and assessing candidates (by the process of selection, discussed in Chapter 4).

(g) *Notifying applicants* of the results of the selection process.

Movements towards flexibility and multi-skilling have encouraged a slightly different approach, which is oriented more towards 'fitting the job to the person' than 'fitting the person to the job'. In a highly innovative market, technological environment or organisational culture, for example, rigid job descriptions would not be suitable. In order to 'thrive on chaos' (Tom Peters' well-known phrase), organisations should be able to look at the skills and attributes of the people they employ, and gifted outsiders, and ask: 'What needs doing that this person would do best?' In a relatively informal environment, where all-round knowledge/skills and experience are highly valued and suitable external labour resources scarce (say, in management consultancy), this approach would give much-needed flexibility. The organisation would try to recruit 'excellent', flexible, motivated and multi-skilled personnel, without reference to any specific job, as defined by a job description. They would form an available 'resource' for any tasks or requirement that arose.

However, the 'selection' approach ('fitting the person to the job') is still by far the most common, and is suitable for most organisations with fairly defined goals and structures.

The human resources department will handle much of this activity, but if there is no such department, there are still strong arguments for centralising the process to some extent, in order to take advantage of experience and to economise on effort. Standardisation and central control should be applied, for example, to equal opportunities, pay provisions and performance standards, where fairness must be seen to operate. Standardisation and central control should be applied, for example, to equal opportunities, pay provisions and performance standards: contexts where legal compliance is involved, or where fairness must be seen to operate.

Activity 2

Suggest five advantages of centralising the recruitment function rather than giving departmental or section managers responsibility for recruiting their own staff.

2.1 Recruitment policy

Detailed procedures for recruitment should only be devised and implemented within the context of a coherent *policy,* or code of conduct.

A typical recruitment policy might deal with:

(a) internal advertisement of vacancies;

(b) efficient and courteous processing of applications;

(c) fair and accurate provision of information to potential recruits; and

(d) selection of candidates on the basis of qualification, without discrimination on any grounds.

In 1994, the Institute of Personnel and Development issued a Recruitment Code, that seeks to establish a model of good practice for recruitment.

> **RECRUITMENT CODE**
>
> 1. Job advertisements should state clearly the form of reply desired, in particular, whether this should be a formal application form or by curriculum vitae. Preferences should also be stated if handwritten replies are required.
> 2. An acknowledgement of reply should be made promptly to each applicant by the employing organisation or its agent. If it is likely to take some time before acknowledgements are made, this should be made clear in the advertisement.
> 3. Applicants should be informed of the progress of the selection procedures, what there will be (eg group selection, aptitude tests etc), the steps and time involved and the policy regarding expenses.
> 4. Detailed personal information (eg religion, medical history, place of birth, family background etc) should not be called for unless it is relevant to the selection process.
> 5. Before applying for references, potential employers must secure the permission of the applicant.
> 6. Applications must be treated as confidential.
> 7. The code also recommends certain courtesies and obligations on the part of the applicants.

2.2 Recruitment procedure

Detailed *procedures* should be devised in order to make recruitment activity systematic and consistent throughout the organisation (especially where it is decentralised in the hands of line managers). Apart from the human resourcing requirements which need to be effectively and efficiently met, there is a *marketing* aspect to recruitment, as one 'interface' between the organisation and the outside world: applicants who feel they have been unfairly treated, or recruits who leave because they feel they have been misled, do not enhance the organisation's reputation in the labour market or the world at large.

Basic procedures involved in recruitment are as follows.

(a) Obtain approval or authorisation for engagement (in accordance with the human resource budget).

(b) Prepare, or update and confirm job description and specification, as appropriate to the job requisition received from the departmental head.

(c) Select media of advertisement or other notification of the vacancy.

(d) Prepare advertising copy, and place advertisement.

(e) Screen replies, at the end of a specified period for application.

(f) Shortlist candidates for initial interview.

(g) Advise applicants accordingly.

(h) Draw up a programme for the selection process which follows.

We will now go on to discuss some of these procedures in more detail.

3 JOB ANALYSIS AND DESCRIPTION

3.1 Job analysis (or job appraisal)

According to the British Standards Institution this is defined as follows.

Definition

Job analysis is 'the determination of the essential characteristics of a job', the process of examining a job to identify its component parts and the circumstances in which it is performed. Analysis may be carried out by observation for routine or repetitive jobs. Irregular jobs with a lot of invisible work (planning, man management, creative thinking and so on) will require interviews and discussions with superiors and with the people concerned.

Opportunities for analyses occur when jobs fall vacant, when salaries are reviewed, or when targets are being set, and the human resources department should take advantage of such opportunities to review and revise existing job specifications.

Information which should be elicited from a job appraisal is both task-oriented information, and worker-oriented information, including:

(a) *initial requirements of the employee*: aptitudes, qualifications, experience, training required;

(b) *duties and responsibilities of the job*: physical aspects; mental effort; routine or requiring initiative; difficult and/or disagreeable features; consequences of failure; responsibilities for staff, materials, equipment or cash etc;

(c) *environment and conditions of the job*: physical surroundings, with notable features such as temperature or noise; hazards; remuneration; other conditions such as hours, shifts, benefits, holidays; career prospects; provision of employee services - canteens, protective clothing etc; and

(d) *social factors of the job*: size of the department; teamwork or isolation; sort of people dealt with - senior management, the public; amount of supervision; job status.

The product of the analysis is usually a *job specification* - a detailed statement of the activities (mental and physical) involved in the job, and other relevant factors in the social and physical environment.

Job analysis, and the job specification resulting from it, may be used by managers:

(a) in recruitment and selection - for a detailed description of the vacant job;

(b) for appraisal - to assess how well an employee has fulfilled the requirements of the job;

(c) in devising training programmes - to assess the knowledge and skills necessary in a job;

(d) in establishing rates of pay - this will be discussed later in connection with job evaluation;

(e) in eliminating risks - identifying hazards in the job; and/or

(f) in re-organisation of the organisational structure - by reappraising the purpose and necessity of jobs and their relationship to each other.

Activity 3

The fact that a job analysis is being carried out may cause some concern among employees: they may fear that standards will be raised, rates cut, or that the job may be found to be redundant or require rationalisation. How might a job analyst need to carry out his or her work in order to gain employees' confidence?

3.2 Job description

Definition

A job description is a broad description of a job or position at a given time (since jobs are dynamic, subject to change and variation).

It is a written statement of those facts which are important regarding the duties, responsibilities, and their organisational and operational interrelationships. Livy, *Corporate Personnel Management*

In *recruitment,* a job description can be used:

(a) to decide what skills (technical, human, conceptual, design or whatever) and qualifications are required of the job holder. When formulating recruitment advertisements, and interviewing an applicant for the job, the interviewer can use the resulting job specification to match the candidate against the job;

(b) to ensure that the job:
  (i) will be a full time job for the holder and will not under-utilise his capacity by not giving him enough to do; and
  (ii) provides a sufficient challenge to the jobholder - job content may be a factor in the motivation of individuals;

(c) to determine a rate of pay which is fair for the job, if this has not already been decided by some other means.

Job descriptions can also be used in other areas of human resource management.

(a) For job evaluation (used in establishing wage rates).
  (i) A standard format for analysing jobs makes it easier for evaluators to compare jobs.
  (ii) Job descriptions focus attention on the job, not the holder, which is important in the job evaluation process.
  (iii) Job descriptions offer opportunities for the jobholder and his manager to discuss any differences of opinion about what the work involves, allowing fairer and more accurate evaluation.

(b) In induction and training, to help new employees to understand the scope and functions of their jobs and to help managers to identify training needs of jobholders on an ongoing basis.

(c) To pinpoint weaknesses in the organisation structure (such as overlapping areas of authority, where two or more managers are responsible for the same area of work; areas of work where no manager appears to accept responsibility; areas of work where authority appears to be too centralised or decentralised).

Townsend (*Up the Organisation*) suggested that job descriptions are only suited for jobs where the work is largely repetitive and therefore performed by low-grade employees: once the element of judgement comes into a job description it becomes a straitjacket. Management jobs, in particular, are likely to be constantly changing as external influences impact upon them, so a job description is constantly out-of-date. Many of the difficulties that arise with job descriptions have arisen because they encourage demarcation disputes, where people adhere strictly to the contents of the job description, rather than responding flexibly to task or organisational requirements: this in turn leads to costly overmanning practices.

Where job descriptions are used, it should be remembered that:

(a) a job description is like a photograph, an image 'frozen' at one point in time;
(b) a job description needs constant and negotiated revision;
(c) a job description rigidly adhered to can work against flexibility.

3.3 The contents of a job description

A job description should be clear and to the point, and so ought not to be lengthy. Typically, a job description would show the following.

(a) *Job title* and department and job code number. The person to whom the job holder is responsible. Possibly, the grading of the job.

(b) *Job summary* - showing in a few paragraphs the major functions and tools, machinery and special equipment used. Possibly also a small organisation chart.

(c) *Job content* - list of the sequence of operations that constitute the job, noting main levels of difficulty. In the case of management work there should be a list of the main duties of the job, indicating frequency of performance - typically between 5 and 15 main duties should be listed. This includes the degree of initiative involved, and the nature of responsibility (for other people, machinery and/or other resources).

(d) The extent (and limits) of the jobholder's authority and responsibility.

(e) Statement showing relation of the job to other closely associated jobs, including superior and subordinate positions and the liaison required with other departments.

(f) Working hours, basis of pay and benefits, and conditions of employment, including location, special pressures, social isolation, physical conditions, or health hazards.

(g) Opportunities for training, transfer and promotion.

(h) Possibly, also, objectives and expected results, which will be compared against actual performance during employee appraisal - although this may be done as a separate exercise, as part of the appraisal process.

   (i) The names and positions of the people/person who has

      (i) prepared the job description;

      (ii) agreed the job description;

(j) The date of preparation.

Two examples of job descriptions are shown below.

Activity 4

Studying has placed you in a role in which you have to perform a fairly consistent set of duties, in fairly consistent conditions, within a structure that requires you to interact with other people, both superiors and peers (and possibly subordinates). Draw up a job description for yourself.

JOB DESCRIPTION

1. *Job title*: Baking Furnace Labourer.
2. *Department:* 'B' Baking.
3. *Date:* 20 November 19X0.
4. *Prepared by*: H Crust, baking furnace manager.
5. *Responsible to*: baking furnace chargehand.
6. *Age range*: 20-40.
7. *Supervises work* of: N/A
8. *Has regular co-operative contact with*: Slinger/Crane driver.
9. *Main duties/responsibilities*: Stacking formed electrodes in furnace, packing for stability. Subsequently unloads baked electrodes and prepares furnace for next load.
10. *Working conditions*: stacking is heavy work and requires some manipulation of 100lb (45kg) electrodes. Unloading is hot (35° - 40°C) and very dusty.
11. *Employment conditions*:

    Wages £3.60 ph + group bonus (average earnings £219.46 pw)

    Hours: Continuous rotating three-shift working days, 6 days on, 2 days off. NB must remain on shift until relieved.

    Trade Union: National Union of Bread Bakers, optional.

MIDWEST BANK PLC

1. *Job title:* Clerk (Grade 2)
2. *Branch:* All branches and administrative offices
3. *Job summary:* To provide clerical support to activities within the bank
4. *Job content:* Typical duties will include:
   (a) cashier's duties;
   (b) processing of branch clearing;
   (c) processing of standing orders;
   (d) support to branch management.
5. *Reporting structure:*

    Administrative officer/assistant manager
    |
    Supervisor (Grade 3)
    |
    Clerk (Grade 2)

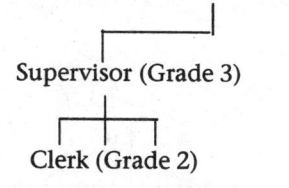

6. *Experience/Education:* experience not required, minimum 3 GCSEs or equivalent
7. *Training to be provided*: initial on-the-job training plus regular formal courses and training
8. *Hours:* 38 hours per week
9. *Objectives and appraisal:* Annual appraisal in line with objectives above.
10. *Salary:* refer to separate standard salary structure.

Job description prepared by: Head office personnel department

4 PERSONNEL SPECIFICATION

Once the job has been clearly defined in terms of its organisational content and operational interrelationships, the organisation can decide what kind of person is needed to fill it effectively.

Definition

A *personnel specification* identifies the type of person the organisation should be trying to recruit: their character, aptitudes, educational or other qualifications, aspirations in their career and other attributes.

Research has been carried out into exactly what a personnel specification ought to assess. Two popular designs are those of Professor Alec Rodger and J Munro Fraser.

Activity 5

Do not continue until you have written out on a piece of paper a definition of each of the following terms as you now understand them.

(a) Job analysis.
(b) Job description.
(c) Personnel specification.

4.1 Seven point plan

Professor Alec Rodger was a pioneer of the systematic approach to recruitment and selection in Britain. He suggested that:

If matching [ie of demands of the job and the person who is to perform it] is to be done satisfactorily, the requirements of an occupation (or job) must be described in the same terms as the aptitudes of the people who are being considered for it.

This was the basis for the formulation of the personnel specification as a way of matching people to jobs on the basis of comparative sets of data: defining job requirements and personal suitability along the same lines.

The *Seven Point Plan* put forward by Professor Rodger in 1951 draws the selector's attention to seven points about the candidate.

(a) Physical attributes (such as neat appearance, ability to speak clearly and without impediment).
(b) Attainment (including educational qualifications).
(c) General intelligence.
(d) Special aptitudes (such as neat work, speed and accuracy).
(e) Interests (practical and social).
(f) Disposition (or manner: friendly, helpful and so on).
(g) Background circumstances.

4.2 Five Point Pattern of Personality

Munro Fraser's Five Point Pattern of Personality (1966) draws the selector's attention to:

(a) impact on others, including physical attributes, speech and manner;
(b) acquired knowledge or qualifications, including education, training and work experience. [Most personnel specifications include achievements in education,

because there appears to be a strong correlation between management potential and higher education];

(c) innate ability, including mental, agility, aptitude for learning;

(d) motivation: individual goals, demonstrated effort and success at achieving them; and

(e) adjustment: emotional stability, tolerance of stress, human relations skills.

4.3 The specification

Note that the personnel specification includes job requirements in terms of a candidate's:

(a) capacities - what he is *capable of*; and
(b) inclinations - what he *will* do.

In other words, behavioural versatility must be accounted for, by considering not only the individual's mental and physical attributes, but his current attitudes, values, beliefs, goals and circumstances - all of which will influence his response to work demands.

Each feature in the specification should be classified as:

(a) *essential* - for instance, honesty in a cashier is essential whilst a special aptitude for conceptual thought is not;

(b) *desirable* - for instance, a reasonably pleasant manner should ensure satisfactory standards in a person dealing with the public;

(c) *contra-indicated* - some features are actively disadvantageous, such as an inability to work in a team when acting as project leader.

PERSONNEL SPECIFICATION: Customer Accounts Manager

	ESSENTIAL	DESIRABLE	CONTRA-INDICATED
Physical attributes	Clear speech Well-groomed Good health	Age 25-40	Age under 25 Chronic ill-health and absence
Attainments	2 'A' levels GCSE Maths and English Thorough knowledge of retail environment	Degree (any discipline) Marketing training 2 years' experience in supervisory post	No experience of supervision or retail environment
Intelligence	High verbal intelligence		
Aptitudes	Facility with numbers Attention to detail and accuracy Social skills for customer relations	Analytical abilities (problem solving) Understanding of systems and IT	No mathematical ability Low tolerance of technology
Interests	Social: team activity		Time-consuming hobbies 'Solo' interests only
Disposition	Team player Persuasive Tolerance of pressure and change	Initiative	Antisocial Low tolerance of responsibility
Circumstances	Able to work late, take work home	Located in area of office	

Activity 6

Now turn your job description for A Student (Activity 4) into a corresponding Personnel Specification, using the 'essential; desirable; contra-indicated' framework, and either the Seven Point Plan or Five Point Pattern.

If you did not do Activity 4, do it now! (You might like to consider into which section of your personnel specification 'laziness' would fall.....)

5 JOB ADVERTISEMENT

The object of recruitment advertising is to home in on the target market of labour, and to attract interest in the organisation and the job.

In a way, it is already part of the *selection* process. The advertisement will be placed where suitable people are likely to see it (say, internally only - immediately preselecting members of the organisation - or in a specialist journal, preselecting those specialists). It will be worded in a way that further weeds out people who would not be suitable for the job (or for whom the job would not be suitable).

5.1 Advertising methods and media

The way in which a job is advertised will depend on:

(a) the type of organisation; and
(b) the type of job.

A factory is likely to advertise a vacancy for an unskilled worker in a different way to a company advertising for a member of the Institute of Personnel and Development for an HRM position. Managerial jobs may merit national advertisement, whereas semi-skilled or unskilled jobs may only warrant local coverage, depending on the supply of suitable candidates in the local area. Specific skills may be most appropriately reached through trade, technical or professional journals, such as those for accountants or computer programmers.

In addition, should the job be advertised within the organisation (internal recruitment) or outside (external recruitment), or both? (The broad issues have already been discussed in relation to management succession in chapter 2.)

The choice of advertising medium will also depend on:

(a) the *cost* of advertising. It is more expensive to advertise in a national newspaper than on local radio, and more expensive to advertise on local radio than in a local newspaper etc;

(b) the *readership and circulation* (type and number of readers/listeners) of the medium, and its suitability for the number and type of people the organisation wants to reach; and

(c) the *frequency* with which the organisation wants to advertise the job vacancy, and the duration of the recruitment process.

Some methods or media for advertising jobs are as follows.

(a) *In-house magazines and notice-boards.* An organisation might advertise vacancies for particular jobs through its own in-house magazine or journal, inviting applications from employees who would like a transfer or a promotion to the particular vacancy advertised. In-house notice boards are a traditional, and still much-used, method of advertising or 'posting' internal vacancies.

> **EXAMPLE: LOGICA**
>
> *Personnel Management* (mid-December 1994) reported an innovative approach to internal recruitment at computer company Logica. As part of a more flexible and international approach (including performance-related pay, appraisal and training), Logica is implementing a global 'resource management system' in which a central database of employees' skills and experiences is being established. 'As well as holding employees' CVs, this will be the first medium to advertise vacancies on a global basis within the company.'

(b) *Professional and specialist newspapers or magazines*, such as *People Management, Accountancy, Marketing* or *Computing*.

(c) Other national newspapers, especially for senior management jobs or vacancies for skilled workers, where potential applicants will not necessarily be found through local advertising. *Local newspapers* would be suitable for jobs where applicants are sought from the local area.

(d) *Local radio, television and cinema*. These are becoming increasingly popular, especially for large-scale campaigns, for large numbers of vacancies.

(e) *Job centres*. On the whole, vacancies for unskilled work (rather than skilled work or management jobs) are advertised through local job centres, although in theory any type of job can be advertised here.

(f) *School and university careers offices*. When an organisation recruits school leavers or graduates, it would be convenient to advertise vacancies through their careers officers. Suitable information should be made available. Ideally, the manager responsible for recruitment in an area should try to maintain a close liaison with careers officers. Some large organisations organise special meetings or *careers fairs* in universities and colleges (the so-called 'milk round'), as a kind of showcase for the organisation and the careers it offers.

(g) Technological media such as the *Internet*. Any personal computer user may access the network, independently or via a service organisation such as CompuServe. According to Michael Forest, executive director of the National Association of Colleges and Employers, there were over 35,000 recruitment sites on the Internet in 1996, compared with only 2,000 a year earlier.

5.2 Content of the advertisement

Preparation of the job information requires skill and attention if it is to fulfil its twin objectives of attraction and preselection. It should be:

(a) concise, but comprehensive enough to be an accurate description of the job, its rewards and requirements;

(b) in a form that will attract the attention of the maximum number of the right sort of people;

(c) attractive, conveying a favourable impression of the organisation, but not falsely so: disappointed expectations will be a prime source of dissatisfaction for an applicant when he actually comes into contact with the organisation;

(d) relevant and appropriate to the job and the applicant. Skills, qualifications and special aptitudes required should be prominently set out, along with special features of the job that might attract - or indeed deter - applicants, such as shiftwork or extensive travel; and

(e) non-discriminatory on the grounds of sex or race (as discussed in detail in chapter 5).

The advertisement, based on information set out in the job description, job and person specifications and recruitment procedures, should contain information about:

(a) the organisation: its main business and location, at least;

(b) the job: title, main duties and responsibilities and special features;

(c) conditions: special factors affecting the job;

(d) qualifications and experience (required, and preferred); other attributes, aptitudes and/or knowledge required;

(e) rewards: salary, benefits, opportunities for training, career development, and so on; and the

(f) application: how to apply, to whom, and by what date.

It should encourage a degree of self-selection, so that the target population begins to narrow itself down. The information contained in the advertisement should deter unsuitable applicants as well as encourage potentially suitable ones.

Activity 7

Select any two job advertisements from a notice board, magazine, journal or newspaper. Note:

(a) the elements of information given;

(b) the 'tone' and style of the advertisement;

(c) the visual presentation, and the impression it makes on you.

Decide what 'sort' of person each advertisement is trying to attract. How (if at all) are the advertisers gong about

(a) attracting that 'sort' of person; and

(b) discouraging applications from others?

5.3 Other methods of reaching the labour market

Various *agencies* exist, through which the employer can reach the public.

(a) *Government agencies* through the Department of Education and Employment.

(b) *Institutional agencies* exist to help their own members find employment: for example, the career services of educational institutions such as schools and colleges, and the employment services of professional institutions and trade unions.

(c) *Private employment agencies* have proliferated in recent years. There is a wide range of agencies specialising in different grades and skill-areas of staff - clerical, technical, professional and managerial. Private agencies generally offer an immediate pool of labour already on their books, and many also undertake initial screening of potential applicants, so that the recruitment officer sees only the most suitable.

Activity 8

Suggest three other ways in which an organisation might, perhaps more informally, recruit staff *without* advertising a vacancy.

5.4 Recruitment consultants

The role of the *recruitment consultant* is to perform the staffing function on behalf of the management of the client organisation: in other words, to fill vacancies with the type and calibre of staff required.

The tasks involved in this include:

(a) analysing, or being informed of, the requirements - the demands of the post, the organisation's preferences for qualifications, personality and so on;

(b) helping to draw up, or offering advice on, job descriptions, person specifications and other recruitment and selection aids;

(c) designing job advertisements;

(d) screening applications, so that those most obviously unsuitable are weeded out immediately;

(e) helping with short-listing for interview;

(f) advising on the constitution and procedures of the interview; and

(g) offering a list of suitable candidates with notes and recommendations.

Much will depend on whether the consultant is employed to perform the necessary tasks, or merely to advise and recommend.

The decision of whether or not to use consultants will depend on a number of factors.

(a) *Cost*. This will be a factor particularly where the desired recruitment is at a low level, since a quality recruitment decision will not be so crucial, and the fees may not therefore be cost-effective.

(b) *The level of expertise and specialist techniques or knowledge which the consultant can bring to the process*. Consultants may be expert in using interview techniques, analysis of personnel specifications and so on. In-house staff, on the other hand, have experience of the particular field (some recruitment consultants specialise - say, in accountancy or computing - but not all) and of the culture of the organisation into which the recruits must fit.

(c) *The level of expertise, and specialist knowledge, available within the organisation*. Even if the consultant is not familiar with the field and organisation, there may be little choice: the cost of training in-house personnel in the necessary interview and assessment techniques may be prohibitive.

(d) Whether there is a *need for impartiality* which can only be filled by an outsider trained in objective assessment. If fresh blood is desired in the organisation, it may be a mistake to have staff selecting clones of the common organisational type.

(e) Whether the use of an outside agent will be *regarded as helpful* by in-house staff. Consultants may be regarded as the tools of the manager who employs them, or as meddlers and outsiders. On the other hand, an outsider will avoid internal office politics.

(f) Whether the *structure and politics of the organisation* allow in-house staff to make decisions of this kind. Consultants are not tied by status or rank and can discuss problems freely at all levels. They are also not likely to fear the consequences of their recommendations for their jobs or career prospects. On the other hand, the organisation may regard in-house selection as an important part of succession and a way of maintaining the organisational culture.

(g) *Time*. Consultants will need to learn about the job, the organisation and the organisation's requirements. The client will not only have to pay fees for this period of acclimatisation: it may require a post to be filled more quickly than the process allows.

(h) *Supply of labour*. If there is a large and reasonably accessible pool of labour from which to fill a post, consultants will be less valuable. If the vacancy is a standard one, and there are ready channels for reaching labour (such as professional journals), the use of specialists may not be cost effective.

6 THE EVALUATION OF RECRUITMENT PROCEDURES

An evaluation of recruitment and selection procedures aims to determine whether the procedures succeed in getting a *suitable* person into a job, at the *time* when the person is required and at an acceptable cost. At a more strategic level, it determines whether recruitment and selection procedures are succeed in achieving the organisation's overall human resource plan.

Connock suggests that auditing the recruitment process can occur at four levels.

(a) *Performance indicators* should be established for each stage of the process. For example, if vacancies are generally known about four weeks before the post needs to be filled then advertisements need to be placed, selection procedures conducted and appointments made within this time. Data can be collected about actual performance and compared with the standards. As Connock says 'Significant variations from the established standards will need to be individually investigated, and remedial action initiated if necessary. Remedial action might include extra staffing for the recruitment section if turn-round times are not being met. One of the major causes of candidate demotivation is a slow turn-round of applications'.

(b) *Cost-effectiveness* of the various methods used should be measured. It may be that a certain advertising medium is too costly for the number of worthwhile responses it generates. Advertising in the national press, for example, may generate a large number of responses, but few of the required quality; meanwhile an insertion in a professional journal with a smaller circulation may generate a higher proportion of potentially suitable candidates.

Connock suggests that a framework is used to determine the cost per person appointed for each method.

Activity 9

What kind of information would you need to record in order to appraise the cost-effectiveness of a recruitment method/medium? Design a framework which lists the costs of various advertising media against different staff and recruitment numbers. Aim to end up with a meaningful figure for the cost per person appointed (and actually entering employment).

(c) *Monitoring the make up of the workforce* and the impact on its constitution of new recruits is essential as part of an equal opportunities policy. This will identify areas where certain groups are under-represented, for example women, disabled people or ethnic minorities. The reasons for this should be investigated and eliminated.

(d) Finally, Connock suggests conducting an *attitude survey* amongst staff who have been recruited, to find out whether they were satisfied with the various stages of their recruitment and selection - did they feel that the job advertisement they responded to gave them a fair idea of the nature of the job? Were they frustrated by the length of time they had to wait for a decision? and so on.

Selection procedures can be evaluated by determining whether selection decisions seem to have been correct in the light of subsequent job performance by the successful candidate.

(a) If tests were used to assess likely potential to perform certain tasks, then the test results can be compared against information about actual performance in the job. If there are regular discrepancies this suggests that the tests may be flawed.

(b) Likewise, if a record is kept of the conclusions made about a candidate in an interview, this can be compared with information gleaned from subsequent appraisal. It may be that some interviewers are consistently more accurate in their judgements than others, and this would mean that those who fall short should be given extra training or perhaps be replaced.

Other methods of evaluating recruitment and selection include 'benchmarking' - comparing the organisation's systems with known examples of good practice used in other organisations. Where a personnel department has adopted the notion of the 'internal customer' it can seek the views of its customers (line managers) and users (job applicants).

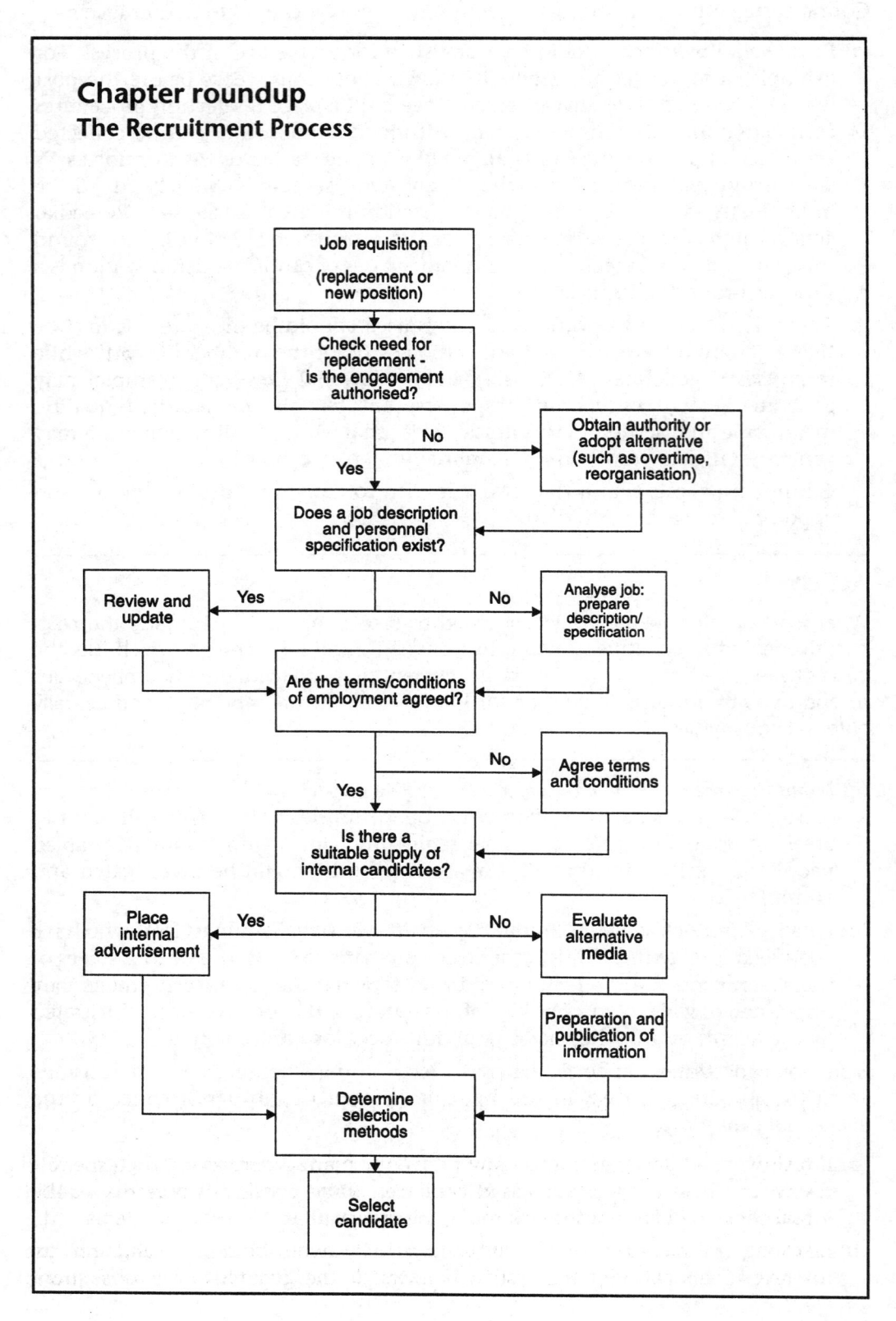

Chapter roundup
The Recruitment Process

```
                    Job requisition
                    (replacement or
                     new position)
                          │
                          ▼
                   Check need for
                   replacement -
                  is the engagement
                     authorised?
                    │         │
                   Yes        No ──▶ Obtain authority or
                    │                 adopt alternative
                    │                 (such as overtime,
                    │                  reorganisation)
                    ▼                          │
              Does a job description  ◀────────┘
              and personnel
              specification exist?
         ┌──── Yes      No ────▶ Analyse job:
         │                        prepare
     Review and                   description/
     update                       specification
         │                              │
         └──────▶ Are the terms/conditions ◀──┘
                 of employment agreed?
                    │         │
                   Yes        No ──▶ Agree terms
                    │                and conditions
                    ▼                     │
                Is there a      ◀─────────┘
                suitable supply of
                internal candidates?
                    │         │
         ┌──── Yes           No ────▶ Evaluate
         │                             alternative
     Place                             media
     internal                            │
     advertisement                       ▼
         │                         Preparation and
         │                         publication of
         │                         information
         │                              │
         └──────▶ Determine  ◀──────────┘
                  selection
                  methods
                     │
                     ▼
                  Select
                  candidate
```

Chapter 3: Recruitment

Quick quiz

1. What is the distinction between recruitment and selection?
2. What factors influence the supply of labour in the external market?
3. What information will a job description usually contain?
4. Which of the following does Professor Rodger's Seven Point Plan personnel specification *not* specifically include?
   - A Physical attributes
   - B Interests
   - C Motivation
   - D Background circumstances
5. What factors are relevant to the decision of where to advertise a job vacancy?
6. List six factors which should be considered when making a decision whether to employ recruitment consultants or to use internal staff for the recruitment process.
7. What are the uses of job descriptions (so far as the personnel function is concerned)? To what extent can it be argued that, in some organisations or situations, job descriptions are dysfunctional?

Solutions to activities

2. (a) The overall priorities and requirements of the organisation will be more clearly recognised and met, rather than the objectives of sub-systems such as individual departments.
   (b) There will be a focal reference point for communication, queries and applications from outside the organisation.
   (c) Communication with the outside world will also be more standardised, and will be more likely to reinforce the overall corporate image of the organisation.
   (d) Potential can be spotted in individuals and utilised in the optimum conditions - not necessarily in the post for which the individual has applied, if he or she might be better suited to another vacant post.
   (e) The volume of administration and the need for specialist knowledge (notably of changing legal and industrial relations requirements) may suggest a specialist function.

3. (a) Communicate: explain the process, methods and purpose of the appraisal.
   (b) Be clearly thorough and competent in carrying out the analysis.
   (c) Respect the work flow of the department, which should not be disrupted.
   (d) Give feedback on the results of the appraisal, and the achievement of its objectives. If staff are asked to co-operate in developing a framework for office training - and then never hear anything more about it - they are unlikely to be responsive on a later occasion.

5. The following definitions were agreed between the Department of Employment and the industrial training boards.
   (a) *Job analysis*. The process of examining a 'job' to identify the component parts and the circumstances in which it is performed.
   (b) *Job description*. A broad statement of the purpose, scope, duties and responsibilities of a particular 'job'.
   (c) *Personnel specification*. An interpretation of the 'job specification' in terms of the kind of person suitable for the job.

8. (a) Unsolicited applications are now frequently made to organisations, especially where there are few advertised vacancies. Some applicants may have heard about impending vacancies through the grapevine.
   (b) Some vacancies may be filled purely by word-of-mouth, and on the recommendation of established workers. If the organisation has a strong

tradition of sons following fathers (say, on the docks, or in mining areas), or if there is a strong cultural type of the acceptable worker, family members vouched for by employees may be taken on for appropriate vacancies. (Some national cultures support this practice more than others.)

(c) 'Head-hunting' has become increasingly popular. Informal approaches are made to successful executives currently employed elsewhere.

9 Connock suggests that a framework such as that shown below be used to determine the cost per person appointed for each method.

JOB DESCRIPTION

Source of application	Number applications	Number of shortlisted candidates	Number offered job	Number commenced employment	Total cost	Cost per head appointed
Local press advert						
National press advert						
Specialist press advert						
Leaflet drop						
etc						
Total						

Further question practice

Now try the following practice questions at the end of the this text

Multiple choice questions	16 to 20
Exam style questions	3

Chapter 4

SELECTION

Introduction

The selection of employees (at all levels, but particularly for key posts) must be approached systematically: the recruiting officer must know what the organisation's requirements are, and must measure each potentially suitable candidate against those requirements. He or she should not waste time and resources investigating candidates who are clearly not suitable for the post in some vital area of skill or personality. ('If only' is not a useful assessment.) On the other hand, no organisation wants to find that it has rejected out of hand someone who goes on to be a 'star' in another (possibly competing) organisation, any more than it wants to get 'stuck' with an employee who can't do the job and doesn't fit in - but looked 'perfect' in the interview! Application forms, interviews and various forms of testing are commonly used to try to reduce the risks by getting as much information about the candidate as possible. Unfortunately, the crystal ball is notoriously unreliable: put the ideal interviewee with the highest IQ and best personality 'score' in a real job, with a real team of workmates, and what happens? No experienced human resource manager would attempt a definite answer.

Your objectives

After completing this chapter you should:

(a) be able to outline a systematic approach to the selection process;

(b) understand the dynamics - and limitations - of selection interviews;

(c) appreciate the value and limitations of selection testing;

(d) be aware of the procedures to be followed once selection has been made.

1 THE SELECTION PROCESS

1.1 Applications

Job advertisements usually ask candidates to fill in a *job application form,* or to send information about themselves and their previous job experience (their CV or *curriculum vitae*), usually with a covering letter briefly explaining why they think they are qualified to do the job.

An application form or CV will be used to find out relevant information about the applicant, in order to decide, at the initial sifting stage:

(a) whether the applicant is obviously unsuitable for the job; or
(b) whether the applicant might be of the right calibre, and worth inviting to interview.

The application form will be designed by the organisation, and if it is to be useful in the sifting process, it should fulfil the following criteria.

(a) It should ask questions which will elicit information about the applicant, which can be compared with the requirements of the job. For example, if the personnel specification requires a minimum of 2 'A'-level passes the application form should ask for details of the applicant's educational qualifications. Similarly, if practical and social interests are thought to be relevant, the application form should ask for details of the applicant's hobbies and pastimes, membership of societies and sporting clubs or teams and so on.

(b) It should give applicants the opportunity to write about themselves, their career ambitions or why they want the job. By allowing applicants to write in their own words at length, it might be possible to obtain some information about their:

(i) neatness;
(ii) intelligence;
(iii) ability to express themselves in writing;
(iv) motivation; and even
(v) character.

An example of an application form is given on the next page.

Activity 1

Suggest four other ways in which an application form could be *badly* designed (both in appearance and content). You may be able to do this from personal experience.

1.2 Selection

A typical selection system will then include the following basic procedures.

(a) Take any initial steps required. If the decision to interview or reject cannot be made immediately, a standard letter of acknowledgement might be sent, as a courtesy, to each applicant. It may be that the job advertisement required applicants to write to the personnel manager with personal details and to request an application form: this would then be sent to applicants for completion and return.

(b) Set each application against key criteria in the job advertisement and specification. Critical factors may include age, qualifications, experience and so on.

(c) Sort applications into 'possible', 'unsuitable' and 'marginal'.

```
┌─────────────────────────────────────────────────────────────┐
│                      APPLICATION FORM                        │
├─────────────────────────────────────────────────────────────┤
│  Post applied for: ..............................  Date:    │
├─────────────────────────────────────────────────────────────┤
│  Surname: Mr/Mrs/Miss/Ms              First names:           │
│  Address:                                                    │
│                                                              │
│  Post Code:                           Telephone:             │
├─────────────────────────────────────────────────────────────┤
│  Age:                      Date of birth:  / /               │
│  Nationality               Marital status:                   │
├─────────────────────────────────────────────────────────────┤
│  EDUCATION AND TRAINING                                      │
│  ┌──────────────────────┬────────┬────────────────────────┐ │
│  │ Place of education   │ Dates  │ Examinations passed/   │ │
│  │ (including schools   │        │ qualifications         │ │
│  │ after 11 years)      │        │                        │ │
│  │                      │        │                        │ │
│  └──────────────────────┴────────┴────────────────────────┘ │
├─────────────────────────────────────────────────────────────┤
│  EXPERIENCE                                                  │
│  ┌──────────────┬────────────┬────────────┬──────┬───────┐  │
│  │ Name of      │ Position   │ Main duties│ From │  To   │  │
│  │ employer and │ held       │            │      │       │  │
│  │ main business│            │            │      │       │  │
│  └──────────────┴────────────┴────────────┴──────┴───────┘  │
├─────────────────────────────────────────────────────────────┤
│  OTHER INFORMATION                                           │
│  Please note your hobbies and interests, and any other       │
│  information you would like to give about yourself or        │
│  your experience.                                            │
│                                                              │
│  State of health (include any disability)                    │
├─────────────────────────────────────────────────────────────┤
│  May we contact any of your previous employers?  Yes☐ No☐    │
│  If yes, please give the names of any managers to whom       │
│  we may apply.                                               │
│  If selected, I would be able to start from  / / .           │
└─────────────────────────────────────────────────────────────┘
```

(d) 'Possibles' will then be more closely scrutinised, and a shortlist for interview drawn up. Ideally, this should be done by both the HR specialist and the prospective manager of the successful candidate, who will have more immediate knowledge of the type of person that will fit into the culture and activities of his department.

(e) Invite candidates for interviews (requiring them to complete an application form, if this has not been done at an earlier stage). Again, if large numbers of interviewees are involved, standard letters should be used (preprinted, or prepared on a word processor using the direct mail facility).

(f) Reinforce interviews with selection testing, if suitable.

(g) Review uninterviewed 'possibles', and 'marginals', and put potential future candidates on hold, or in reserve.

(h) Send standard letters to unsuccessful applicants, informing them simply that they have not been successful.

  (i) 'Rejects' should be briefly, but tactfully, dismissed: 'Thank you for your interest in the post of .... We have given your application careful consideration. I regret to inform you, however, that we have decided not to ask you to attend for an interview. The standard of application was very high ...'.

  (ii) Reserves will be sent a holding letter: 'We will keep your details on file, and should any suitable vacancy arise in future ...'.

We will now go on to look at two of the most popular techniques used for evaluating candidates: interviews and tests.

2 INTERVIEWS

Despite frequent criticism for its inability to elicit reliable or meaningful information about a candidate's likely performance in the *job*, interviewing remains a highly popular technique. According to Smith and Abrahamsen, the selection interview was used by more than 90% of UK organisations in their 1994 study, and the vast majority used it as their main source for decision-making. The interview gives the organisation a chance to assess applicants (and particularly their interpersonal communication skills) directly, and gives applicants a chance to learn more about the organisation, the people and the working environment.

The interview has a three-fold purpose.

(a) Finding the best person for the job.

(b) Making sure that applicants understand what the job is and what the career prospects are. They must be allowed a fair opportunity to decide whether they would want the job if it were offered to them.

(c) Making all applicants feel that they have been given fair treatment in the interview, whether they get the job or not.

In brief, the factors to be considered with regard to conducting selection interviews are:

(a) the impression of the organisation given by the interview arrangements;

(b) the psychological effects of the location of the interview and seating arrangements;

(c) the manner and tone of the interviewers - whether putting the candidate at his ease or 'in the hot seat';

(d) the extent to which the candidate can be encouraged to talk freely (by asking open questions) and honestly (by asking probing questions), in accordance with the organisation's need for information;

(e) the opportunity for the candidate to learn about the job and organisation; and

(f) the control of bias or hasty judgement by the interviewer.

2.1 Preparation of the interview

The interview is a two-way process, but the interviewer must have a clear idea of what the interview is setting out to achieve, and must be in sufficient control to make sure that every candidate is asked questions which cover the same ground and which elicit all the information required within the time available.

The agenda and questions will be based on:

(a) the job description, and what abilities are required of the jobholder;

(b) the personnel specification. The interviewer must be able to judge whether the applicant matches up to the personal qualities required from the jobholder; and

(c) the application form or the applicant's CV: what qualities the applicant claims to possess.

The interview process should be efficiently run to make a favourable impression on the candidates: they should be clearly informed when and where to come, whom to ask for, what to bring with them etc and should be expected by the receptionist or other receiving staff. A waiting room should be available, preferably with cloakroom facilities. Arrangements should have been made to welcome and escort candidates: they should not be placed under the extra stress of being left stranded, getting lost, or being ignored. Accommodation for the interview should be private and free from distractions and interruption.

The layout of the room should be carefully planned. Most interviewers wish to put candidates at their ease, and so it would be inadvisable to put the candidate in a 'hot-seat' across a desk (a psychological barrier) from them. On the other hand, some interviewers might want to observe the candidate's reaction under severe pressure, and deliberately make the layout of the room uncomfortable and off-putting.

Activity 2

Think back to a selection interview you have had, for a job, school or place at your university/college.

(a) What sort of interview did you have: one-to-one? panel? formal or informal?

(b) What impression of the organisation did you get from the whole process?

(c) How well-conducted was the interview, looking back on it?

(d) What efforts (if any) were made to put you at your ease?

2.2 Conduct of the interview

The manner of the interviewers, the tone of their voice, and the way their early questions are phrased can all be significant in establishing the tone of the interview, and the ease with which the candidate can talk freely.

Questions should be paced and put carefully. The interviewer should not be trying to confuse the candidate, plunging immediately into demanding questions or picking on isolated points; neither, however, should (s)he allow the interviewee to digress or gloss over important points. The interviewer must retain control over the information-gathering process.

A variety of questions may be used, to different effects.

(a) *Open questions* or open-ended questions ('Who...? What...? Where...? When...? Why...?') force candidates to put together their own responses in complete sentences. This encourages them to talk, keeps the interview flowing, and is most revealing ('Why do you want to be in HRM?').

(b) *Probing questions* are similar to open questions in their phrasing but aim to discover the deeper significance of the candidate's answers, especially if they are initially dubious, uninformative, too short, or too vague. ('But what was it about HRM that *particularly* appealed to you?')

(c) *Closed questions* are the opposite, inviting only 'yes' or 'no' answers: ('Did you...?', 'Have you...?'). A closed question has the following effects.

   (i) It elicits an answer only to the question asked. This may be useful where there are small points to be established ('And did you pass your exam?') However, there may be other questions and issues that the interviewer has not anticipated but which will emerge if interviewees are given the chance to express themselves by an open question.

   (ii) It does not allow the candidates to express their personality, or to interact with the interviewer on a deeper level.

   (iii) It makes it easier for candidates to conceal things ('You never *asked* me....').

   (iv) It makes the interviewer work very hard.

(d) *Multiple questions* are just that: two or more questions are asked at once. ('Tell me about your last job? How did your knowledge of HRM help you there, and do you think you are up-to-date or will you need to spend time studying?') This type of question can be used to encourage the candidate to talk at some length, without straying too far from the point. It might also test the candidate's ability to listen, and to handle large amounts of information. On the other hand candidates may simply choose the part of the question they feel most comfortable with and ignore the rest.

(e) *Problem-solving questions* present the candidate with a situation and ask him to explain how he would deal with it. ('How would you motivate your staff to do a task that they did not want to do?'). Such questions are used to establish whether the candidate will be able to deal with the sort of problems that are likely to arise in the job, or whether he has sufficient technical knowledge (in which case a line manager rather than the HR manager might be the best person to ask the questions and judge the responses).

(f) *Leading questions* lead the candidate to give a certain reply. ('We are looking for somebody who likes detailed figure work. How much do you enjoy dealing with numbers?' or 'Don't you agree that...?'. 'Surely...?').

The danger with this type of question is that the candidate will give the answer that he thinks the interviewer wants to hear, but it might also legitimately be used to deal with highly reticent or nervous candidates, simply to encourage them to talk.

Activity 3

Identify the type of question used in the following examples, and discuss the opportunities and constraints they offer the interviewee who must answer them.

(a) 'So, you're interested in a Business Studies degree, are you, Jo?'

(b) 'Surely you're not interested in Business Studies, Jo?'

(c) 'How about a really useful qualification like a Business Studies degree, Jo? Would you consider that?'

(d) 'Why are you interested in a Business Studies degree, Jo?'

(e) 'Why particularly Business Studies, Jo?'

The interviewer must listen carefully to the responses and evaluate them so as to judge what the candidate:

(a) wants to say;

(b) is trying *not* to say;

(c) is saying - but doesn't mean, or is lying about (according to Fletcher around 20% of candidates admit to lying at interviews);

(d) is having difficulty saying.

In addition, the interviewer will have to be aware when he:

(a) is hearing something he needs to know;

(b) is hearing something he *doesn't* need to know;

(c) is hearing only what he expects to hear; and/or

(d) is not hearing clearly - when his or her own attitudes, perhaps prejudices, are getting in the way of an objective response to the candidate.

Candidates should be given the opportunity to ask questions. Indeed, well-prepared candidates should go into an interview knowing what questions they want to ask. The choice of questions might well have some influence on how the interviewers assess a candidate's interest in and understanding of the job. Moreover, there is information that the candidate will need to know about the organisation and the job, and about:

(a) terms and conditions of employment (although negotiations about detailed terms may not take place until a provisional offer has been made); and

(b) the next step in the selection process - whether there are further interviews, when a decision might be made, or which references might be taken up.

2.3 Types of interview

Individual or *one-to-one interviews* are the most common selection method. They offer the advantages of direct face-to-face communication, and opportunity to establish *rapport* between the candidate and interviewer: each has to give attention solely to the other, and there is potentially a relaxed atmosphere, if the interviewer is willing to establish an informal style.

The disadvantage of a one-to-one interview is the scope it allows for a biased or superficial decision.

(a) The candidate may be able to disguise lack of knowledge in a specialist area of which the interviewer knows little.

(b) The interviewer's perception may be selective or distorted, and this lack of objectivity may go unnoticed and unchecked.

(c) The greater opportunity for personal rapport with the candidate may cause a weakening of the interviewer's objective judgement: (s)he may favour someone (s)he got on with over someone who was unresponsive but better-qualified. Again, there will be no cross-check with another interviewer.

Panel interviews are designed to overcome such disadvantages. A panel may consist of two or three people who together interview a single candidate: most commonly, an HR specialist and the departmental manager who will have responsibility for the successful candidate. This may be more daunting for the candidate (depending on the tone and conduct of the interview) but it has several advantages.

(a) The HR and line specialists gather the information they each need about the candidate at the same time, cutting down on the subsequent information-sharing stage, and making a separate subsequent interview with one or the other unnecessary.

(b) The questions each specialist wants put to the candidate (related to their respective fields of activity and expertise) will be included, and the answers will be assessed by the specialist concerned: they will also be able to give the candidate information, both about the employment aspects of the position, and about the departmental task-related aspects.

(c) The interviewers can discuss their assessment of the candidate's abilities, behaviour and personality. They can thus gain a more complete picture, and can modify any hasty, superficial or biased judgements.

Large formal panels, or *selection boards,* may also be convened where there are a number of individuals or groups with an interest in the selection. This has the advantage of allowing a number of people to see candidates, and to share information about them at a single meeting: similarly, they can compare their assessments on the spot, without a subsequent effort at liaison and communication.

Offsetting these administrative advantages, however, there are severe drawbacks to the effectiveness of the selection board as a means of assessment.

(a) Questions tend to be more varied, and more random, since there is no single guiding force behind the interview strategy. The candidate may have trouble switching from one topic to another so quickly, especially if questions are not led up to, and not clearly put - as may happen if they are unplanned. Candidates are also seldom allowed to expand their answers, and so may not be able to do justice to themselves.

(b) If there is a dominating member of the board, the interview may have greater continuity - but that individual may also influence the judgements of other members.

(c) Some candidates may not perform well in a formal, artificial situation such as a board interview, and may find such a situation extremely stressful. The interview will thus not show the best qualities of someone who might nevertheless be highly effective in the work context and in the face of work-related pressures.

(d) Research consistently shows that board members rarely agree with each other in their judgements about candidates.

2.4 The limitations of interviews

Interviews are criticised because they fail to provide accurate predictions of how a person will perform in the job. The main reasons why this might be so are as follows.

(a) Limited scope and relevance. An interview is necessarily too brief to 'get to know' candidates in the kind of depth required to make an accurate prediction of their behaviour in any given situation. In addition, an interview is an artificial situation: candidates may be 'on their best behaviour' or, conversely, so nervous that they do not do themselves justice. Neither situation reflects what the person is 'really like'.

> *Among the qualities which neither the interview nor intelligence tests are able to assess accurately are the candidate's ability to get on with and influence his colleagues, to display qualities of spontaneous leadership and to produce ideas in a real-life situation.* **Plumbley**

(b) Errors of judgement by interviewers. These might include the following.

   (i) The *halo effect* - a tendency for people to make an initial general judgement about a person based on a single obvious attribute, such as being neatly dressed, or well-spoken, or having a public school education. This single attribute will colour later perceptions, and might make an interviewer mark the person up or down on every other factor in their assessment.

   (ii) *Contagious bias* - a process whereby an interviewer changes the behaviour of the applicant by suggestion. The applicant might be led by the wording of questions or non-verbal cues from the interviewer, and change what (s)he is doing or saying in response.

   (iii) A possible inclination by interviewers to *stereotype* candidates on the basis of insufficient evidence. Stereotyping groups people together who are assumed to share certain characteristics (women, say, or vegetarians), then attributes certain traits to the group as a whole (emotional, socialist etc). It then (illogically) assumes that each individual member of the supposed group will possess that trait.

   (iv) *Incorrect assessment* of qualitative factors such as motivation, honesty or integrity. Abstract qualities are very difficult to assess in an interview.

   (v) *Logical error*. For example, an interviewer might decide that a young candidate who has held two or three jobs in the past for only a short time will be unlikely to last long in any job. (Not necessarily so.)

Activity 4

What assumptions might an interviewer make about *you*, based on your:

(a) accent, or regional/national variations in your spoken English;
(b) school;
(c) clothes and hair-style
(d) stated hobbies, interests, 'philosophies'; and
(e) taste in books and TV programmes.

To what extent would any of these assumptions be fair?

For objectivity, you might like to conduct this Activity in class. What assumptions do you make about the person sitting next to you?

(c) Lack of skill and experience in interviewers. The problems with inexperienced interviewers are not only bias, but:
  (i) inability to evaluate information about a candidate properly;
  (ii) failure to compare a candidate against the requirements for a job or a personnel specification;
  (iii) bad planning of the interview;
  (iv) failure to take control of the direction and length of the interview;
  (v) a tendency either to act as an inquisitor and make candidates feel uneasy or to let candidates run away with the interview;
  (vi) a reluctance to probe into facts and challenge statements where necessary.

While some interviewers may be experts from the human resources function, it is usually thought desirable to include line managers in the interview team. They cannot be full-time interviewers, obviously: they have their other work to do. No matter how much training they are given in interview techniques, they will lack continuous experience, and probably not give interviewing as much thought or interest as they should. A simplified set of criteria may help, which is in non-HR-specialist's terminology, and is clearly related to relevant items on the job specification.

3   SELECTION TESTING

In some job selection procedures, an interview is supplemented by some form of selection test. According to Smith and Abrahamsen more than 40% of organisations use some form of testing (such as personality, intelligence or work sampling) as an integral part of their selection process. The interviewers must be certain that the results of such tests are reliable, and that a candidate who scores well in a test will be more likely to succeed in the job. The test will have no value unless there is a direct relationship between ability in the test and ability in the job. The test should be designed to be *discriminating* (to bring out the differences in subjects), *standardised* (so that it measures the same thing in different people, providing a consistent basis for comparison) and *relevant* to its purpose.

The science of measuring mental capacities and processes is called 'psychometrics'; hence the term 'psychometric testing'. There are five types of test commonly used in practice:

(a) intelligence tests;
(b) aptitude tests;
(c) tests of interests;
(d) personality tests;
(e) proficiency tests.

3.1   Intelligence tests

Tests of *general* intellectual ability typically test memory, ability to think quickly and logically, and problem solving skills. An article in *Personnel Management* magazine (December 1993) referred to the continuing influence of 'cognitive ability' tests and suggests that reliance on such measures may increase. This is because uncertainty in UK employers' minds about the validity of A-level and GCSE results and the wide variation in degree classes between higher educational institutions may lead them to seek alternative reassurance of general intellectual ability.

Most people have experience of IQ tests and the like, and few would dispute their validity as good measures of *general* intellectual capacity. This is what is known as 'face' validity: in other words candidates believe in such tests and indeed, in tests generally.

3.2 Aptitude tests

Aptitude tests are designed to predict an individual's potential for performing a job or learning new skills. There are various accepted areas of aptitude, as follows.

(a) Reasoning - verbal, numerical and abstract.

(b) Spatio-visual ability - practical intelligence, non-verbal ability and creative ability.

(c) Perceptual speed and accuracy - clerical ability.

(d) 'Manual' ability - mechanical, manual, musical and athletic.

With a few possible exceptions most of the areas of aptitude mentioned above are fairly easily measurable and, so long as it is possible to determine what particular aptitudes are required for a job, it is likely that aptitude tests will be useful for selection.

3.3 Tests of interests

Tests of interests are generally designed to shed light on a person's likely behaviour in different work situations. To take an obvious example, it might be expected that somebody who likes playing rugby will be a good team worker.

3.4 Personality tests

Personality tests may measure a variety of characteristics, such as an applicant's skill in dealing with other people, his ambition and motivation or his emotional stability. Probably the best known example is the 16PF, originally developed by Cattell in 1950. This is described as follows in *Personnel Management* (February 1994).

> *The 16PF comprises 16 scales, each of which measures a factor that influences the way a person behaves.*
>
> *The factors are functionally different underlying personality characteristics, and each is associated with not just one single piece of behaviour but rather is the source of a relatively broad range of behaviours. For this reason the factors themselves are referred to as source traits and the behaviours associated with them are called surface traits.*
>
> *The advantage of measuring source traits, as the 16PF does, is that you end up with a much richer understanding of the person because you are not just describing what can be seen but also the characteristics underlying what can be seen.*
>
> *The 16PF analyses how a person is likely to behave generally, including, for example, contributions likely to be made to particular work contexts, aspects of the work environment to which the person is likely to be more or less suited, and how best to manage the person.*

The validity of such tests has been much debated, but it seems that some have been shown by research to be valid predictors of job performance, so long as they are used properly (*Personnel Management*, December 1993).

3.5 Proficiency tests

Proficiency tests are perhaps the most closely related to an assessor's objectives, because they measure ability to do the work involved. An applicant for an audio typist's job, for example, might be given a dictation tape and asked to type it. This is a type of attainment test, in that it is designed to measure abilities or skills already acquired by the candidate.

3.6 Trends in the use of tests

In the December 1993 article in *Personnel Management*, Clive Fletcher identifies the following six trends in the use and development of tests.

(a) Continuing enthusiasm for personality measures.

(b) The continuing influence of cognitive ability tests.

(c) A focus on certain popular themes - sales ability or aptitude, customer orientation, motivation, teamworking and organisational culture are mentioned.

(d) The growing diversity of test producers and sources (meaning more choice, but also more poor quality measures).

(e) Expanded packages of tests, including tapes, computer disks, workbooks and so on.

(f) A growing focus on fairness: the most recent edition of the 16PF test, for example, has been scrutinised by expert psychologists 'to exclude certain types of content, such as dated material, content that might lead to bias, material that might be unacceptable in an organisational setting and anything considered to be strongly socially desirable or undesirable'.

3.7 Limitations of psychometric testing

Psychometric testing has grown in popularity in recent years, but you should be aware of certain drawbacks.

(a) There is not always a direct (let alone predictive) relationship between ability in the test and ability in the job: the job situation is very different from artificial test conditions.

(b) The interpretation of test results is a skilled task, for which training and experience is essential. It is also highly subjective (particularly in the case of personality tests), which belies the apparent scientific nature of the approach.

(c) Additional difficulties are experienced with particular kinds of test. For example:
   (i) an aptitude test measuring arithmetical ability would need to be constantly revised or its content might become known to later applicants;
   (ii) personality tests can often give misleading results because applicants seem able to guess which answers will be looked at most favourably;
   (iii) it is difficult to design intelligence tests which give a fair chance to people from different cultures and social groups and which test the *kind* of intelligence that the organisation wants from its employees: the ability to score highly in IQ tests does not necessarily correlate with desirable traits such as mature judgement or creativity, merely mental agility. In addition, 'practice makes perfect': most tests are subject to coaching and practice effects.

(d) It is difficult to exclude bias from tests. Many tests (including personality tests) are tackled less successfully by women than by men, or by some candidates born overseas than by indigenous applicants because of the particular aspects chosen for testing. This is a particular problem in countries, such as the UK, where equal opportunities legislation makes it illegal to discriminate in employment on the basis of sex or race.

Activity 5

The following is a classic IQ test 'odd man out' question from an old '11+' paper.

'Which is the odd man out?

MEASLES, STEAMER, LEAVE, OMELETTE, COURAGE.'

(a) What is the answer?

(b) How might this question discriminate against certain tested groups?

EXAMPLE: PREDICTIVE VALIDITY SCALE

Smith and Abrahamsen in 1994 referred to a scale that predicts how well a candidate will perform at work if offered that job. This is known as a predictive validity scale. The scale ranges from 1 (meaning a method that is right every time) to 0 (meaning a method that is no better than chance). On this basis, they produced the following results.

Method	% use	Predictive validity
Interviews	92	0.17
References	74	0.13
Work sampling	18	0.57
Assessment centres	14	0.40
Personality tests	13	0.40
Cognitive tests	11	0.54
Biodata	4	0.40
Graphology	3	0.00

The results are most revealing as they show a pattern of employers relying most heavily on the least valid selection methods for their recruitment purposes. Interviews, in particular (and for the reasons given earlier) seem not much better than tossing a coin.

3.8 Group selection methods

Group selection methods might be used by an organisation as the final stage of a selection process as a more 'natural' and in-depth appraisal of candidates. Group assessments tend to be used for posts requiring leadership, communication or teamworking skills: advertising agencies often use the method for selecting account executives, for example. They consist of a series of tests, interviews and group situations over a period of two days, involving a small number of candidates for a job. Typically, six or eight candidates will be invited to the organisation's premises for two days. After an introductory session to make the candidates feel at home, they will be given one or two tests, one or two individual interviews, and several group situations in which the candidates are invited to discuss problems together and arrive at solutions as a management team. Techniques in such programmes include:

(a) group role-play exercises, in which they can explore (and hopefully display) interpersonal skills and/or work through simulated managerial tasks;

(b) case studies, where candidates' analytical and problem-solving abilities are tested in working through described situations/problems, as well as their interpersonal skills, in taking part in (or leading) group discussions of the case study.

These group sessions might be thought useful because:

(a) they give the organisation's selectors a longer opportunity to study the candidates;

(b) they reveal more than application forms, interviews and tests alone about the ability of candidates to persuade others, negotiate with others, and explain ideas to others and also to investigate problems efficiently. These are typically management skills;

(c) they reveal more about how the candidate's personalities and attributes will affect the work team and his own performance. Stamina, social interaction with others (ability to co-operate and compete), intelligence, energy, self confidence or outside interests will not necessarily be meaningful in themselves (as analysed from written tests), but may be shown to affect performance in the work context.

4 THE OFFER AND CONTRACT OF EMPLOYMENT

Once an eligible candidate has been found, a provisional offer can be made, by telephone or in writing, subject to satisfactory references.

The organisation should be prepared for its offer to be rejected at this stage. Applicants may have received and accepted other offers. They may not have been attracted by their first-hand view of the organisation, and may have changed their mind about applying; they may only have been testing the water in applying in the first place, gauging the market for their skills and experience for future reference, or seeking a position of strength from which to bargain with their present employers. A small number of eligible applicants should therefore be kept in reserve.

4.1 References

References provide further confidential information about the prospective employee. This may be of varying value, as the reliability of all but the most factual information must be in question. A reference should contain:

(a) straightforward factual information confirming the nature of the applicant's previous job(s), period of employment, pay, and circumstances of leaving; and

(b) opinions about the applicant's personality and other attributes. These should obviously be treated with some caution. Allowances should be made for prejudice (favourable or unfavourable), charity (withholding detrimental remarks), and possibly fear of being actionable for libel (although references are privileged, as long as they are factually correct and devoid of malice).

At least two *employer* references are desirable, providing necessary factual information, and comparison of personal views. *Personal* references tell the prospective employer little more than that the applicant has a friend or two.

Written references save time, especially if a standardised letter or form has been pre-prepared. A simple letter inviting the previous employer to reply with the basic information and judgement required may suffice. (If the recruiting officer wants a more detailed appraisal of the applicant's suitability, brief details of the post in question may be supplied, but the previous employer's opinion will still be an ill-informed and subjective judgement.) A standard form to be completed by the referee may be more acceptable, and might pose a set of simple questions about:

(a) job title;
(b) main duties and responsibilities;
(c) period of employment;
(d) pay/salary; and
(e) attendance record.

If a judgement of character and suitability is desired, it might be most tellingly formulated as the question: 'Would you re-employ this individual? (If not, why not?)'

Telephone references may be time-saving if standard reference letters or forms are not available. They may also elicit a more honest opinion than a carefully prepared written statement. For this reason, a telephone call may also be made to check or confirm a poor or grudging reference which the recruiter suspects may be prejudiced.

The pen is more double-edged than the sword!

'I am delighted to write a reference for X, now that I no longer employ him.'

'The person who gets Y to work for him will be fortunate indeed.'

'I cannot speak too highly of Z's ability.'

'I can honestly say that things have not been the same since P left.'

Activity 6

(a) At the end of a recent selection process one candidate was outstanding, in the view of everyone involved. However, you have just received a very bad reference from her current employer. What do you do?

(b) For fun, rephrase the following comments in the way that you might expect to see them appear in a letter of reference.

  (i) Mr Smith is habitually late
  (ii) Remains immature
  (iii) Socially unskilled with clients
  (iv) Is rather dull

4.2 Work permits

A combination of new immigration rules and the European Union has complicated the recruitment and selection of non-UK nationals. *People Management* (12 January 1995) reported as follows.

(a) The general principle is that people coming to the UK for employment require a work permit. 'Employment' includes paid and unpaid employment, self-employment and engagement in business or any professional activity. (This does not affect short 'business visits'.) Work permits are generally issued for 1 to 2 years and not more than 4 years.

(b) Nationals from the European Economic Area (EEA) have a right to work anywhere in the EEA without permits. This covers the EU, *plus* Norway, Iceland and Switzerland.

(c) In order to get a work permit for an overseas employee, the UK employer has to show:

  (i) that there is no one in the EU who can fill the post in question; and that
  (ii) the business requires the post to be filled by someone of the individual's particular calibre.

(d) The Employment Department tends to require less information where the post is a transfer within an international group; is at board level (or equivalent); is in a skill area recognised to be scarce in the EU; or is essential to a project which will bring investment and jobs into the UK.

4.3 Contracts of employment

Once the offer of employment has been confirmed and accepted, the contract of employment can be prepared and offered.

A contract of employment may be written, oral or a mixture of the two. At the one extreme, it may be a document drawn up by solicitors and signed by both parties; at the other extreme it may consist of a handshake and a 'See you on Monday'. Senior personnel may sign a contract specially drafted to include terms on confidentiality and restraint of trade. Other employees may sign a standard form contract, exchange letters with the new employer or supply agreed terms orally at interview. Each of these situations, subject to the requirements (outlined below) as to written particulars, will form a valid contract of employment, as long as there is agreement on essential terms such as hours and wages.

4.4 Written particulars of employment

Although the contract need not be made in writing, the employer must give an employee (who works at least eight hours a week) a written statement of certain particulars of his or her employment, within two months of the beginning of employment (*Trade Union Reform and Employment Rights Act* (TURERA), 1993). This requirement applies to all employees except merchant seamen, employees working wholly or mainly outside the UK, and those who have a written contract of employment which gives all the necessary details.

The statement should identify the following.

(a) The names of *employer* and *employee*.
(b) The *date* on which employment began (important if it becomes necessary to decide what period of notice should be given).
(c) Whether any service with a previous employer forms part of the employee's *continuous period* of employment (important if the employee wished to claim for redundancy or unfair dismissal).
(d) *Pay* - the scale or rate of pay and the intervals at which it is to be paid.
(e) *Hours of work* (including any specified 'normal working hours') rest pauses, shifts and so on.
(f) Any *holiday* entitlements (including fixed dates, if any, and qualifying periods) and *holiday pay* entitlement (including any right to accrued holiday pay on termination of employment).
(g) *Sick leave* and *sick pay* entitlement (if any) including requirements for medical certificates, and maximum time lost before termination of the contract.
(h) *Pensions* and pension *schemes* (unless statutory, ie prescribed by legislation)
(i) Length of *notice* of termination to be given on either side (or the expiry date if employed for a fixed term).
(j) The *title* of the job which the employee is employed to do.
(k) Details of *disciplinary procedures* and *grievance procedures,* (for employers of 20+ employees: section 9, Employment Act 1989), works rules, union or staff association membership.
(l) Rules on *health and safety at work* (by custom only).

It is sufficient to refer to separate booklets or notices (on pension schemes, disciplinary/ grievance procedures and so on) where the relevant details can be found: not all the information needs to go in the written statement!

The purpose of these rules is to ensure that the employee has precise information of the terms on which he is employed. Some employers invite the employee to countersign and return a second copy of the particulars as evidence that he has received them. But the statement is not the contract itself - it is merely written evidence, so if the particulars are found to contain an error, that does not bind either party to the erroneous terms: the true agreed terms of the 'contract' prevail.

4.5 Implied terms

Express terms are those which are explicitly and specifically offered and accepted as part of the contract of employment. Since it would not be practicable or desirable for all aspects of a contract of employment to be codified exhaustively into a written agreement, *common law* (made up of decisions in the courts which act as precedents for all later cases) 'implies' a number of terms. Even if no express terms have been agreed, the courts have nevertheless taken certain duties and entitlements to be implied by the nature of employment with regard to the following areas.

(a) *Employers' duties*. For example, on:
  (i) *pay*. If there is no express agreement, the employee is entitled to 'reasonable' remuneration, and to receive an itemised pay slip showing pay and deductions;
  (ii) *provision of work*. The employer has an implied obligation to provide the work for which employees were engaged, or to protect the employees against (or compensate them for) extended loss of earnings as a result of lack of work;
  (iii) *health and safety*. In addition to statutory duties (provided for by legislation), the employer has an implied common law duty to take 'reasonable care' of employees by:
    (1) selecting proper staff;
    (2) providing adequate materials; and
    (3) providing a safe system of working (including protection, warnings etc).
(b) *Employees' duties*. The employee has a basic duty of faithful service to the employer.

Activity 7

Suggest what you think 'faithful service' means: what does an employee 'owe' his or her employer?

A severe breach of these common law implied duties can entitle the injured party to regard it as a breach of the contract of employment. In that case, the employer may dismiss the offending employee, or the employee may claim damages from the employer.

In addition, there may be *collective implied terms*. Terms of employment, such as wages and working conditions, are often negotiated on a collective basis by an employer (or employers' association) and trade unions. These collectively agreed terms are generally implied to be agreed between the individual employee and employer, even if they are not expressly stated in the contract between them, as long as the terms are reasonable, properly negotiated and known to the employee.

Statutory implied terms are duties imposed on the parties by statute, or Act of Parliament. Whatever the express terms of the employment contract, the law of the land overrides them; an employer cannot force employees to abide by a contract that denies their statutory rights with regard to:

(a) wage payments;
(b) maternity leave;
(c) time off work;

(d) health and safety; and
(e) employment protection.

This legislation will be discussed in relevant chapters of this book.

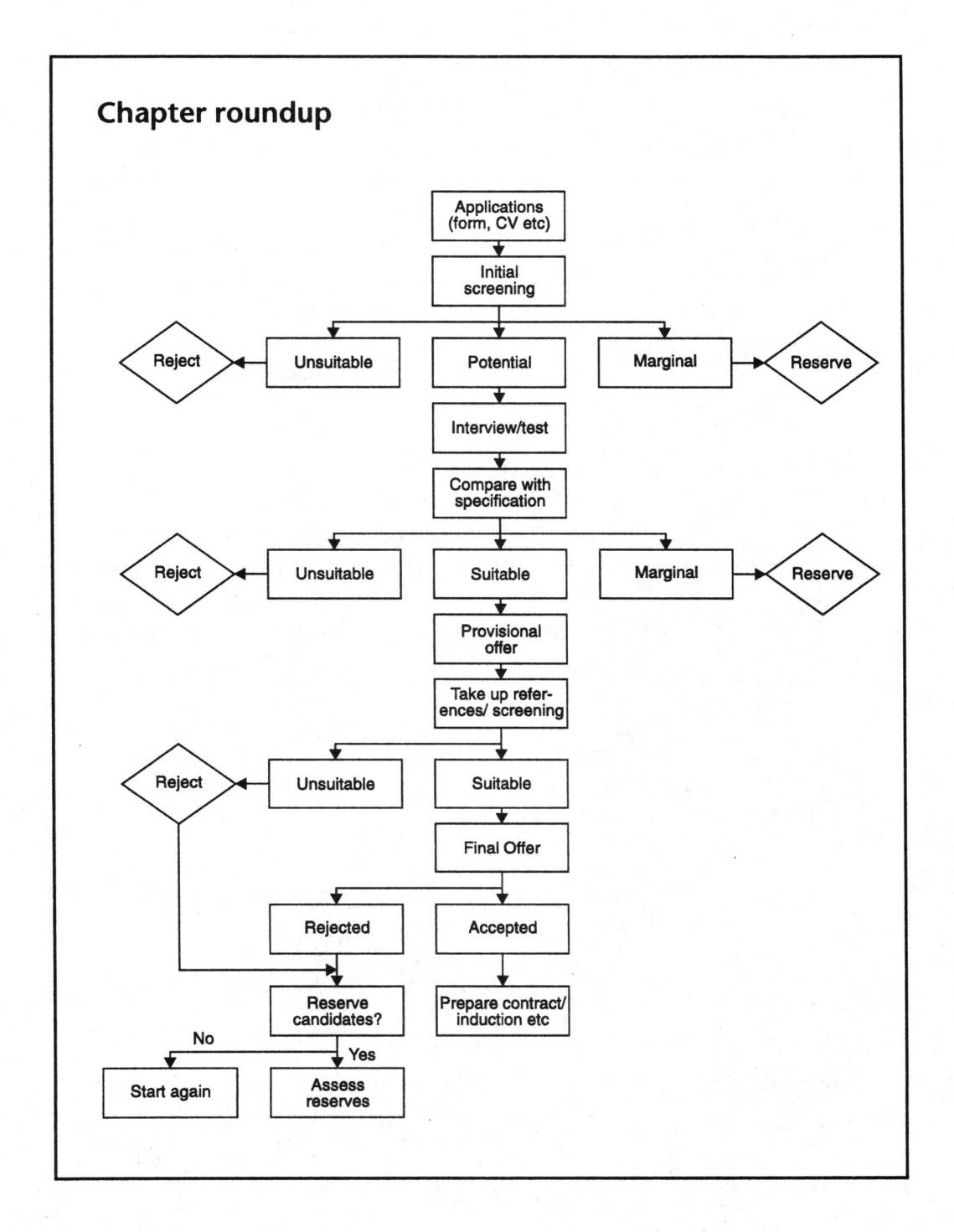

Chapter roundup

```
                    Applications
                    (form, CV etc)
                          ↓
                    Initial
                    screening
          ┌───────────────┼───────────────┐
          ↓               ↓               ↓
   Reject ← Unsuitable  Potential    Marginal → Reserve
                          ↓
                    Interview/test
                          ↓
                    Compare with
                    specification
          ┌───────────────┼───────────────┐
          ↓               ↓               ↓
   Reject ← Unsuitable  Suitable     Marginal → Reserve
                          ↓
                    Provisional
                    offer
                          ↓
                    Take up refer-
                    ences/ screening
                  ┌───────┴───────┐
                  ↓               ↓
        Reject ← Unsuitable     Suitable
                                  ↓
                                Final Offer
                          ┌───────┴───────┐
                          ↓               ↓
                       Rejected         Accepted
                          ↓               ↓
                    Reserve           Prepare contract/
                    candidates?       induction etc
                   ↙       ↘
                 No         Yes
                 ↓           ↓
             Start again   Assess
                           reserves
```

Quick quiz

1 A job selection interview has several aims. If you were conducting one, though, you should not be concerned with:

A comparing the applicant against the job/personnel specification;

B getting as much information as possible about the applicant;

C giving the applicant information about the job and organisation; and

D making the applicant feel he has been treated fairly;

79

Business Basics: Human Resource Management

NOTES

2 Amon Leigh-Hewman is interviewing a candidate for a vacancy in his firm. He asks a question about the candidate's views on a work-related issue. The candidate starts to answer, and sees to his horror that Amon in pursing his lips and shaking his head slightly to himself. 'Of course, that's what some people say', continues the candidate, 'but I myself ...' Amon smiles. His next question is 'Don't you think that ...?'

Amon is getting a distorted view of the candidate because of:

A   the halo effect

B   contagious bias

C   stereotyping

D   logical error.

3 Selection tests such as IQ tests and personality tests may not be effective in getting the right person for the job for several reasons. Which of the following criticisms is false, though?

A   Test results can be influenced by practice and coaching rather than genuine ability

B   Subjects are able (and tend) to deliberately falsify results

C   Tests do not eliminate bias and subjectivity

D   Tests are generally less accurate predictors of success than interviews

4 What can be done to improve the effectiveness of selection interviews?

5 What are the relative merits and drawbacks of the panel and one-to-one interviews in personnel selection?

6 What matters should be identified in the written particulars of employment supplied to employees?

7 Distinguish between:

(a) express terms;

(b) implied terms in common law;

(c) collective implied terms; and

(d) statutory implied terms.

Solutions to activities

1   (a) Boxes too small to contain the information asked for.

   (b) Forms which are (or look) so lengthy or complicated that prospective applicants either complete them perfunctorily or give up (and apply to another employer instead).

   (c) Illegal (eg discriminatory) or offensive questions.

   (d) Lack of clarity as to what (and how much) information is required.

3   (a) Closed. (The only answer is 'yes' or 'no', unless Jo is prepared to expand on it, at his or her own initiative.)

   (b) Leading. (Even if Jo was interested, (s)he would get the message that 'yes' would not be what the interviewer wanted, or expected, to hear.)

   (c) Leading closed multiple! ('Really useful' leads Jo to think that the 'correct' answer will be 'yes': there is not much opportunity for any other answer, without expanding on it unasked.)

   (d) Open. (Jo has to explain, in his or her own words.)

   (e) Probing. (If Jo's answer has been unconvincing, short, or vague, this question forces a more specific answer.)

5 (a) 'Steamer'. (The others share national connotations: German measles, French leave, Spanish omelette, Dutch courage.)

   (b) The answer presupposes a knowledge of expressions which are rooted in a European context and, in some cases, are old-fashioned and dependent on a middle-class upbringing and education.

6 (a) It is quite possible that her current employer is desperate to retain her. Disregard the reference, or question the referee by telephone, and seek another reference from a previous employer if possible.

   (b) The phrases given are 'translations' by Adrian Furnham (Financial Times, December 1991) of the following.

   (i) 'Mr Smith was occasionally a little lax in time keeping'

   (ii) 'Clearly growing out of earlier irresponsibility'

   (iii) 'At her best with close friends'

   (iv) 'Got a well deserved lower second'

7 The courts have implied the following duties on the part of the employee:

   (a) Reasonable competence to do the job.

   (b) Obedience to instructions (unless this would force him to endanger himself or break the law).

   (c) Accountability for any money or property received in the course of employment (such as commissions, 'gifts' etc).

   (d) 'Reasonable' care and skill in the performance of the job.

   (e) Personal service - in other words, not delegating or 'subcontracting' the duties agreed in the (personal) employment contract, without the employer's consent.

Further question practice

Now try the following practice questions at the end of this text

Multiple choice questions	21 to 27
Exam style question	4

Chapter 5

DISCRIMINATION AND EQUAL OPPORTUNITY

Introduction

Sexual and racial discrimination have become such high-profile issues that you should be aware of obvious abuses: 'White Anglo-Saxon Protestant Males only need apply' is not an acceptable recruitment policy!

However, the 1990s have seen the range of discrimination issues widening to include disability, age and sexual orientation. Moreover, the concept of indirect discrimination has forced employers to examine the implications of previously 'fair-seeming' practices. (If you encourage word-of-mouth recruitment, for example, in a predominantly white male workforce, you are - indirectly - discriminating against women and racial minorities by not allowing them the same opportunity to hear about the jobs.)

An increasingly aware and powerful consumer base has brought the issue of discrimination home to employers in a new way. They still need to comply with the law, and Codes of Practice by which they could be taken to an Industrial Tribunal in the event of a dispute. But they are also starting (slowly) to realise that discriminatory policies and practices risk alienating not only existing and potential employees, but the customers on whom their business depends.

Your objectives

After completing this chapter you should:

(a) understand the nature and causes of discrimination at work;

(b) be aware of the legislative framework;

(c) be able to outline the practical implications of non-discrimination for HRM;

(d) be aware of related issues such as sexual harassment.

1 DISCRIMINATION AT WORK

1.1 Women in employment

Despite the fact that women have contributed directly to the national product since medieval times - on the land and in home-based industries such as textiles - the acceptance of women in paid employment has been a slow process which is even now having to be enforced by law.

> *The introduction of the typewriter, the development of shorthand, and the invention of telephone and light office machines ... led to women's real breakthrough into office work. With the great expansion in the number of office jobs, many of a new type, women were seen less as a threat to the existing labour force than as a much needed additional resource.*
> **Baroness Seear,** *Corporate Personnel Management,* ed. Livy

The World Wars, prompting many women into the munitions industry, changed the nature of 'acceptable' employment for women. In professional employment, however, - apart from teaching, nursing and social work - women remained heavily outnumbered for many years.

The distribution of women in the UK workforce today is still heavily concentrated in categories such as textiles, footwear, clothing and leather, hotel and catering, retail distribution, professional and scientific services, and miscellaneous services. A significant percentage of the women employed in these categories work part-time.

Only in recent decades has there been a widespread challenge to sex segregation in employment - the idea that there are 'men's jobs' and 'women's jobs', with only a few genuinely 'unisex' categories of work. Reasons for this discrimination include:

(a) social pressures on the woman to bear and rear children, and on the man to make a lifetime commitment to paid work as the 'breadwinner'. Employers assumed - and sometimes still assume - that women's paid work would be short-term or interrupted, and that training and development was therefore hardly worthwhile;

(b) the nature of earlier industrial work, which was physically heavy: legal restrictions were placed on women's employment in areas such as mines, night work in factories etc;

(c) lack of organisation of women at work and influence in trade unions (except in industries like textiles), up until the 1970s and 1980s;

(d) the reinforcing of segregation at home and at school: for example, lack of encouragement to girls to study mathematical and scientific subjects;

(e) career ladders which fail to fast-track women. Apprenticeships, for example, are rarely held by girls.

In addition, organisations, like banks, which have traditionally developed staff on the assumption of a lifetime career with the one employer, have tended to assume that women are unlikely to want a lifetime career. Commitments to geographical mobility are similarly assumed to be undesirable to women; and

(f) child-bearing and family responsibilities. Part-time work has enabled many women to continue in paid employment, but tends to apply to jobs which carry little prospect for promotion.

Many of these assumptions are being re-examined, and we will look a bit later at some of the measures being taken to remove the barriers to women in employment.

> *The mixture of the sexes involves no risk but is highly beneficial. It raises the tone of the male staff by confining them during many hours of the day to a decency of conversation and demeanour which is not always to be found where*

men alone are employed.
Mr Scudamore, *Post Office Telegraph Report*, 1872 *(quoted by* Baroness Seear, *Corporate Personnel Management).*

1.2 Ethnic minorities in employment

In its Annual Report of 1984, the Commission for Racial Equality noted that the level of unemployment for black people was nearly twice as high as that for white people. The Home Office Research Unit listed four causes of high minority unemployment.

(a) Because immigration has mainly occurred in the last thirty years, the ethnic minority population is much younger than the population as a whole: young people find it particularly hard to get jobs when vacancies are scarce.

(b) Again because of fairly recent arrival, minority workers may not have UK-accepted occupational skills and qualifications, and may perhaps have poor English as well.

(c) Direct racial discrimination in favour of white labour, when this is in ample supply.

(d) Concentration of minorities in certain industrial sectors, types of firm and occupations (perhaps as a result of discrimination) which are contracting (hitherto mainly in the manufacturing sector), insecure or low-status.

The Research Unit concluded that the first two factors would diminish with time, highlighting further the need to address the issue of racial discrimination.

The number of allegations of unlawful racial discrimination at work to the Commission for Racial Equality (CRE) has continued to rise (to around 1,500 in 1994) and a CRE survey of 168 large companies showed that 55% had no racial equality action plan, and 12% not even a racial equality policy.

In January 1995, the CRE launched a new initiative in the drive for equal opportunities, with its benchmarking standard for employers, *Racial Equality Means Business*. This aims to move the issue beyond compliance with legislation, and even beyond commitment to the moral principle of equality, to a recognition of its business benefits. Companies which have implemented practical policies and action plans on racial equality - including Midland Bank, Littlewoods and WH Smith - claim to have found measurable benefits in terms of staff morale and performance, and customer loyalty.

Reasons for adopting such plans included:

(a) good HR practice, in attracting and retaining the best people;

(b) compliance with the CRE's Code of Practice (1984), which is used by industrial tribunals;

(c) widening the recruitment pool;

(d) other potential benefits to the business through its image as a good employer, and through the loyalty of customers in areas of ethnic diversity.

At the launch, however, the CRE Chairman also criticised companies that did nothing except use 'equal opportunities designer labels' to make recruitment advertisements look good.

1.3 Other disadvantaged groups

It should be remembered that discrimination may operate in all kinds of areas: not just on grounds of sex, but of sexual orientation or marital status; on grounds of religion or politics as well as race and colour; and on grounds of age.

Chapter 5: Discrimination and equal opportunity

Activity 1

Have you ever felt discriminated against at school, work or your university/college? On what grounds: your sex, colour, age, background? What was the effect of the discrimination on your plans and attitudes?

Two further forms of discrimination specifically legislated against are:

(a) failure to provide equal opportunities to suitably qualified *disabled persons*; and

(b) non-engagement or dismissal on the grounds of a *conviction for a criminal offence*, once the offender is rehabilitated and his conviction 'spent'.

(The relevant legislation in these cases is discussed below in Section 2 of this chapter.)

1.4 Age and employment

Despite demographic and educational changes and associated skill shortages among the younger population, a certain amount of discrimination is still directed at more mature workers.

In January 1991, the Institute of Personnel and Development issued a statement, *Age and Employment*, to encourage policies and practices which lead to the employment of qualified individuals regardless of age. The IPD statement says that the use of age-related criteria should be challenged in every aspect of employment decision-making, including recruitment, selection for training, counselling, development, and promotion, and selection for redundancy. However, it is still not against the law in the UK to specify age requirements in recruitment.

2 THE LEGISLATIVE FRAMEWORK

2.1 Equal Pay Act 1970

The Equal Pay Act (passed in 1970, but effective from 1975) was the first major attempt to tackle sexual discrimination. It was intended 'to prevent discrimination as regards terms and conditions of employment between men and women'.

(a) Where there is an element of sex discrimination in a collective agreement, this must be removed to offer a 'unisex' pay rate.

(b) Where a job evaluation scheme is operated to determine pay rates, a woman can claim equal pay for a job which has been rated as equivalent under the scheme.

(c) Where job evaluation is not used, a women can claim equal pay for work that is 'the same or broadly similar' as the work of a man in the same establishment, ('broadly similar' having to be interpreted in the courts, in many cases. The defending employer must show differences of 'practical importance' in the two jobs).

The Equal Pay (Amendment) Regulations 1984 established the right to equal pay for 'work of equal value', so that a woman would no longer have to compare her work with that of a man in the same or broadly similar work, but could establish that her work has equal value to that of a man in the same establishment.

> **Case Study: Equal pay for work of equal value**
>
> *Case: Hayward v Cammell Laird Shipbuilders Ltd.* The applicant, a trained canteen cook, claimed that her work was equal in value to that of male tradesmen employed as painter, thermal installation engineer and joiner. The industrial tribunal found in her favour. (The employers subsequently appealed to the Employment Appeals Tribunal, which ruled that the same pay and overtime rates did not in fact have to be paid to the cook since, when her terms and conditions of work overall were taken into account, she was not unfavourably treated.)

2.2 Equal opportunity

In Britain, two main Acts have been passed to deal with inequality of opportunity.

(a) The Sex Discrimination Act 1975, outlawing certain types of discrimination on the grounds of sex or marital status.

(b) The Race Relations Act 1976, outlawing certain types of discrimination on grounds of colour, race, nationality, or ethnic or national origin.

There are two types of discrimination, under the Acts.

Definitions

(a) *Direct discrimination* occurs when one interested group is treated less favourably than another (except for exempted cases). It is unlikely that a prospective employer will practise direct discrimination unawares.

(b) *Indirect discrimination* occurs when a policy or practice is fair in form, but discriminatory in operation: for example, if requirements or conditions are imposed, with which a substantial proportion of the interested group can not comply.

The employer must, if challenged, justify the conditions on non-racial or non-sexual grounds. It is often the case that employers are not aware that they are discriminating in this way and this concept was a major breakthrough when introduced by the Acts.

Activity 2

Suggest four examples of practices that would constitute indirect discrimination on the grounds of sex.

In both equal opportunity Acts, the obligation of non-discrimination applies to all aspects of employment, including advertisements, recruitment and selection programmes, access to training, promotion, disciplinary procedures, redundancy and dismissal.

In both Acts, too, there are certain exceptions, in which discrimination of a sort may be permitted.

(a) In relation to women, the most important of these are 'genuine occupational qualifications', which include:
   (i) reasons of physiology (not physical strength);
   (ii) reasons of decency or privacy, closely defined;
   (iii) special welfare consideration;
   (iv) the provision of personal services promoting welfare or education; and
   (v) jobs affected by legal restrictions, particularly jobs likely to involve work outside the UK, where 'laws or customs are such that the duties could not, or could not effectively, be performed by a woman'.

Chapter 5: Discrimination and equal opportunity

(b) In the case of ethnic minorities, the exceptions are:
  (i) dramatic performances, where the dramatis personae requires a person of a particular racial group;
  (ii) artists or photographic models for advertising purposes, for reasons of authenticity; and
  (iii) where personal services are rendered for the welfare of the particular group.

The legislation does *not* (except with regard to training) permit *positive discrimination* - actions which give preference to a protected person, regardless of genuine suitability and qualification for the job. In particular, there is no quota scheme such as operates for registered disabled persons (as discussed a bit later): there is no fixed number or percentage of jobs that must be filled by women or members of ethnic minorities, regardless of other criteria.

The organisation may, however, set itself *targets* for the number of such persons that they will *aim* to employ - if the required number of eligible and suitably qualified people can be recruited - as part of an equality action plan.

Training may (RRA ss 37-38, SDA ss 47-48) be given to particular groups exclusively, if the group has in the preceding year been substantially under-represented. It is also permissible to encourage such groups to:

(a) apply for jobs where such exclusive training is offered; and
(b) apply for jobs in which they are under-represented.

A training body (other than the employer) running such a positively discriminating scheme must be either permitted by the Act, or specially designated by application to the Secretary of State for Employment.

The Equal Opportunities Commission and Commission for Racial Equality have powers, subject to certain safeguards, to investigate alleged breach of the Acts, to serve a 'non-discrimination notice', and to follow-up the investigation until satisfied that undertakings given (with regard to compliance and information of persons concerned) are carried out.

Marital status

The Sex Discrimination Act also makes it unlawful to discriminate against married people, for example if an employer believes that a single man will be able to devote more time to the job. (Oddly, perhaps, there is no equivalent protection for single people.)

2.3 Disability

The Disability Discrimination Act 1995 contains the following key points.

(a) A disabled person is defined as a person who has a physical or mental impairment that has a substantial and long-term (more than 12 months) adverse effect on his ability to carry out normal day to day activities. Severe disfigurement is included, as are progressive conditions such as HIV even though the current effect may not be substantial.

(b) The effect includes mobility, manual dexterity, physical co-ordination, and lack of ability to lift or speak, hear, see, remember, concentrate, learn or understand or to perceive the risk of physical danger.

(c) The Act makes it unlawful to discriminate against a disabled person/employee:
  (i) in deciding who to interview or who to employ, or in the terms of an employment offer;
  (ii) in the terms of employment and the opportunities for promotion, transfer, training or other benefits, or by refusing the same;
  (iii) by dismissal or any other disadvantage.

(d) The employer has a duty to make reasonable adjustments to working arrangements or to the physical features of premises where these constitute a disadvantage to disabled people.

(e) The provisions regarding employment do not apply to an employer who has fewer than 20 employees.

Activity 3

Examine the university/college where you are studying, plus any large shop (like a supermarket) you know well. What facilities have been provided for disabled people (staff, students and customers)? What problems remain? Are there any disabled people on the staff? If so, what are their jobs?

2.4 Rehabilitation of Offenders

Another non-discrimination requirement affecting recruitment is the Rehabilitation of Offenders Act 1974. A conviction for criminal offences is 'spent' after a period of time (which varies according to the severity of the offence). After this period, an offender is 'rehabilitated' and is not obliged to disclose the nature of his offence or details of his conviction. Failure to disclose is therefore not justifiable grounds for non-engagement (or dismissal). There are exceptions, however, including life imprisonment, prison sentences over 30 months, and convictions for doctors, lawyers, teachers, accountants and police officers.

The Police Act 1997 will make it easier for recruiters to screen out applicants who have a criminal record. It will establish the Criminal Records Agency, administering a new system of conviction certificates that employers can ask job applicants to provide.

The Institute of Personnel and Develpment conducted a survey on diversity in 1996, and reported the opinions of recruitment consultancies around the UK. Typical views included:

'Of all the things to put off a client, a criminal record is the worst.'

'As far as I am concerned, if they've done it once, they might do it again.'

2.5 Religion

Under the Fair Employment Act of 1989, employers in Northern Ireland are required to monitor the religious composition of their workforce and draw up affirmative action programmes, with targets, to protect Catholics. (The level of Catholics recruited is now greater than their proportion in the labour force; before 1990 it was lower.)

3 THE PRACTICAL IMPLICATIONS

The practical implications of the legislation for employers are set out in Codes of Practice, issued by the Commission for Racial Equality and the Equal Opportunities Commission. These do not have the force of law, but may be taken into account by Industrial Tribunals, where discrimination cases are brought before them. Many organisations now establish their own policy statements or codes of practice on equal opportunities: apart from anything else, a statement of the organisation's position may provide some protection in the event of complaints.

3.1 Formulating an effective policy

In an article in *Administrator* in June 1992, John Green suggested that many organisations make minimal efforts to avoid discrimination, paying lip-service to the idea only to the extent of claiming 'We are an Equal Opportunities Employer' on advertising literature. He goes on to explore the factors necessary to turn such a claim into reality.

(a) *Support* from the top of the organisation for the formulation of a practical policy.

(b) A working party drawn from - for example - management, unions, minority groups, the HR function and staff representatives. This group's brief will be to produce a draft Policy and Code of Practice, which will be approved at senior level.

(c) *Action plans and resources* (including staff) to implement and monitor the policy, publicise it to staff, arrange training and so on.

(d) *Monitoring*. The numbers of women and ethnic minority staff can easily be monitored:

   (i) on entering (and applying to enter) the organisation;

   (ii) on leaving the organisation; and

   (iii) on applying for transfers, promotions or training schemes.

   (It is less easy to determine the ethnic origins of the workforce through such methods as questionnaires: there is bound to be suspicion about the question's motives, and it may be offensive to some workers.)

(e) *Positive action*: the process of taking active steps to encourage people from disadvantaged groups to apply for jobs and training, and to compete for vacancies. (Note that this is not positive discrimination.) Examples might be: using ethnic languages in job advertisements, or implementing training for women in management skills.

3.2 Recruitment and selection

This is an area of particular sensitivity. There is always a risk that a disappointed job applicant, for example, will attribute his lack of success to discrimination, especially if the recruiting organisation's workforce is conspicuously lacking in representatives of the same ethnic minority, sex or group. The implications are obviously wide and attention should be given to the following.

(a) *Advertising*.

   (i) Any wording that suggests preference for a particular group should be avoided (except for genuine occupational qualifications).

   (ii) Employers must not indicate or imply any 'intention to discriminate'.

   (iii) Recruitment literature should state that the organisation is an Equal Opportunities employer.

   (iv) The placing of advertisements only where the readership is predominantly of one race or sex is construed as indirect discrimination. This includes 'word-of-mouth' recruiting from the existing workforce, if it is not broadly representative.

(b) *Recruitment agencies*. Instructions to an agency should not suggest any preference;

(c) *Application forms*. These should include no questions which are not work-related (such as domestic details) and which only one group is asked to complete;

(d) *Interviews*.

   (i) Any non-work-related question must be asked of all subjects, if at all, and even then, some types of question may be construed as discriminatory. (You cannot, for example, ask only women about plans to have a family or care of dependants, or ask - in the most offensive case - about the Pill or PMT.)

(ii) It may be advisable to have a witness at interviews, or at least to take detailed notes, in the event that a claim of discrimination is made.

(e) *Selection tests*. These must be wholly relevant, and should not favour any particular group. Even personality tests have been shown to favour white male applicants;

(f) *Records*. Reasons for rejection, and interview notes, should be carefully recorded, so that in the event of investigation the details will be available.

3.3 Other initiatives

In addition to responding to legislative provisions, some employers have begun to address the underlying problems of equal opportunities, with measures such as the following.

(a) Putting equal opportunities higher on the agenda by appointing Equal Opportunities Managers (and even Directors) who report directly to the Personnel Director.

(b) Flexible hours or part-time work, 'term-time' or annual hours contracts (to allow for school holidays) to help women to combine careers with family responsibilities. Terms and conditions, however, must not be less favourable.

(c) Career-break or return-to-work schemes for women.

(d) Fast-tracking school-leavers, as well as graduates, and posting managerial vacancies internally, giving more opportunities for movement up the ladder for groups (typically women and minorities) currently at lower levels of the organisation.

(e) Training for women-returners or women in management to help women to manage their career potential. Assertiveness training may also be offered as part of such an initiative.

(f) Awareness training for managers, to encourage them to think about equal opportunity policy.

(g) The provision of workplace nurseries for working mothers.

(h) Positive action to encourage job and training applications from minority groups.

(i) Alteration of premises to accommodate wheelchair users, blind or partially sighted workers and so on.

(j) Practices to be reviewed for discrimination against employees of a particular marital status or sexual orientation. (For example, British Airways' extension of its concessionary travel scheme to partners of gay employees. Entitlement to a dead partner's pension is another big issue for partners in homosexual and even heterosexual partnerships: most schemes only recognise husbands or wives as beneficiaries.)

Chapter 5: Discrimination and equal opportunity

Case study: Opportunity 2000

The Opportunity 2000 campaign (led by the voluntary organisation Business in the Community) was launched on 28 October 1991, with an initial 62 organisations - mostly household names. Each set out and published its goals for employing and promoting women during the years up to 2000. Highlights (reported in the Financial Times, 29 October 1991) include:

- *J. Sainsbury*: More than 95,000 staff, about two-thirds women, are employed in more than 320 supermarkets and 60 DIY stores. At the end of last financial year 40 per cent of management were women.

  New measures included scholarships to female weekend employees going on to higher education to take courses in areas in which women are traditionally under-represented, such as retailing, information technology, transport studies and engineering.

- *IBM (UK)*: The computer group set four goals: 'To contribute externally to the advancement of women in the national workforce; ensure that the company takes full advantages of the economic potential of women in the workforce; encourage women employees to realise their full potential; and increase the representation of women in senior management positions.' To achieve these IBM aimed for 30 per cent of graduate intake to be female.

- *BBC:* The BBC has been one of the leading organisations in setting numerical targets for the promotion of women. Existing targets are for the following female/male ratios: 30:70 for senior executive grades; 40:60 senior management; 40:60 management.

- These targets are to be reviewed every five years and further targets are set for the year 2000. It intends to introduce more sophisticated monitoring procedures, further flexible working arrangements, and a policy to tackle harassment at work.

- *British Airways:* Of 50,000 British Airways staff worldwide, 32 per cent are women. Principle goals are: for women employed at all levels to reflect the proportion of women in the total UK workforce. (1991: 32 per cent; 2000: 42 per cent). Women managers in the UK workforce to reflect the proportion of women in full-time employment in the total UK workforce. (1991: 20 per cent; 2000: 27 per cent.)

- The first awards for best practice under Opportunity 2000 were made in 1995, and included Avon Cosmetics' flexible working scheme, childcare arrangements and community programme, and Royal Mail's implementation of a workplace nursery at its biggest sorting office at Mount Pleasant in London.

Activity 4

How many women and racial minority groups are represented among your peers in the university/college where you are studying? Examine its prospectus, the courses offered, and any statements published about equal opportunities: what evidence is there of a coherent equality policy? Identify good and bad practices (if any) that you are aware of.

What more do you think could and should be done?

4 SEXUAL HARASSMENT

Definition

Sexual harassment may be defined as any unwanted conduct with sexual connotations, physical or verbal. It is currently a matter of concern to the European Commission, the British courts and employing organisations. The IPD issued a statement on the matter in 1992.

There is nothing new about harassment in itself, but there are several reasons why it is receiving greater attention. An increasingly diverse workforce, changing attitudes to equal opportunities and acceptable behaviour at work, fuller understanding of the impact of harassment on individuals and organisations, specific legal remedies for victims - all these have put the issue on the business agenda.... Since harassment causes much avoidable demoralisation, stress, anxiety and even sickness among employees, the IPM [now IPD] encourage all attempts to eliminate it for these reasons alone. Yet such efforts also clearly make business sense: a climate free from hostility enables people to contribute far more effectively to the success of the organisation which employs them, and to achieve higher levels of job satisfaction. Furthermore, employers can face legal proceedings if they allow harassment to occur.

Harassment at Work: an IPD Statement, October 1992

The definition of sexual harassment is helpfully set out in the 1991 EU Code of Conduct as:

(a) 'unwanted conduct of a sexual nature, or other conduct based on sex affecting the dignity of women and men at work';

(b) 'unwelcome physical, verbal or non-verbal conduct'; and

(c) 'conduct that denigrates or ridicules or is intimidatory or physically abusive of an employee because of his or her sex, such as derogatory or degrading abuse or insults which are gender-related and offensive comments about appearance or dress'.

The essential characteristic of sexual harassment is that it is unwanted by the recipient

However defined, the problem is a serious one. A survey conducted earlier this year by Alfred Marks, a UK employment agency, showed that a hair-raisingly high 60 per cent of 5,000 of its employees had experienced some kind of sexual harassment during their working lives, most of them several times. Some victims said they became embarrassed and humiliated, others angry and bad-tempered. People suffer, it seems, but do nothing about it. Only one in 20 complained to personnel departments, and in half the cases nothing was done as a result...

The vast majority of private companies - 80 per cent in the UK, according to Alfred Marks, and even more elsewhere in Europe - have no policy to deal with sexual harassment at all. Financial Times 23 October 1991

More recently, according to *The Times* (20 March 1997), Tania Clayton, an employee of the Hereford and Worcester Fire Brigade, was awarded £200,000 in damages for suffering 'three years of intimidation, insults and cruelty' from her male colleagues.

Compliance with the EU code is only voluntary, and there is no specific law against sexual harassment in Europe: indeed, it is not mentioned in law at all. However, it has been ruled that proven sexual harassment is unlawful sex discrimination, under the Sex Discrimination Act.

Chapter 5: Discrimination and equal opportunity

> ### Case examples: What is sexual harrassment?
>
> **Case:** *Strathclyde Regional Council v Porcelli* **1986**
>
> Sexual harassment was ruled 'a particularly degrading and unacceptable form of treatment which it must be taken to have been the intention of Parliament to restrain.'
>
> **Case:** *Wileman v Minilec Engineering Ltd* **1988**
>
> Although the words 'sexual harassment' do not appear in the Sex Discrimination Act, it is 'legal shorthand for activity which is easily recognisable as "subjecting her to any other detriment" within the meaning of the Act'.

4.1 Handling sexual harassment

Recommendations to organisations for handling sexual harassment in the EU Code of Conduct - and the IPD statement on sexual harassment - include the following.

(a) The issuing of a clear policy statement or corporate Code of Conduct, with communication and awareness training (especially for managers) to highlight the seriousness of the offence.

(b) The implementation of counselling procedures, giving advice to victims, and hopefully resolving problems by informal means, but - if not - also planning further proceedings.

(c) The design of complaints procedures, both:

   (i) informal, including person-to-person reproof (a clear statement by the victim to the offender that the conduct is unwelcome) and intervention by a trusted third party; and

   (ii) formal. Provision should be made for confidentiality to be guaranteed, and for an investigator of the same sex as the victim to be available to follow up complaints.

(d) The implementation of disciplinary action. Rules should be defined, including protection of the complainant from further victimisation as a result of the action.

The problem of workplace harassment can be resolved only by developing and implementing preventative policies and procedures. Introducing an effective policy creates a climate of greater confidence to challenge harassment and may lead, in the short term, to more people coming forward; the long-term impact of eliminating harassment will be positive for both employer and employees. There is a mistaken belief that the absence of complaints is indicative that there is no problem. Employers who receive few, or no, complaints about harassment should not be complacent.

The right policies and procedures enable employers to tackle individual incidents quickly and effectively. The goal is to develop a working environment in which harassment is known to be unacceptable and where individuals are confident enough to bring complaints without fear of ridicule or reprisal. This requires an organisational culture where everybody feels a personal responsibility to ensure that the dignity of colleagues, clients and customers is not abused. Harassment at Work; an IPD Statement, October 1992

Activity 5

Give five examples of conduct that you would consider to be sexual harassment, assuming in all cases that the conduct is 'unwarranted' by the object of it.

> ### Case studies: ICI and Leicester City Council
>
> ICI (among others including Reading and Brighton councils and the Midland Bank) have issued a policy statement on sexual harassment at work. The statement deplored any 'unwanted conduct with sexual connotations, whether physical or verbal, which is offensive to the recipient. It may be a single example of grossly offensive behaviour or repeated more minor examples of such behaviour.'
>
> Measures instituted by ICI include reporting, investigation and disciplinary procedures. (This is part of a package of Equal Opportunity measures including improved maternity pay, childcare assistance, and the promotion of less traditional working patterns like job sharing and term-time working.)
>
> 'Leicester City Council has specially trained a number of women to act as "listening posts" for victims to talk to. Their task is to advise and act as confidantes; the response has been so overwhelming that some of the confidantes have complained of stress from so much listening'.
>
> *Financial Times* 23 October 1991

Chapter roundup

- Discrimination of certain types is illegal on grounds of:
  - sex and marital status (Sex Discrimination Act 1975);
  - colour, race, nationality and ethnic or national origin (Race Relations Act 1976);
  - disability (Disability Discrimination Act 1995) and
  - spent convictions (Rehabilitation of Offenders Act 1975).
- In addition, age discrimination has recently been highlighted as an undesirable feature of employment practice, and sexual harassment has been ruled to be sexual discrimination under UK law.
- Employers should note the implications of the Acts for both:
  - direct discrimination - less favourable treatment of a protected group; and
  - indirect discrimination - when requirements or conditions cannot be justified on non-racial grounds and work to the detriment of a protected group.
- Specific legislation (Equal Pay Act 1970) covers the offer of equal pay to a woman as to a man for work that is:
  - similarly evaluated in a job evaluation scheme;
  - 'the same or broadly similar' to the man's; or
  - 'of equal value' (Equal Pay (Amendment) Regulations).

Chapter 5: Discrimination and equal opportunity

Quick quiz

1 Under the Race Relations Act 1976, which of the following is a prohibited form of discrimination?

   A   Auditioning black men only for the part of Othello
   B   Specifying the race of models for an advertisement for reasons for authenticity
   C   Offering training exclusively to a racial group which has so far been under-represented
   D   Setting selection tests relevant to a particular cultural tradition

2 Matt Black and Di Gloss run a small DIY shop. They're recruiting an assistant. Matt puts up an ad on the notice board of his Men's Club. It says: 'Person required to assist in DIY shop. Fulltime. Aged under 28. Contact ...' Two candidates turn up for interview the following day: a man and a woman (who's heard about the job by word of mouth, through Di). Matt interviews them both, asking work-related questions. He also asks the woman whether she has children and how much time she expects to spend dealing with family matters.

   Under the Sex Discrimination Act 1975, Matt has laid himself open to allegations of:

   A   one count of discrimination
   B   two counts of discrimination
   C   three counts of discrimination
   D   no discrimination at all

3 List four causes of high minority unemployment in the UK
4 List two possible causes of low disabled employment.
5 List five possible measures that might support an equal opportunities policy in an organisation.
6 What is 'sexual harassment'? Give two examples.

Solutions to activities

2   (a) Advertising a vacancy in a primarily male environment, where women would be less likely to see it.
    (b) Offering less favourable terms to part-time workers (given that most of them are women).
    (c) Specifying age limits which would tend to exclude women who had taken time out of work for child-rearing.
    (d) Asking in selection interviews about plans to have a family (since this might be to the detriment of a woman, but not a man).

5   Examples you might have thought to include:
    (a) Inappropriate physical contact or proximity, taken to be suggestive
    (b) Derogatory comments about (most commonly) 'girls' or 'women' in general
    (c) Gender-related insults such as the use of animal names to describe women
    (d) Comments about appearance and dress which are sexually suggestive or gender-related
    (e) Sexual innuendoes and jokes

Further question practice

Now try the following practice questions at the end of this text.

Multiple choice questions	28 to 33
Exam style questions	5

Chapter 6

TRAINING AND DEVELOPMENT

Introduction

Providing the organisation with the most suitable human resources for the task and environment is an on-going process. It involves not only recruitment and selection, but the training and development of employees - prior to employment, or at any time during their employment, in order to help them meet the requirements of their current and potential future job.

The term 'industrial training', used in connection with training in a work context, includes a wide range of activities: commercial training, competence or skills training, management development, apprenticeships and so on.

The main purpose of industrial training is to raise competence and therefore performance standards. From the perspective of HR management, however, it is also concerned with personal development, helping individuals to expand and fulfil their potential (and therefore also, theoretically, motivating them to higher performance, by offering them the opportunity for personal growth).

Your objectives

After completing this chapter you should:

(a) appreciate the role of training in an organisation;
(b) be able to outline a systematic approach to training;
(c) understand how training needs and objectives can be determined;
(d) be able to suggest how learning theory impacts on training plans;
(e) be able to discuss a range of training methods and media;
(f) understand how training schemes might be validated and evaluated;
(g) appreciate the particular requirements and methods of management training and development;
(h) understand how organisations can help employees to manage their careers.

1 THE ROLE OF TRAINING IN THE ORGANISATION

1.1 Attitudes to training

As we suggested in our introduction, training has a dual role. It is, ideally, both:

(a) task oriented; and

(b) worker-oriented.

The organisation will need to control its training activity to ensure that it really is developing and releasing into the organisation skills that will improve its performance. At the same time, the potential of the employees/trainees must be considered if training is going to be successful, and willingly applied to the job. There is even an argument that training has benefits - in terms of employee satisfaction, morale, enhanced capability and flexibility - quite independently of specific performance objectives. The human resource manager may get 'caught in the middle' between the varied (and possibly conflicting) expectations of managers and trainees.

> *Training is to some extent a management reaction to change, eg changes in equipment and design, methods of work, new tools and machines, control systems, or in response to changes dictated by new products, services, or markets. On the other hand, training also induces change. A capable workforce will bring about new initiatives, developments and improvements - in an organic way, and of its own accord. Training is both a cause and an effect of change.*
>
> Bryan Livy: *Corporate Personnel Management*

Easy assumptions about training and, within each organisation, specific training programmes, should constantly be challenged if the desired outcome from training is to be achieved.

(a) *'Training is a matter for the HR department.'* Yes it is - but not exclusively. Line managers are conversant with the requirements of the job, and the individuals concerned; they are also responsible for the performance of those individuals. They should be involved in:

   (i) the identification of training needs and priorities;

   (ii) training itself. A specialist trainer may be used as a catalyst, but the experience of line personnel, supervisors and senior operatives will be invaluable in ensuring a practical and participative approach; and

   (iii) follow-up of performance, for the validation of training methods.

   In addition, experience and learning opportunities in the job itself are very important, and the individual employee should be encouraged in self-learning, and in the 'ownership' of his own development at work.

(b) *'The important thing is to have a training programme.'* The view that training in itself is such a Good Thing that an organisation can't go wrong by providing some is a source of inefficiency.

   (i) The individual needs and expectations of trainees must be taken into account. The purpose of training must be clear, to the organisation (so that it can direct training effort and resources accordingly) and to the individual, so that he feels it to be worthwhile and meaningful - without which the motivation to learn will be lost. If individuals feel that they are training in order to grow and develop, to find better ways of working, or to become more a part of the organisation culture, they will commit themselves to learning more thoroughly than if they feel they are only doing it to show willing, to fulfil the human resource plan, or whatever.

(ii) It is too easy to run old or standard programmes, without considering that:

    (1) the learning needs of current trainees may be different from past ones;

    (2) the requirements of the job may not all be susceptible to classroom or study methods: are the most relevant needs being met?

    (3) the training group may not be uniform in its needs: the training package may be off-target for some members.

(c) *'Training will improve performance.'* It *might* - and *should*, all other things being equal - but a training course is not a simple remedy for poor performance. Contingency theory ('It all depends') must be applied to situations where employee performance is below the desired standard. An employee who is adequately *trained* to perform may still not be *able* or *willing* to do so, because of badly designed working methods or environment, faulty equipment, inappropriate supervision, poor motivation, lack of incentive, or non-work factors, such as health, domestic circumstances and so on. In particular, it must be remembered that performance is not just a product of The System, but a product, and manifestation, of human behaviour. Training methods, and their expected results, must take into account human attitudes, values, emotions and relationships.

Activity 1

Why are you taking a Business Studies (or other) degree? What do you expect to 'get out of it'? What kinds of 'satisfaction' does it give you. (Think not just about course content and the qualification itself, but about other skills, disciplines and experiences you are gaining.)

1.2 The systematic approach to training

Definition

According to the Department of Employment, *training* is 'the systematic development of the attitude/knowledge/skill/behaviour pattern required by an individual in order to perform adequately a given task or job.'

The application of systems theory to the design of training has gained currency in the West in recent years. A *training system* uses scientific methods to programme learning, from:

(a) the identification of training needs; this is a product of job analysis and specification (what is required in order to do the job) and an assessment of the present capacities and inclinations of the individuals (their 'pre-entry' behaviour); via

(b) the design of courses, selection of methods and media; to

(c) the measurement of trained performance - the 'terminal behaviour' expected on the job - against predetermined proficiency goals.

Requirements of the job → Learning gap = training need → Learning/training → Improved job performance (terminal behaviour)

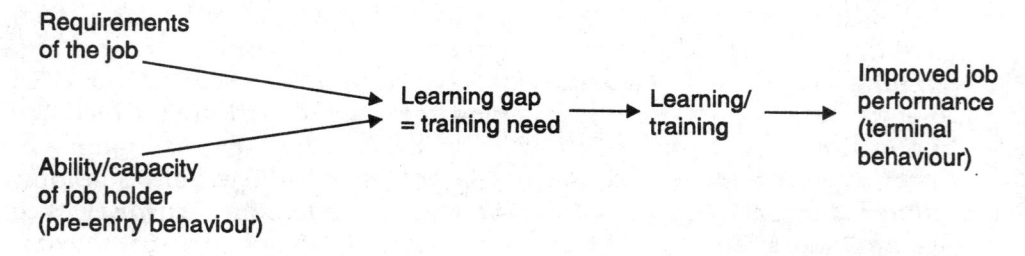

Ability/capacity of job holder (pre-entry behaviour) →

Figure 6.1. Training system

We will look at this system in more detail.

2 TRAINING NEEDS AND OBJECTIVES

The training needs of individuals and groups will vary enormously, according to the nature of the job and particular tasks, the abilities and experience of the employees. As suggested earlier, training should not be a 'shot in the dark'; the homogeneity of the training group cannot be assumed; clear and obtainable objectives are essential to the efficiency and effectiveness of the training programme.

Some training requirements will be obvious and 'automatic'.

(a) If a piece of legislation is enacted which affects the organisation's operations, training in its provisions will automatically be indicated: so, for example, HR staff will need to be trained if and when various EU Directives are enacted in UK law.

(b) The introduction of new technology similarly implies a training need.

(c) An organisation seeking accreditation for its training scheme, or seeking a British Standard (say, for quality systems - see below), will have certain training requirements imposed on them by the approving body.

In other cases, qualitative indicators might be taken as symptoms of a need for training: absenteeism, high labour turnover, grievance and disciplinary actions, crises, conflict, poor motivation and performance. Such factors will need to be investigated to see what the root causes are, and whether training *will* solve the problem.

Alternatively, a regular programme of formal training needs analysis may be carried out as discussed below.

2.1 Training for quality: BS EN ISO 9000

The British Standard for Quality Systems (BS EN ISO 9000: formerly BS 5750) which many UK organisations are working towards (often at the request of customers, who perceive it to be a 'guarantee' that high standards of quality control are being achieved) includes training requirements. As the following extract shows, the Standard identifies training needs for those organisations registering for assessment, and also shows the importance of a systematic approach to ensure adequate control.

> *The training, both by specific training to perform assigned tasks and general training to heighten quality awareness and to mould attitudes of all personnel in an organisation, is central to the achievement of quality.*
>
> *The comprehensiveness of such training varies with the complexity of the organisation.*
>
> *The following steps should be taken:*
>
> *1 Identifying the way tasks and operations influence quality in total*
>
> *2 Identifying individuals' training needs against those required for satisfactory performance of the task*
>
> *3 Planning and carrying out appropriate specific training*
>
> *4 Planning and organising general quality awareness programmes*
>
> *5 Recording training and achievement in an easily retrievable form so that records can be updated and gaps in training can be readily identified.*
>
> BSI, 1990

2.2 Training needs analysis

Definition

Training needs may be identified as the gap between the requirements of the job and the actual current performance of the job-holders. In other words:

Required level of competence minus present level of competence = training need.

The *required level of competence* for the job can be determined by the following.

(a) Job analysis.

(b) Skills analysis, for more skilled jobs. Here, not only the task- and worker-oriented requirements of the job are identified, but also the skill elements of the task, such as the following.

  (i) What sensory information (cues and stimuli) need to be recognised?
  (ii) What senses (vision, touch, hearing etc) are involved?
  (iii) What left-hand/right-hand/foot operations are required?
  (iv) What counter-balancing operations are required?
  (v) What interactions with other operatives are required?

(c) Role analysis, for managerial and administrative jobs requiring a high degree of co-ordination and interaction with other.

(d) Existing records, such as job specifications and descriptions, person specifications, the organisation chart (depicting roles and relationships) and so on.

The *present level of employees' competence* (which includes not only skill and knowledge, but inclination or willingness as well) can be measured by an appropriate pre-test of skills, knowledge, performance, attitude and so on. Assessment interviews and the ongoing system of performance appraisal may also be used. (Appraisal is discussed in Chapter 7.)

2.3 Competence analysis

We have so far used the word 'competence' in its general sense of 'capability', but you should be aware that it now carries more technical connotations, as part of a revolution in the approach to vocational and professional qualifications and training.

Competence-based education and training focuses on the output of the learning process (what the trainee should be able to do at the end of it) rather than its input (a scheme of learning, or a syllabus of topics to be covered). The idea has been around for some time, having its roots in teacher education in the US, but only gained currency in the UK in the 1980s. In 1986, the Manpower Services Commission launched a Standards Development Programme, while a review of vocational qualifications led to the establishment of the National Council for Vocational Qualifications (NCVQ). This has responsibility for developing criteria for a new qualification framework based on *standards of competence,* against which candidates are assessed, rather than a syllabus, or body of knowledge, tested by examinations.

In practice, this has involved analysing real jobs in a given occupational area in order to find out what 'acceptable performance' in the job entails. Standards of competence identify the key roles of the occupation and break them down into areas or *units of competence*. These in turn are formulated as statements of:

(a) the specific activities a jobholder should be able to perform (*elements of competence*);

(b) how well (*performance criteria*);

(c) in what contexts and conditions (listed in a *range statement*); and

(d) with what 'underpinning' *knowledge and understanding*.

The NCVQ *accredits* suitably (re)structured qualifications, awarded by bodies such as training councils and professional bodies, as NVQs (National Vocational Qualifications) at a range of levels (1-5). Among the professional bodies the Association of Accounting Technicians (AAT) for example, has already implemented a competence-based training and assessment scheme, leading to an NVQ Levels 2, 3 and 4 in progressive stages. NVQs are designed to be vocationally relevant and nationally recognised, since the standards of competence being assessed are devised by 'lead bodies' made up of highly qualified representatives of the occupation or profession nationwide. There are over 160 lead bodies: some are industry-specific (retail, construction and so on); some are more broadly occupational (training and development, accountancy and administration, marketing and so on).

In general terms, Connock (*HR Vision*) suggests that competence definition and analysis may be a useful approach within an organisation, as a way of assessing its future requirements, and providing data to underpin recruitment, training, appraisal, potential assessment, succession planning and reward strategies. Connock suggests that, being systematic and based on real-life observable behaviour, competence analysis provides a thorough and objective picture of job requirements at different levels, and one that is relevant to the circumstances and values of the organisation. He does recognise, however, that achieving definitions of competence is a long and complex task, and tends therefore to be over-simplistic and quickly outdated.

2.4 Training objectives

The training department manager will have to make an initial investigation into the problem of the gap between job or competence requirements and current performance or competence. (As we noted earlier, it may be that shortcomings in the capacities and inclinations of employees would *not* be improved by training, but require a review of the work environment, systems and procedures, work methods, technology, industrial relations, leadership style, motivation and incentives.)

If it is concluded that the provision of training would improve work performance, training *objectives* can then be defined. They should be clear, specific and related to observable, measurable targets, ideally detailing:

(a) behaviour - what the trainee should be able to do;

(b) standard - to what level of performance; and

(c) environment - under what conditions (so that the performance level is realistic).

(Note that this corresponds directly to the approach used for standards of competence.)

Objectives are usually best expressed in terms of active verbs: at the end of the course the trainee should be able to describe .... or identify .... or distinguish x from y .... or calculate .... or assemble .... and so on. It is insufficient to define the objectives of training as 'to give trainees a grounding in ....' or 'to encourage trainees in a better appreciation of ....': this offers no target achievement which can be quantifiably measured.

Activity 2

Here is a quick test to see how well you have kept up!

(a) What are the two basic purposes of training?
(b) Is training a reaction to change or a cause of change?
(c) Training will improve performance. True or false?
(d) What is the systematic approach to training?
(e) Training needs may be identified as ... what?
(f) What is a standard of competence?
(g) How should training objectives be expressed?

The answers can all be found in the first two sections of this chapter.

3 LEARNING THEORY

Having identified training needs and objectives, the manager will have to decide on the best way to approach training: there are a number of types and techniques of training, which we will discuss below.

There are different schools of learning theory which explain and describe the learning process in very different ways.

(a) Behaviourist psychology concentrates on the relationship between 'stimuli' (input through the senses) and 'responses' to those stimuli. 'Learning' is the formation of new connections between stimulus and response, on the basis of experience or 'conditioning'. We modify our responses in future according to whether the results of our behaviour in the past have been good or bad. We get *feedback* on the results of our actions, which may be rewarding ('positive reinforcement') or punishing ('negative reinforcement') and therefore an incentive or a deterrent to similar behaviour in future. Trial-and-error learning, and carrot-and-stick approaches to motivation, work on this basis.

(b) The cognitive (or 'information processing') approach argues that the human mind takes sensory information and imposes organisation and meaning on it: we interpret and rationalise. We use feedback information on the results of past behaviour to make rational decisions about whether to maintain successful behaviours or modify unsuccessful behaviours in future, according to our goals and our plans for reaching them.

Whichever approach it is based on, learning theory offers certain useful propositions for the design of effective training programmes.

(a) The individual should be *motivated* to learn. The advantages of training (to the trainee) should be made clear, according to the individual's motives - money, opportunity, valued skills or whatever.

(b) Clear *objectives and standards* should be set, so that each task has some meaning. Each stage of learning should present a challenge, without overloading trainees or making them lose confidence. Specific objectives and performance standards for each stage will help trainees in the control process that leads to learning, providing targets against which performance will constantly be measured and adjusted accordingly.

(c) There should be timely, relevant *feedback* on performance and progress. This will usually be provided by the trainer, and should be concurrent - or certainly not long delayed. If progress reports or performance appraisals are given only at the year end, for example, there will be no opportunity for behaviour adjustment or learning in the meantime.

(d) Positive and negative *reinforcement* should be judiciously used. Recognition and encouragement enhances trainees' confidence in their competence and progress. Punishment for poor performance - especially without explanation and correction - discourages the learner and creates feelings of guilt, failure and hostility, but helpful or constructive criticism is likely to be beneficial.

(e) Active *participation* is more telling than passive reception (because it motivates the individual to learn and enhances concentration and recollection). If a high degree of participation is impossible, *practice* and *repetition* can be used to reinforce receptivity, but participation has the added effect of encouraging 'ownership' of the process of learning and changing - committing the individual to it as his or her *own* goal, not just a process imposed by management.

3.1 Learning styles

It is believed that the way in which people learn best will be different according to the 'type' of person they are: in other words, there are learning 'styles' which suit different individuals.

Peter Honey and Alan Mumford have drawn up a popular classification of four learning styles.

(a) *Theorist*

This person seeks to understand underlying concepts before applying them in practice, and to take an intellectual, 'hands-off' approach based on logical argument. Such a person prefers training:

(i) to be programmed and structured;

(ii) to allow time for analysis; and

(iii) to be provided by teachers who share his preference for concepts and analysis.

Theorists find learning difficult if they have a teacher with a different style (particularly an activist style), material which skims over basic principles, a programme which is hurried and unstructured, or which encourages them to learn 'hands-on' by trial and error before they have studied the theory.

(b) *Reflector*

People who like to observe phenomena, think about them and then choose how to act are called reflectors. Such people need to work at their own pace and would find learning difficult if forced into a hurried programme, or required to attempt tasks before having a chance to observe and think about them first.

Reflectors are able to produce carefully thought-out conclusions after research and reflection but tend to be fairly slow, non-participative (unless to ask questions) and cautious.

(c) *Activist*

These are people who like to deal with practical, active problems and who do not have much patience with theory. They require training based on hands-on experience.

Activists are excited by participation, experimentation and pressure, such as making presentations and attempting new projects. Although they are flexible and optimistic, they may rush at things without due preparation, take risks and then get bored.

(d) *Pragmatist*

These people only like to study if they can see its direct link to practical problems - they are not interested in theory for its own sake. They are particularly good at learning new techniques in on-the-job training which they see as useful improvements. Their aim is to implement action plans and/or do the task better. Such a person is business-like and realistic, but may discard as impractical, good ideas which only require some development. They may even regard training, other than direct task-oriented training, as a waste of time.

The implications for management are that people react to problem situations in different ways and that, in particular, training methods should where possible, be tailored to the preferred style of trainees.

Activity 3

John, Paula, Ringo and Georgette are learning French, as part of their firm's initiative to develop staff in a European market.

(a) John reckons that since he does not actually speak to clients, the whole scheme is a waste of time. He claims to be too busy to attend classes.

(b) Paula loves the classes, because they simulate real conversational situations. The trainees have to use whatever vocabulary they have to get their meaning across, guided and corrected by the tutor: Paula doesn't like learning grammatical rules - she's happy to pick up the phrases to fit the situations.

(c) Ringo doesn't mind the teaching method either. He doesn't say anything for the first few minutes, though, just picks up what he can, gets it straight (allowing Paula to make the mistakes) and then comes out with a fluent response.

(d) Georgette is lost. She feels frustrated because, although she has learned the phrase for a given situation she is not sure it will apply in other contexts. She takes home a book of grammar at night, to bone up on the general principles and rules.

Who represents which learning style? What style has the course been designed for?

3.2 The learning cycle

Another useful model is the *experiential learning cycle* devised by David Kolb. Kolb suggested that classroom-type learning is 'a special activity cut off from the real world and unrelated to one's life': a teacher or trainer directs the learning process on behalf of a passive learner. Experiential learning, however, involves doing, and puts the learner in an active problem-solving role: a form of *self-learning* which encourages the learner to formulate and commit himself to his own learning objectives.

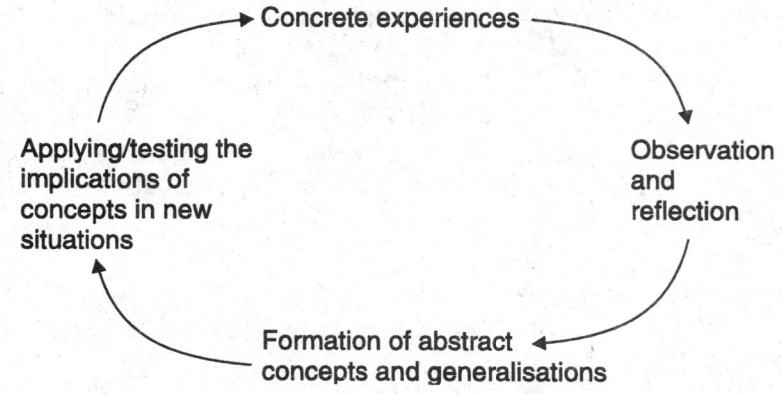

Figure 6.2 The learning cycle

Say an employee interviews a customer for the first time (concrete experience). He observes his own performance and the dynamics of the situation (observation) and afterwards, having failed to convince the customer to buy his product, he analyses what he did right and wrong (reflection). He comes to the conclusion that he had failed to listen to what the customer really wanted and feared, underneath her general reluctance: he realises that the key to communication is listening (abstraction/generalisation). In his next interview he applies his strategy to the new set of circumstances (application/testing). This provides him with a new experience with which to start the cycle over again.

Act
↓
Analyse actions
↓
Understand principles
↓
Apply principles

This is the model for many of the modern approaches to training, and particularly management development, which recommend experiential learning - 'learning by doing', or self-learning.

In effect, it involves elements of *all* the learning styles identified by Honey and Mumford.

4 TRAINING METHODS AND MEDIA

Training methods and media must next be evaluated, and a programme designed. There are a variety of options, discussed below, including:

(a) formal training and education; by internal or external residential courses, day courses or lectures, distance learning, programmed learning or computer-aided learning;

(b) on-the-job training - including induction, coaching and job-rotation; and

(c) awareness-oriented training - including T groups (leaderless groups that are assigned problems to solve without guidance), assertiveness training and neuro-linguistic programming (NLP).

4.1 Formal training and education

Internal courses are sometimes run by the training department of larger organisations. Skills may be taught at a technical level, related to the organisation's particular product and market, or in aspects such as marketing, teambuilding, interviewing or information technology management. Some organisations encourage the wider development of staff by offering opportunities to learn languages or other skills. Some of this is accomplished informally - for example, by encouraging foreign-language discussion groups in meal breaks.

One way of conveniently decentralising training (as well as quickly developing training courses to meet emerging needs) is the use of computer-based training (CBT) and Interactive Video (IV), through teaching equipment in offices or even trainees' homes. Training programmes may be developed by the organisation or by outside consultants - or bought 'off the shelf': the software (or 'courseware') can then be distributed, so that large numbers of dispersed staff can learn about new products or procedures quickly and simultaneously.

External courses vary, and may involve:

(a) day-release, which means that the employee attends a local college on one day of the week;

(b) evening classes, or 'distance learning' (a home study or 'correspondence' course, plus limited face-to-face teaching) which make demands on the individual's time outside work;

(c) full-time but brief introductory or revision courses for examinations, for example, by professional bodies;

(d) a sponsored full-time course at a university for 1 or 2 years. This might be the case, for example, for a manager doing an MBA degree.

Formal training tends to have disadvantages in some contexts.

(a) An individual will not benefit from formal training unless he/she wants to learn. The individual's superior may need to provide encouragement in this respect.

(b) If the subject matter of the training course does not relate to an individual's job, the learning will not be applied, and will quickly be forgotten. Many training managers provide courses without relating their content to the specific task needs of individuals attending them.

(c) Individuals may not be able to accept that what they learn on a course applies in the context of their own particular job. For example, a manager may attend a course on people management which suggests a participatory style of leadership, but on returning to the job(s) he may consider that participation would be impossible, because the staff are too young or too inexperienced. (This frequently occurs in industries which are undergoing rapid change: managers experienced in traditional work practices, who have always been discouraged from taking risks, are suddenly asked to be 'entrepreneurs' and are justifiably suspicious).

(d) Immediate and relevant *feedback* on performance and progress may not be available from the learning process, especially if knowledge is 'tested' at wide intervals. This will lower the learner's incentive and sense of direction.

(e) It does not suit activists or pragmatists.

Activity 4

(a) What kind of learner are you?

(b) What kind of learner is your present course designed for?

(c) Appraise your course according to the criteria given on pages 102 - 103: incentives, objectives, feedback, reinforcement and participation.

4.2 On-the-job training

On-the-job training is very common, especially when the work involved is not complex. (Trainee managers require more coaching, and may be given assignments or projects as part of a planned programme to develop their experience.) This type of training will only be successful if:

(a) the assignments have a specific purpose from which the trainee can learn and gain experience;

(b) the trainee is a pragmatist and/or activist. A theorist or reflector will need to get away from the pressures of the workplace to think through issues and understand the underlying principles before applying new techniques;

(c) the organisation is tolerant of any mistakes which the trainee makes. Mistakes are an inevitable part of on-the-job learning, and if they are punished the trainee will be reluctant to take further risks; and will be de-motivated to learn.

In addition, there may be real risks involved in throwing people in at the deep-end: the cost of mistakes or inefficiencies may be high and the pressure on learners great.

An important *advantage* of on-the-job training is that it takes place in the environment of the job itself, and in the context of the work group in which the trainee will have to operate. The style of supervision, personal relations with colleagues, working conditions and pressures, the culture of the office/shop floor and so on, will be absorbed as part of the training process.

(a) There will be no re-adjustment to make, as there will be when a trainee transfers externally-acquired knowledge, skills and academic attitudes to the job, the work place and work group.

(b) The work group itself will be adapting to the dynamics of the trainee's situation: it will adjust to his or her new capacities and inclinations. All too often, trainees return from a course to find that they cannot apply their new-found ideas and skills: supervisors are set in their ways, colleagues resent any perceived superiority, the tasks and methods stay the same. Learning within the work group also prevents trainees from becoming isolated and introverted (concentrating on their own learning process).

(c) The perceived relevance of the training to the job and performance criteria is much greater, and therefore the training is felt to be of greater value.

(d) There is greater opportunity for relevant, performance-related *feedback*, which is an integral part of the learning process (both as a means by which the individual recognises the need to adjust his or her behaviour, and as a motivating factor, with the knowledge of progress and success). Feedback on performance in a non-work environment may leave doubts in the trainees' minds as to the value of their progress when they return to the job.

Different *methods* of on-the-job training include:

(a) *induction:* introducing new recruits or transferred employees to their new job and workplace. We will look at this in more detail below;

(b) *coaching:* the trainee is put under the guidance of an experienced employee who shows the trainee how to do the job. This is sometimes called 'sitting with Nellie'. The length of the coaching period will depend on the complexity of the job and the previous experience of the trainee. According to *People Management*, March 1997 this approach should be treated with more respect. Ryder Trucks, for example, found that on-the-job training and learning from colleagues were the only ways a new employee could hope to deal with the complexities of the paperwork and the company's procedures;

(c) *job rotation:* the trainee is given several jobs in succession, to gain experience of a wide range of activities. (Even experienced managers may rotate their jobs, to gain wider experience; this philosophy of job education is commonly applied in the Civil Service, where an employee may expect to move on to another job after a few years);

(d) *temporary promotion:* an individual is promoted into a superior's position whilst the superior is absent. This gives the individual a chance to experience the demands of a more senior position;

(e) *'assistant to' positions*: a junior manager with good potential may be appointed as assistant to the managing director or another executive director. In this way, the individual gains experience of how the organisation is managed 'at the top'; and

(f) *project or committee work:* trainees might be included in the membership of a project team or committee, in order to obtain an understanding of inter-departmental relationships, problem-solving and particular areas of the organisation's activity.

You will note that most of these are forms of experiential learning: learning by doing.

4.3 Induction training

From his first day in a job, a new recruit must be helped to find his bearings. There are limits to what any person can pick up in a short time, so the process of 'getting one's feet under the table' will be a gradual one. Induction is an ongoing process.

On the first day, a manager or HR officer should welcome the new recruit. The manager might discuss in broad terms what he requires from people at work, working conditions, pay and benefits, training opportunities and career opportunities. He should then introduce the new recruit to the person who will be his immediate supervisor.

The immediate supervisor should then take over the on going process of induction. Here is a general checklist.

(a) Pinpoint the areas that the recruit will have to learn about in order to start work. Some things (such as detailed technical knowledge) may be identified as areas for later study or training, while others (say, some of the procedures and systems with which the recruit will have to deal) will have to be explained immediately. A list of learning priorities should be drawn up, so that the recruit, and the supervisor, are clear about the rate and direction of progress required.

(b) Explain first of all the nature of the job, and the goals of each task, of the recruit's job and of the department as a whole. This will help the recruit to work to specific targets and to understand how each task relates to the overall objectives of the department - or even the organisation as a whole.

(c) Explain about hours of work and stress the importance of time-keeping. If flexitime is operated, explain how it works. Any other work practices, customs and rules should be explained clearly.

(d) Explain the structure of the department: to whom the recruit will report, to whom (s)he can go with complaints or queries and so on.

(e) Introduce the recruit to people in the workplace. (S)he should meet the departmental manager and all the members of the immediate work team (and perhaps be given the opportunity to get to know them informally). One particular colleague may be assigned to the recruit as a *mentor* for the first few days, to answer routine queries and 'show him (or her) the ropes'. The layout of the premises, procedures for lunch hours or holidays, rules about smoking or eating at work and so on will then be taught informally.

(f) Plan and implement an appropriate training programme for whatever technical or practical knowledge is required. Again, the programme should have a clear schedule and set of goals so that the recruit has a sense of purpose, and so that the programme can be efficiently organised to fit in with the activities of the department.

(g) Coach and/or train the recruit; check regularly on his progress, as demonstrated by performance, reported by the mentor, and/or as perceived by the recruit. Feedback information will be essential to the learning process, correcting any faults at an early stage and building the confidence of the recruit.

(h) Integrate the recruit into the culture of the workplace. Much of this may be done informally: (s)he will pick up the prevailing norms of dress, degree of formality, attitude to customers etc. However, the supervisor should try to 'sell' the values and style of the organisation and should reinforce commitment to those values by rewarding evidence of loyalty, hard work and desired behaviour.

After three months, six months and/or one year the performance of a new recruit should be formally appraised and discussed. This should dovetail into a regular employee appraisal programme.

Activity 5

Did you have any form of induction into student life?

Compare your experience to the checklist given above. How effective did you feel your induction was? What difference did it make to your confidence in your studies?'

4.4 Awareness-oriented training

An 'alternative' approach to training is to encourage trainees to gain insight into their own behaviour, and to try and change any negative or restricting attitudes that may be preventing them from attaining more effective performance.

Such approaches vary from the relatively straightforward 'encounter group' principle, which allows people to analyse and practise interpersonal skills in a controlled group, to the more controversial concept of 'neuro-linguistic programming' (NLP).

T groups

Group learning is not common in industry but is more common in organisations such as the social services departments of local government authorities. The purpose of group learning is to:

(a) give each individual in a training group (or T group) a greater insight into his own behaviour;

(b) to teach an individual how he appears to other people, as a result of responses from other members of the group;

(c) to teach an understanding of intra-group processes, and how people inter-relate; and

(d) to develop each individual's skills in taking action to control such intra-group processes.

Assertiveness training

Definition

Assertiveness may be described as clear, honest and direct communication. It is not to be confused with 'bossiness' or aggression. Aggressive behaviour is competitive and directed at 'beating' someone else: assertion is based on equality and co-operation. Assertion is a simple affirmation that every individual has certain rights and can stand by them in the face of pressures from other people; that there is middle ground between being powerful and powerless, between the role of 'top dog' and 'door mat'.

It means:

(a) not being dependent on the approval of others;
(b) not feeling guilty if you do not put other people's needs first all the time;
(c) having the confidence to receive criticism openly and give it constructively;
(d) avoiding conflict without having to give up your own values and wants;
(e) being able to express your own values and feelings without guilt or fear;
(f) making clear requests for what you want.

You can see that much of this is to do with awareness of one's own feelings, and attitudes about one's role and rights as a person. Training is therefore partly a matter of identifying, challenging and changing attitudes.

Assertiveness training commonly uses group role-play exercises to:

(a) test individuals' natural reactions in situations;
(b) analyse what the assertive alternative would be; and
(c) allow individuals to *practise* being assertive without the pressures of real-life scenarios. There are practical techniques and skills which can be taught - as well as habits of mind which can be developed - in order to achieve an assertive approach to situations such as asking for what you want, saying 'no', and giving and receiving criticism.

Assertiveness training is popularly seen as a prime means of remedying under-achievement in women, or of helping women to avoid exploitation at work. It is likely to be part of a 'Women Into Management' or similar training and education programme. The techniques and insights involved are likely to be of benefit to men as well, but it has been recognised that it is primarily women who are disadvantaged in western society by the failure to distinguish between assertion and aggression, submission and conflict-avoidance.

Activity 6

Suggest four areas in which you think women might benefit from assertiveness training.

Neuro-linguistic programming (NLP)

Defintion

NLP is a technique which emerged in the USA in the 1970s. It is based on:

(a) identifying and breaking down the behaviour patterns found in 'excellent' performers; and

(b) communicating these patterns to people who wish to emulate their performance; in a way that

(c) overcomes the restricted thinking processes and limiting self-beliefs that typically hold those people back.

Typical NLP techniques include the following.

(a) The development of detached self-awareness or self-consciousness, so that trainees become able to monitor their own behaviour constantly and objectively. This is achieved through 'disassociation' - the attainment of a detached state in which they can observe and evaluate themselves dispassionately and as if from 'outside' the situation.

(b) Conditioning, such as that used by behaviourist psychologists. Positive and negative responses can be evoked by stimuli with which they have become associated in the mind. If you have spent many happy times with friends, for example, the stimulus (the sight of them) will become associated with the response (happiness), and you will tend thereafter to feel happy at the sight of your friends, or even thinking about them, or visualising their faces. A trainee can thus be conditioned to recall a 'trigger' stimulus (a person, image, place or event) in order to summon up associated feelings (of confidence, calmness or energy, say) which may be useful. This technique is called 'anchoring'.

(c) Developing the ability to establish rapport with others through 'matching' behaviour. The principle of rapport is that people feel comfortable with people who are like themselves in some way. 'Matching' is a technique of observing the behaviour of others and adapting your behaviour to theirs in some way - say, in the amount of gesturing they use, the volume of their voice, or the heartiness of their manner.

(d) Developing the ability to shift perspectives - to view things from another person's point of view - using 'mental mapping' and visualisation techniques. This can be used to help people with work relationships.

(e) The 'mental rehearsal' of events and plans. This operates as a form of practice, and also gives the mind positive suggestions (as if the event has already successfully taken place), giving confidence and therefore - usually - enhanced actual performance.

(f) Using words as powerful tools of suggestion and understanding.

Case study: NLP, training breakthrough

'Staff trained by NLP techniques acquire flexibility of thinking, choice of behaviour and control over their feelings; they are better equipped to handle themselves and others and to produce operational results. NLP also enables people to measure their results through sensory processes, giving them a very real sense of what they are achieving.'

Deception?

'This raises ... questions about the extent to which people should appear to be something they are not in order to achieve a particular result. Much the same question could be levelled at job applicants; how far should they go at a selection interview to persuade the interviewer they are an appropriate choice and would fit into the organisation?

NLP does not aim to resolve people's ethical problems; it aims to give them better quality information and more flexibility so they may make their own choices about behaviour.'

Or manipulation?

'Possibly because of the speed with which NLP produces results, some people have regarded it warily and are concerned that it is potentially manipulative. In reality these fears are unfounded; of course, NLP could be misused, but so could any other technique you might consider. The concern tends to arise when there is a confusion between influencing and manipulation. We all influence others all the time; it is not possible to exist and not exert an influence on those around us.'

Carol Harris - director of the Association for NLP, *Personnel Management*, July 1992.

5 VALIDATION AND EVALUATION OF TRAINING SCHEMES

Implementation of the training scheme is not the end of the story. The scheme should be validated and evaluated.

(a) *Validation* means observing the results of the course, and measuring whether the training objectives have been achieved.

(b) *Evaluation* means comparing the actual costs of the scheme against the assessed benefits which are being obtained. (If the costs exceed the benefits, the scheme will need to be re-designed or withdrawn.)

5.1 Validation

There are various ways of validating a training scheme.

(a) *Trainee reactions to the experience*: asking the trainees whether they thought the training programme was relevant to their work, and whether they found it useful. This form of monitoring is rather inexact, and it does not allow the training department to measure the results for comparison against the training objective.

(b) *Trainee learning*: measuring what the trainees have learned on the course, perhaps by means of a test at the end of a course.

(c) *Changes in job behaviour following training*: studying the subsequent behaviour of the trainees in their jobs to measure how the training scheme has altered the way they do their work. This is possible where the purpose of the course was to learn a particular skill.

(d) *Impact of training on organisational goals*: seeing whether the training scheme (and overall programme) has contributed to the overall objectives of the organisation. This too is a form of monitoring reserved for senior management, and would perhaps be discussed at board level in the organisation. It is likely to be the main component of a cost-benefit analysis.

Validation is thus the measurement of terminal behaviour (trained work performance) in relation to training objectives.

5.2 Evaluation

The training course should only go ahead if the likely benefits are expected to exceed the costs of designing and running it. The problem here is not so much in estimating the costs, but in estimating the potential benefits.

(a) Costs will be the costs of the training establishment, training materials, the time (with pay) of the staff attending training courses, their travelling expenses, the salaries or fees of training staff, and so on.

(b) Benefits might be measured in terms of:

  (i) quicker working and therefore reductions in overtime or staff numbers;

  (ii) greater accuracy of work;

  (iii) more extensive skills and versatility for labour flexibility; and

  (iv) enhanced job satisfaction and reduced labour turnover.

As you will appreciate, the benefits are more easily stated in general terms than quantified in monetary terms.

Activity 7

What technique of training validation is employed in the following cases?

(a) You fill out a Lecturer Assessment Form at the end of term.

(b) You take an exam at the end of the year.

(c) You write an essay on HRM.

(d) You fill out a questionnaire on how you feel about sexual harassment.

(e) The university asks new applicants to state why they chose that course and provider: was it by recommendation?

(f) You fill out a report for the Careers Office (in several years' time) on your career progress.

6 MANAGEMENT DEVELOPMENT

You might subscribe to the 'trait theory' of leadership, that some individuals are born with the personal qualities to be a good manager, and others aren't. There might be some truth in this view, but very few individuals, if any, can walk into a management job and do it well without some guidance, experience or training.

In every organisation, there should be some arrangement or system whereby:

(a) managers gain *experience*, which will enable them to do another more senior job in due course of time;

(b) subordinate managers are given *guidance* and *counselling* by their bosses;

(c) managers are given suitable *training* and *education* to develop their skills and knowledge; and

(d) managers are enabled to plan their future and the opportunities open to them in the organisation.

If there is a planned programme for developing managers, it is called a *management development programme*. Note, however, that a 'programme' is no substitute for the individual's own commitment to *self-development:* the support of creating and using learning opportunities in the job.

6.1 The value of management development

Drucker has suggested that management development should be provided for all managers, not just the ones who are considered promotable material (and not just men, though this direct quote does seem to suggest this!)

> *The promotable man concept focuses on one man out of ten - at best one man out of five. It assigns the other nine to limbo. But the men who need management development the most are not the balls of fire who are the ... promotable people. They are those managers who are not good enough to be promoted but not poor enough to be fired. Unless they have grown up to the demands of tomorrow's jobs, the whole management group will be inadequate, no matter how good ... the promotable people. The first principle of manager development must therefore be the development of the entire management group.*

On the other hand, Handy noted that '... it remains true that career planning in many organisations is not a development process so much as a weeding-out process'.

The *Financial Times,* 13 November 1991, put forward four possible views of management training. (Note: these are extreme 'types' - not real people!)

(a) *Cynics* believe that it is a waste of time, and despise the resulting Smart-Alecs and 'course junkies'. They believe that management practices are either learnt through experience, or cannot be taught. Many believe that people are basically 'untrainable' anyway: 'They certainly do not take seriously the "proof" that training works, arguing that what can be taught is not ... relevant.' Moreover, they subscribe to the view that: 'Those who can, manage; those who can't, become management trainers.'

(b) *Sceptics* are less hostile but not entirely convinced. They believe that training can help - but that not all training courses are clear or helpful in practice, and even if they are, the benefits tend to wear off. 'Back in the work place, the idealistic practices are ignored or even punished and hence discontinued. Most believe the solution lies in selecting people who are already well-trained or at least trainable.'

(c) *Enthusiasts* 'simply cannot see how people are expected to manage without being explicitly taught and trained'. They both reward training attendance, and use it as a reward. They take training needs audits, course appraisal and follow-up very seriously.

(d) *Naive proponents* 'are proselytisers of the near miraculous benefits of such-and-such a course, test, guru or concept. If only, they argue, people were to go on a course, understand and live its message, all would be well with the organisation.' They innocently embrace personal testimony and glossy brochure claims for courses.

Activity 8

Suggest three reasons why an organisation should give attention to management training and development.

6.2 Management education and training

Approaches to management development fall into three main categories.

(a) *Management education* - study for an MBA (Masters in Business Administration) degree or DMS (Diploma in Management Studies), for example.

(b) *Management training* - largely off-the-job formal learning activities.

(c) *Experiential learning* - learning by doing.

The last of these categories has gained in popularity in recent years, with methods such as Management by Objectives being claimed to offer a higher degree of relevance to performance and 'ownership' by the trainee.

Constable and McCormick, however, in their influential report 'The Making of British Managers', suggest that there is still a place for a systematic education and training programmes featuring study for professional qualifications and the design of in-house training courses. Such a programme is the basis of efforts to ensure that managers are (and can demonstrate that they are) properly trained, through the *Management Charter Initiative* (MCI), a government backed body which seeks to improve standards of management training through the competence-based approach.

Constable and McCormick formulated a useful distinction between management education, training and development.

(a) '*Education* is that process which results in formal qualifications up to and including post-graduate degrees.'

(b) *Training* is 'the formal learning activities which may not lead to qualifications, and which may be received at any time in a working career'; for example, a course in human resource forecasting or counselling skills.

(c) '*Development* is broader again: job experience and learning from other managers, particularly one's immediate superior, are integral parts of the development process.'

It is important to realise that 'education and training' no longer implies bookwork, academic and theory-based studies. W A G Braddick (*Management for Bankers*) suggests the kind of shift in focus that has occurred in management development methods in recent years. (The notes are ours.)

From	To	Notes
Principles	Specifics	(Every organisation is unique)
Precepts	Analysis/diagnosis	(Address the issues)
Theory-based	Action-centred	(Understand it - and do it)
Academic	Real time problems	(Tackle 'live' problems)
Functional focus	Issue and problem focus	(Deal with 'whole' activities)
Excellent individual	Team members and leaders	(Develop people - together)
Patient	Agent	(Learn actively, take control)
One-off	Continuous	(Keep learning)

Thus management education and training now tends to focus on the real needs of specific organisations, and to be grounded in practical skills. In-house programmes and on-the-job techniques have flourished, as have techniques of off-the-job learning which *simulate* real issues and problems: case study, role play, desk-top exercises, leadership exercises and so on.

Activity 9

'Does getting wet, cold and generally miserable in the countryside help you to become a better manager?' Supporters of outward bound courses believe it does, but critics question the value of having highly-paid and specialised executives tramping around the woods honing boy scout-level skills.

Is outdoor training not just a way of keeping ageing physical exercise teachers, sadistic ex-corporals and overpaid consultants employed? And is it just an expensive fad in training, no better or worse than classroom teaching?'

Financial Times, January 1993

What do you think?

6.3 Encouraging management development

Constable and McCormick reported in 1987 that:

> *The total scale of management training is currently at a very low level. The general situation will only improve when many more companies conscientiously embrace a positive plan for management development. This needs to be accompanied by strong demand on the part of individual managers for continuing training and development throughout their careers.*

Recommendations of the report 'The Making of British Managers' included the following.

'Senior management

1. Create an *atmosphere* within the organisation where continuing management training and development is the norm.
2. Utilise *appraisal procedures* which encourage management training and development.
3. Encourage individual managers, especially by *making time available* for training.
4. Provide *support* to local educational institutes to provide management education and training (E & T).
5. Integrate in-house training courses into a wider system of management E & T. *Make the subject matter of in-house courses relevant to managers' needs.* Work closely with academic institutions and professional institutions to ensure that the 'right' programmes are provided.

Individual managers

1. Actively want and seek training and development and to 'own' their own career.
2. Recognise what new skills they require, and seek them out positively
3. Where appropriate, join a professional institute and seek to qualify as a professional member.'

By September 1992, a report in *Personnel Management Plus* (September 1992) suggested that the UK lead spending on management training in Europe, with a rise of 15% (compared with 14% in Germany and only 2% in Belgium, for example). Of total spending, 37% went on internally-run programmes, 35% on in-house programmes run by consultants, and 28% on external courses through training organisations. 'Managing people' and 'Communication skills' were the most popular courses.

The HR view?

> *Management training is now a huge industry. Consultancy companies, magazines and human resource departments are exclusively dedicated to teaching people how to manage more effectively and efficiently.*
>
> *The newly inducted, the freshly promoted, the diagnosed incompetent as well as high flyers are sent on courses on such subjects as time management, communication skills and finance for non-specialists.*

But do these courses work? Can they be measured in some way and be shown to have a desirable effect?

A lot of sweat, tears and ink has been spilled over this apparently simple question. Hard-headed types want evidence that the expense is justified by increased productivity and revenue.

On the other hand, human resources managers seem happy enough if they get the feeling, through ratings on a feedback form, that participants have 'enjoyed' the course.

Financial Times, 13 November 1991

6.4 Career development

Note that management development includes career development and succession planning by the organisation. This will require attention to a number of matters outside the scope of education and training courses.

(a) The types of *experience* a potential senior manager will have to acquire. It may be desirable for a senior manager, for example, to have experience of:

  (i) both line and staff/specialist management - in order to understand how authority is effectively exercised in both situations, and the potentially conflicting cultures/objectives of the two fields;

  (ii) running a whole business unit (of whatever size) in order to develop a business, rather than a functional or sub-unit perspective. This is likely to be a vital transition in a manager's career, from functional to general management; and

  (iii) dealing with head office, from a subsidiary management position - in order to understand the dynamics of centralised/decentralised control and politics.

Activity 10

See if you can suggest two more areas of experience that might be useful for a manager to acquire in order to enhance his or her prospects.

(b) The individual's *guides and role models* in the organisation. It is important that individuals with potential should measure themselves against peers - assessing weaknesses and strengths - and emulate role models, usually superiors who have already 'got what it takes' and proved it. Potential high fliers can be fast-tracked by putting them under the guidance of effective motivators, teachers and power sources in the organisation.

At any stage in a career, a *mentor* will be important. The mentor may occupy a role as the employee's teacher/coach/trainer, counsellor, role model, protector or sponsor/ champion, spur to action or improvement, critic and encourager. In May 1993 the FT reported that 40% of British companies now have a mentoring scheme, and a further 20% are thinking about creating one.

(c) The level of *opportunities and challenges* offered to the developing employee. Too much responsibility too early can be damagingly stressful, but if there is not some degree of difficulty, the employee may never explore his full potential and capacity.

6.5 PDPs and EDPs

Personal development hunt plans (PDPs) are essentially action plans for people's career development which put the onus on them - the individual employees - to seek and organise training. A draft report of the Institute of Employment Studies (reported in *People Management*, 12 January 1995) found that the number of large employers

Chapter 6: Training and development

looking to introduce PDPs is rapidly increasing.

'Organisations no longer feel they can take prime responsibility for the future careers and development of their employees, and the PDP approach clearly places the development ball in the employee's court.'

The most popular PDP schemes take account of people's wider needs and aspirations, rather than focusing simply on skills required to do their current job better.

This trend is also reflected in *employee development programmes* (EDPs), company-run schemes which offer employees a wide range or 'menu' of development opportunities, not necessarily related to their job. The effect of such schemes is to develop a culture in which learning and adaptability is valued - a 'learning culture' - as well as to enhance employee satisfaction and morale. Expense has hitherto confined EDPs to large companies such as Ford, Unipart and Rover, but the National Commission on Education released a briefing paper in January 1994 calling for a national body to help medium-sized firms and a consortia of smaller firms to develop such programmes.

Business Basics: Human Resource Management

Chapter roundup

- A systematic approach to training can be illustrated in a flowchart as follows.

Training

Human resource planning

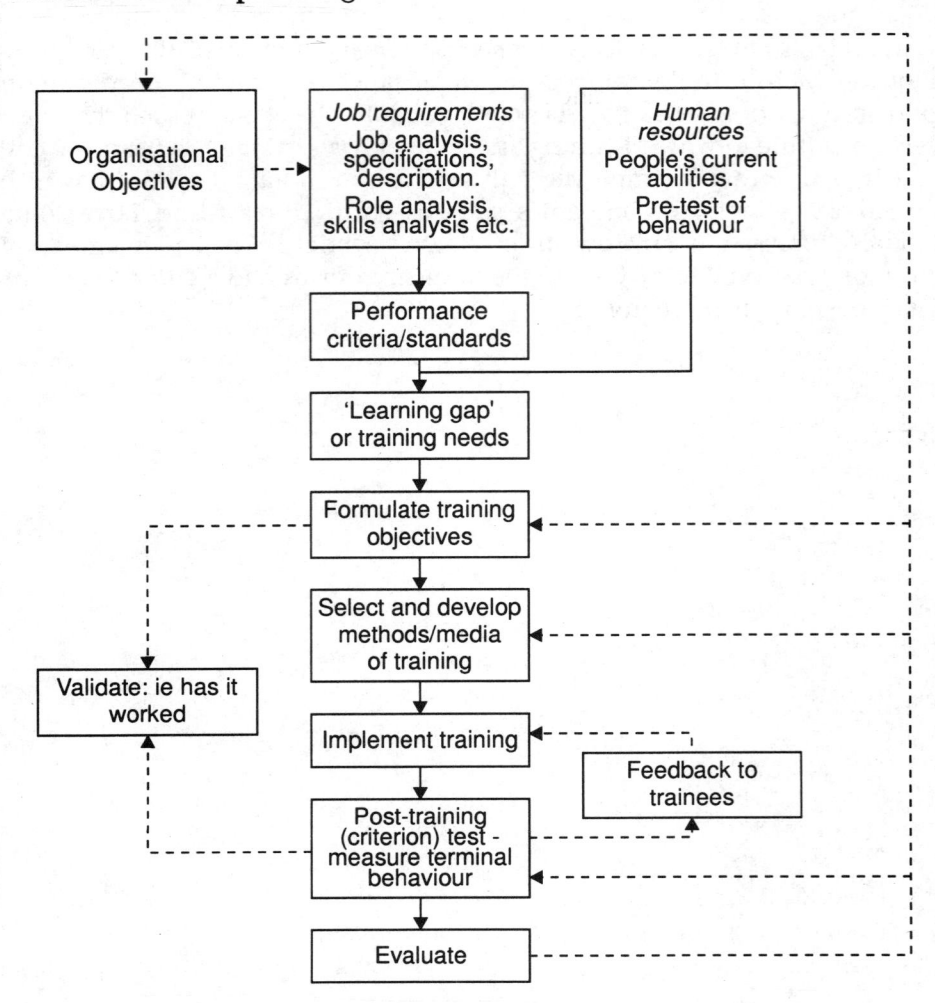

```
         Organisational      Job requirements          Human
         Objectives       -> Job analysis,             resources
                             specifications,           People's current
                             description.              abilities.
                             Role analysis,            Pre-test of
                             skills analysis etc.      behaviour
                                      |
                                      v
                             Performance
                             criteria/standards
                                      |
                                      v
                             'Learning gap'
                             or training needs
                                      |
                                      v
                             Formulate training
                             objectives
                                      |
                                      v
         Validate: ie has it  Select and develop
         worked               methods/media
                              of training
                                      |
                                      v
                              Implement training   <--  Feedback to
                                      |                 trainees
                                      v
                              Post-training
                              (criterion) test -
                              measure terminal
                              behaviour
                                      |
                                      v
                              Evaluate
```

- Management development is a process whereby managers:
    o   gain experience;
    o   receive instruction and guidance from their superiors;
    o   enhance their ability and potential through training and education;
    o   plan their future and the opportunities open to them in the organisation.

This is a collaborative activity of the organisation and the individual manager.

Chapter 6: Training and development

Quick quiz

1 How do 'training needs' arise in an organisation? How would you carry out a 'training needs analysis' if required to do so?
2 Outline the role of:
   (a) motivation;
   (b) feedback; and
   (c) 'reinforcement'
   in the learning process.
3 Draw the 'experiential learning curve' designed by Kolb. Choose any task you have done today, and show how the learning cycle would help you to do it better next time.
4 What are the advantages and disadvantages of 'on-the job' training methods?
5 Outline the process of induction.
6 What is assertiveness?
7 Distinguish between management education and training and development, with examples of methods for each.
8 What is a mentor?
9 What are PDPs and EDPs?

Solutions to activities

3 John is a pragmatist: Paula an activist; Ringo a reflector; Georgette a theorist. The course seems tailored for activists: reflectors would cope, but might not contribute enough to keep the classes going.

6 (a) It has been suggested that women are more prone to the 'compassion trap' - a sense of obligation to put everyone else's needs before your own all the time.

   (b) Women also suffer from attitudes towards money, particularly the sense that it is not 'feminine' to know about or talk about (let alone argue about) money. This discomfort combined with a lack of self-esteem and self-assertion can make negotiating salary levels a nightmare for many women, who may be aware that they are not paid what they are worth.

   (c) The same kind of attitudes to power and authority make it difficult for women to criticise, confront and direct male subordinates and colleagues.

   (d) The failure of victims of sexual harassment to come forward may indicate another area in which assertiveness could be of value.

7 (a) Trainee reaction
   (b) Trainee learning
   (c) Change in behaviour (attitude) following training (reading Chapter 5!)
   (d) Impact of training on the organisation's goals, as a result of training (ie satisfied trainees)
   (e) Impact of training on *your* goals.

8 (a) The prime objective of management development is improved performance capacity - both from the managers *and* from those they manage.

   (b) Management development secures management succession: a pool of promotable individuals in the organisation.

   (c) The organisation's showing an interest in the career development of staff may motivate them and encourage loyalty. (This will be especially important if the firm intends to rely on management succession to fill senior management positions.)

Business Basics: Human Resource Management

9 The *FT* article goes on to give three arguments in favour of this type of training.

(a) Experimental versus theoretical learning. Since the 1960s, when encounter groups thrived, trainers have claimed that real learning occurs when people are put in difficult, novel and problematic situations and not when they study elaborate theories or abstract ideas.

(b) Emotions not ideas. Most training courses are about ideas, concepts, skills and models. They involve brain work and traditional classroom activities. But outdoor trainers claim that modern management is as much about self-confidence and courage.

(c) Team membership not leadership. There are plenty of leadership courses but not too many for those who have to follow. Despite mouthing platitudes about teams and team work, Anglo-Americans come from an individualistic, not a collective, culture. Team work does not come easily or naturally.

10 (a) International operations - if the organisation is in (or moving into) the international arena. Understanding of cultural differences is crucial to effective strategic and people management.

(b) Other disciplines and organisations. Some consultancies and banks, for example, offer secondment with business organisations, development agencies or the civil service. Organisations often encourage potential high-fliers (and sometimes HR specialists) to gain experience in different areas of the business.

Further question practice

Now try the following questions at the end of this text

Multiple choice questions	34 to 41
Exam style questions	6

Chapter 7

PERFORMANCE APPRAISAL

Introduction

The general purpose of 'performance appraisal' is to improve the efficiency of the organisation by ensuring that the individuals within it are performing to the best of their ability, and (perhaps) also developing their potential for improvement. Within this overall aim, staff appraisals are used for:

(a) *reward review* - assessing whether an employee is deserving of a bonus or pay increase;

(b) a review of *past performance*, for identifying problems and unutilised potential, planning (and following-up) training and development programmes; and

(c) the identification of *potential*, as an aid to planning career development.

This used to be regarded as a process which started with an appraisal form and ended with a (frequently perfunctory) chat about it. But in the late 1980s, emphasis shifted more towards the setting of the goals and priorities on which performance would be assessed: an approach known as 'performance management'.

Your objectives

After completing this chapter you should:

(a) understand the purposes of performance appraisal;

(b) be able to outline systematic appraisal procedures;

(c) appreciate the human relations problems with appraisal;

(d) be aware of 'performance management' and other trends in appraisal;

(e) be able to suggest techniques for the identification of potential.

1 THE PURPOSES OF PERFORMANCE APPRAISAL

In his book *Human Resource Management* (1988), George Thomason identifies the variety of objectives of appraisals.

(a) Establishing what actions are required of the individual in a job in order that the objectives for the section or department are realised.

(b) Establishing the key or main results which the individual will be expected to achieve in the course of his or her work over a period of time.

(c) Assessing the individual's level of performance against some standard, to provide a basis for remuneration above the basic pay rate.

(d) Identifying the individual's levels of performance to provide a basis for informing, training and personal development.

(e) Identifying those persons whose performance suggests that they are promotable at some date in the future and those whose performance requires improvement to meet acceptable standards.

(f) Establishing an inventory of actual and potential performance within the undertaking to provide a basis for human resource planning.

(g) Monitoring the initial selection procedures against the subsequent performance of recruits, relative to the organisation's expectations.

(h) Improving communication about work tasks between different levels in the hierarchy.

Whatever the purpose of appraising staff in a particular situation, the review should be a systematic exercise, taken seriously by assessor and subject alike.

It may be argued that such deliberate stock-taking is unnecessary, since managers are constantly making judgements about their subordinates and (should be) giving their subordinates feedback information from day to day. However, it must be recognised that:

(a) managers may obtain random impressions of subordinates' performance (perhaps from their more noticeable successes and failures), but rarely form a coherent, complete and objective picture;

(b) they may have a fair idea of their subordinates' shortcomings - but may not have devoted time and attention to the matter of improvement and development;

(c) judgements are easy to make, but less easy to justify in detail, in writing, or to the subject's face;

(d) different assessors may be applying a different set of criteria, and varying standards of objectivity and judgement, which undermines the value of appraisal for comparison, as well as its credibility in the eyes of the appraisees;

(e) unless stimulated to do so, managers rarely give their subordinates adequate feedback on their performance, especially if the appraisal is a critical one.

Activity 1

From the above, what matters do you think need formulating into a formal, standardised system? There are three major issues.

2 APPRAISAL PROCEDURES

A typical system would involve:

(a) identification of *criteria* for assessment, perhaps based on job analysis, performance standards, person specifications and so on;

(b) the preparation by the subordinate's manager of an *appraisal report*;

(c) an *appraisal interview*, for an exchange of views about the results of the assessment, targets for improvement, solutions to problems and so on;

(d) review of the assessment by the assessor's own superior, so that the appraisee does not feel subject to one person's prejudices. Formal appeals may be allowed, if necessary to establish the fairness of the procedure;

(e) the preparation and implementation of *action plans* to achieve improvements and changes agreed; and

(f) *follow-up*: monitoring the progress of the action plan.

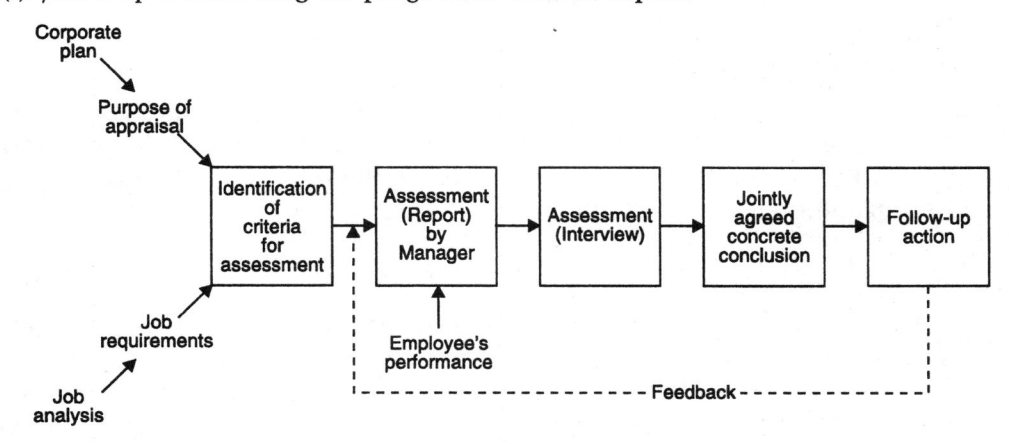

Figure 7.1 Appraisal procedures

There may not need to be standard forms for appraisal - elaborate form-filling procedures should be avoided - as long as managers understand the nature and extent of what is required, and are motivated to take it seriously. Most systems, however, provide for appraisals to be recorded, and report forms of various lengths and complexity may be designed for standard use.

2.1 The basis of appraisal

The basis of appraisal must first be determined. Assessments must be related to a common standard, so comparisons can be made between individuals. On the other hand, they should be related to meaningful performance criteria, which take account of the critical variables in each different job. A blanket approach may provide a common standard, but may not offer a significant index for job performance.

In particular, there is the question of whether *personality* or *performance* is being assessed: in other words, what the individual is, or what he does. According to Livy

> *Personal qualities have questionable validity as a measure of performance, and may introduce unreliability since they are prone to ambiguity and have moral connotations ... In practical terms, this ... has encouraged the use of results-based appraisals (such as Management By Objectives) and the development of job-related performance criteria.*

It is now generally considered that personality is only relevant where there is reason to suspect that it is a factor in poor performance: as long as the employee is achieving the desired results, personality characteristics are not a useful measurement.

Various appraisal techniques have been formulated.

Overall assessment

This is the simplest method, simply requiring the manager to write in narrative form his judgements about the appraisee, possibly with a checklist of personality characteristics and performance targets to work from. There will be no guaranteed consistency of the criteria and areas of assessment, however, and managers may not be able to convey clear, effective judgements in writing. Kay Rowe studied several such schemes and concluded:

> *A few suggested careful thought and a conscientious effort to say something meaningful, but the vast majority were remarkable for their neutrality. Glib, generalised, enigmatic statements abounded.*

Guided assessment

Assessors are required to comment on a number of specified characteristics and performance elements, with guidelines as to how terms such as 'application', 'integrity' and 'adaptability' are to be interpreted in the work context. This is a more precise, but still rather vague method.

Grading

Grading adds a comparative frame of reference to the general guidelines, whereby managers are asked to select one of a number of levels or degrees to which the individual in question displays the given characteristic. These are also known as rating scales, and were much used in standard appraisal forms. Their effectiveness depends to a large extent on:

(a) the relevance of the factors chosen for assessment. These may be nebulous personality traits, for example, or clearly defined job factors such as job knowledge, performance against targets, or decision-making;

(b) the definition of the agreed standards of assessment. Grades A-D might simply be labelled 'Outstanding - Satisfactory - Fair - Poor', in which case assessments are subject to much variation and subjectivity. They may, on the other hand, be more closely related to work priorities and standards, using definitions such as 'Performance is good overall, and superior to that expected in some important areas', or 'Performance is broadly acceptable, but employee needs training in several major areas and/or motivation is lacking.'

Numerical values may be added to ratings to give rating scores. Alternatively a less precise *graphic scale* may be used to indicate general position on a plus/minus scale.

Factor: job knowledge

High ————✓———— Average ————————— Low

Behavioural incident methods

These concentrate on employee behaviour, which is measured against typical behaviour in each job, as defined by common 'critical incidents' of successful and unsuccessful job behaviour reported by managers. Time and effort are required to collect and analyse reports and to develop the scheme, and it only really applies to large groups of people in broadly similar jobs. However, it is firmly rooted in observation of real-life job behaviour, and the important aspects of the job, since the analysis is carried out for key tasks, (those which are identified as critical to success in the job and for which specific standards of performance must be reached).

The behavioural equivalent of the graphic scale (illustrated above) for a manager's key task of 'marketing initiative' might appear as:

| Produces no new ideas for marketing. Appears apathetic to competitive challenge | Produces ideas when urged by head office. Ideas not clearly thought out nor enthusiastically applied | Produces ideas when urged by head office and gives full commitment to new programmes | Spontaneously generates new ideas for marketing and champions them through head office approval. Ideas related to identified needs and effective in practice |

Results-orientated schemes

All the above techniques may be used with more or less results-orientated criteria for assessment - but are commonly based on trait or behavioural appraisal. A wholly results-orientated approach (such as Management by Objectives) sets out to review performance against specific targets and standards of performance agreed in advance by manager and subordinate together. This is closer to the approach known as *performance management*. The advantages of this are that:

(a) the subordinate is more involved in the appraisal of his own performance, because he is able to evaluate his success or progress in achieving specific, jointly-agreed targets;

(b) the manager is therefore relieved, to an extent, of his role as critic, and becomes a counsellor. A primarily *problem-solving* approach (what does the employee require in order to do his job better?) may be adopted; and

(c) learning and motivation theories suggest that clear and known targets are important in modifying and determining behaviour.

The effectiveness of the scheme will still depend on the targets set, however, (are they clearly defined? realistic?) and the commitment of both parties to make it work. The measurement of success or failure is only part of the picture: reasons for failure and opportunities arising from success must be evaluated.

Activity 2

Study the appraisal form on the following page. This is based on a genuine example reproduced in a book published in 1982. Can you suggest any ways in which the form could be improved for the 1990s?

2.2 360-degree feedback

360-degree feedback, also known as 'multi-rater instruments' and 'multi-source assessment', is based on the recognition that the employee's immediate boss is not the only (or necessarily the best) person to assess his or her performance. According to Peter Ward (who introduced the system at Tesco in 1987) in a feature in *People Management* (9 February 1995):

> *Traditional performance measurement systems have rarely operated on more than one or two dimensions. However, 360-degree feedback is designed to enable all the stake-holders in a person's performance to comment and give feedback. This includes the current (and perhaps previous) boss (including temporary supervisors), peers and co-workers, subordinates and even external customers. Finally, the employee's own self-assessment is added and compared.*

Performance Classification

Outstanding performance is characterised by high ability which leaves little or nothing to be desired. Personnel rated as such are those who regularly make significant contributions to the organisation which are above the requirements of their position. Unusual and challenging assignments are consistently well handled.

Excellent performance is marked by above-average ability, with little supervision required. These employees may display some of the attributes present in 'outstanding' performance, but not on a sufficiently consistent basis to warrant that rating. Unusual and challenging assignments are normally well handled.

Satisfactory Plus performance indicates fully adequate ability, without the need for excessive supervision. Personnel with this rating are able to give proper consideration to normal assignments, which are generally well handled. They will meet the requirements of the position. 'Satisfactory plus' performers may include those who lack the experience at their current level to demonstrate above-average ability.

Marginal performance is in instances where the ability demonstrated does not fully meet the requirements of the position, with excessive supervision and direction normally required. Employees rated as such will show specific deficiencies in their performance which prevent them from performing at an acceptable level.

Unsatisfactory performance indicates an ability which falls clearly below the minimum requirements of the position. 'Unsatisfactory' performers will demonstrate marked deficiencies in most of the major aspects of their responsibilities, and considerable improvement is required to permit retention of the employee in his current position.

Personal Characteristics Ratings

1. – Needs considerable improvement – substantial improvement required to meet acceptable standards.
2. – Needs improvement – some improvement required to meet acceptable standards.
3. – Normal – meets acceptable standards.
4. – Above normal – exceeds normally acceptable standards in most instances.
5. – Exceptional – displays rare and unusual personal characteristics.

P & O
October 1982 **4168B/1** Reverse

Personnel Appraisal: Employees in Salary Grades 5-8

Date of Review	Time on Position	S.G.	Age	Name
	Yrs. Mths.		Yrs.	
Period of Review	Position Title			Area

Important: Read guide notes carefully before proceeding with the following sections

Section One

Performance Factors	N/A	U	M	SP	E	O	Section Two	Personal Characteristics
								1 2 3 4 5
Administrative Skills							Initiative	
Communications – Written							Persistence	
Communications – Oral							Ability to work with others	
Problem Analysis							Adaptability	
Decision Making							Persuasiveness	
Delegation							Self-Confidence	
Quantity of Work							Judgement	
Development of Personnel							Leadership	
Development of Quality Improvements							Creativity	

Section Three
Highlight Performance Factors and particular strengths/weaknesses of employee which significantly affect Job Performance

Overall Performance Rating (Taking into account ratings given)

Prepared by: Signature .... Date .... Position Title ....

Section Four
Comments by Reviewing Authority

I.R. Review Initial .... Date ....

Signature .... Date .... Position Title ....

Section Five
Supervisor's Notes on Counselling Interview

Signature .... Date .... Position Title ....

Section Six
Employee's Reactions and Comment

Signature .... Date ....

This information is usually collected (anonymously) through questionnaires, either on paper or on disk.

The advantages of 360-degree feedback are said to be as follows.

(a) It highlights every aspect of the individual's performance, and allows comparison of the individual's self-assessment with the views of others. (Rather revealing, in most cases.)

(b) Feedback tends, overall, to be balanced, covering strengths in some areas with weaknesses in others, so it is less discouraging.

(c) The assessment is based on the real, normal work environment and circumstances - not artificial (eg interview) situations or isolated incidents. The feedback is thus felt to be fairer and more relevant, making it easier for employees to accept the assessment and the need for change and development.

Ward warns of potential pitfalls, however. If 360-degree feedback is to be successful, the organisation needs to avoid:

(a) negative emphasis: feedback on weaknesses should be balanced by positive feedback on strengths and potential, to encourage the employee to develop;

(b) a 'flavour of the month approach', where the technique and its results are seen as interesting - but no thought has been given to follow-up action;

(c) lack of confidentiality. Respondents must be anonymous, or they may fear to tell the truth in an assessment (especially of a boss!);

(d) poor communication of the purpose of the exercise. It can be daunting, and employees need to understand that it is not a political exercise, or a 'rod' to beat anyone with: they are not being asked to 'rat' on anyone!

(e) lack of action and support. The organisation must support the employee in the development suggested by the feedback.

Activity 3

Peter Ward gives an example of the kind of questionnaires that might be used as the instrument of 360-degree feedback.

'A skill area like "communicating", for example, might be defined as "the ability to express oneself clearly and to listen effectively to others". Typical comments would include "Presents ideas or information in a well-organised manner" (followed by rating scale); or: "Allows you to finish what you have to say".'

Rate yourself on the two comments mentioned here, on a scale of 1-10. Get a group of friends, fellow-students, even a tutor or parent, to write down, anonymously, on a piece of paper their rating for you on the same two comments. Keep them in an envelope, unseen, until you have a few.

Compare them with your self-rating. If you dare...

2.3 Interview and counselling

The extent to which any discussion or counselling interview is based on the written report varies in practice. For certain purposes - say, mutually agreed programmes for further training of the individual under review - the report may be distributed to the appraisee in advance of the interview, so that he has a chance to make an independent assessment for discussion with his manager.

Maier (*The Appraisal Interview*) identifies three types of approach to appraisal interviews.

(a) The *tell and sell* method. The manager tells the subordinate how he has been assessed, and then tries to 'sell' (gain acceptance of) the evaluation and the improvement plan. This requires unusual human relations skills in order to convey constructive criticism in an acceptable manner, and to motivate the appraisee to alter his behaviour.

(b) The *tell and listen* method. The manager tells the subordinate how he has been assessed, and then invites him to respond. The manager therefore no longer dominates the interview throughout, and there is greater opportunity for counselling as opposed to pure direction. The employee is encouraged to participate in the assessment and the working out of improvement targets and methods: it is an accepted tenet of behavioural theory that participation in problem definition and goal setting increases the individual's commitment to behaviour and attitude modification. Moreover, this method does not assume that a change in the employee will be the sole key to improvement: the manager may receive helpful feedback about how job design, methods, environment or supervision might be improved. Again, however, the interviewer needs to be a talented and trained listener and counsellor.

(c) The *problem-solving* approach. The manager abandons the role of critic altogether, and becomes a counsellor and helper. The discussion is centred not on the assessment, but on the employee's work problems. The employee is encouraged to think solutions through, and to commit himself to the recognised need for personal improvement. This approach encourages intrinsic motivation through the element of self-direction, and the perception of the job itself as a problem-solving activity. It may also stimulate creative thinking on the part of employee and manager alike, to the benefit of the organisation's adaptability and methods. Again, the interviewer will require highly-developed skills, and the attitudes of both parties to the process will need to be got right.

EXAMPLE: APPRAISAL INTERVIEWS

In 1995, Saville and Holdsworth (the largest occupational psychology practice in the world) conducted a survey into attitude towards appraisal interviews in the UK. They found that:

(a) 96% of their survey group had conventional appraisal systems

(b) of these, 31% had self-appraisal

(c) 11% had upward appraisal

(d) 7% included peer appraisal

(e) 74% expressed an interest in finding out more about 360 degree feedback.

Cuming suggests that, unlike the conventionally-used attitude surveys which concentrate on the compensatory aspects of employment (on the basic assumption that work is intrinsically unpleasant, and that management's task is to render it more satisfactory by pay, fringe benefits, friendly treatment, pride in the company and so on), the appraisal interview should ask positive and thought-provoking questions which focus on the employee's hopes and frustrations.

(a) Do you fully understand your job? Are there any aspects you wish to be made clearer?

(b) What parts of your job do you do best?

(c) Could any changes be made in your job which might result in improved performance?

(d) Have you any skills, knowledge, or aptitudes which could be made better use of in the organisation?

(e) What are your career plans? How do you propose achieving your ambitions in terms of further training and broader experience?

2.4 Follow-up

After the appraisal interview, the manager may complete his report, with an overall assessment, assessment of potential and/or the jointly-reached conclusion of the interview, with recommendations for follow-up action.

The manager should then discuss the report with the counter-signing manager (usually his or her own superior), resolving any problems encountered in making the appraisal or report, and agreeing on action to be taken. The report form may then go to the management development adviser, training officer, or other relevant people, for follow-up.

Follow-up procedures will include:

(a) informing appraisees of the results of the appraisal, if this has not been central to the review interview. Some people argue that there is no point making appraisals if they are not openly discussed, but unless managers are competent and committed to reveal results in a constructive, frank and objective manner, the negative reactions on all sides may outweigh the advantages;

(b) carrying out agreed actions on training, promotion and so on;

(c) monitoring the appraisee's progress and checking that *(s)he* has carried out agreed actions or improvements; and

(d) taking necessary steps to help the appraisee attain improvement objectives, by guidance, providing feedback, upgrading equipment, altering work methods or whatever.

2.5 Upward appraisal

A notable modern trend, adopted in the UK by companies such as BP, British Airways and others, is upward appraisal, whereby employees are not rated by their superiors but by their subordinates. The followers appraise the leader. For example, in 1996 Halifax Building Society (as it then was) launched a new performance management system that included upward appraisal, but in this case staff were asked to comment on the effectiveness of management teams rather than individual managers.

The advantages of upward appraisal were set out as follows in an article by Adrian Furnham in the *Financial Times* (March 1993).

(a) Subordinates tend to know their superior better than superiors know their subordinates. They see their bosses and know their moods, foibles and preferences, their adequacies, skills, strengths and limitations and things they do and do not like doing.

(b) As all subordinates rate their managers statistically, these ratings tend to be more reliable - the more subordinates the better. Instead of the biases of individual managers' ratings, the various ratings of the employees can be converted into a representative view. If the employees have very differing views of their bosses this can present problems, but represents very significant data meriting further investigation.

(c) Subordinates' ratings have more impact because it is more unusual to receive ratings from subordinates. It is also surprising to bosses because, despite protestations to the contrary, information often flows down organisations more smoothly and comfortably than it flows up. When it flows up it is qualitatively and quantitatively different. It is this difference that makes it valuable.

Activity 4

Suggest the two major problems that might be experienced with upward appraisal.

3 PROBLEMS WITH APPRAISAL

In theory, such appraisal schemes may seem very fair to the individual and very worthwhile for the organisation, but in practice the system often goes wrong.

(a) Appraisal interviews are often defensive on the part of the subordinate, who believes that criticism may herald financial disadvantage or lost promotion opportunity. The superior may be defensive too, not being able to reconcile the role of judge and critic with the human relations aspect of the interview and maybe feeling uncomfortable about 'playing God' with the employee's future.

(b) The superior might show conscious or unconscious bias in his report or may be influenced by his rapport with the interviewee, in the face-to-face phase. Systems with no clearly-defined standard criteria will be particularly prone to the subjectivity of the assessor's judgements.

(c) The manager and subordinate may both be reluctant to devote time and attention to appraisal. Their experience in the organisation may indicate that the exercise is a waste of time (especially if there is a lot of form-filling) with no relevance to the job, and no reliable follow-up action.

(d) The organisational culture may simply not take appraisal seriously: interviewers are not trained or given time to prepare, appraisees are not encouraged to contribute, or the exercise is perceived as a 'nod' to Human Relations with no practical results.

EXAMPLE: APPRAISAL INTERVIEWS

Kay Rowe conducted a study of appraisal systems, based on 1,440 completed appraisal forms from six organisations. In a famous article ('An appraisal of appraisals', *Journal of Management Studies*, 1964) which seems to have lost none of its relevance with age she concluded that:

(a) appraisers are reluctant to appraise;

(b) interviewers are reluctant to interview; and

(c) there is no follow-up.

3.1 Appraisal: good or bad for motivation?

The effect of appraisal on motivation is a particularly tricky issue.

(a) *Feedback on performance* is regarded as vital in motivation, because it enables an employee to evaluate his achievement and make future calculations about the amount of effort required to achieve objectives and rewards. Even negative feedback can have this effect - and is more likely to spur the employee on to post-appraisal action.

(b) Agreement of challenging but attainable *targets* for performance or improvement also motivates employees by clarifying goals and the value (and 'cost' in terms of effort) of incentives offered.

(c) A *positive approach* to appraisal allows employees to solve their work problems and apply creative thinking to their jobs.

However, people rarely react well to criticism - especially at work, where they may feel that their reward or even job security is on the line. In addition, much depends on the self-esteem of the appraisee.

(a) If the appraisee has a high self-image, he may be impervious to criticism: he will be able to deflect it - and the greater the criticism, the harder he will work to explain it away. If such a person is *not* criticised, he will be confirmed in his behaviour and sense of self-worth, which will motivate him to continue as he is: this is fine if he is doing a good job, but *not* if he is doing a bad job and simply being given a 'soft' appraisal.

(b) If the appraisee has a low self-image, he may be encouraged by low levels of criticism, and this may help to improve his performance. Heavy criticism of a person of low self-esteem can, however, be psychologically damaging.

3.2 Improving the system

The appraisal scheme should itself be assessed (and regularly re-assessed) according to the following general criteria.

(a) *Relevance*
   (i) Does the system have a useful purpose, relevant to the needs of the organisation and the individual?
   (ii) Is the purpose clearly expressed and widely understood by all concerned, both appraisers and appraisees?
   (iii) Are the appraisal criteria relevant to the purposes of the system?

(b) *Fairness*
   (i) Is there reasonable standardisation of criteria and objectivity throughout the organisation?
   (ii) Is there reasonable objectivity?

(c) *Serious intent*
   (i) Are the managers concerned committed to the system - or is it just something the personnel department thrusts upon them?
   (ii) Who does the interviewing, and are they properly trained in interviewing and assessment techniques?
   (iii) Is reasonable time and attention given to the interviews - or is it a question of 'getting them over with'?
   (iv) Is there a genuine demonstrable link between performance and reward or opportunity for development?

(d) *Co-operation*
   (i) Is the appraisal a participative, problem-solving activity - or a tool of management control?
   (ii) Is the appraisee given time and encouragement to prepare for the appraisal, so that he can make a constructive contribution?
   (iii) Does a jointly-agreed, concrete conclusion emerge from the process?
   (iv) Are appraisals held regularly?

(e) *Efficiency*
   (i) Does the system seem time-consuming compared to the value of its outcome?
   (ii) Is it difficult and costly to administer?

Activity 5

What role can you see for the HR function in improving performance appraisal (in general terms), and what political factors do you think might hamper its influence?

4 PERFORMANCE MANAGEMENT AND OTHER TRENDS

4.1 Performance management

In an article in *Personnel Management* in September 1993, Clive Fletcher commented on 'the break-up of the traditional, monolithic approach' to performance appraisal.

Connock (*HR Vision*, 1991) agrees:

> *In the late 1980s the emphasis moved from performance appraisal to performance management. Whilst setting clear and measurable objectives was always a major part of earlier schemes, the emphasis was more on the appraisal of past performances. Under performance management there is a dual emphasis: on setting key accountabilities, objectives, measures, priorities and time scales for the following review period and appraising performance at the end of the period.*

Connock suggests four reasons for this shift in emphasis.

(a) Competitive pressures mean that if organisations do not improve they will not survive.

(b) It is now widely realised that corporate missions and strategic objectives can be more effectively implemented by linking them to individual objectives.

(c) The new focus on quality in many companies means that quality standards have to be set or refined and this has fed through to the performance management processes.

(d) Performance-related pay is being used more and more widely. If it is to be used effectively, 'clear objectives, measures and time scales are necessary from which judgements about the individual's contribution can be made'.

Activity 6

Can you anticipate any advantages for employees from a performance management system?

4.2 Other trends in appraisal

Current and likely future trends in the design and operation of performance appraisal systems were described in the 1993 *Personnel Management* article by Clive Fletcher.

(a) Increased use of self-appraisal and appraisal by peers, because of delayering, the spread of matrix management and wider geographical distribution of staff mean that former appraisers (the individuals' immediate bosses) now have too wide a span of control (too many appraisees) to deal with, or see them too seldom to appraise effectively.

(b) Increased use of upward appraisal.

(c) The practice of having several appraisers contribute to the process, with one then feeding back a representative view of the appraisee's performance (as in 360-degree feedback).

(d) The increasing adoption of a 'competency' framework for describing performance development. Conversely, the use of 'rating scales' appears to be in decline.

(e) A view of development as something that takes place *within* the current position or through a lateral move rather than through promotion. This is a consequence of the downsizing and delayering that has taken place in many organisations.

(f) An increased use of assessment centres and psychometric tests in appraisal instead of relying on the limited perspectives of individual appraisers.

(g) Performance appraisal is becoming a less centralised, more 'line driven' process than it has been. This is complemented by a general movement in the field of human resources management towards a more strategic role, devolving many of the day to day concerns of personnel management to line managers. As Fletcher says, 'greater line management ownership [of performance management] should help focus the process more effectively on the needs of appraisers and appraisees and raise commitment to making it work'.

5 THE IDENTIFICATION OF POTENTIAL

The review of potential is the use of appraisal to forecast the direction in which an individual is progressing, in terms of his career plans and skill development, and at what rate. It can be used as feedback to the individual, to indicate the opportunities open to him in the organisation in the future. It will also be vital to the organisation in determining its management succession plans.

Information for potential assessment will include:

(a) strengths and weaknesses in existing skills and qualities;

(b) possibilities and strategies for improvement, correction and development;

(c) the goals, aspirations and attitudes of the appraisee, with regard to career advancement, staying with the organisation and handling responsibility; and

(d) the opportunities available in the organisation, including likely management vacancies, job rotation/enrichment plans and promotion policies for the future.

No single review exercise will mark an employee down for life as 'promotable' or otherwise. The process tends to be an on-going one, with performance at each stage or level in the employee's career indicating whether he might be able to progress to the next step. However, this approach based on performance in the current job is highly fallible: hence the 'Peter principle' of L J Peter, who pointed out that managers tend to be promoted from positions in which they have proved themselves competent until one day they reach a level at which they are no longer competent - promoted 'to the level of their own incompetence'!

Moreover, the management succession plan of an organisation needs to be formulated in the long term: there is a long lead time involved in equipping a manager with the skills and experience needed at senior levels and the organisation must develop people if it is to fill the shoes of departing managers without crisis.

Some idea of *potential* must therefore be built into appraisal. It is impossible to predict with any certainty how successful an individual will be in what will, after all, be different circumstances from anything he has experienced so far. However, some attempt can be made to:

(a) determine key *indicators of potential*: in other words, elements believed to be essential to management success; and/or

(b) *simulate* the conditions of the position to which the individual would be promoted, to assess his performance.

5.1 Key indicators of potential

Various research studies (by employing organisations and by theorists) have been carried out into exactly what makes a successful senior manager (and could be identified in junior people to indicate that they might *become* successful senior managers).

The following are some of the factors identified.

(a) General effectiveness (track record in task performance and co-worker satisfaction).

(b) Administrative skills (planning and organising, making good decisions).

(c) Interpersonal skills or intelligence (being aware of others, making a good impression, persuading and motivating).

(d) Intellectual ability or analytical skills (problem-solving, mental agility).

(e) Control of feelings (tolerance of stress, uncertainty and so on).

(f) Leadership (variously defined, but demonstrated in follower loyalty and commitment).

(g) Imagination and intuition (for creative decision-making and innovation).

(h) 'Helicopter ability' (the ability to rise above the particulars of a situation, to see the whole picture, sift out key elements and conceive strategies - the ability to 'see the wood for the trees').

(i) Orientation to work (being motivated by work rather than non-work satisfactions; self-starting, rather than needing to be motivated by others).

(j) Team work (ability and willingness to co-operate with others).

(k) Taste for making money (empathy with the profit motive: ambition for self and business).

(l) 'Fit' (having whatever mix of all the above skills, abilities and experience the business organisation needs - being in the right place at the right time).

Activity 7

Which of these indicators of potential do you think *you* possess?

Various techniques can be used to measure these attributes, including:

(a) written tests (for intellectual ability);

(b) simulated desk-top tasks or case studies (for administrative skills, analytical and problem-solving ability);

(c) role play (for negotiating or influencing skills, conflict resolution or team working);

(d) leadership exercises (testing the ability to control the dynamics of a team towards work-related objectives);

(e) personality tests (for work orientation, motivation and so on);

(f) interviews (for interpersonal skills, attitudes and so on); and

(g) presentations or speeches (for communication skills).

Note the use of *simulated* activity, such as case study or role play, to give potential managers experience of managerial tasks. An alternative approach might be to offer them *real* experience (under controlled conditions) by appointing them to assistant or deputy positions or to committees or project teams, and assessing their performance. This is still no real predictor of their ability to handle the *whole* job, on a continuous basis and over time, however, and it may be risky, if the appraisee fails to cope with the situation.

5.2 Assessment centres

Definition

Assessment centres (ACs) are an increasingly used approach, which started with the War Office Selection Board methods during the Second World War.

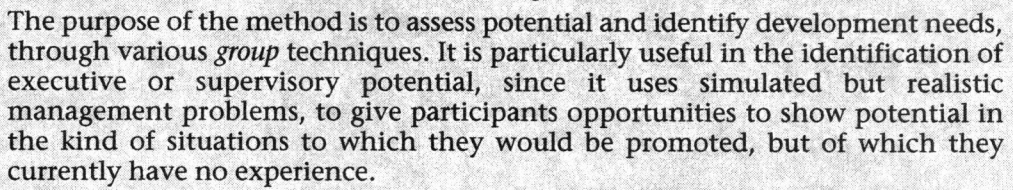

The purpose of the method is to assess potential and identify development needs, through various *group* techniques. It is particularly useful in the identification of executive or supervisory potential, since it uses simulated but realistic management problems, to give participants opportunities to show potential in the kind of situations to which they would be promoted, but of which they currently have no experience.

Trained assessors - usually line managers two levels above the participants, and perhaps consultant psychologists - use a variety of games, simulations, tests and group discussions and exercises. Observed by the assessors, participants may be required to answer questionnaires about their attitudes, complete written tests, prepare speeches and presentations, participate in group role-play exercises, work through simulated supervisory tasks, and undertake self-appraisal and peer-rating. They are assessed on a range of factors, such as assertiveness, energy, initiative and creativity, stress-tolerance, sensitivity, abilities in persuasion, communication, and decision-making.

An assessment report is then compiled from the assessors' observations, test scores and the participant's self-assessment. This is discussed in a feedback counselling interview.

Advantages of assessment centres include:

(a) a high degree of acceptability and user confidence; avoidance of single-assessor bias;

(b) reliability in predicting potential success (if the system is well-conducted);

(c) the development of skills in the assessors, which may be useful in their own managerial responsibilities;

(d) benefits to the assessed individual, including experience of managerial/supervisory situations, opportunity for self-assessment and job-relevant feedback, and opportunities to discuss career prospects openly with senior management.

The cost of the scheme must, however, be considered. A well-run centre with trained and practised assessors requires considerable expense of managerial time, and the time of participants, as well as the fixed costs of setting up the programme, whether it is designed internally or bought 'off the shelf'.

Activity 8

From your knowledge of similar techniques used in selection, and the criteria for good appraisal systems, what pitfalls will need to be avoided by the 'designer' of an assessment centre programme?

> **EXAMPLE: ROVER**
>
> Rover's approach to ACs was reported in *Personnel Management* (June 1991). 'An internal study, comparing appointments made using ACs with those resulting from more traditional interview approaches, suggested that decisions arising from ACs were more robust and reliable.'
>
> However, Rover experienced problems with:
>
> (a) the absence of learning and development experience for trainees (as opposed to observation opportunities for the employer)
>
> (b) the acceptability and relevance of simulations to the participants
>
> (c) the lack of clarity and visibility in assessment criteria
>
> (d) the subjectivity of assessments
>
> (e) the bulk of recorded data resulting from ACs, obscuring the true assessment of outcomes.
>
> Rover revised their AC system in 1989, and applied it to reorganisation in the HR function itself. Major features of the new programme included the following.
>
> (a) To establish clear and rigorous assessment criteria, a *competence-based model* was adopted, using a 'map' of eight themes or dimensions of competence: strategy, business, resource management, communication, quality, professional consultancy and organisation development.
>
> The map was developed with senior human resource managers, using brainstorming and workshop sessions, and later refined in discussion. Its concise nature and use of language culturally and organisationally specific to Rover, generated interest and established credibility with senior managers and, subsequently, with participants.
>
> (b) It was decided to give *learning and development* equal priority to assessment. Rover made the assessment criteria freely available to participants and offered them enrolment by self-assessment. Thus simulations and exercises were developed which would observe and measure agreed competence benchmarks and provide a challenging and satisfying development experience: for example, an exercise involving the development of HR strategy for Rover.
>
> (c) Scores in all tests were built up into *individual profiles*, which could be used to identify relative strengths and development needs: *personal development plans* were later agreed with each individual.
>
> 'In conclusion, we found that the shift from assessment to *development centre* approaches has been very successful. Using competence-based criteria gives greater visibility and credibility to the process and offers spin-off benefits in performance appraisal, training objectives and for succession and development planning purposes. Challenging exercises that reflect real business issues are more acceptable to participants and offer more realistic assessment.'

This approach was echoed by Martin Gillespie, the Training and Development Executive for Tarmac Professional Services (as reported in *People Management*, February 1997). Tarmac has a philosophy of growing its own senior managers and directors and run various programmes for managers, including a two-year executive development programme. The competition for this fast-track programme is fierce and Tarmac use an assessment centre, that places a stress on development, for select entrants.

Chapter roundup

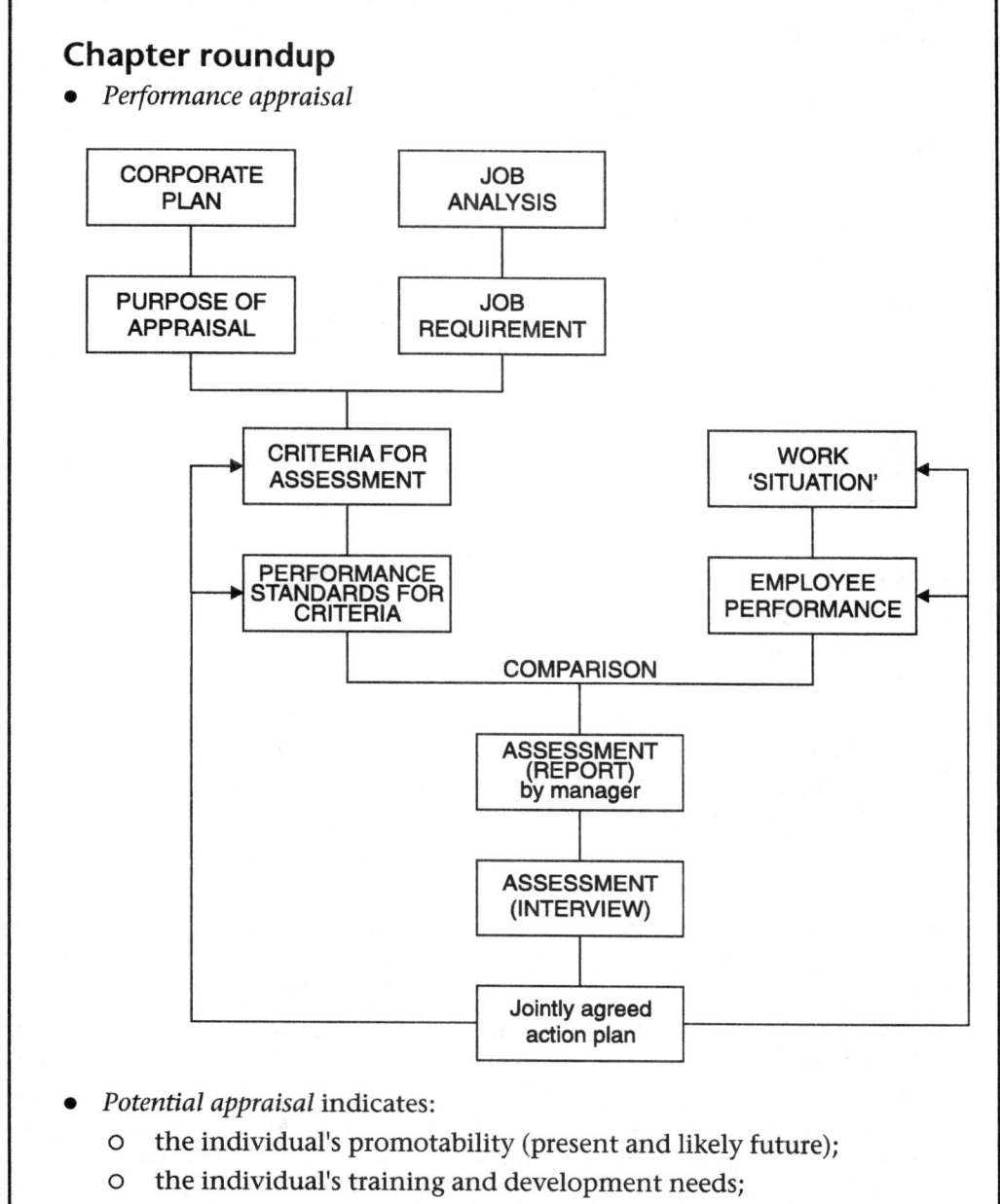

- *Performance appraisal*

```
CORPORATE PLAN          JOB ANALYSIS
     |                       |
PURPOSE OF APPRAISAL    JOB REQUIREMENT
            \           /
         CRITERIA FOR ASSESSMENT          WORK 'SITUATION'
                  |                              |
         PERFORMANCE STANDARDS          EMPLOYEE PERFORMANCE
         FOR CRITERIA
                     \       COMPARISON       /
                        ASSESSMENT (REPORT) by manager
                                  |
                        ASSESSMENT (INTERVIEW)
                                  |
                        Jointly agreed action plan
```

- *Potential appraisal* indicates:
    - the individual's promotability (present and likely future);
    - the individual's training and development needs;
    - the direction and rate of progress of the individual's development;
    - the future (forecast) management resource of the organisation; and
    - the management recruitment, training and development needs of the organisation.

Quick quiz

1. What are the purposes of appraisal?
2. What bases or criteria of assessment might an appraisal system use?
3. Outline a results-orientated approach to appraisal, and its advantages.
4. What is 360-degree feedback, and who might be involved?
5. What follow-up procedures should be used after an appraisal?
6. What kinds of criticism might be levelled at appraisal schemes by a manager who thought they were a waste of time?

Business Basics: Human Resource Management

7 What is the difference between performance appraisal and performance management?

8 What techniques might be used to measure an employee's potential to become a successful senior manager?

9 What is an assessment centre?

Solutions to activities

1 There is clearly a need for a system which tackles the basic problems of:

(a) the definition of criteria: desired traits and standards against which individuals can be consistently and objectively assessed. Assessors must be aware of factors which affect their judgements;

(b) recording assessments. Managers should be encouraged to utilise a standard and understood framework, but still allowed to express what they consider important, and without too much form-filling; and

(c) getting the appraiser and appraisee together, so that both contribute to the assessment and plans for improvement and/or development.

2 Amongst the points you might have made are the following.

(a) Some of the wording has an old-fashioned ring to it ('salary grades 5-8', 'reviewing authority')

(b) Many organisations have now dispensed with rating scales on the grounds that they are contentious, and they don't adequately distinguish attributes that are very significant from those that are less so.

(c) The term 'weaknesses' is used whereas many organisations would use a term like 'areas for improvement'.

There are other points to be made. Alternatively you may think the form is fine as it is, and these objections are merely faddish 'political correctness'.

4 Problems with upward appraisal include fear of reprisals or vindictiveness (or extra form-processing). Some bosses in strong positions might refuse to act, even if a consensus of staff suggested that they should change their ways.

5 The HR function has a role to play in encouraging line management to carry out systematic appraisal, and in overcoming some of the causes of managerial reluctance to appraise. Education in the potential benefits of and constructive approaches to appraisal may help, starting to build a culture where appraisal is perceived to be a primary problem-solving tool and keystone of managerial effectiveness. The HR specialist(s) should design, and instruct managers in the use of, workable procedures and documentation for appraisal.

However, a change in attitudes and practice such as would be required in many organisations will not be easy to achieve, particularly since part of the attitude problem is likely to be the feeling that appraisal is being imposed on line managers by the HR function, which does not understand the operational difficulties. Ultimately, the cultural change may have to come from the HR department's own practices: the HR manager will have to lead by example, to show that it can be done.

6 (a) Fletcher identifies a major advantage of performance management as the separation of performance appraisal from performance related pay awards. ('Organisations ... are tending to have a session on objective setting and review, tied in to the start of the business year, with a more developmentally-oriented appraisal session at a later date. Any performance-related pay element is usually related to the former.')

This takes some of the fear and inhibition out of the appraisal part of the process.

(b) Objective-setting gives employees the security and satisfaction of both understanding their jobs and knowing exactly what is expected of them. (A 1995 report by the Audit Commission, entitled 'Calling the Tune', showed that local authorities who operated a comprehensive performance management system also scored highly in staff attitude surveys on 'know how' and 'feel good' factors. In other words, objective-setting and appraisal help staff to feel that they understand more about their work, and 'feel good' about it.)

(c) Joint-objective setting and a developmental approach are positive and participatory, helping employees' to accept and 'own' - commit to - change and improvement.

8 An article in *Personnel Management* (June 1991) suggested the following 'design shortcomings' which frequently occur, but should be avoided.

(a) Inadequate specification of the target competencies against which participants are assessed.

(b) Exercises which bear little relation either to the competencies being assessed, or to the organisation's cultural practices.

(c) Little or no assessor training and selection.

(d) Inadequate selection and briefing of candidates, so that some are 'lost' from the start.

(e) Inefficient programming and scheduling of the events.

(f) Inadequate or non-existent follow-up action, feedback, counselling and implementation of recommendations.

Further question practice

Now try the following practice questions at the end of this text

Multiple choice questions	**42 to 48**
Exam style question	**7**

Chapter 8

MOTIVATION AND REWARDS

Introduction
The word motivation is commonly used in different contexts to mean:

(a) goals, or outcomes that have become desirable for a particular individual. These are more properly 'motivating factors' - since they give people a reason for behaving in a certain way (in pursuit of a chosen goal): thus we say that money, power or friendship are our 'motives' for doing something;

(b) the mental process of choosing desired outcomes, deciding how to go about them, assessing whether the likelihood of success warrants the amount of effort that will be necessary, and setting in motion whatever behaviour is required. Whether we are 'motivated' to do something will depend on how far we think our goals will be fulfilled by doing it;

(c) the social process by which the behaviour of an individual is influenced by others. 'Motivation' in this sense usually applies to the attempts of organisations to get workers to put in more effort by offering them certain rewards (financial and non-financial) if they do so.

In this chapter, we cover some basic motivation theories (which explain the first two meanings), then concentrate on 'motivation' in the third sense, which is the practical responsibility of HRM.

Your objectives
After completing this chapter you should:

(a) be able to define motivation and discuss its impact on work performance;
(b) be able to outline the need theories, two-factor theory and expectancy theory of motivation;
(c) appreciate the range of rewards that might act as 'motivators';
(d) be able to outline how 'job satisfaction' might be offered to employees;
(e) be able to discuss the significance of pay as a motivator.

1 MOTIVATION AND PERFORMANCE

Motivation, as it most nearly concerns HRM, is the controlling of the work environment and the offering of rewards in such a way as to encourage extra performance from employees. As rational purposive beings (who act deliberately in pursuit of goals), employees consciously or unconsciously decide whether it is 'worth their while', or desirable, to put forth what Charles Handy called 'E factors' - energy and effort - in a given work situation. The decision of whether more 'E' is worth putting in is reached by considering what rewards or incentives are available for doing so.

Activity 1

Come up with five more words beginning with 'e' that signify extra input to an individual's work and would therefore classify as 'E factors'.

1.1 Rewards and incentives

You may already realise that not all the rewards or incentives that an organisation can offer its employees are directly related to *monetary* rewards. The satisfaction of *any* of the employee's wants or needs may be seen as a reward for past or future performance.

Different individuals have different goals, and get different things out of their working life: in other words they have different *orientations* to work. There are any number or reasons (some of which are formulated in 'need' theories of motivation as discussed below) why a person works, or is motivated to work well.

(a) The 'human relations' school of management theorists regarded *work relationships* as the main source of satisfaction and reward offered to the worker. The desire to fit in with co-workers and maintain their friendship was thought to act as a powerful motivator.

(b) Later writers suggested a wide range of motivations, including:

 (i) *job satisfaction*, interest and challenge in the job itself - rewarding work;

 (ii) *participation* in decision-making - responsibility and involvement; and

 (iii) the *culture* of the organisation, which itself can offer a range of psychological and physical rewards.

 We will be discussing each of these in section 5 of this chapter.

(c) *Pay* has always occupied a rather ambiguous position, but since people need money to live, it will certainly be *part* of the reward 'package' an individual gets from his work.

(d) Ivan Robertson, *Motivation: Strategies, Theory and Practice* (1992) concludes that there is no universal motivator that can galvanise the whole of a workforce into action:

> *Far from being alike in capacity, some people are intrinsically and perhaps even genetically more motivated than others, and so put greater effort into anything they are called upon to do.* Financial Times, January 1993

1.2 Why is motivation important for HRM?

You may be wondering whether motivation is really so important. It could be argued that if a person is employed to do a job, he will do that job and no question of motivation arises. If the person doesn't want to do the work, he can resign. The point at issue, however, is the *efficiency* with which the job is done. It is suggested that if individuals can be motivated, by one means or another, they will work more efficiently (and productivity will rise) or they will produce a better quality of work. There is some debate as to what the actual effects of improved motivation are, whether efficiency or quality, but it has become widely accepted that motivation is beneficial to the organisation.

Barnard suggested that management needs to understand what motivates employees and act to encourage such motivation; otherwise, many employees will tend to act in a negative way, contrary to the aims of the organisation.

If all those who may be considered potential contributors to an organisation are arranged in order of willingness to serve it, the scale descends from possibly intense willingness through neutral or zero willingness to intense opposition or hatred. The preponderance of persons in a modern society always lies on the negative side with reference to any existing or potential organisation.

Human resource managers need to be aware, however, that motivation is not an exact science - which may leave them open to allegations of naivety (or worse) from line managers. In particular the case for *job satisfaction* as a factor in improved performance is not proven. You should be clear in your own mind that although it seems obviously a Good Thing to have employees who enjoy their work and are interested in it, there is no reason why the organisation should want a satisfied work force unless it makes the organisation function better: it is good for human reasons, but it must be (at least plausibly) relevant to organisational efficiency or effectiveness.

It is another point of debate whether intrinsic satisfaction motivates employees to improved performance, or whether it works more the other way around: the perception of success and achievement from good performance is itself an important source of satisfaction.

We will now look at how motivation works, in theory.

1.3 Motivation theory

One way of grouping the major theories of motivation is by distinguishing between:

(a) *content theories;* and

(b) *process theories*.

Definitions

Content theories assume that human beings have an innate package of 'motives' which they pursue; in other words, that they have a set of needs or desired outcomes and will act in such a way as to fulfil them.

Process theories explore the process through which outcomes become desirable and are pursued by individuals. This approach assumes that people are able to select their goals and choose the paths towards them, by a conscious or unconscious process of calculation.

Maslow's hierarchy of needs theory and Herzberg's two-factor theory are two of the most important content theory approaches. Expectancy theory is the major approach of the process theory. It takes a *contingency approach,* by stressing the number of variables that influence the individual's decision in each case: there is no 'one best way' to motivate people.

Activity 2

What do you think is your main 'motive' for studying for this degree? In other words, what is the main thing you expect to get out of it?

2 NEED THEORIES

Need theories suggest that the desired outcome of behaviour in individuals is the *satisfaction of innate needs*. ('Innate' means 'existing from birth (rather than acquired)'.)

2.1 Human 'needs'

The American psychologist Abraham Maslow argued that man has seven *innate needs*. Maslow's categories are as follows.

- Physiological needs — avoiding cold and hunger, etc
- Safety needs — freedom from threat, but also security, order, predictability
- Love needs — for relationships, affection, sense of belonging
- Esteem needs — for competence, achievement, independence, confidence and their reflection in the perception of others: recognition, appreciation, status, respect
- Self-actualisation needs — for the fulfilment of personal potential: 'the desire to become more and more what one is, to become everything that one is capable of becoming'
- Freedom of inquiry and expression needs — for social conditions permitting free speech, encouraging justice, fairness and honesty
- Knowledge and understanding need — to gain and order knowledge of the environment, to explore, learn, experiment

According to Maslow, the last two needs are the channels through which we find ways of satisfying all the other needs: they are the basis of satisfaction. The first two needs are essential to human survival. Satisfaction of the next two is essential for a sense of adequacy and psychological health. Maslow regarded self-actualisation as the ultimate human goal, although few people ever reach it.

David McClelland, writing in the 1950s, identified three types of motivating needs (in which you will recognise some of Maslow's categories).

(a) *The need for power.* People with a high need for power usually seek positions of leadership in order to influence and control.

(b) *The need for affiliation.* People who need a sense of belonging and membership of a social group tend to be concerned with maintaining good personal relationships.

(c) *The need for achievement.* People who need to achieve have a strong desire for success and a strong fear of failure.

2.2 Maslow's hierarchy of needs theory

In his motivation theory, Maslow put forward certain propositions about the motivating power of needs. (Note that the model was not constructed specifically around people's needs at work, although it can be applied to them as well as general life needs.) He suggested that Man's needs can be arranged in a 'hierarchy of relative pre-potency'. This means that there are 'levels' of need, each of which is dominant until it is satisfied; only then does the next level of need become a motivating factor.

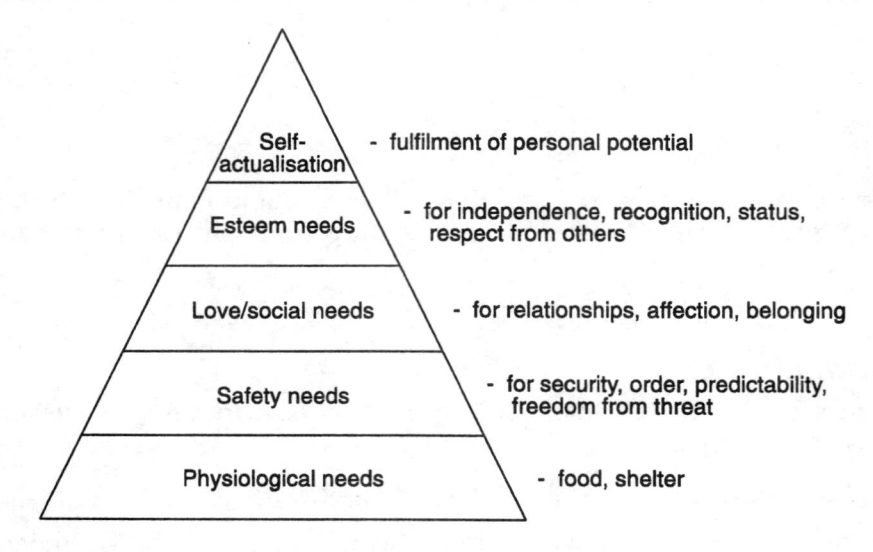

- Self-actualisation — fulfilment of personal potential
- Esteem needs — for independence, recognition, status, respect from others
- Love/social needs — for relationships, affection, belonging
- Safety needs — for security, order, predictability, freedom from threat
- Physiological needs — food, shelter

There is a certain intuitive appeal to Maslow's theory. After all, you are unlikely to be concerned with status or recognition while you are hungry or thirsty - primary survival needs will take precedence. Likewise, once your hunger is assuaged, the need for food is unlikely to be a motivating factor. Unfortunately, research does not bear out the proposition that needs become less powerful as they are satisfied, except at this very primitive level of primary needs (such as hunger and thirst). How much recognition or friendship is 'enough'?

Activity 3

Where are you, at the moment, in the hierarchy of needs? In other words, which category of needs (if any) is uppermost in your mind and in the way you are directing your activities?

2.3 Theory - not fact

The hierarchy of needs is only a theory - *not* an established or empirical fact - and there are various major problems associated with it.

(a) Empirical verification for the hierarchy is hard to come by.

(b) *Maslow may simply have reflected American middle class values and the pursuit of the good life, and may not have hit on fundamental universal truths about human psychology.*
    Buchanan and Huczynski, *Organisational Behaviour*

Several research studies have indicated that cultural patterns affect work behaviour and the success of management techniques: what works in one context may simply not work in another.

(c) It is difficult to predict behaviour using the hierarchy: the theory is too vague. It is impossible to define how much satisfaction has to be achieved before the individual progresses to the next level in the hierarchy. Different people emphasise different needs (and some people are clearly able to suppress even their basic physiological and safety needs for the sake of a perceived 'higher cause', or for the sake of other people). Also, the same need may cause different behaviour in different individuals. (Consider how many ways of achieving self-esteem or fame there are!)

(d) Application of the theory in work contexts presents various difficulties. (Since Maslow did not base his model in the work context, this is not a serious criticism of the model's validity - but does pose problems for managers attempting to derive practical techniques from it.) The role of pay is problematic, since it arguably acts as an instrument of, or 'stands in' for, a wide range of other rewards - status, recognition, independence and so on. Moreover, as Drucker notes, a 'want' changes in the act of being satisfied: 'incentives' such as remuneration, once regularly provided, come to be perceived as 'entitlements', and their capacity to create dissatisfaction, to become a deterrent to performance, outstrips their motivatory power. Self-actualisation, too, is difficult to offer employees in practice, since its nature is so highly subjective.

3 TWO-FACTOR THEORY

In the 1950s, the American psychologist Frederick Herzberg interviewed 203 Pittsburgh engineers and accountants and asked two 'critical incident' questions. The subjects were asked to recall events which had made them feel good about their work, others which made them feel bad about it. Analysis revealed that the factors which created satisfaction were different from those which created dissatisfaction.

In his book *Work and the Nature of Man* Herzberg reported on the factors which commonly cause job dissatisfaction and those which cause job satisfaction.

He saw two basic needs of individuals:

(a) the need to avoid unpleasantness, satisfied (temporarily, and in a rather negative way) by environmental factors; and

(b) the need for personal growth, satisfied at work only by 'motivator factors'.

Herzberg suggests that: 'when people are dissatisfied with their work it is usually because of discontent with the *environmental factors*'. Herzberg calls these *'hygiene' factors* because at best they are essentially preventative rather than motivating. They are designed to prevent or minimise dissatisfaction but do not give satisfaction, in the same way that sanitation minimises threats to health, but does not give good health. They are also called 'maintenance' factors.

These environmental, or hygiene, factors include:

(a) company policy and administration;
(b) salary;
(c) the quality of supervision;
(d) interpersonal relations;
(e) working conditions;
(f) job security.

Satisfaction with environmental factors is not lasting. In time, dissatisfaction will occur. For example, an individual might want a pay rise which protects his income against inflation. If he is successful in obtaining the rise he wants, he will be satisfied for the time being, but only until next year's salary review.

3.1 Motivator factors

Motivator factors, on the other hand, create job satisfaction and are effective in motivating an individual to superior performance and effort. These factors fulfil the individual's need for a sense of self-actualisation or personal growth, and consist of:

(a) status (although this may be a hygiene factor as well as a motivator factor);
(b) advancement;
(c) gaining recognition;
(d) being given responsibility;
(e) challenging work;
(f) achievement; and
(g) growth in the job.

In suggesting means by which motivator satisfactions could be supplied, Herzberg encouraged managers to study the job itself (the type of work done, the nature of tasks, levels of responsibility) rather than conditions of work. 'Dissatisfaction arises from environment factors - satisfaction can only arise from the job.'

If there is sufficient challenge, scope and interest in the job, there will be a lasting increase in satisfaction and the employee will work well; productivity will be above 'normal' levels. The extent to which a job must be challenging or creative in order to provide motivation will depend on each individual, his ability, his expectations and his tolerance for delayed success.

Herzberg specified three typical means whereby jobs can be redesigned to improve motivation.

Definitions

(a) *Job enrichment*, or 'the planned process of up-grading the responsibility, challenge and content of the work'.
(b) *Job enlargement*, the process of increasing the number of operations in which a worker is engaged and so moving away from narrow specialisation of work.
(c) *Job rotation*, or the planned operation of a system whereby staff members exchange positions with the intention of breaking monotony in the work and providing fresh job challenges.

We will discuss these later in this chapter, when we consider job satisfaction as a motivator in more detail.

Activity 4

Note down all the things that:

(a) you regard as basics of any course such as the one you are doing; and
(b) you positively like about studying for this course at this college.

Do the factors you have listed in (a) correspond to Herzberg's 'hygiene' factors: are they things that make studying 'comfortable' but don't really 'switch you on' to extra effort?

Do the factors you have listed in (b) correspond to Herzberg's 'motivator' factors: do they make you want to work harder, for their sake?

4 EXPECTANCY THEORY

The expectancy theory of motivation is a process theory, based on the assumptions that human beings are purposive and rational (in other words, aware of their goals and capable of directing their behaviour towards those goals).

Essentially, the theory states that the strength of an individual's motivation to do something will depend on the extent to which he expects the results of his efforts, if successfully achieved, to contribute towards his personal needs or goals.

In 1964 Victor Vroom, another American psychologist, worked out a formula by which human motivation could actually be assessed and measured, based on expectancy theory.

Vroom suggested that the strength of an individual's motivation is the product of two factors.

(a) The strength of his preference for a certain outcome. Vroom called this *valence*. It may be represented as a positive or negative number, or zero - since outcomes may be desired, avoided or considered with indifference.

(b) His expectation that that outcome will in fact result from a certain behaviour. Vroom called this *subjective probability*: it is only the individual's expectation, and depends on his perception of the link between behaviour and outcome. As a probability, it may be represented by any number between 0 (no chance) and 1 (certainty).

In its simplest form, the expectancy equation therefore runs: $F = V \times E$.

Force or strength of motivation to do x	=	Valence (strength of preference for outcome y)	×	Expectation (that doing x will result in y)

This is what you would expect: if either valence or expectation have a value of zero, there will be no motivation.

(a) An employee may have a high *expectation* that behaviour x (increased productivity) will result in outcome y (promotion) - because of past experience, or a negotiated productivity deal, for example. However, if he is *indifferent* to that outcome (perhaps because he doesn't want the responsibility that promotion will bring), V = 0, and he will not be motivated to more productive behaviour.

(b) If the employee has a great desire for outcome y (promotion) - but doesn't have high *expectations* that behaviour x (increased production) will secure it for him (say, because he has been passed over previously), E = 0, and he will still not be highly motivated.

(c) If V = -1, (because the employee actively fears responsibility and doesn't want to leave his work group), the value for motivation will be negative, and the employee may deliberately *under*-produce.

Expectancy theory attempts to measure the strength of an individual's motivation to act in a particular way. It is then possible to compare 'F' (force of motivation) values for a range of different behaviours, to discover which behaviour the individual is most likely to adopt. It is also possible to compare 'F' values for different individuals, to see who is most highly motivated to behave in the desired (or undesirable) way.

Activity 5

Analyse the force of your motivation to study HRM, in terms of expectancy theory.

5 NON-MONETARY REWARDS

5.1 Job design

Definition

There is no particular mystique about *'job design'*: it is merely the way in which tasks are fragmented or grouped to form a given job, and what decisions are made about specialisation, discretion, autonomy, variety and other job elements.

Early job design

Frederick Taylor was an early exponent of systematic job design. His techniques (called 'scientific management') were based on the 'micro-division' of labour.

(a) Decide on the optimum degree of task fragmentation, breaking down a complex job into its simplest component parts.

(b) Decide on the most efficient way of performing each component.

(c) Train employees to carry out a single task in the 'best' way.

Scientific management was based on a production-line organisation of work, and offered some efficiencies.

(a) Each task was so simple and straightforward that it could be learned with very little training.

(b) Since skills required were low, the effects of absenteeism and labour turnover were minimised: workers could be shifted from one task to another very easily.

(c) Tasks were closely defined, standardised and timed (by work study methods), so output and quality were more easily predicted and controlled.

Problems of task fragmentation

The question of 'job design' acquired its prominence when human relations theorists became interested in the motivational aspects of the job itself, and the role of 'job satisfaction' in employee performance. It was recognised that jobs made up of low-skilled, repetitive tasks (of which there will inevitably be some, in any organisation's operations) could offer little satisfaction to the workers performing them, being socially isolating, meaningless and monotonous.

Studies of human behaviour at work also suggested that the existence of such tasks poses problems for management.

(a) Monotony, and the experience of boredom, is part of what may be called *'industrial fatigue'*. Tasks which provide little mental stimulation for the worker may result in inattention, daydreaming or preoccupation with other things, such as social interactions and diversions. Errors and even accidents may result from this. If the worker has *no* social outlet, however, the strain of monotony is even worse.

(b) Stress is related specifically to high-workload, *low-discretion* jobs. Its symptoms - including nervous tension, withdrawal and low morale - will invariably affect performance.

(c) Motivation may suffer, unless particular efforts are made to compensate the workers for lack of satisfaction in the work itself.

(d) If such tasks are perceived to be the lot of the worker ('us'), under the control of management ('them'), relations between manager and workers may be hampered.

A systematic approach to job design as a source of job satisfaction and its relationship to job design, was first put forward by Frederick Herzberg in the 1950s.

Job design for job satisfaction

Herzberg's theory suggested that the job itself can be a source of satisfaction, offering various ways of meeting the individual's needs for personal growth. A similar prescription was drawn up by other theorists. Concepts such as combining tasks, forming natural work units, establishing client relationships, vertical loading (ie increased delegation, reduced controls) and feedback were said to result in enhancement of work experience in five *core job dimensions*:

(a) skill variety;

(b) task identity;

(c) task significance;

(d) autonomy;

(e) feedback.

The experience of these dimensions was said to meet employee growth needs and lead to high motivation and satisfaction, high quality performance and low absenteeism/turnover rates.

Interest therefore came to be focused on 'job enrichment' as a job design technique.

Definition

Job enrichment is planned, deliberate action to build greater responsibility, breadth and challenge of work into a job.

Job enrichment is thus a 'vertical' extension of the job design, which might include:

(a) removing controls;

(b) increasing accountability;

(c) creating natural work units;

(d) providing direct feedback;

(e) introducing new tasks; or

(f) allocating special assignments.

It would be wrong, however, to suppose that job enrichment alone will automatically make employees more productive.

> *Even those who want their jobs enriched will expect to be rewarded with more than job satisfaction. Job enrichment is not a cheaper way to greater productivity. Its pay-off will come in the less visible costs of morale, climate and working relationships.*
>
> Handy

Job enrichment was popular throughout the 1970s and contributed significantly to the 'quality of working life movement', and the high-profile work organisation experiments (now defunct) of companies such as Volvo, Saab-Scania and Atlas Copco, the introduction of autonomous working groups and so on.

Definition

Job enlargement is frequently confused with job enrichment, though it should be clearly defined as a separate technique. Job enlargement, as the name suggests, is the attempt to widen jobs by increasing the number of operations in which a job holder is involved. This has the effect of lengthening the time cycle of repeated operations. By reducing the number of repetitions of the same work, the dullness of the job should also be reduced. Job enlargement is therefore a 'horizontal' extension of an individual's work.

Arguably, job enlargement is limited in its ability to improve motivation since, as

Herzberg points out, to ask a worker to complete three separate tedious, unchallenging tasks is unlikely to motivate him more than asking him to fulfil one single tedious, unchallenging task.

5.2 Empowerment

It might have been expected that the world economic recession of the 1980s and 1990s would divert management theorists' attention away from such issues. (As Buchanan and Huczynski note: 'The quality of working life is less important when there is little work to be had.')

Nevertheless, the theories offered managers ideas about what their subordinates look for and get out of their work, and what variables can be manipulated to give them greater challenge and satisfaction in their work. Relatively simple managerial changes, for example giving more direct feedback on performance, or reducing the number of formal controls on employee behaviour, can affect the employee's experience of the core job dimensions (listed above).

In addition, recessionary pressures have encouraged processes such as delayering (cutting out levels of mainly middle-management) and downsizing, leading to 'flatter hierarchies', with more delegation and more decentralisation of authority. All this involves shifting responsibility to employees further 'down' the management hierarchy, a process recently given the broad name of *empowerment*.

'Empowerment' has been variously defined: like HRM, it means different things to different people. For example, an article in *Personnel Management* in November 1993 included definitions from a number of leading figures and personnel practitioners.

(a) 'What (companies) mean by empowerment varies dramatically ... many of them are really talking about firing middle management. But companies which are really serious are talking about the orderly distribution of power and authority.'

(b) 'To me it means people using their own judgement in the interests of the organisation and the customer within a disciplined context.'

(c) 'The purpose of empowerment is to free someone from rigorous control by instructions and orders and giving them freedom to take responsibility for their ideas and actions, to release hidden resources which would otherwise remain inaccessible.'

The argument, in a nutshell, is that by empowering workers (or 'decentralising' control of business units, or devolving/delegating responsibility, or removing levels in hierarchies that restrict freedom), not only will the job be done more effectively but the people who do the job will get more out of it.

This thinking is very much in line with that of the neo-human relations theorists such as Maslow, Herzberg and McGregor who believed that organisational effectiveness is determined by the extent to which people's 'higher' psychological needs for growth, challenge, responsibility and self-fulfilment are met by the work that they do.

Chapter 8: Motivation

> **EXAMPLE: HARVESTER RESTAURANTS**
>
> The validity of this view and its relevance to modern trends appears to be borne out by the approach to empowerment adopted by Harvester restaurants, as described in *Personnel Management*. The management structure comprises a branch manager and a 'coach', while everyone else is a team member. Everyone within a team has one or more 'accountabilities' (these include recruitment, drawing up rotas, keeping track of sales targets and so on) which are shared out by the team members at their weekly team meetings. All the team members at different times act as 'co-ordinator' - the person responsible for taking the snap decisions that are frequently necessary in a busy restaurant. Apparently all of the staff involved agree that empowerment has made their jobs more interesting and has hugely increased their motivation and sense of involvement.

Activity 6

How, other than by *asking* employees (through feedback, interviews or attitude surveys), might an organisation assess whether its employees were satisfied or not?

5.3 Participation and democratic leadership

Related to job satisfaction and empowerment is the theory that if a superior invites his subordinates to participate in planning decisions which affect their work, if the subordinates voluntarily accept the invitation, and if results about actual performance are fed back regularly to the subordinates so that they can make their own control decisions, then the subordinate will be motivated:

(a) to be more efficient;

(b) to be more conscious of the organisation's goals;

(c) to raise his planning targets to reasonably challenging levels;

(d) to be ready to take appropriate control actions when necessary.

What exactly does participation involve and why might it be a good thing? Handy commented that:

> *Participation is sometimes regarded as a form of job enlargement. At other times it is a way of gaining commitment by workers to some proposal on the grounds that if you have been involved in discussing it, you will be more interested in its success. In part, it is the outcome of almost cultural belief in the norms of democratic leadership. It is one of those 'good' words with which it is hard to disagree.*

The advantages of participation should perhaps be considered from the opposite end: what would be the disadvantages of *not* having participation? Then, employees would be told what to do, and would presumably comply with orders. However, their compliance might not be enthusiastic, and they might not be psychologically committed to their work.

Participation can involve employees and make them committed to their task, but only if:

(a) it is genuine. It is very easy for a boss to pretend to invite participation from his subordinates but end up issuing orders. If subordinates feel the decision has already been taken, they might resent the falsehood of management efforts to discuss the decision with them;

(b) the efforts to establish participation are continual and pushed over a long period of time and with a lot of energy. However, 'if the issue or the task is trivial, or foreclosed, and everyone realises it, participative methods will boomerang. Issues that do not affect the individuals concerned will not, on the whole, engage their interest' *(Handy)*;

(c) the purpose of the participation of employees in a decision is made quite clear from the outset. If employees are consulted to make a decision, their views should carry the decision. If, however, they are consulted for advice, their views need not necessarily be accepted;

(d) the individuals really have the abilities and the information to join in decision-making effectively; and

(e) the manager wishes for participation from his subordinates, and does not suggest it because he thinks it is the Done Thing.

> *It is simply naive to think that participative approaches are always more effective than authoritarian styles of management or vice versa. The critics as well as the advocates of participative management would therefore be wise to direct their energies towards identifying the situations in which a variety of decision-making styles are effective, rather than towards universalistic claims for the applicability or otherwise of any single approach.*
> Hopwood

5.4 Quality as a motivator

Quality circles seem to have emerged first in the United States, but it was in Japan that they were adopted most enthusiastically. The modern success story of Japanese industry has prompted Western countries to imitate many of the Japanese working methods, with the result that quality circles are now re-appearing in American and West European companies.

Definition

A *quality circle* consists of a voluntary group of employees, perhaps about eight in number, which meets regularly to discuss problems of quality and quality control in their area of work, and perhaps to suggest ways of improving quality. The quality circle has a leader or supervisor who directs discussions and possibly also helps to train other members of the circle.

Ideally, quality circles should be given more responsibility than merely suggesting or even championing improvements: commitment may be increased if the members of quality circles also have responsibility for implementing their recommendations. In practice, quality circles may become 'talk shops' for problem-solving, inter-disciplinary communication and suggestion/idea generation. Even so, their value should not be underestimated, particularly since they represent a genuine attempt to encourage an impetus towards quality at the lower levels of the organisation hierarchy: most initiatives aimed at improving quality - and quality awareness among staff - are activated and driven from above, by management. A bottom-up approach such as quality circles may encourage greater ownership by staff of quality values.

Benefits claimed to arise from the use of quality circles include:

(a) greater motivation and involvement of employees;

(b) improved productivity and quality of output;

(c) greater awareness of problems by operational staff; and

(d) greater awareness of quality and service issues, market and individual customer needs etc.

5.5 Culture as a motivator

Definition

'*Culture*' is the shared value system of an organisation: its customs, unwritten rules, special vocabulary, mottoes and legends; its 'style'; the things it believes in, as a body; in short, 'the way we do things round here'.

Peters and Waterman (*In Search of Excellence*) argue that employees can be 'switched on' to extraordinary loyalty and effort by the culture of the organisation, in the following circumstances.

(a) *The cause is perceived to be in some sense great.* Peters and Waterman call this 'reaffirming the heroic dimension' of work. Commitment comes from believing that a task is inherently worthwhile: devotion to quality values, and to the *customer*, and his needs and wants, is an important motivator in this way. 'Owing to good luck, or maybe even good sense, those companies that emphasise quality, reliability, and service have chosen the *only* area where it is readily possible to generate excitement in the average down-the-line employee. They give people pride in what they do. They make it possible to love the product.' Shared values and good news swapping - a kind of folklore of past success and heroic endeavour - create a culture or 'climate' where intrinsic motivation is a driving force.

(b) *They are treated as winners.* 'Label a man a loser and he'll start acting like one.' Repressive control systems and negative reinforcement break down the employee's self-image. Positive reinforcement, good news swapping, attention from management and so on, enhance the employee's self-image and create positive attitudes to work and to the organisation.

(c) *They can satisfy their dual needs* to:
   (i) be a conforming, secure part of a team; and
   (ii) be a 'star' in their own right.

Activity 7

Take the example of a branch of McDonald's. How strong a 'culture' does the company create? What visible or audible signs are there of this culture?

5.6 Non-cash incentive schemes

Incentive and recognition schemes are increasingly focused not on cash, but on non-cash awards. According to a feature in *Personnel Management,* September 1992: 'Traditionally aimed at sales people, gifts and travel incentives have been spreading slowly to other areas and are now used to add interest to quality schemes and encourage money saving ideas ... to enable managers to show gratitude to staff for such things as continuous improvement and teamwork ... to lift morale'.

(a) British Telecom - in the wake of large scale voluntary redundancies - launched an up-beat 'Living our values' initiative, including the awarding of gifts to employees exemplifying the organisation's values and being role models to others.

(b) British Aerospace has preserved its quality awards, despite job losses. Teams receive gold pens, watches, ties or scarves for a PSB (Problem Solution Benefit).

(c) ICL used to offer symbolic awards of bronze, silver and gold medals, but has now replaced these with a gift catalogue (called the 'Excellence Collection') from which nominees choose rewards they value: 'Change is essential if recognition schemes are going to succeed ... This is one of the problems with this kind of programme. If you don't update it from time to time, it just gets tired.' (*Personnel Management*, September 1992).

(d) Abbey Life's top performers are given the opportunity to attend conventions in exotic foreign locations, with partners (and without an onerous work content): length of stay and luxury of location depend on performance.

(e) Trusthouse Forte 'has launched a drive to cut employee turnover through an incentive scheme which awards air mileage in return for staff loyalty ... In addition to the basic retention programme, THF is also offering further incentives to staff, including 500 miles for the employee of the month and 1,000 for employee of the year, with another 200 miles for staff receiving a complimentary letter from a guest.' (*Personnel Management*, February 1991)

More recently, *People Management* (September 1995) cited other organisational examples, which included:

(a) Taylor Walker has introduced a points-based incentive scheme for all its staff. Points are awarded for sales, customer care, progress in training and for general 'above and beyond' performance. Points can be exchanged for items from a catalogue of gifts.

(b) Midland Bank offers travel vouchers, at the discretion of the branch manager, for a variety of things, including referrals, balancing and exceptional effort, in order to recognise achievement within the branch.

Such schemes can be regarded by some staff as manipulative, irrelevant ('awards are being made for things that are part of normal duties: no special effort required') or just plain gimmicky. (The general secretary of the staff union at Sun Alliance has been quoted as saying: 'I have worked for a firm which rewarded its top salespeople with a cruise. I can't imagine anything worse than being trapped on a yacht with a lot of other life assurance salesmen'!) However, it is generally considered that such schemes can be effective as incentives, team-building exercises, and, perhaps more fundamentally, ways of expressing recognition of achievement - without which staff may feel isolated, undervalued or neglected.

6 PAY AS A MOTIVATOR

Pay has a central - but ambiguous - role in motivation theory. It is not mentioned explicitly in any need list, but it may be the means to an infinite number of specific ends, offering the satisfaction of many of the various needs. Individuals may also have needs unrelated to money, however, which money cannot satisfy, or which the pay system of the organisation actively denies. So to what extent is pay an inducement to better performance: a motivator or incentive?

6.1 What do people want from pay?

Employees need income to live. The size of their income will affect their standard of living. However, people tend not to be concerned to *maximise* their earnings. They may like to earn more, but are probably more concerned:

(a) to earn *enough* pay; and

(b) to know that their pay is *fair* in comparison with the pay of others both inside and outside the organisation.

Equity (perceived fairness of pay in relation to the job and to the pay of others) is often more important than maximising income, once the individual has enough pay to maintain a satisfactory lifestyle. Yet Edgar Schein's 'Economic Man' model - which assumes that people will adjust their effort if offered money - is still the basis of payment-by-results schemes, bonuses, profit-sharing and other monetary incentives.

Payment systems then have to tread the awkward path between *equity* (a fair and objectively-derived rate for the job, preserved differentials and so on) and *incentive* (an offered reward to stimulate extra effort and attainment by particular individuals and groups).

6.2 Pay as a hygiene factor

Pay is one of Herzberg's hygiene rather than motivator factors. It gets taken for granted, and so is more usually a source of dissatisfaction than satisfaction. (Lawler suggested that in the absence of information about how much colleagues are earning, individuals guess their earnings and usually over-estimate. This then leaves them dissatisfied because they resent earning less than they *think* their colleagues are getting!)

However, pay is the most important of the hygiene factors, according to Herzberg. It is valuable not only in its power to be converted into a wide range of other satisfactions (perhaps the only way in which organisations can - at least indirectly - cater for individual employee's needs and wants through a common reward system) but also as a consistent measure of worth or value, allowing employees to compare themselves and be compared with other individuals or occupational groups inside and outside the organisation.

The Affluent Worker research of Goldthorpe, Lockwood et al (1968) illustrated an *instrumental* orientation to work (the attitude that work is not an end in itself, but a means to other ends). The highly-paid Luton car assembly workers experienced their work as routine and dead-end. The researchers concluded that they had made a rational decision to enter employment offering high monetary reward *rather* than intrinsic interest: they were getting out of their jobs what they most wanted from them.

The Luton researchers did not claim that all workers have an instrumental orientation to work, however, but suggested that a person will seek a suitable balance of:

(a) the rewards which are important to him; and

(b) the deprivations he feels able to put up with.

Even those with an instrumental orientation to work have limits to their purely financial aspirations, and will cease to be motivated by money if the deprivations - in terms of long working hours, poor conditions, social isolation or whatever - become too great. In other words, if the 'price' of pay is too high.

High taxation rates may also weight the deprivation side of the calculation; workers may perceive that a great deal of extra effort will in fact earn them little extra reward.

6.3 Pay from the organisation's point of view

We should also consider pay from the organisation's point of view. Wages and salaries are:

(a) a cost, which appears in the cost of the product or service to the market;

(b) an investment: money spent on one resource or factor of production (labour) in the hope of a return; and also

(c) a potentially crucial environmental variable, as an incentive and motivator, a source of job satisfaction or dissatisfaction, political power or conflict.

The objectives of pay from the organisation's point of view are:

(a) to attract and retain labour of a suitable type and quality from the labour market;

(b) to fulfil perceived (or enforced) social responsibilities with regard to 'reasonable' remuneration for services; and

(c) to motivate employees to achieve and maintain desired levels of performance.

Activity 8

How do you feel personally about pay as a motivator? Where would you draw the line between extra money and the hardships required to earn it?

6.4 Cash incentives: do they work?

Organisations are obliged to *reward* or *remunerate* employees for the amount and standard of work agreed in the contract of employment: to give a fair day's pay for a fair day's work. In addition, the organisation may wish to offer monetary *incentives* (or 'carrots') to employees, if they will work longer or more productively. We will discuss various monetary incentives (like performance-related pay, or profit-sharing) in Chapter 9, but following our discussion of pay as a motivator, you should be aware of a number of difficulties associated with incentive schemes based on monetary reward.

(a) Increased earnings simply may not be an incentive to some individuals. An individual who already enjoys a good income may be more concerned with increasing his leisure time, for example.

(b) Workers are unlikely to be in complete control of results. External factors, such as the general economic climate, interest rates and exchange rates may play a part in *profitability* in particular. In these cases, the relationship between an individual's efforts and reward may be indistinct, and so not part of the 'expectancy' calculation.

(c) Both teamworking and specialisation may mean that particular employees cannot be specifically credited with the success of their particular products. This may lead to frustration amongst employees who think their own results are being adversely affected by inefficiencies elsewhere in the team or organisation.

(d) Even if employees *are* motivated by money, the effects may not be altogether desirable. An instrumental orientation may encourage self-interested performance at the expense of teamwork: it may encourage attention to output at the expense of quality, and the lowering of standards and targets (in order to make bonuses more accessible).

Research also indicates that workers suspect that if they achieve high levels of output and earnings, they will make it look too easy (and costly) and that management will set higher performance targets to reduce future earnings. Work groups therefore tend to restrict output to a level that they feel is 'fair', but 'safe'.

Chapter roundup

- Motivation is a term used in different contexts to refer to:
  - goals or outcomes that have become desirable for a particular individual, as in: 'he is motivated by money';
  - the mental process of choosing a goal and deciding whether and how to achieve it, as in: 'he is motivated to work harder';
  - the social process by which the behaviour of an individual is influenced by others, as in: 'the manager motivates his team'.
- *Content* theories suggest that man has a package of needs: the best way to motivate an employee is to find out what his needs are and offer him rewards that will satisfy those needs.
  - Abraham Maslow identified seven innate needs of all individuals and arranged them in a hierarchy, suggesting that an individual will be motivated to satisfy each category, starting at the bottom before going on to seek higher order satisfactions.
  - Frederick Herzberg identified two basic need systems: the need to avoid unpleasantness and the need for personal growth. He suggested factors which could be offered by organisations to satisfy both types of need: 'hygiene' and 'motivator' factors respectively.
- Process theories do not tell managers what to offer employees in order to motivate them, but help managers to understand the dynamics of employees' decisions about what rewards are worth going for. They are generally variations on the *expectancy* model: $F = V \times E$.
- Various means have been suggested of improving job satisfaction but there is little evidence that a satisfied worker actually works harder. Likewise, participation in decisions, involvement in product quality or enthusing employees about the corporate culture may or may not have an impact.
- Pay is the most important of the 'hygiene' factors, but it is ambiguous in its effect on motivation.

Quick quiz

1. What are the seven needs identified by Maslow? Incorporate the relevant needs in a simple diagram of the hierarchy.
2. List five motivator and five hygiene factors.
3. Explain the formula '$F = V \times E$'.
4. Distinguish between job enrichment and job enlargement.
5. What is 'empowerment'?
6. Are people better motivated if they are allowed to participate in decisions?
7. What is organisation 'culture'?
8. 'People will work harder and harder to earn more and more pay.' Do you agree? Why (or why not)?
9. Give four features of a well-designed incentive scheme.

Solutions to activities

1. Excitement, expenditure, efficiency, effectiveness, endeavour, excellence, empathy - and so on!

6. (a) There is little evidence that a satisfied worker actually works harder - so increased productivity per se will not imply satisfaction on the part of the work force. They may be motivated by fear, or work methods may have been improved.-

   (b) There is, however, support for the idea that satisfied workers tend to be loyal, and stay in the organisation.

       (i) *Labour turnover* (the rate at which people leave an organisation) may therefore be an indication of dissatisfaction in the workforce - although there is a certain amount of natural wastage.

       (ii) *Absenteeism* may also be an indication of dissatisfaction, or possibly of genuine physical or emotional distress.

   (c) There is also evidence that satisfaction correlates with mental health - so that symptoms of stress or psychological failure may be a signal to management that all is not well.

7. McDonalds has a notoriously strong (Americanised) culture, which 'travels' all over the world. Signs include name badges, uniforms (especially the hats), special names for products (Mc-everything...), slogans ('There's nothing quite like a McDonalds') and so on.

Further question practice

Now try the following practice questions at the end of this text.

Muliple choice questions	49 to 55
Exam style questions	8

Chapter 9

PAY AND BENEFITS

Introduction

In the previous chapter, we introduced pay (financial reward) and its role as a motivator. We noticed that there is a dilemma for management in the dual requirements in reward systems for:

(a) *equity* - pay rates for the job that are fair in relation to others, that accurately reflect the relative worth of the job; and

(b) *incentive* - the need to be able to offer extra reward for extraordinary effort and attainment: 'dangling the carrot'.

In this chapter we discuss how reward systems can be designed to fulfil either or both of these requirements.

'Benefits' consist of items or awards which are, traditionally, supplementary to normal pay. Some - such as pensions and sick pay - are entitlements under the law, so the common term 'fringe benefits' is misleading. But there are also 'perks', such as staff discounts or medical insurance, which are at the discretion of the organisation, as part of its recruitment, retention or incentive structures.

Your objectives

After completing this chapter, you should:

(a) understand the purposes and methods of job evaluation;

(b) appreciate other influences on pay levels;

(c) be aware of a range of salary and wage systems;

(d) be able to suggest and evaluate a number of monetary incentive schemes;

(e) be aware of a range of statutory and discretionary benefits available to employees;

(f) be aware of the legal framework on pay and benefits.

1 JOB EVALUATION

Definition

Job evaluation is a systematic method of arriving at a wage or salary structure, so that the rate of pay for a job is felt to be *fair* in comparison with other jobs in the organisation.

Any job for which a wage or salary is offered has been evaluated in some way or other in order to arrive at the amount of payment to be made. To this extent it might be said that all organisations which pay employees have job evaluation. However, the term 'job evaluation' is mostly used nowadays with greater precision to describe a formal standardised method for ranking jobs and grouping them into grades. Invariably, such systems are used primarily as the basis for a payment structure ... .

Institute of Administrative Management, **1976**

The British Institute of Management (*Job Evaluation*) gives the following definition. 'Job evaluation is the process of analysing and assessing the content of jobs, in order to place them in an acceptable rank order which can then be used as a basis for a remuneration system.'

The advantages of a job-evaluated salary structure are as follows.

(a) The salary structure is based on a formal study of work content, and the reasons for salary differentials between jobs has a rational basis that can be explained to anyone who objects to his salary level or grading in comparison with others.

(b) The salary structure should be well balanced, even in an organisation that employs people with a wide range of different technical skills (such as engineers, accountants and salesmen).

(c) The salary structure is based on job content, and not on the personal merit of the jobholder himself. The individual jobholder can be paid personal bonuses in reward for his efforts, and when he moves to another job in the organisation, his replacement on the job will be paid the rate for the job, and will not inherit any personal bonuses of his predecessor.

(d) Regular job evaluation should ensure that the salary structure reflects current changes in the work content of jobs, and is not outdated, so that pay differentials remain fair.

(e) A job-evaluated salary structure might protect an employer from the accusation that rates of pay discriminate between different types of worker - notably between men and women, who by law (The Equal Pay Act 1970) should be paid the same rate for 'like work', 'work rated as equivalent' or 'work of equal value'.

(f) Analysis of job content and worth are available for use in recruitment, selection, training and other human resource contexts.

Job-evaluated salary structures do have some flaws, however.

(a) They pay a fair rate for a job only in the sense that differentials are set according to *relative* worth. Job evaluation does not make any recommendations about what the general level of pay ought to be, in monetary terms. Indeed it cannot do so without reference to outside factors such as rates fixed by collective bargaining, statutory obligation or local custom. (Such factors are discussed in Section 2 of this chapter.)

(b) Many job evaluation methods suggest that job evaluation is a scientific and accurate technique, whereas in fact there is a large element of subjective judgement involved in awarding points or ratings, and evaluations can be unfair.

(c) Job evaluated salary structures can get out-of-date. There ought to be periodic reviews, but in practice, an organisation might fail to review jobs often enough.

Activity 1

Based on what you have learned about motivation, what other problems might be caused by job evaluation, from a human point of view?

1.1 Methods of job evaluation

In large organisations, it is impossible to evaluate every individual job, because the process would be too long and costly. Instead, selected key jobs are evaluated, and provide a benchmark for the evaluation of other similar jobs. Ideally, the key jobs chosen for analysis should be jobs comparable with those in other organisations, for which a market rate of pay is known. Some information for evaluation may already be available in the form of job descriptions.

It may be said that, even in its more quantitative or analytical forms, job evaluation is 'systematic' rather than 'scientific'. The number of different inputs and environmental variables make an element of subjectivity inevitable, despite refinements aimed at minimising it.

Non-analytical approaches to job evaluation make largely subjective judgements about the whole job, its difficulty, and its importance to the organisation relative to other jobs. (Ranking is a method of this type.)

Analytical methods of job evaluation identify the component factors or characteristics involved in the performance of each job, such as skill, responsibility, experience, mental and physical efforts required. Each component is separately analysed, evaluated and weighted: degrees of each factor, and the importance of the factor within the job, are quantified. (Examples of such methods include points rating and factor comparison.) These methods involve detailed analysis and a numerical basis for comparing jobs as like to like.

Activity 2

Why might there still be an element of subjectivity in this analysis?

It is undoubtedly desirable to achieve objectivity, to reduce the resentment commonly felt at the apparent arbitrariness of pay decisions. If job evaluation were truly objective, it would be possible to justify differentials on a rational basis, the organisation would have a balanced and economical pay structure based on contribution, and employers would be safe from accusations of unfair pay decisions.

Despite the element of subjectivity even in the more analytical methods of job evaluation, it may be true to say that any form of job evaluation is useful, minimising the (real or perceived) arbitrariness of pay decisions, and removing personality or discriminatory issues from pay reviews.

According to a survey of more than 300 organisations, which was conducted by the Institute of Personnel and Development in 1994, job evaluation is alive and well, despite its criticisms (*People Management*, September 1995). The survey found more than half of the responding organisations operated formal job evaluation and, of those that did not, half intended to introduce it. Two thirds expressed reasonable satisfaction with their job evaluation scheme, although 43% intended to make some changes in the future.

We shall describe five methods of job evaluation.

(a) Ranking
(b) Classification
(c) Factor comparison
(d) Points rating
(e) The HAY-MSL method.

Ranking method

In a ranking system of job evaluation, each job is considered as a whole (rather than in terms of job elements) and ranked in accordance with its relative importance or contribution to the organisation. Having established a list of jobs in descending order of importance, they can be divided into groups, and jobs in each group given the same grade and salary.

The advantage of the ranking method is that it is simple and unscientific. In a small organisation, it might be applied with fairness.

However, the job evaluators need to have a good personal knowledge of every job being evaluated, and in a large organisation they are unlikely to have it. Without this knowledge, the ranking method would not produce fair evaluations. This is why more complex methods of job evaluation have been devised.

Classification method

This is similar to the ranking method, except that instead of ranking jobs in order of importance and then dividing them into grades, the classification method begins with deciding what grades there ought to be (say, grades A, B, C, D and E, with each grade carefully defined) and then deciding into which grade each individual job should be classified: is the job a grade C or a grade D job?

The advantages and disadvantages of this method are the same as those of ranking.

Factor comparison method

This is an analytical method of job evaluation. It begins with the selection of a number of qualitative factors on which each job will be evaluated. These qualitative factors might include, for example, technical knowledge, physical skill, mental skill, responsibility for other people, responsibility for assets or working conditions.

Key benchmark jobs are then taken, for which the rate of pay is considered to be fair (perhaps in comparison with similar jobs in other organisations). Each key job is analysed in turn, factor by factor, to decide how much of the total salary is being paid for each factor. So if technical skill is 50% of a benchmark job paying £10,000, the factor pay rate for technical skill (within that job) is £5,000. When this has been done for every benchmark job, all the different rates of pay for each factor are correlated, to formulate a ranking and pay scale for that factor.

Other (non-benchmark) jobs are then evaluated by analysing them factor by factor. In this way a salary or grading for the job can be built up. For example, analysis of a clerk's job factor by factor might be:

Factor	Proportion of job		Pay rate for factor (as established by analysis of benchmark jobs)	Job value £
Technical skills	50%	×	£12,000 pa	6,000
Mental ability	25%	×	£16,000 pa	4,000
Responsibility for others	15%	×	£10,000 pa	1,500
Other responsibilities	10%	×	£5,000 pa	500
				12,000

The Institute of Administrative Management comments about the factor comparison method that: 'the system links rates closely to existing levels for key benchmark jobs and depends heavily on careful allocation of money values to each factor of the benchmark jobs. It is not easy to explain to employees, and is best suited to situations where the range of jobs is limited and of a fairly simple nature.' It is not well-suited to the evaluation of office jobs.

Points rating method

Points rating is probably the most popular method of formal job evaluation. It begins with listing a number of factors which are thought to represent the qualities being looked for in the jobs to be evaluated. (Remember that jobs are being evaluated, not jobholders themselves, and the qualities listed should relate to the jobs themselves.) In a typical evaluation scheme, there might be from 8-12 factors listed. The factors will vary according to the type of organisation, but they might include:

(a) skill - education, experience, dexterity, qualifications;

(b) initiative;

(c) physical or mental effort;

(d) dealing with others;

(e) responsibility for subordinates, or the safety and welfare of others;

(f) responsibility for equipment, for a process or product, for materials;

(g) job conditions - such as monotony of working, working in isolation, unavoidable work hazards.

A number of points is allocated to each factor, as a maximum score. In this way, each factor is given a different weighting according to how important it is thought to be. Each job is then examined, analysed factor by factor, and a points score awarded for each factor, up to the maximum allowed. The total points score for each job is found by adding up its points score for each factor. The total points scored for each job provides the basis for ranking the jobs in order of importance, for grading jobs, if required, and for fixing a salary structure.

Points rating has the advantage of flexibility in that the factors selected are best suited for the particular types of job being evaluated, and the importance given to each factor is decided by the allocation of points. It also provides a rank order of jobs according to the numbers of points, without determining the money value of the job. This allows the pattern of grades and salary rates to be determined as separate operations. Like all systems, it has some disadvantages; the selection of factors, the points score allocated to a job, and the points weighting given each factor remain subjective judgements.

The Institute of Administrative Management

The HAY-MSL method

The HAY-MSL method of job evaluation is a points method, whereby points are awarded for significant elements of a job and the importance of individual jobs relative to others is measured by comparing their total points scores. The job elements by which jobs are compared are, in effect:

(a) *know-how*: the amount of skill, knowledge and experience needed to do the job, including the ability to handle people;

(b) *problem solving*: this is concerned with the amount of discretion and judgement the jobholder must exercise, the frequency of problems that call for decisions to be made by the jobholder and the extent to which the jobholder is expected to contribute new ideas;

(c) *accountability*: this is the assessment of whether the jobholder is responsible and accountable for small or large areas of work, and whether the activities of the jobholder affect the organisation to a larger or smaller extent in terms of money (revenues and expenditures).

The HAY-MSL system lends itself better to higher levels of management than to lower-ranking jobs. For example, in the case of a financial controller, technical know-how, the ability to solve finance-related problems, and stewardship over the company's money place him high on the HAY-MSL scheme.

Activity 3

Draw up a table showing the characteristics, advantages and disadvantages of each of the methods of job evaluation discussed above (leaving aside HAY-MSL).

2 OTHER FACTORS IN SETTING REMUNERATION LEVELS

We have discussed the role of job evaluation in determining the relative value of jobs, but there are other factors not related to job *content* which affect the rates an organisation will actually want to pay.

2.1 Equity

Wilfred Brown defined equity as

> *the level of earnings for people in different occupations which is felt by society to be reasonably consistent with the importance of the work which is done, and which seems relatively fair to the individual.*

In other words, pay must be *perceived* and felt to match the level of work, and the capacity of the individual to do it: it must be 'felt fair'. Pay structures should allow individuals to feel that they are being rewarded in keeping with their skill, effort and contribution, and with the rewards received by others for their relative contributions.

2.2 Negotiated pay scales

Pay scales, differentials and minimum rates may have been negotiated at plant, local or national level, according to various environmental factors:

(a) legislation and government policy (on equal pay, for example, or increases in line with inflation);

(b) the economy (levels of inflation; unemployment, affecting labour supply and demand, and therefore market rates); and

(c) the strength of the employers and unions/staff associations in negotiation.

2.3 Individual performance in the job

> *A growing number of organisations, commentators and academics assert that paying for individual skills, contribution and competence is more relevant to the needs of today than traditional job-based evaluation ... Placing the heaviest emphasis on job requirements discounts the importance of other compensatable factors - particularly individual capability and performance.*
> Murlis and Fitt, *Personnel Management*, May 1991

Individuals in organisations are paid for three things.

(a) *Input factors:* what the individual brings to work, such as the specific attributes of the individual's competence like intelligence, personality, qualifications, experience and expertise. Payment for skill and competence is widespread within the education system in some professional contexts.

(b) *Process factors:* elements of the person which are thought to be required for the job to be performed, like effort, skills, decision-making ability, commitment, enthusiasm and judgement. Payment for process factors is at the root of reward-related appraisal procedures which incorporate rating scales of some kind.

(c) *Output factors:* such as the achievement of targets, profits, production levels, quality and productivity. Payment for output is well established in certain fields (like sales management) but is more questionable in others where the link between the individual's performance and the achievement of the organisation is more tenuous.

2.4 Market rates

Thomason suggests that if an employer were free to pay what he liked, he would pay

> *the lowest rate consistent with securing enough labour in quantity to satisfy his production needs and ... to ensure ... a sufficient contribution to the enterprise's tasks to allow it to survive.*

This is the *market rate* for the given type of labour. It will vary with supply/demand factors, such as:

(a) the relative scarcity of particular skills; and

(b) the extent of labour mobility in response to pay levels or differentials, which may dictate the need for higher rates of pay to retain employees, or to attract them from other organisations. Pay may or may not act as an incentive to change employers, depending on the availability of work elsewhere, the employee's loyalty, willingness to face risk and change, and the attractions of his present job which may not be measurable in financial terms: work relationships, conditions and so on.

Factors which distort or dilute the effect of the forces of supply and demand on labour pricing include the following.

(a) The organisation's ability to pay may necessitate lower than market rates, in lean times.

(b) The bargaining strength of unions may weaken or strengthen the position of a group of employees in negotiation with their employers.

(c) Government action, including incomes policies, equal pay legislation and anti-inflationary measures may restrict or secure pay rates. The minimum wage, in particular, traditionally prevented outright exploitation of labour, even if employers wished to pursue it.

(d) Internal differentials and job evaluated salary structures make it difficult for employers to justify a conspicuously low rate of pay for one type of job, or in response to market fluctuations.

(e) The culture and value systems of the organisation will influence the attitude of management towards the market rate, and whether age, length of service, motivation, employee aspirations and/or other factors are taken into account in the determination of pay, rather than fluctuations in supply and demand.

Business Basics: Human Resource Management

Job evaluation form

Key job code _____   Department _____
Job type _____   Job holder studied _____
Date _____   Employee number _____

Task number

Description

Factor	Rating			Comments
	Points	Weighting	Total	

Skills and knowledge
    Education/qualifications
    Experience
    Dexterity				

Skills sub-total				
Initiative				

Responsibility
    People
    Equipment
    Resources				

Responsibility sub-total				

Effort
    Mental
    Physical				

Effort sub-total				

Communication
    Oral
    Written				

Communication sub-total				
Interpersonal skills				

Conditions of work
    Hazards
    Isolation
    Monotony				

Conditions sub-total				
TOTAL				
RANKING				
COMMENTS				

2.5 Why should an organisation pay more than the market rate?

Activity 4

Before you read on, consider the question yourself. Why *should* an employer pay any more than he has to, in order to obtain the right number and calibre of staff? (A good point for discussion with your fellow students, perhaps.)

One may list the general arguments for paying *over* market rate as follows.

(a) The offer of a notably higher remuneration package than market rate may be assumed to generate greater interest in the labour market. The organisation will therefore have a wider field of selection for the given labour category, and will be more likely to have access to the most skilled/experienced individuals. If the organisation establishes a reputation as a 'wage leader' it may generate a consistent supply of high-calibre labour.

(b) There may be benefits of high pay offers for employee loyalty, and better performance resulting from the (theoretically) higher calibre and motivation of the workforce.

(c) Even if a cheap supply of labour were available, and the employer could get away with paying a low rate, the ideology or ethical code of an organisation may make him reluctant to do so. A socially responsible employer may wish to avoid the exploitation of labour groups, such as immigrants, who may not be aware of general market rates.

(d) An employer might adopt a socially responsible position not purely for ethical reasons, but to maintain a respected image and good relations with government, interest groups, employee representatives and the general public (potential customers/consumers).

(e) Survival and immediate profit-maximisation are not necessarily the highest objective of any organisation. Employers *in* growth markets, or hoping to diversify into new markets, cannot afford a low-calibre, high-turnover workforce. Notably innovative organisations can be seen to be offering higher than market rate on salaries (eg Mars) or remuneration packages including profit-related bonuses (eg Sainsbury's): moreover, their financial performance bears out their view that pay is an investment. To an extent, this pay strategy stems from the culture or value system of the organisation, the importance it attaches to loyalty, innovation and initiative, and its willingness to pay more to attract and retain such higher-level attributes: quantity may not be the prime employment criterion.

On the other hand, there are substantial cost savings in paying lower rates. It cannot be assumed that high remuneration inevitably leads to higher motivation and better performance. Not everybody has an instrumental orientation to work: money may not be the prime incentive - and pay is often a source of dissatisfaction rather than satisfaction, whatever its level.

If the organisation's ability to maintain high rewards in the future is in doubt, management ought also to be aware that the disappointment and culture shock of reversing a high-remuneration policy is very great.

The constituents of a remuneration policy must therefore embrace such crucial factors as the objectives of the organisation, its finances, cash flow and profitability, the state of the labour market, expected demand and supply of various types of labour, any government regulations on pay, anticipated contraction or expansion of the organisation, as well as the personal aspirations and inclinations of the workforce.

3 PAYMENT SYSTEMS

3.1 Salary administration

Salary administration is not to be confused with payroll administration, which is usually a financial function. It refers to the process by which levels of pay for staff employees are determined, monitored and controlled.

'Salary administration itself is not something that can be looked at in isolation. Salary administration is an attempt to achieve the objectives formulated in a salary policy, which itself ought ideally to be a plan - not simply to pay fair and equitable salaries, but to relate and reconcile career aspirations in terms of current and potential earnings, and personal commitment to total organisation objectives. A host of variables is involved.'

Livy, *Corporate Personnel Management*

The aims of salary administration are therefore broadly concerned with:

(a) obtaining and retaining suitable staff, within the requirements of the human resource plan;

(b) developing and maintaining a *salary structure* which:

   (i) is felt to be equitable, for jobs with similar responsibilities, and consistent in the differentials between differently valued jobs;

   (ii) takes market rates into account;

   (iii) is adjusted in line with cost-of-living increases;

   (iv) is flexible enough to accommodate changes in market rates, organisational structure and so on; and

   (v) rewards performance and responsibility by providing for progression;

(c) *reviewing* salary levels and differentials;

(d) operating the system so that it is easily understood and *seen to be fair* by staff; and

(e) controlling salary and administrative *costs* to the organisation.

3.2 Salary structures

Armstrong identifies the main objectives in designing a coherent salary structure as being

to provide for internal equity in grading and paying staff and to maintain competitive rates of pay' and notes that *'neither of those objectives can be achieved if a chaotic set of rates exists which has evolved over the years and is altered at whim or because of a panic reaction to difficulties in recruitment or retention.*

A salary structure may be designed using any, or a combination, of three main types:

(a) a graded structure, based on job evaluation;

(b) rate for age scales; and

(c) progression curves.

We will discuss each of these briefly in turn.

Graded salary

A typical structure of this type consists of a series of salary grades, to which all jobs are allocated on the basis of job evaluation. For each grade, there is a salary *scale* or range: minimum and maximum salary levels for jobs in that grade.

The *range,* and *overlap* of the scales between grades, will require careful thought because of the consequences for promotions, and transfers between grades. For example, the range must be wide enough to allow for progression: people in similarly-graded jobs may perform differently, and should be rewarded accordingly. There should also be an overlap, in recognition that an experienced person performing well in a given job may be of more value than a new or poor performer in the next grade up.

Chapter 9: Pay and benefits

The number of different scales in the structure will then depend on the number of distinct grades of jobs (according to job evaluation), the width and overlap of each scale, and the range of appropriate salaries in the organisation from the most junior to the most senior job.

Flexibility must be built into the system. Changes in job content and/or market rates should prompt re-grading. Moreover, the main principal of the structure is that progression within a grade is *performance related*, with the assumption that a normally competent individual eventually reaches the scale maximum, unless he is promoted out of the grade first. Again, flexibility may be required, for example in the case of an individual whose performance is outstanding, but for whom there are no immediate openings for promotion: discretionary payment of a salary *above* the grade maximum may be made, in order to maintain the individual's loyalty and motivation.

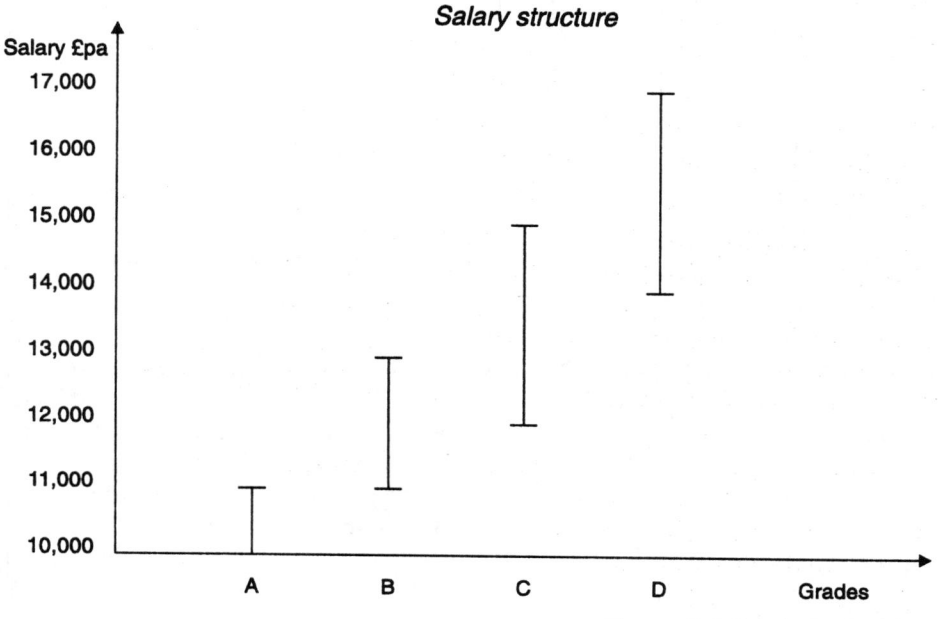

Figure 9.1 Graded salary structure

Rate for age systems

A rate for age system links the *age* of staff to defined scales or rates, for certain jobs, particularly where there are young employees who are being trained or carrying out junior, routine work. Incremental scales for age are based on the assumption that the value of staff to the organisation is directly related to greater experience and maturity.

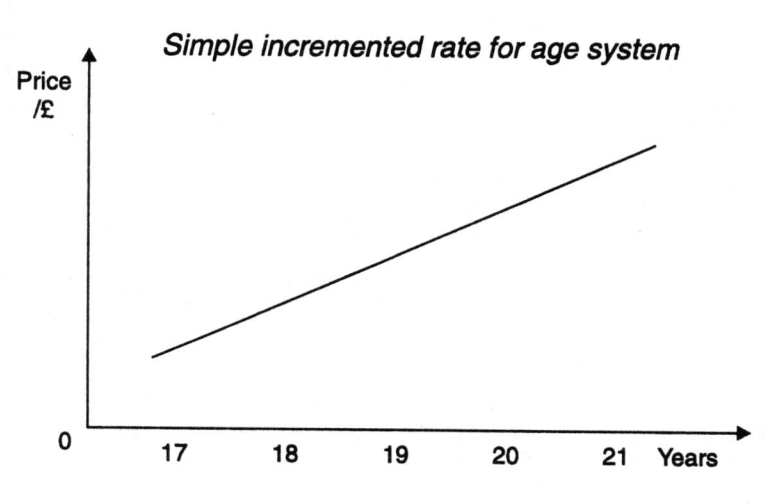

Figure 9.2 Rate for age systems

Such systems are, in their simplest form, easy to administer, because no evaluation of the relative merit of specific employees has to be made: they are, therefore, perceived to be entirely equitable, but may not have a motivating effect unless a system is used which relates pay to performance as well as age, by applying scales for merit at each age.

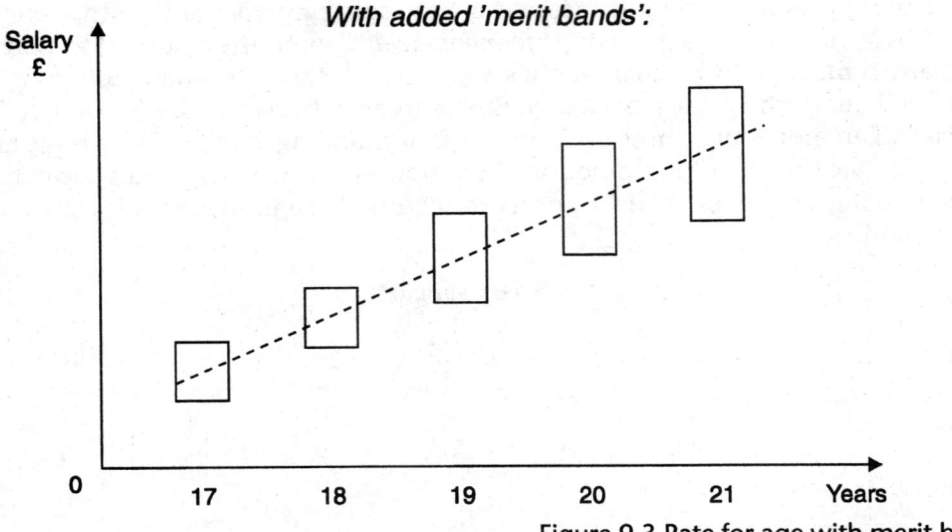

Figure 9.3 Rate for age with merit bands

Salary progression curve

The salary progression or *maturity curve* also aims to relate salary increases to maturity and experience, but in the longer term. It is most relevant to staff whose value is measured in terms of their professional ability rather than pure job content: for example, scientific and professional jobs. It is assumed that salary starts at the market rate for the person's *qualifications*, and that he or she will subsequently develop as a result of experience at a standard rate. In fact, some will develop faster than others, so the curve is only a guideline.

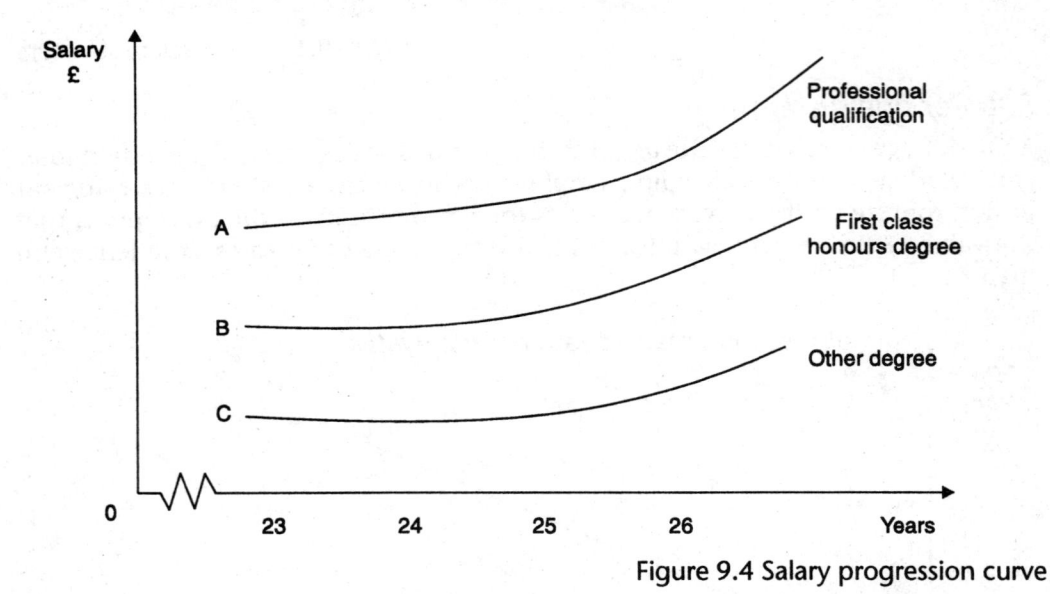

Figure 9.4 Salary progression curve

Activity 5

How is *incentive* added in each of the three systems discussed? In other words, what potential for higher earnings is offered an employee who works harder or better than another?

3.3 Salary review

Salary reviews may be carried out as a general exercise, when all or most salaries have to be increased to keep pace with market rates, cost of living increases or negotiated settlements. *General reviews* are often carried out annually (government regulations permitting) during inflationary periods: this may or may not create problems in financing individual merit awards as well.

Individual salary reviews are carried out to decide on merit awards. Again, these are usually held annually - with interim reviews, possibly, for trainees and younger staff who are making fast progress. Some companies phase reviews throughout the year rather than hold them all at once; this is more difficult to administer but does diffuse the tension of a general review period.

Guidelines for salary review will be necessary to minimise the subjectivity of discretionary payments. The total cost of all merit increases, or minimum/maximum amounts for increases, might be specified.

A *salary review budget* will determine the increase that can be allocated for awards, as a percentage of payroll costs for the department. The size of the budget will depend on:

(a) how average salaries in each grade differ from the target salary (the mid-point): ideally, they should correspond, but may be too high or low. A high ratio indicates that *earnings drift* has taken place, and salaries have moved towards the upper end of the scale - which may or may not correspond to the merits of the staff concerned; and

(b) the amount the company estimates it will be able to pay, based on forecast revenue, profit, and labour cost savings elsewhere (perhaps from highly-paid employees leaving, and recruits entering at lower-paid levels: this is called *salary attrition*).

Salary structures, job evaluation schemes, progression policies and salary review procedures all aim to make salary administration a scientific process. But they cannot entirely succeed. Salary administration is as much art as science and, inevitably, there are problems which can only be solved by exercising judgement in the light of circumstances.

                         Armstrong, *Handbook of Personnel Management Practice*

3.4 Problems of perceived fairness

Perceived equity and fair differentials are important elements in any salary structure, if it is to achieve its aim of attracting, holding (and to some extent, motivating) employees. Apart from the subjective aspects of assessment, grading and discretionary increment systems, there are typically problems associated with:

(a) *distortion of the salary structure,* as discussed above, by factors such as salary attrition and drift. Jobs should be meticulously graded and re-graded: non-merit-related awards should be controlled, and where averages appear to be dropping, the situation should be explained to staff;

(b) *the squeezing of differentials.* Some employees may benefit from negotiated increases, overtime and bonuses, which their superiors may not get. This upward pressure may be a cause of dissatisfaction to higher-grade employees who feel that their particular contribution is not being acknowledged. The only solution is to maintain differentials between the target salary for the supervisorial grade, and the average earnings (with overtime) of the subordinates. Panic measures, creating a knock-on effect on all other grades, should be avoided: the overall span of salary levels should be wide enough to allow for 15-20% differentials to be maintained between each grade;

(c) *salary limits*. There may be a problem motivating individuals who have reached the top of their grade scale but cannot be promoted out of the grade. The situation must be made quite clear to employees: secrecy will only deprive the employee of a perceived goal (promotion) which will be a further source of demotivation. Special bonuses may also be allowed, in exceptional circumstances; and

(d) *market rates*. Where market rates exist and can be determined, they will influence salary levels. However, they may (say, where a category of staff is in short supply) indicate salaries higher than internal job evaluation would: differentials are upset, and employees see apparent injustice. It may not be possible to recruit and retain suitable staff without sacrificing equity to some extent. Jobs subject to such market pressures should, however, be noted as exceptions in the salary structure or 'red-circled'. Adjustments may therefore be made later, as a result of regular audits of market rates, and anomalies may disappear as market rates deflate.

3.5 Wage systems

The wage pay structure is much like the salary structure, incorporating differentials in grades (with fixed rates for each job, or brackets allowing for merit payments), but influenced by pay bargaining and market forces.

Frequently, however, there is little in the way of a formal structure: perhaps only categories of skilled, semi-skilled and unskilled labour. Differentials may be arbitrary, grades overlapping and indistinct, and grading/re-grading a highly subjective and contentious issue.

Pay rates may be divided into:

(a) basic time rate (payment at a fixed rate per hour, according to hours worked); and

(b) piecework rate (varying according to output).

The most common individual payment-by-results (PBR) scheme is *straight piecework*: payment of a fixed amount per unit produced, or operation completed (*money piecework*), or payment of a fixed amount for the standard time allowed for the job (*time piecework*). Under the last system, a worker is paid basic piecework rate for the time allowed for the job: if he completes it in less time, he is in effect gaining a bonus since he is still paid for the allowed time.

The current trend is for the basic : incentive ratio to be 3:1 or 4:1, to minimise fluctuations and to control the upward drift of earnings. Overtime and shift (premium) rates will also be incorporated, along with special allowances for dangerous or dirty work.

3.6 Single status schemes

In fact, wage payment systems have been replaced by salaries in many organisations, as part of *single status* or *staff status* schemes. These represent an attempt to harmonise the payment systems operating in an organisation, mainly by removing the distinction between the treatment of manual and white-collar staff. Such agreements:

> *represent more than just a change of payment system and an improvement in manual workers' conditions of work. The employers involved were consciously attempting to change the relationship between workers and management. They wanted to encourage responsibility, pride in work, and co-operation, and hoped thereby to increase efficiency.*
>
> **Lupton and Bowey**, *Wages and Salaries*

Activity 6

What advantages and disadvantages for the organisation and workers can you see from single status schemes?

4 INCENTIVE SCHEMES

In our discussion of salary structures and wage payment systems, we noted where incentives could be built into fixed scales of pay: where payments could be linked directly to performance, so that employees could see a clear relationship between working well or better, and earning more. Various *incentive schemes* might also, or alternatively, be applied, such as:

(a) performance related pay;

(b) bonus schemes; and

(c) profit-sharing.

4.1 Performance related pay (PRP)

Definition

Performance related pay (PRP) (or part of it) is related to output (in terms of the number of items produced, or time taken to produce a unit of work), or results achieved (performance to defined standards in key tasks, according to plan).

The most common individual PRP scheme for wage earners is straight piecework: payment of a fixed amount per unit produced, or operation completed.

For managerial and other salaried jobs, however, a form of management by objectives will probably be applied so that:

(a) key results can be identified and specified, for which merit awards (on top of basic salary) will be paid;

(b) there will be a clear model for evaluating performance and knowing when, or if, targets have been reached and payments earned; and

(c) the exact conditions and amounts of awards can be made clear to the employee, to avoid uncertainty and later resentment.

For service and other departments, a PRP scheme may involve *bonuses* for achievement of key results, or *points schemes*, where points are awarded for performance on various criteria (efficiency, cost savings, quality of service and so on). Certain points totals (or the highest points total in the unit, if a competitive system is used) then win cash or other awards.

Personnel Management, November 1990, reported research into the benefits and problems of performance related pay.

(a) *Benefits of PRP cited*
  (i) Improves commitment and capability
  (ii) Complements other HR initiatives
  (iii) Improves business awareness
  (iv) Better two-way communications
  (v) Greater supervisory responsibility.

(b) *Potential problems cited*
  (i) Subjectivity

(ii) Supervisors' commitment and ability

(iii) Translating appraisals into pay

(iv) Divisive/against team working

(v) Union acceptance/employee attitudes.

> *In the wrong hands, PRP can do more harm than good, so organisations considering PRP should consider carefully whether it is appropriate for them ... Other payment systems which do not seek to directly link individual performance and reward may be more suited to the aims of the business.*

People management (September 1996) reported several local authorities who had withdrawn from their PRP schemes. PRP was adopted by around 70 councils between 1988 and 1991: the figure is now in decline. The London Borough of Brent dropped PRP because of the difficulty in measuring performance and a general unease about its position in local government. Cambridgeshire County Council axed its PRP scheme as part of an overhaul of salary policy, while the London Borough of Lewisham abandoned PRP in favour of other programmes such as Investors in People, and ISO 9000, claiming that it demotivated more people than it inspired.

4.2 Suggestion schemes

Another variant on performance-based pay is the *suggestion scheme*, where payments or prizes are offered to staff to come up with workable ideas on improving efficiency or quality, new marketing initiatives or solutions to production problems. The theory is that there is in any case motivational value in getting staff involved in problem-solving and planning. Staff are often in the best position to provide practical and creative solutions to their work problems or the customer's needs. However, an added incentive will help to overcome any reluctance on the part of staff to put forward ideas (because it is seen as risky, or doing management's job for them, or whatever).

Wherever possible, the size of the payment should be related to the savings or value added as a result of the suggestion - either as a lump sum or percentage. Payments are often also made for a 'good try' - an idea which is rejected but considered to show initiative, effort and judgement on the part of the employee. *People Management* (9 February 1995) reported that British Gas had plans to offer 'scratch' cards with £1, £2, and £5 prizes to employees whose ideas are *rejected*, in a bid to encourage more people to put forward ideas.

Suggestion schemes usually apply only to lower grades of staff, on the grounds that thinking up improvements is part of the supervisor's or manager's normal job, but with the increase of worker empowerment and 'bottom-up' quality initiatives, such as quality circles, they are becoming more widespread in various forms.

Whichever system is used, results-oriented payments should:

(a) offer real incentives, sufficiently high after tax to make extraordinary effort worthwhile, perhaps 10-30% of basic salary;

(b) relate payments to criteria over which the individual has control (otherwise he will feel helpless to ensure his reward, and the expectancy element in motivation will be lacking);

(c) make clear the basis on which payments are calculated, and all the conditions that apply, so that individuals can make the calculation of whether the reward is worth the extra level of effort;

(d) be flexible and sensitive enough to reward different levels of achievement in proportion, and with provision for regular review and adaptation to the changing needs of the particular organisation.

4.3 Bonus schemes

Bonus schemes are supplementary to basic salary, and have been found to be popular with entrepreneurial types, usually in marketing and sales. Bonuses are both incentives and rewards.

Group incentive schemes typically offer a bonus for a group (equally, or proportionately to the earnings or status of individuals) which achieves or exceeds specified targets. Offering bonuses to a whole team may be appropriate for tasks where individual contributions cannot be isolated, workers have little control over their individual output because tasks depend on each other, or where team building is particularly required.

It may enhance team spirit and co-operation as well as provide performance incentives, but it may also create pressures within the group if some individuals are seen to be 'not pulling their weight'.

Long-term, large-group schemes may be applied *factory-wide*, as an attempt to involve all employees in the organisation and objectives of production. Typically, bonuses would be calculated monthly on the basis of improvements in output per man per hour against standard, or value added (to the cost of raw materials and parts by the production process).

Value added schemes work on the basis that improvements in productivity (indicated by a fall in the ratio of employment costs to sales revenue) increases value added, and the benefit can be shared between employers and employees on an agreed formula. So if sales revenue increases and labour costs (after charges for materials, utilities and depreciation have been deducted) stay the same, or sales revenue remains constant but labour costs decrease, the balance becomes available. There has been an increase in such schemes in recent years (for example, at ICI).

4.4 Profit-sharing schemes and employee shareholders

Profit-sharing schemes offer employees (or selected groups of them) bonuses, perhaps in the form of shares in the company, related directly to profits. The formula for determining the amounts may vary, but in recent years, a straightforward distribution of a percentage of profits above a given target has given way to a value added related concept. The profit formula itself is not easily calculated - profit levels being subject to accounting conventions - so care will have to be taken to publish and explain the calculations to employees if the scheme is not to be regarded with suspicion or as simply another fringe benefit.

Profit-sharing is in general based on the belief that all employees can contribute to profitability, and that that contribution should be recognised. If it is, the argument runs, the effects may include profit-consciousness and motivation in employees, commitment to the future prosperity of the organisation and so on.

The actual incentive value and effect on productivity may be wasted, however, if the scheme is badly designed.

(a) A perceivably significant sum should be made available to employees - once shareholders have received appropriate return on their investment - say, 10% of basic pay.

(b) There should be a clear, and not overly delayed, link between effort/performance and reward. Profit shares should be distributed as frequently as possible - consistent with the need for reliable information on profit forecasts and targets and the need to amass a significant pool for distribution.

(c) The scheme should only be introduced if profit forecasts indicate a reasonable chance of achieving the above: profit-sharing is welcome when profits are high, but the potential for disappointment is great.

(d) The greatest effect on productivity arising from the scheme may in fact arise from its use as a focal point for discussion with employees, about the relationship between their performance and results, and areas and targets for improvement. Management must be seen to be committed to the principle.

4.5 Examples: profit-sharing and employee shareholders

Several hundred companies already operate some sort of profit-sharing scheme and according to a survey by the British Institute of Management, published in November 1978, almost all of them considered their scheme to be fairly, or very 'successful'. (The criteria by which 'success' is judged, however, will presumably vary from firm to firm.)

The main reasons given in the survey for the success of a profit-sharing scheme were that:

(a) it encouraged given employees to identify with the company;

(b) it provided an incentive to work harder;

(c) it made staff profit-conscious;

(d) employees were able to earn more money;

(e) it helped to retain staff; and

(f) it was generally liked by employees.

It appears that profit related pay schemes have become increasingly popular. The number has tripled since 1990, stimulated by government support and extra tax incentives, although these were reduced in the budget of November 1996.

However, *Personnel Management* (May 1991) reported the results of a study of an employee share ownership scheme (operated as a voluntary Save as You Earn related scheme) in a Midlands factory.

'In the event, we concluded there had been no change in attitudes which we felt should be attributed to the scheme,' they report. 'If this is correct, it is hard to see how it could have had any effect on the behaviour of the employees and any significant advantage to the firm.'

There were also very few joiners. Researchers say many workers on low incomes are unwilling to make a five-year or seven-year savings commitment. They warn that this could lead to such schemes becoming the preserve of higher-paid staff, intensifying the 'them' and 'us' attitudes of British industry.

Share ownership has little effect on class divisions, according to a survey of employees in two privatised utilities carried out by Leicester University. This revealed that only 10% believed that 'them and us' attitudes were replaced with a sense of common purpose because of share ownership.

Although 80% of the sample of nearly 450 employees were employee shareholders, 65% said that it made no difference to how careful they were with the company's equipment, and 70% felt it did not make people work harder.

Activity 7

What would make you work harder at your studies than you do? Think seriously about it ... Consider not just what 'carrots' you could be offered, but how your attitudes to the work might be changed.

5 BENEFITS

Benefits consist of items or awards which are supplementary to normal pay. Some - such as pensions and sick pay - are essential entitlements, so the common term 'fringe benefits' is perhaps misleading. Certain provisions for the maintenance of adequate standards of living have been underwritten by the state, which has legislated for employees and employers alike to bear some of the cost. They are awarded to anyone who meets certain qualifying conditions, and as such are independent of the employer's discretion and performance considerations. Other benefits such as cars, medical insurance and 'perks', are more in the nature of optional extras and as such may be part of the recruitment, retention and incentives strategies of the organisation.

Some organisations operate on the belief that pay and benefits form a whole package, the composition of which is flexible and can be adapted to personal and organisational circumstances. This means that employees and employers alike get a more complete picture of the total value of the remuneration, and its cost to the company.

Remuneration levels are set with consideration of bonuses and benefits as well: this may be important for senior staff, for whom there may be tax advantages in taking certain benefits instead of higher basic salary. This total remuneration concept has become so accepted that any decline in the value of benefits is seen as an erosion of remuneration.

The emphasis on benefits and the ingenuity shown in their provision vary with economic circumstances and with the impact of any incomes policy, but more recently they have appeared in conjunction with annual wage and salary demands. It must always be recognised, nevertheless, that, however generous they are, they can never be an adequate substitute for an inadequate base rate or an illogical salary structure or for tangible recognition of the effect of inflation.   Ream, *Personnel Administration*

An organisation might run what has been called a cafeteria system, whereby a range of benefits are on offer, and employees can choose from them up to their allowed budget. This offers the element of choice, and may increase the value of the benefit to the individual, since it answers his real needs or wants. According to an article in *Personnel Management* (December 1994) 'The number of firms offering their employees flexible benefits has risen by more than 50% in the last year, with perks ranging from childcare vouchers to personal pensions.' A scheme at Admiral Insurance, for example, allows employees to spend a sum worth up to 13% of their basic salary on benefits from a menu including an extra day's annual leave (valued at £9.32 per month), membership of a sports club (£20 per month) or vouchers. 'Unspent' allowance can be taken in cash. All staff receive 'care' benefits, including 20 days' holiday, discounts on motor insurance, death-in-service and sickness benefits, interest-free season ticket loans and loans for work related training.

5.1 Pension schemes

Pensions are generally regarded as the most important benefit after basic pay: they are a kind of deferred pay, building up rights to a guaranteed income on retirement (or to dependants, on death). They are financed by contributions from the company, with facilities for contribution by employees as well.

Most organisations see a need for more than token pension arrangements, because:

(a) social responsibility dictates the need to provide reasonable security especially for loyal and long-serving employees;

(b) a good pension scheme will be attractive to potential staff, and an inducement to loyalty for existing staff. (Note, however, that pensions are no longer the 'golden handcuff' they once were; pension rights must be preserved for early leavers, or transferred to another scheme. Pensions are more portable than they were before 'personal pensions' were introduced in 1988);

(c) a good pension scheme may have industrial relations benefits in demonstrating the organisation's long-term interest and care of its employees.

Pension schemes are complex affairs, and will usually require advice or administrative service from pensions specialists. There are legal and tax considerations as well as organisational needs and circumstances.

Many firms set up occupational pension schemes for their employees, either as:

(a) self-administered funds, where the firm's contributions (and the employees', if it is a contributory scheme) are invested by fund managers and controlled by trustees; or

(b) life office schemes, which are conducted through a contract with a life assurance office.

Concerns about potential for abuse of pension scheme funds were highlighted by the Maxwell affair. In 1992-3, a Commons Select Committee and an independent commission (the Goode Committee) reported on the operation of pension funds, with particular regard to the accountability and roles of trustees, fund managers, auditors and advisers. Following the recommendations, the government issued a White Paper: 'Security, Equality, Choice: the Future for pensions', (June 1994) which became the Pensions Act 1995. Provisions include the following.

(a) The formation of a pensions 'watchdog', the Occupational Pensions Regulatory Authority, which will have the power to enforce forthcoming regulations. There will also be a compensation scheme to protect members from loss as a result of fraud or misappropriation of funds.

(b) Schemes will be required to maintain a minimum solvency level, to be maintained by a schedule of contribution payments agreed by the trustees.

(c) Members will have the right to select some of the trustees of the pension scheme (at least one-third, for schemes with 100 members or more, or one trustee for smaller schemes). Professional advisors (auditors and legal advisers) will be independent and responsible to the trustees. Previously trustees, actuaries and advisors, were appointed by, and accountable to, the *employer*.

(d) Men and women have to be treated equally in their entitlement to pension *benefits* accruing after 17 May 1990 (the date of a judgment in the European Court of Justice). The government also intends to equalise the *state pension age* at 65: the change will be brought in gradually over ten years, starting in 2010.

(e) The link between SERPS (the State Earnings-Related Pension Scheme) and occupational schemes which have 'contracted-out' of SERPS will be broken. From 1997 contracted-out employees lose their future entitlement to SERPS in full. Schemes will 'only' be required to ensure that they provide benefits of a good enough standard to satisfy the government. (This is not as outrageous as it sounds: occupational schemes are generally enormously more generous than SERPS.)

(f) Members will be entitled to more information about their scheme, written in plain English.

Activity 8

Consider how important a pension seems to you now - and how it might seem in later life. Get a pensions leaflet from your bank or building society and see what a personal pension involves, including 'contracting-out of SERPS'. What kind of security does it offer? (Do try and do this. Don't worry: a salesperson won't jump on you if you ask for a leaflet!)

5.2 Sick pay

It is understandable that sickness or other enforced absence from work would haunt workers with the prospect of lost earnings, unless there was some sort of provision for genuine sufferers. Many employers supplement the state benefit by additional sick pay schemes, which may be tailored to the organisation's particular objectives (looking after long-serving employees, or generosity from the outset to attract recruits).

Statutory Sick Pay is paid under the Social Security and Housing Benefit Act 1982. It is related to annually reviewed earnings bands, and is payable for eight weeks in any tax year or in any single spell of illness. Payment is made only on the fourth successive qualifying day of illness, unless illnesses are separated by less than 14 days. Employers may wish to limit claims during holiday periods, and can do so by designating as 'qualifying days' only one day in each holiday week, so that payment will not have to be made until the fourth week of absence.

DSS advice and literature (*The Employers' Guide to Statutory Sick Pay*) is available to help in the details of administering the scheme.

Records of payment must be kept for at least three years in a readily inspected form. They must show:

(a) each employee's period of incapacity;

(b) agreed qualifying days;

(c) amounts paid out; and

(d) reason for any absence that has not ranked for payment.

Sick pay schemes are sometimes blamed for increases in *absenteeism*, since the incentive to go in to work, unless genuinely ill, has been removed with the threat of lost earnings. However, this is a complicated situation, particularly with a flexible definition of 'sickness'.

(a) The nature of certain work may cause more illnesses: 'jet-lag' for travelling executives, for example, or digestive complaints for shift workers.

(b) Stress may account for a number of odd days off for superficially unconvincing reasons: fatigue, headaches, emotional distress.

(c) Alcohol is a significant cause of absences on Mondays.

(d) Hourly paid, closely supervised employees may have to take days off and claim sickness, in order to attend to pressing personal matters.

(e) Employees may simply hate the idea of coming in to work, and absenteeism may therefore be:

   (i) a symptom of very serious organisational problems; and/or

   (ii) a safety valve for discontent, possibly preventing industrial unrest.

Control over absences will therefore depend on a good absence-recording system, sensibly operated and interpreted by supervisors and managers. Claims of sickness should be taken on trust as far as possible (unless there is positive proof of malingering) but the supervisor might point out to frequent absentees that even short intermittent absences affect the work and work group, and cannot be tolerated indefinitely. An illness or diagnosis may be confirmed by referring the employee to a company doctor - although disciplinary action cannot be taken against an employee who refuses to be examined (unless it is a condition of employment).

A common procedure is likely to require an absent employee to:

(a) notify the office as soon as possible on the first day;

(b) give as much information as possible about the nature and likely duration of the illness;

(c) record the illness absence, on return to work;

Business Basics: Human Resource Management

(d) arrange for a medical certificate to be sent to the office for absences of seven days or more;

(e) notify management if the illness is highly infectious or dangerous (since other staff will have to be checked and warned).

According to *People Management* (April 1997), companies are increasingly using pre-employment medical 'gatekeeping' to reduce their susceptibility to sickness absenteeism. Thus, candidates whose physical or psychological fitness for the job is in doubt, may have their offers of employment removed. It remains to be seen whether this increasingly common practice will contravene the Disability Discrimination Act 1995.

5.3 Maternity leave and benefits

Following EC Directive 92/85, provisions on maternity came into force in the UK under the Trade Union Reform and Employment Rights Act (TURERA) 1993, and Maternity Allowance and Statutory Maternity Pay Regulations 1994.

A woman who has completed the required periods of continuous employment (two years) in the service of an organisation has the following rights. (We go into some detail because this is likely to be of interest to many students.)

(a) To take time off for ante-natal care, starting at the 11th week before the estimated week of confinement (EWC), with 21 day's notice required.

(b) Not to be dismissed for reasons connected with pregnancy. It would automatically be 'unfair dismissal', unless the employee had become incapable of doing her work adequately and no reasonable alternative was available.

(c) To take up to 29 weeks' leave *after* having her baby (a total of 40 weeks, leave) of which 18 weeks is leave with *statutory maternity pay* (SMP). Under TURERA 1993, a total of 14 weeks' maternity leave and 18 weeks SMP are available to *all* women, regardless of length of service and hours worked. The period of leave can be extended by four weeks, for medical reasons.

(d) To return to her old job with no less favourable pay, seniority and pensions rights than before. The only exceptions are small businesses with fewer than five employees, and situations where her job is made redundant, in which case suitable alternative employment must be offered. Twenty-one days' notice must be given of the woman's intention to return; the employer may ask for confirmation but not earlier than 11 weeks after the birth. (In the case of women with less than two years' service, no notice is required: TURERA 1993.)

(e) To accrue pension and other benefits (excluding pay) during 14 weeks' maternity leave, based on what she would have been paid if she had been working normally. However, she will only be required to pay contributions on the contractual pay or statutory maternity pay actually received (Social Security Act 1989).

Statutory maternity pay (SMP) will start at any time from the 11th week before the EWC, and will last for 18 weeks. If a woman is absent with a pregnancy-related illness, statutory or occupational sick pay will apply until the sixth week before the EWC: then SMP will be 'triggered'. A woman will be eligible for SMP if she has been continuously employed by the organisation for 26 weeks into the 15th week before EWC and her average earnings are over a certain amount per week. She will be paid 90% of her average earnings for 6 weeks, followed by a flat rate per week for the following 12 weeks. Women with less than 26 weeks' service may be eligible for a maternity allowance from the DSS.

In addition, the new provisions include the health and safety of pregnant women: this will be discussed in the following chapter.

5.4 Holidays

Holidays are another benefit which is usually very much taken for granted. The UK average is three weeks' paid holiday, with four or five weeks for management.

There are few legal obligations governing entitlement in the UK, except for the Factories Act (women and young persons to be allowed Christmas Day, Good Friday and bank holidays). There is an EU recommendation that employees should be given four week's holiday a year, but this has no legal force. The 'right' to holidays is therefore whatever is set out and agreed in the terms and conditions of employment. The length of holidays has increased over the years in the UK: in a number of instances, additional holiday entitlement has been granted instead of reduction in working hours.

Employees should check their organisation's regulations and/or available statements of terms and conditions with regard to:

(a) basic entitlement to public and other holidays;

(b) how entitlement is calculated (calendar year, year from date of joining?) and what happens in the case of someone joining or leaving the organisation during the 'holiday year' thus defined;

(c) any restrictions on when individuals can take a holiday, how much at a time, and who gets precedence if too many people want to be away at the same time; and

(d) additional holiday entitlements - traditionally for seniority (in the hierarchy, and in terms of age or length of service).

5.5 Cars

Cars are another highly regarded benefit in the UK, and are still perceived as necessary in order to attract and retain managerial staff, despite the reduction in tax benefits in recent years. Cars for those whose work requires them to travel extensively (sales and service staff) are obviously a necessary investment for the company.

A company car saves the user the personal cost of acquisition, and usually also running costs, although this advantage has been reduced by legislation in recent years. It is costly for the organisation to lease and maintain a fleet, however, and there may be political problems of preserving status differentials (since not everybody can have a Porsche).

5.6 Other benefits

Other benefits might also be on offer.

(a) *Transport assistance.* Examples may include loans for the purchase of annual season tickets, or bulk buying of tickets by employers for distribution to staff.

(b) *Housing assistance,* perhaps in the form of:
  (i) allowances to staff who have been transferred or relocated - removal and travelling expenses, lodging, conveyancing fees and so on; or
  (ii) assistance with house purchase - bridging loan, preferential mortgage terms.

(c) *Medical benefits* - say, medical insurance, to provide private medical facilities in the event of illness or accident. Some medical services may also be provided at the workplace.

(d) *Catering services* - most commonly, subsidised food and drink at the workplace or Luncheon Vouchers.

(e) *Recreational facilities* - subsidy and organisation of social and sports clubs or provision of facilities such as a gymnasium or bar.

(f) *Allowances* - for telephone costs, professional subscriptions or work related reading matter.

(g) *Discounts* or preferential terms on the organisation's own products/services. Bank employees, for example, may receive: a mortgage subsidy; discounts on unit trusts or insurance products; bonus interest on accounts or savings plans; or reduced interest rates on overdrafts and loans.

Activity 9

Which, of all the benefits mentioned, would you think were the most important to people?

6 PAYROLL

In many, or perhaps most, organisations running the payroll and the PAYE system (which includes Statutory Sick Pay and Statutory Maternity Pay) will be the responsibility of the accounts department. However the HR function will be involved in setting rates of pay, awarding bonuses and so on, so there will be a good deal of liaison between the two functions.

With this in mind it will be useful for you to have an outline knowledge of how the figures on a payslip are calculated. You may also want to check payslips that you receive if you have a part-time job, say. There is probably no need to learn this (unless your tutor says otherwise): it is for interest only. Bear in mind that we are simplifying things somewhat for the purposes of illustration.

Let us suppose that you have just got your first job after graduating (as a trainee HR manager) at an annual salary of £15,000.

You will be paid in twelve monthly instalments giving you a gross monthly salary of £1,250. Unfortunately in the UK you have to pay income tax and National Insurance on this amount, so your net pay will be less than this.

Your net pay - the amount you actually end up with - is worked out as follows. The various deductions are explained in the notes that follow the calculations.

	Notes	£	Figures shown on payslip £
Gross pay		1,250.00	1,250.00
Pay adjustment	1	(337.08)	
Taxable pay		912.92	
Income tax at 20%	2	68.33	
Income Tax at 25%	3	131.38	
Total income tax			(199.71)
Pay after income tax			1,050.29
National insurance	4		
On the first £269 at 2%		5.38	
On the next £981 at 10%		98.10	
Total National Insurance			(103.48)
Net pay			946.81

Notes

1 The pay adjustment reduces the amount of pay that you have to pay tax on. Every year you get a 'personal allowance' of tax free pay and you usually get one twelfth of this per month. The single person's personal allowance is £4,045 for 1997/98 so you get £4,045 ÷ 12 = £337.08 per month, giving you *taxable* income of £912.92. The free pay is only deducted for the purposes of calculating tax: it is not taken away from the money that you get.

2 The first £4,100 of your taxable income is taxed at the rate of 20%. Again you get one twelfth of this £4,100 per month so you pay 20% tax on £4,100 ÷ 12 = £341.67 × 20% = £68.33.

3 The next £22,000 worth of income is taxed at 23% *. Again you get a twelfth per month. £22,000 ÷ 12 = £1,833.33. However you only have another £571.25 (912.92 - 341.67) of taxable income so only this amount is charged to tax. £571.25 × 23% = £131.38.

* Tax is charged at 40% for earnings above this level, but this does not apply in this case.

4 National Insurance is calculated on the full amount of your gross pay. The first £269 per month suffers National Insurance at 2% and the next amount (up to £1,746) suffers NI at 10%. NI is not payable by the employee above this level.

We have ignored various complications about rounding and so on in the illustration above to keep things simple.

In practice the Inland Revenue (who collect Income Tax) and the DSS (who collect NI) issue sets of tables that make it much easier to do the calculations. In fact, in practice, if you work for a company that has more than three or four employees it is worth buying a computer package that takes all the pain out of payroll calculations. Even so, payroll also involves a good deal of form-filling for the government, especially at the end of a tax year (April), and this can impose quite a heavy administrative burden upon an organisation.

Activity 10

It's pretty gruesome to give the government all this money isn't it?

Assuming the above figures apply, how much do you cost your employer a month to employ?

We have already discussed legal aspects of pay such as Equal Pay (Chapter 5) and pensions (Section 5 of this chapter). Here are some more Acts that affect payroll administration.

6.1 Employment Protection (Consolidation) Act 1978

Every employee must receive a statement showing gross and net amounts payable to him, variable and fixed deductions, and methods of calculation. If such an itemised pay statement is not provided, the employee may go to Industrial Tribunal to get repayment of the sum of un-notified deductions.

The employer must make deductions for income tax under Schedule E (known as PAYE: Pay As You Earn) from salary paid to employees under a contract of service.

6.2 Wages Act 1986

Under the Truck Acts (1831-1940), all manual employees had to be paid in cash. The Department of Employment released a statement in March 1987, saying that

> *the Government ... foresee a steady growth in non-cash methods of wage payment, which should reduce opportunities for crime and end unfair distinctions between the terms and conditions of employment of blue-collar and white-collar workers.*

The Wages Act repealed former legislation, so that the method of wage payment for all workers will now be entirely a matter for negotiation and contractual agreement between them and their employers. The Act does not remove any existing contractual right an individual may have to payment in cash, however, nor does it require an employer to change over to non-cash methods of wage payment.

Part 1 of the Act also introduced an important new set of rights for all workers against unlawful deductions from wages or payments to employers. Deductions or payments will be unlawful unless provided for:

(a) in statute, such as income or National Insurance;

(b) in the contract of employment, such as union dues;

(c) with the prior written agreement of the worker.

Any worker who believes an employer has not followed the provisions of the Act laying down what deductions and payments are lawful, now has a right to complain to an industrial tribunal.

Wages councils were established to regulate terms and conditions, principally in retailing, catering and clothing manufacture, but these were abolished under the Trade Union Reform and Employment Rights Act (TURERA) 1993: there is no longer a statutory minimum remuneration in those areas of business.

Chapter roundup

- Job evaluation is the process of analysing and assessing the content of jobs, in order to place them in an acceptable rank order which can then be used as a basis for a remuneration system.
- Salary structures most commonly consist of a graded structure, with a range (or scale) of salaries within each grade, and an overlap of pay scales between grades.
- Incentives are built into graded salary systems on a limited basis. In addition, many organisations operate incentive or Performance Related Pay (PRP) schemes, such as bonus schemes, suggestion schemes and profit-sharing.
- Remuneration can be seen as a whole package of pay and benefits, including
  - pension, sick pay and maternity leave, as statutory entitlements;
  - extended holiday entitlement (and a range of other (potentially flexible) 'perks').

Chapter 9: Pay and benefits

Quick quiz

1. Outline the advantages and disadvantages of job evaluation.
2. Distinguish between analytical/quantitative and non-analytical/qualitative approaches to job evaluation.
3. Why might an organisation wish to offer rates of pay above the market level?
4. How can performance related awards be built into a:
   (a) graded salary structure;
   (b) rate for age system;
   (c) salary progression curve?
5. What are the problems of monetary incentives?
6. What is the 'total remuneration' concept?
7. What is the amount of a woman's entitlement to Statutory Maternity Pay and what are the qualifying conditions?
8. What should be on an itemised pay slip?

Solutions to activities

1. (a) Analyse the organisation's structure and fix a rate for the job irrespective of the personal merits of the jobholder, or fluctuations in performance. This can depress employee motivation.
   (b) Job evaluation assumes that people are commodities who can be made to fit defined roles and supports rigid hierarchical organisation. It may prevent labour flexibility and multiskilling and may undermine attempts to foster a people-centred organisation culture.
   (c) Employees might be suspicious of the process of job analysis and its purposes. They will need to be told clearly that they are not being appraised, personally, for the purpose of setting pay rates.

2. (a) The factors for analysis are themselves qualitative, not easy to define and measure. Mental ability and initiative are observable in jobholders, but not easily quantifiable as an element of the job itself.
   (b) Assessment of the importance and difficulty of a job cannot objectively be divorced from the context of the organisation and jobholder. The relative importance of a job is a function of the culture and politics of the organisation, the nature of the business and not least the personal power of the individual in the job. The difficulty of the job depends on the ability of the jobholder and the favourability or otherwise of the environment/technology/work methods/management.
   (c) The selection of factors and the assignment of monetary values to factors remain subjective judgements.

Business Basics: Human Resource Management

3

Scheme	Characteristics	Advantages	Disadvantages
Ranking method	Whole job comparisons are made to place them in order of importance.	Easy to apply and understand.	No defined standards of judgement - differences between jobs are not measured.
Job classification method	Job grades are defined and jobs are slotted into the grades by comparing the whole job description with the grade definition.	Simple to operate and standards of judgement are provided in the shape of the grade definition.	Difficult to fit complex jobs into one grade without using excessively elaborate definitions.
Factor comparison method	Separate factors are identified as a proportion of the job and valued in comparison with benchmark jobs.	Uses benchmark jobs which are considered to be fairly paid.	Hard to explain. Depends on accuracy of benchmark rates. Limited applicability.
Points rating methods	Separate factors are scored to produce an overall points score for the job.	The analytical process of considering separate defined factors provides for objectivity and consistency in making judgements.	Complex to install and maintain - judgement is still required to rate jobs in respect of different factors.

5   Graded: accelerated progression through a grade, promotion out of it, or discretionary added payments. Rate for age: added merit bands. Progression curve: added bands or steeper curves.

6   Single status schemes can save an organisation administrative and overtime costs, and may improve employee flexibility and industrial relations. For manual workers, there are clear advantages in receiving a wider range of benefits and an annual salary (which at least improves their borrowing position).

However, there may be an increase in labour costs overall. For the workers, too, there is a drawback, in monthly - instead of weekly - payments. There is also a perceived loss of status for salaried workers in the achievement of parity by previous wage-earners: this may affect their morale, although the organisation culture will have a lot to do with whether harmonisation is perceived as threatening or equitable and exciting.

9   In a survey of 2,000 people in full-time employment in France, Britain, Germany and Italy, it was discovered that:

(a) most workers think a staff restaurant is a more important benefit than a company car (84% of workers, in 'cuisine-conscious' France!);

(b) company cars were also rated less important than pensions or private health insurance. *Personnel Management Plus*, September 1992

10 Your employer pays you £946.81 along with your £199.71, to the Inland Revenue on your behalf, and £228.48 to the DSS, a total of £1,375. More than your gross pay, you will observe, because the employer also has to pay National Insurance amounting to 10% of your gross pay.

Further question practice

Now try the following practice questions at the end of this text

Multiple choice questions	56 to 62
Exam style question	9

Chapter 10

WELFARE, HEALTH AND SAFETY

Introduction

Welfare is a 'state of faring or doing well, freedom from calamity etc, enjoyment of health etc'. In human resource terms, welfare consists of 'efforts to improve conditions of living for ... a group of employees or workers'.

There is quite a long history in the UK of employees providing welfare to their employees. The Quaker Cadbury family used to provide housing for its employees at Bourneville. Similarly, coal mining employers, such as the mine owners of Lanarkshire, provided cottages for miners and their families, although they did not assist retired miners or bereaved families of miners. Other employers provided company stores, and schools for educating employees' children. On the other hand, there is also a long history in the UK of employers exploiting employees, without any provision of welfare benefits - the sweat shops of East London are only one of many examples.

As far health and safety are concerned, you should readily appreciate the value of a working environment that offers protection from ill-health and accidents. Such measures are important.

(a) primarily, to protect employees from pain and suffering. This point is so obvious that we need not develop it further, but if you have witnessed a serious accident, you might agree that it is an unforgettable and most unpleasant experience;

(b) because an employer has legal obligations for the health and safety of employees;

(c) because accidents and illness cost the employer money; and

(d) because the company's image will suffer if its health and safety record is bad.

Your objectives

After completing this chapter you should:

(a) appreciate the range of circumstances in which welfare benefits and services may be offered;

(b) be able to outline a coherent health and safety policy;

(c) be aware of the legal provisions with regard to health and safety;

(d) understand the causes (and prevention) of accidents in the workplace;

(e) appreciate the range of issues covered by 'occupational health';

(f) appreciate the role and methods of counselling in the workplace;

(g) be aware of provisions for employees to have time off work.

1 WELFARE

A certain number of welfare benefits are provided by the State, and the 'Welfare State' refers to 'a state in which socialist principles have been put into effect with the purpose of ensuring the welfare of all who live in it'. In spite of the socialist origins of state welfare, there is no questioning in the UK of the idea that a welfare state should exist (providing state pensions, unemployment pay, supplementary benefits, state education, and a National Health Service), although politicians might argue about how much should be spent on it, and how far alternatives should be encouraged.

Benefits to employees from employers that are required by law, or conceded in negotiations with trade unions, do not constitute welfare in the proper meaning of the word. Employers provide welfare to employees when they give benefits without being forced to, under no duress or pressure.

Employers might want to provide welfare:

(a) because of a genuine concern for the lives of their employees;
(b) to improve the morale and loyalty of employees; or
(c) because other companies and organisations are offering similar benefits, and they need to do the same in order to attract and retain the calibre of staff they require.

Suppose a 20-year old person enters the company at £10,000 per year, works there for 30 years, receives an eight percent per year increase, retires at half salary and lives to the age of 75. That person represents a £2.5 million investment to the company and the number just goes up from there. For a person who reaches top management, the figure can easily hit five to ten times that figure.

If that corporation had a machine worth this kind of money, they'd build a fence around it, polish it, show it off and have someone specially trained to provide whatever it needed to remain productive. We really think people need to be treated with the same level of respect for the investment they represent.

Administrator, October 1985

A case can, however, be made *against* the provision of discretionary welfare.

(a) Welfare is provided for by the state: why should other organisations duplicate services?
(b) It is irrelevant or even counter to organisational objectives (notably, profit maximisation).
(c) Welfare services have not been shown to increase loyalty or motivation: they are largely taken for granted, and as such are more likely to be a source of disappointment and dissatisfaction at any shortcomings than a source of satisfaction. Even gratitude or appreciation is not a prime motivator.
(d) The non-work affairs and interests of employees are not the business of employers. If this attitude prevails in some situations (so that if the employee commits an offence outside work, this is not sufficient grounds for dismissal) it should prevail in others.

The case *for* welfare rests mainly on the concept of the social responsibility of organisations towards their employees. Martin (*Welfare at Work*) suggested that:

Staff spend at least half their waking time at work or in getting to it or leaving it. They know they contribute to the organisation when they are reasonably free from worry, and they feel, perhaps inarticulately, that when they are in trouble they are due to get something back from the organisation. People are entitled to be treated as full human beings with personal needs, hopes and anxieties; they are employed as people; they bring themselves to work, not just their hands, and they cannot readily leave their troubles at home.

The economic arguments are not as weak as they may seem. Welfare may not have a positive effect on morale and productivity - but anxiety, stress and distress invariably have a *negative* effect which should be alleviated where possible in the interests of effectiveness. In other words, welfare is a hygiene factor.

1.1 Welfare benefits and services

We have already discussed benefits, in Chapter 9. Additional help may be offered in special situations such as:

(a) providing for employees who have a long-term illness, especially an industry related illness (perhaps caused by working practice or environment);

(b) provision of medical care over and above statutory facilities, which may include the availability of private treatment and convalescence facilities;

(c) help at times of bereavement; or

(d) help with schooling and transport for the families of employees posted abroad or moved around within the country.

Individual welfare *services* may be offered in a number of circumstances.

Sickness

Support and counsel may be required, particularly during prolonged absence, if these are not available from family or state. Absent employees should be kept in touch with, in order to identify needs: not in the spirit of checking up in case of malingering, or pointing out that paid sick leave has been used up, but offering concern and encouragement. In the first instance, a letter might be sent by the line manager, expressing concern and best wishes, and offering help or a visit. If a visit is requested or judged necessary, it might be made by a colleague, manager, personnel or welfare specialist. The aims of such a visit will depend on the circumstance, but may include encouragement, alleviation of loneliness, advice or help with domestic problems, alleviation of anxiety about the future and so on.

There should also be policies in regard to specific illnesses such as *Aids* and *HIV*. The fear and prejudice surrounding the Acquired Immune Deficiency Syndrome and Human Immunodeficiency Virus require positive commitment:

(a) to prevent discrimination on the grounds of sexual orientation, since the diseases are still widely associated in people's minds with a homosexual lifestyle;

(b) to protect the employment rights and working life of HIV-positive employees;

(c) to prevent unnecessary fear among employees, while promoting safe practices;

(d) to give support to HIV-positive employees, employees with HIV-positive partners and so on.

Employee education and counselling programmes are considered helpful by companies which run them, such as Body Shop, but they should not be considered a replacement for non-discrimination policies. The Body Shop, along with Barclays Bank and over 40 other companies, are signatories to the National Aids Trust's 'Companies Act!' charter, which highlights HIV and Aids as equal opportunities issues.

Domestic problems

Situations such as marital breakdown, depression, alcoholism (or other addictions) or bereavement are, above all, private, but are likely to be carried in to work: in any case, a cry for help should not be ignored. Advice may be as simple as putting the employee in touch with appropriate organisations or qualified counsellors. In the case of bereavement, help may be given with funeral arrangements or legal matters and possibly with payment of debts. Welfare officers should not be regarded purely as 'agony aunts', but may be a first port of call in difficulties. (Alcoholism is increasingly regarded as a matter of occupational health, and will be dealt with later in this chapter.)

Activity 1

Does your college/university have provision for welfare services? What are they? How well publicised are they? Ask for a leaflet, if there are not notices or entries in the Student Hand Book. List the issues which are highlighted by the counselling or welfare programme.

Preparation for retirement

Retirement is a major life crisis and should be prepared for, through in-house or local classes on how to cope, how to use leisure time and so on. Welfare for elderly employees, prior to retirement, may also consist of help with employment problems: transfer to light or designated duties, exemption from shiftwork or whatever. (This is discussed in Chapter 13.)

Preparation for redundancy

Like retirement, redundancy requires psychological as well as circumstantial adjustment: counselling, as well as help with retraining, redeployment or job search might be given. (This is also discussed in Chapter 13.)

1.2 Who is responsible for welfare?

Most examples of welfare provision do not affect the relationship between line managers and the people who work for them. Occasionally, however, the manager might become closely involved - especially in cases of ill-health or bereavement - visiting employees or their families at their homes in times of distress, and setting in motion on their behalf the procedures to obtain company welfare benefits. However, employees may not wish to share problems with their boss, and line managers may not be qualified to give advice or direct people to where it can be found. Human resource managers are a realistic alternative - but their other responsibilities (providing management services) may not be consistent with providing in-depth help to individual employees: they may not have the time, and there may be a conflict of interest if employees' problems are work related.

A welfare officer - an expert counsellor with time and interest for individual casework - may therefore be appointed. This is still a sensitive role, however: it exists dependent on the organisation, so a conflict of interests may still arise.

2 HEALTH AND SAFETY

2.1 Surely health and safety precautions are obvious?

In 1972, the Royal Commission on Safety and Health at Work reported that unnecessarily large numbers of days were being lost each year through industrial accidents, injuries and diseases, because of the 'attitudes, capabilities and performance of people and the efficiency of the organisational systems within which they work'.

Since 1972, major legislation has been brought into effect in the UK, most notably the Health and Safety at Work Act 1974, plus Regulations and Codes of Practice under the Act, which implement the provisions of six EU directives on health and safety issues: the Management of Health and Safety at Work Regulations 1992.

Since 1972, society as a whole has become more aware of health and safety, through:

(a) legislation requiring health warnings and descriptions of contents of goods;

(b) the raising of issues such as unsafe toys, food labelling, flammable materials in furniture, and asbestos poisoning;

(c) experience of notorious disasters in factories, railway stations and so on; and

(d) improvements in the general quality of life and environments.

However, it would be wrong to paint too optimistic a picture of employers' performance on health and safety.

(a) Legislation sets bare minimum standards for (and levels of commitment to) health and safety. ('The law is a floor'). It does not represent satisfactory - let alone best - practice for socially responsible organisations.

(b) Health and safety are still regarded with a negative attitude by many managers. Provisions are costly, and have no immediately quantifiable benefit. Like other forms of risk management - such as insurance - they are perceived as a regrettable necessity, which would be avoided if it were safe to do so, given the constraints of legal obligations, trade union pressure and the threat of adverse publicity from a disaster.

(c) Positive discipline (setting mechanisms and systems which theoretically prevent hazardous behaviour) only goes so far, and irresponsible or ignorant behaviour can still cause accidents - where operators disobey safety instructions on machinery, for example.

(d) New health and safety concerns are constantly emerging, as old ones are eradicated. For example:

   (i) new technology and ergonomics may make physical labour less stressful, but it creates new hazards and health risks, such as a sedentary, isolated lifestyle, and problems associated with working long hours at VDUs or shift working;

   (ii) new issues in health are constantly arising, such as passive smoking in the workplace or alcohol abuse, with the increasing stress of work in highly competitive sectors.

Activity 2

How many notorious workplace disasters can you think of? What were the main costs to the organisations concerned?

2.2 The Health and Safety at Work Act 1974

In the UK, the Health and Safety at Work Act 1974 provides for the introduction of a system of approved codes of practice, prepared in consultation with industry, so that an employee, whatever his employment, should find that his work is covered by an appropriate code of practice. The codes have a legal status but are not statutory in the sense that they must be followed. They are more like the Highway Code, in the sense that in a road accident, failure to obey the Highway Code would be evidence of failure in the driver's duty of care, and so open the driver to prosecution and awards for damages.

Employers also have specific duties under the 1974 Act.

(a) All systems (work practices) must be safe.

(b) The work environment must be safe and healthy (well-lit, warm, ventilated and hygienic).

(c) All plant and equipment must be kept up to the necessary standard (with guards on machines and so on).

In addition, information, instruction, training and supervision should be directed towards safe working practices, and the safety policy should be clearly communicated to all staff.

The *employee* also has a duty:

(a) to take reasonable care of himself and others;

(b) to allow the employer to carry out his duties (including enforcing safety rules); and

(c) not to interfere intentionally or recklessly with any machinery or equipment.

2.3 Safety Representative Regulations 1978

The Safety Representative Regulations provide for *safety representatives* to be appointed by a recognised trade union, and for *Safety Committees* to be set up at the request of employee representatives, to monitor safety measures and to assist (or 'police') the employer in providing a healthy and safe place of work.

The employer must:

(a) produce a *written statement of his safety measures* and the means used to implement them. This statement should be brought to the notice of his employees (only an employer who has less than five employees is exempt from this requirement);

(b) *consult with safety representatives* appointed by recognised trade unions with a view to the effective maintenance of adequate safety measures;

(c) *appoint a safety committee* if requested to do so by the safety representatives, to keep safety measures under review.

An employer may not make any charge to his employees for the cost of safety measures or equipment which it is his legal duty to take or provide.

Activity 3

What aspects of your studying environment (if any) do you think are:

- a hindrance to your work?
- a source of dissatisfaction?
- a hazard to your health and/or safety?

2.4 EU directives

In 1989 and 1990 the European Council of Ministers agreed to a framework directive on health and safety, together with five other directives on:

- health and safety requirements for the workplace;
- safety and health requirements for the use of work equipment at work;
- the use of personal protective equipment;
- the manual handling of loads where there is a risk, particularly of back injury to workers; and
- health and safety requirements for work with display screen equipment.

The EU directives were implemented on 31 December 1992. In fact most of the matters addressed by the directives were already covered to some extent by existing UK legislation and regulations in particular the Health and Safety at Work Act 1974, but the requirements of the display screen equipment directive were new. (These are discussed in more detail below.)

Under the EU directives employers have the following additional general duties.

(a) They must carry out risk assessment, generally in writing, of all work hazards. Assessment should be continuous.

(b) They must introduce controls to reduce risks.

(c) They must assess the risks to anyone else affected by their work activities.

(d) They must share hazard and risk information with other employers, including those on adjoining premises, other site occupiers and all subcontractors coming on to the premises.

(e) They should revise safety policies in the light of the above, or initiate safety policies if none were in place previously.

(f) They must identify employees who are especially at risk.

(g) They must provide fresh and appropriate training in safety matters.

(h) They must provide information to employees (including temps) about health and safety.

(i) They must employ competent health and safety advisers.

Employees also have an additional duty under the new regulations to inform their employer of any situation which may be a danger, although this does not reduce the employer's responsibilities in any way because his risk assessment programme should have spotted the hazard in any case.

The workplace directive

The workplace directive deals with matters that have been statutory requirements for many years in the UK under legislation such as the Offices, Shops and Railway Premises Act 1963, although in some cases the requirements have been more clearly defined. The following provisions are made.

(a) *Equipment*. All equipment should be properly maintained.

(b) *Ventilation*. Air should be fresh or purified.

(c) *Temperature*. The temperature must be 'reasonable' inside buildings during working hours. This means not less than 16° where people are sitting down, or 13° if they move about to do their work.

(d) *Lighting* should be suitable and sufficient, and natural, if practicable. Windows should be clean and unobstructed.

(e) *Cleaning* and *decoration*. Floors, walls, ceilings, furniture, furnishings and fittings must be kept clean.

(f) *Room dimensions* and *space*. Each person should have at least 11 cubic metres of space, ignoring any parts of rooms more than 3.1 metres above the floor or with a headroom of less than 2.0 metres.

(g) *Floors* must be properly constructed and maintained (without holes, not slippery, properly drained and so on).

(h) *Falls* or *falling objects*. These should be prevented by erecting effective physical safeguards (fences, safety nets, ground rails and so on).

(i) *Glazing*. Windows should be made of safe materials and if they are openable it should be possible to do this safely.

(j) *Traffic routes*. These should have regard to the safety of pedestrians and vehicles alike.

(k) *Doors* and *gates*. These should be suitably constructed and fitted with any

Chapter 10: Welfare, health and safety

necessary safety devices (especially sliding doors and powered doors and doors opening in either direction).

(l) *Escalators* and *travelators* should function safely and have readily accessible emergency stop devices.

(m) *Sanitary conveniences* and *washing facilities* must be suitable and sufficient. This means that they should be properly ventilated and lit, properly cleaned and separate for men and women. 'Sufficient' means that undue delay is avoided!

(n) *Drinking water.* An adequate supply should be available with suitable drinking vessels.

(o) *Clothing.* There should be suitable accommodation for outdoor clothing, which should be able to dry out if wet. Facilities for changing clothing should be available where appropriate.

(p) *Rest facilities* and *eating facilities*. These must be provided unless the employees' workstations are suitable for rest or eating, as is normally the case for offices.

Activity 4

Reassess your answer to Activity 3 in the light of these specific provisions!

Manual handling and protective equipment

The manual handling regulations are very well summarised by John Barrell (*Administrator,* October 1992).

> *More than a quarter of accidents reported each year to the enforcing authorities are associated with this activity. Back injuries are the most common and no place of work is immune. Offices and shops produce these injuries as much as do factories, hospitals and warehouses.*
>
> *The Manual Handling Operation Regulations will in the first instance require every employer, so far as is reasonably practicable to avoid the need for his employees to undertake any manual handling activities which will involve the risk of their becoming injured ... However, if the cost of avoiding such risk is unreasonable the employer will be required to carry out an assessment of all manual handling operations which are to be retained ... Where the (compulsory) assessment reveals risk to employees, steps must be taken to reduce those risks to the lowest level reasonably practicable ... .*
>
> *Employees will have two duties under these regulations: to make full and proper use of equipment and systems provided by the employer: and to inform their employer of any injury or conditions which may affect their ability to safely undertake manual handling operations. The Manual Handling Regulations will not apply on board ships and aircraft.*

The regulations on protective equipment require employers to provide such equipment where necessary, maintain it properly, and provide training in its use. Employees have a duty to report defects.

Health and safety and workstations

If you have ever worked for a long period at a VDU you may personally have experienced some discomfort. Back ache, eye strain and stiffness or muscular problems of the neck, shoulders, arms or hands are frequent complaints. The common, if somewhat inaccurate, term for this is Repetitive Strain Injury or RSI. The *Financial Times* reported in October 1991 that RSI now accounts for more than half of all work-related injuries in the US and that in Australia it has reached almost epidemic proportions. Disorders seem to arise from poor equipment, environment and posture, which lead to muscles being starved of oxygen, the build up of waste

195

products in the body and the compression of nerves.

Although the Health and Safety Commission (HSC) issued helpful guidelines on working with VDUs some time ago, these did not have legal force, and employers had remained free to ignore the problem if they wished. However, the EU directive on workstations were implemented at the end of 1992. Any new workstations put into service after this date have to meet new requirements and existing workstations must have been adapted to comply or have been replaced by the end of 1996.

The main provisions of the directive are as follows.

(a) *VDUs:* these must not flicker, must be free from glare, and must swivel and tilt.
(b) *Keyboards:* again they must tilt and must be free from glare; the workspace in front of them must be 'sufficient' for the operators to rest their forearms.
(c) *Desks:* these must be free from glare; there must be enough space to allow 'flexible' arrangement of all equipment and documents. Measurements are not specified.
(d) *Chairs:* the seat must be adjustable in height, and the back in height and angle; footrests must be made available if required.
(e) *Lighting:* there must be 'appropriate contrast' between the screen and its background; windows must have some form of blinds.
(f) *Heat* and *humidity* levels must be 'adequate' on the one hand and not uncomfortable on the other.
(g) *Radiation* must be reduced to negligible levels.
(h) *Breaks:* screen work must be 'periodically interrupted by breaks or changes in activity'.
(i) *Eyesight:* the employer must offer free eyesight testing at regular intervals and provide any special glasses that may be needed for screen work.
(j) *Consultation:* employees must be consulted about health and safety measures.
(k) *Training:* training in the proper use of equipment must be provided.

2.5 Health and safety in pregnancy

The EU directive on pregnancy and maternity (discussed in connection with maternity leave in Chapter 9) also tackled the issue of health and safety. Pregnant women, those who have recently given birth and those who are breastfeeding are recognised as special groups requiring protection. The provisions have been incorporated into UK law in Schedule 3 of the Trade Union Reform and Employment Rights Act, 1993 and the Management of Health and Safety at Work (Amendment) Regulations, 1994.

Provisions include the following.

(a) Every employer must undertake a *risk assessment* if the workforce includes women of child-bearing age (c.20-45), and if the work is of a kind that could involve risk to women in any of the three categories mentioned above. All risks to health and safety must be taken into account, whether from processes, working conditions or physical, biological or chemical agents. (Risks already specifically mentioned in legislation, regulations and codes include working with lead, lifting objects, excessive use of VDUs, exposure to radiation, changes in air pressure and so on.) Heat, stress, exhaustion and mental stress are also potential hazards.
(b) The work of pregnant women must be adjusted to remove the risk. This may involve transferring night workers to day work, removing the need to lift heavy objects, or reducing travel in the job.
(c) If the work hours or conditions cannot be made safer, alternative safer work

must be offered. This must be suitable for the woman and not substantially less favourable in terms and conditions.

(d) If no safer alternative work exists, the woman must be suspended on full terms and conditions, for the period of risk.

(e) The woman has the right to refuse night work on medical grounds.

These duties apply once the employer has been notified in writing that a woman is pregnant or falls into one of the other categories. The employee must, on request, product a certificate from a registered medical practitioner or midwife. Failure to identify and eliminate risks is a criminal offence under the Act, and is also a failure of the general duty to provide a safe system of work, opening the employer to various statutory claims for damages.

3 ACCIDENTS

Apart from obviously dangerous equipment in offices, there are many hazards to be found in the modern working environment. Many accidents could be avoided by the simple application of common sense and consideration by employer and employee; and by safety consciousness encouraged or enforced by a widely acceptable and well-publicised safety policy.

Common causes of injury include:

(a) slippery or poorly maintained floors;

(b) frayed carpets;

(c) trailing electric leads;

(d) obstacles in gangways;

(e) standing on chairs (particularly swivel chairs) to reach high shelving;

(f) staircases used as storage facilities;

(g) lifting heavy items without bending properly; and

(h) removing the safety guard on a machine to free a blockage.

3.1 The cost of accidents

The costs of accidents to the employer include:

(a) time lost by the injured employee;

(b) time lost by other employees who choose to, or must of necessity, stop work at the time of or following the accident;

(c) time lost by supervision, management and technical staff following the accident;

(d) a proportion of the cost of first aid materials, or even medical staff;

(e) the cost of disruption to operations at work;

(f) the cost of any damage to the equipment or any cost associated with the subsequent modification of the equipment;

(g) the cost of any compensation payments or fines resulting from legal action. An employer may be liable to his employee in tort if the employee is injured as a result of either:

   (i) the employer's failure to take reasonable care in providing safe premises and plant, a safe system of work and competent fellow employees; or

   (ii) the employer's breach of a statutory duty - say, to fence dangerous machinery;

(h) the costs associated with increased insurance premiums;

(i) reduced output from the injured employee on return to work;

(j) the cost of possible reduced morale, increased absenteeism, increased labour turnover among employees;

(k) the cost of recruiting and training a replacement for the injured worker.

Although the injured employee's damages may be reduced if his injury was partly a consequence of his own contributory negligence, due allowance is made for ordinary human failings. In particular:

(a) an employee is not deemed to consent to the risk of injury because he is aware of the risk. It is the employer's duty to provide a safe working system;

(b) employees can become inattentive or careless in doing work which is monotonous or imposes stress. This factor too must be allowed for in the employer's safety precautions;

(c) it is not always a sufficient defence that the employer provided safety equipment and rules: the employer has some duty to encourage if not to insist on its proper use;

(d) many dangers can be caused by carelessness or other fault of an otherwise competent employee, possibly by mere thoughtlessness. It is the employer's duty to be watchful and to keep such tendencies in check;

(e) employees do not work continuously. The employer's duty is to take reasonable care for their safety in all acts which are normally and reasonably incidental to the day's work.

Activity 5

If a person went to wash a tea-cup after use, at his or her office, and slipped on a slippery surface in the kitchen and was injured, who would be at fault?

3.2 Preventive action

The prevention of accidents requires efforts on the part of employees and management, including those responsible for the design of the operating system and its staffing. Some of the steps, which might be taken to reduce the frequency and severity of accidents are:

(a) developing a safety consciousness among staff and workers and encouraging departmental pride in a good safety record;

(b) developing effective consultative participation between management, workers and unions so that safety and health rules can be accepted and followed;

(c) giving adequate instruction in safety rules and measures as part of the training of new and transferred workers, or where working methods or speeds of operation are changed;

(d) materials handling, a major cause of accidents, to be minimised and designed as far as possible for safe working and operation;

(e) ensuring a satisfactory standard from the safety angle for both basic plant and auxiliary fittings such a guards and other devices;

(f) good maintenance - apart from making sound job repairs, temporary expedients to keep production going should not prejudice safety.

In general, the appropriate code of practice for the industry/work environment should be implemented in full.

3.3 Factories Act 1961

The 1961 Act applies only to a factory, defined as a place where manufacturing or processing work is done for the purposes of gain, and where the main purpose of the premises involves manual labour. This includes buildings ancillary to a place of manufacture and also a slaughterhouse, a laundry, a shipyard, a film set and premises where packing takes place (among other specified categories).

The occupier of a factory has an absolute duty to fence securely all prime movers (machines which provide power), all transmission machinery and every dangerous part of any machinery. Machinery is dangerous if it can be reasonably foreseen that injury to any person can occur in the ordinary course of use.

(a) It is no defence to show that there is no practicable means of fencing the machine. If it cannot be used when adequately fenced, then it should not be used at all.

(b) The fencing should be substantial and kept in position at all times when the machine is in motion, although not when it is being examined or lubricated.

(c) It is only the dangerous parts which need to be fenced. If that is done there is no duty to fence the rest of the machine.

(d) A fence is sufficiently secure even though it does not prevent *reckless* employees from circumventing it.

3.4 Investigation and report of accidents

Safety inspections should be carried out to locate and define faults in the system that allow accidents to occur. They may be carried out as a comprehensive audit, working through a checklist, or by using random spot checks, regular checks of particular risk points or statutory inspections of particular areas, such as lifts, hoists, boilers or pipelines.

It is essential that checklists used in the inspection process should identify corrective action to be taken, and allocate responsibility for that action. There should be reporting systems and control procedures to ensure that inspections are taking place and that findings are being acted on.

Accident-reporting systems will be particularly important, but it must be emphasised to staff that the report is not an exercise in itself but a management tool, designed to:

(a) identify problems; and

(b) indicate corrective action.

Statistical trends should be monitored to reveal areas where recurring accidents suggest the need for special investigation, but only more serious incidents will have to be followed-up in depth. Follow-up should be clearly aimed at preventing recurrence - not placing blame.

3.5 Fire

The general regulations relating to fire, contained in the Offices, Shops and Railway Premises Act 1963, were reinforced in the Fire Precautions Act 1971 and the Fire and Safety at Sports Places Act 1987. The main provisions are that:

(a) there must be adequate means of escape kept free from obstructions;

(b) all doors out of the building must be capable of opening from the inside;

(c) all employees should know the fire alarm system;

(d) there must be an effective and regularly tested fire alarm system; and

(e) there must be fire-fighting equipment easily available and in working order.

Fire represents a further area for preventive action. The main causes of fire in industry and commerce tend to be associated with electrical appliances and installations, and smoking is a major source of fires in business premises. The Fire Protection Association (of the UK) suggests the following guidelines for fire prevention and control:

(a) management should accept that fire prevention policies and practices must be established and reviewed regularly;

(b) management should be aware of the possible effects and consequences of fires, in terms of loss of buildings, plant and output, damage to records, effects on customers and workers etc;

(c) fire risks should be identified, particularly as regards sources of ignition, presence of combustible materials, and the means by which fires can spread;

(d) the responsibility for fire prevention should be established;

(e) a fire officer should be appointed; and

(f) a fire prevention drill should be established and practised.

The Fire Protection Association provides detailed guidelines for fire prevention, and checklists for use in assessing the adequacy of existing procedures and in designing new procedures.

Activity 6

Identify anything that strikes you as being hazardous about the working environment depicted on page 202.

4 OCCUPATIONAL HEALTH

Occupational health programmes are concerned largely with the effects of the working environment on workers. This may involve:

(a) identifying substances, conditions or processes which are actually or potentially hazardous, and in what circumstances;

(b) identifying the effect of methods and processes of work on the human body and mind; and

(c) exercising control over the working environment and substances used in the course of work, so as to minimise risk.

Thus, occupational health is concerned with toxic substances (such as lead oxide, chlorine, asbestos, and radiation), and with protective measures against all of these, as well as less obvious sources of hazard at work, including noise, fatigue and physical and mental stress (excessive demands on the body and mind). Increasingly, it is also concerned with personal substance abuse (such as smoking and alcoholism) and their direct or indirect affect on the workplace and work performance.

4.1 Ergonomics

Ergonomics is taken from the Greek - ergos (work) and nomos (natural laws).

Definition

Ergonomics is usually described as the scientific study of the relationship between man and his working environment. This sphere of scientific research explores the demands that can arise from a working environment and the capabilities of people to meet these demands.

Through this research, data is made available to establish machines and working conditions which, apart from functioning well, are best suited to the capacities and health requirements of the human body. Computer consoles and controls, office furniture, factory layout and so on can be designed so that the individual expends minimal energy and experiences minimal physical strain in any given task.

Industrial psychology increasingly enters into this field. Apart from purely mechanical considerations - in what position should a worker be sitting in order to exert maximum force over a long period of time without physical strain or fatigue? - the ergonomist must now take into account the increasing problems of the worker as information processor. The perceptual limitations of the worker can also be measured, and systems designed which do not make unreasonable demands on the worker's attention span or capacity to absorb information: one example might be the use of sound signals to attract attention to visual displays or equipment.

4.2 Shift work

We described briefly how shift work systems work in Chapter 2. The effects of shift work on workers have been well researched.

(a) *Physiological or medical effects* - a disruption of body-temperature, digestion and sleep patterns, resulting from the disorientation of the body's regular 24-hour cycle. Some people suffer more from the physical disruption than others: in particular, diabetics, epileptics and those prone to digestive disorders should be screened by management, and excluded from shift work for health reasons

(b) *Psychological effects*. The experience of variety can be stimulating. On the other hand, the fatigue and sense of physical disorientation can be stressful and those with strong security or structure needs may feel threatened by a lack of rhythm in working life.

(c) *Social effects*. Some forms of shiftwork involve a high degree of social and family disruption, though others - in particular double-day working - very little.

4.3 Stress

Definition

> *Stress* is a term which is often loosely used to describe feelings of tension or exhaustion - usually associated with too much, or overly demanding, work. In fact, stress is the product of demands made on an individual's physical *and mental* energies: monotony and feelings of failure or insecurity are sources of stress, as much as the conventionally considered factors of pressure, overwork and so on.

It is worth remembering, too, that demands on an individual's energies may be stimulating as well as harmful: many people, especially those suited to managerial jobs, work well under pressure, and even require some form of stress to bring out their best performance. (It is excessive stress that can be damaging: this may be called strain.) This is why we talk about the management of stress, not about its elimination: it is a question of keeping stress to helpful proportions and avenues.

Harmful stress, or strain, can be identified by its effects on the individual and his performance. Symptoms usually include:

(a) *nervous tension*. This may manifest itself in various ways: irritability and increased sensitivity, preoccupation with details, a polarised perspective on the issues at hand, or sleeplessness. Various physical symptoms - such as skin and digestive disorders - are also believed to be stress-related;

(b) *withdrawal*. This is essentially a defence mechanism which may manifest itself as unusual quietness and reluctance to communicate, or as physical withdrawal in the form of absenteeism, poor time-keeping, or even leaving the organisation;

(c) *low morale*: low confidence, dissatisfaction, expression of frustration or hopelessness;

d) signs that the individual is repressing the problem, trying to deny it. Forced cheerfulness, boisterous playfulness or excessive drinking may indicate this.

(It is worth noting that some of these symptoms - say, absenteeism - may or may not be *correctly* identified with stress. There are many other possible causes of such problems, both at work (lack of motivation) and outside (personal problems). The same is true of physical symptoms such as headaches and stomach pains: these are not invariably correlated with personal stress.

All these things can adversely affect performance, however, which is why stress management has become a major workplace issue. Considerable research effort has been directed to:

- investigating the causes of stress;
- increasing awareness of stress in organisations; and
- designing techniques and programmes for stress control.

Stress can be caused or aggravated by:

(a) *personality*. Competitive, sensitive and insecure people feel stress more acutely;

(b) ambiguity or conflict in the *roles* required of an individual. If a person is unsure what is expected of him at work, or finds conflict between two incompatible roles (employee and mother of small children, say), role stress may be a problem;

(c) *insecurity, risk and change*. A manager with a high sense of responsibility who has to initiate a risky change, and most people facing career change, end or uncertainty, will feel this kind of stress;

(d) *management style*. A recent American report pointed out particular management traits that were held responsible by workshop interviewees for causing stress and health problems (high blood pressure, insomnia, coronary heart disease and alcoholism). These included:

   (i) unpredictability. Staff were under constant threat of an outburst;

   (ii) destruction of workers' self esteem - making them feel helpless and insecure;

   (iii) setting up win/lose situations - turning work relationships into a battle for control; and

   (iv) providing too much - or too little - stimulation.

Activity 7

What sources of stress are there in your own lifestyle? Are you aware of the symptoms of stress in yourself? What do you do (if anything) to control your stress?

Greater *awareness* of the nature and control of stress is a feature of the modern work environment. *Stress management techniques* are increasingly taught and encouraged by organisations, and include:

(a) counselling;

(b) time off or regular rest breaks;

(c) relaxation techniques (breathing exercises, meditation);

(d) physical exercise and self-expression as a safety valve for tension;

(e) delegation and planning (to avoid work-load related stress); and

(f) assertiveness (to control stress related to insecurity in personal relations).

In addition, *job* training can increase the individual's sense of competence and security and *ecological* control can be brought to bear on the problem of stress, creating conditions in which stress is less likely to be a problem: well designed jobs and environments, and an organisation culture built on meaningful work, mutual support, communication and teamwork.

However, these strategies may offer only a limited impact. As reported in *People Management* (October 1996) stress may cost the UK anything between £3.7 billion and £11 billion a year through sickness absence and health costs. The Trades Union Congress (TUC), which conducted a survey on 7,000 health and safety officers, found more than two-thirds said stress was their biggest concern. They identified the main sources as being new management techniques, such as just-in-time production and teamworking. According to the report, for example, team-based pay is often linked to low absenteeism and accident rates, as well as meeting production targets. Thus, peer pressure to achieve the pay award means that accidents may go unreported and people may take holidays instead of sick leave.

4.4 Sick Building Syndrome (SBS)

SBS is an illness (comparatively recently identified) associated with the workplace. Symptoms include lethargy, stuffy nose, dry throat, headache and itching eyes: once away from the workplace, staff are free from these problems. Factors in the workplace suspected to contribute to SBS include air-conditioning, and open-plan office space where there is perceived to be little control over the indoor environment. A report by the Health and Safety Executive (HSE) (reported in *Personnel Management*, September 1992) found that 30-50% of new or refurbished buildings may affect people in this way, but that the causes (and therefore the cure) are uncertain.

4.5 Passive smoking

Following a 1992 Australian court case in which an employer was held to have been negligent in not protecting a non-smoking employee from the ill effects of exposure to colleagues' smoking, smoking policies have rapidly been introduced by many organisations.

One report suggests that 'The risks of passive smoking are greater than these posed by any other indoor man-made pollutant released into the general environment'. A recent Health Education Authority campaign has called for environmental tobacco smoke to be added to the list of substances which can be controlled in the workplace under the Control of Substances Hazardous to Health (COSHH) Regulations.

Amid the publication of conclusive scientific evidence as to the harmful effects, the publicity surrounding it (including advice on segregation of smokers and non-smokers from the HSE), and a (January 1993) EU directive on separate rest rooms for smokers and non-smokers to be implemented within three years, there is considerable pressure on employers to act. It is no longer possible for an employer to plead ignorance of the risks as a defence against civil action by an employee whose health has been damaged by passive smoking at work.

In *Personnel Management* (August 1992), the options for a smoking policy were identified as a total smoking ban, or the provision of separate smoking rooms.

The components of a well-implemented smoking policy at work are consultation, sensitivity to the needs of smokers and plenty of warning. An industrial tribunal, quoted in the article, suggested that a fair way of introducing new rules on smoking, which would protect the employer from smoker-employee claims of breach of contract or constructive dismissal (in effect, 'forcing' the employee to resign), would be:

(a) to discuss the new rules in advance with staff in a sensitive and sympathetic way and perhaps hold a ballot to establish the level of support;

(b) to give proper notice of the change in the rules of employment; and

(c) to attempt to seek alternative measures for those who cannot desist from their habit overnight, either by moving smokers into an office where smoking is allowed or allowing smoking in some parts of the building or even outside.

In 1995, a number of local authorities introduced hard-line anti-smoking policies (*People Management*, August 1995). After Stockport County Council paid out £40,000 in passive smoking claims, organisations are much more wary and heed the pressure from non-smokers. Derby County Council have introduced a total smoking ban for new employees: existing employees will be allowed two 10 minute breaks per day to smoke in designated areas. Brent Council has introduced a uniform ban saying 'Smoking is regarded as a fire hazard and a health risk'. For Newham Council, persistent offenders will face disciplinary action. There will be no smoking areas in any of its buildings, and staff will be actively discouraged from smoking outside council premises.

> **Case study: Chase Manhattan Bank, Bournemouth**
>
> In January 1991, Chase Manhattan introduced a smoking policy in its Bournemouth headquarters. The policy was devised by a working party (including a consultant) with the agreed aims: 'To introduce a smoking policy which would:
>
> (a) recognise the employer's obligations to its employees regarding health and safety;
>
> (b) improve the working environment at Chase Manhattan with regard to general cleanliness etc; and
>
> (c) best attempt to respect the wishes of smokers.'
>
> After communication and consultation, it was decided to make the office a non-smoking site with designated smoking areas (which were designed to be well-ventilated and pleasant, but away from areas of public circulation). A policy statement was inserted in the staff handbook, and given to all potential recruits: breach of smoking regulations was to be considered a matter for disciplinary action. Details of assistance were given for those smokers who wished to give up, but there was no pressure on people to change their behaviour - other than its location.
>
> Chase Manhattan have found that the necessity for smoking breaks has not caused a significant drop in performance. The working environment is considered cleaner and more pleasant. Health hazard awareness has risen. Initial worries - about alienating smokers, handling the need for smoking breaks, fire hazards and so on - were overcome by systematic consultation and briefing.

4.6 Alcohol policy

An Industrial Relations Service (IRS) Employment Trends Survey in August 1992 highlighted alcoholism and alcohol awareness as a major and growing issue.

As far back as 1981, the Government suggested the need for an agreed policy on alcohol, in its booklet *The Problem Drinker at Work*. In 1990, the Health Education Authority (HEA) launched a major campaign on alcohol awareness at work, and in 1992, it commissioned research which showed that 70% of organisations in the UK had formal or informal policies on alcohol.

Business Basics: Human Resource Management

> *It is estimated that one in 10 employees in Britain has an alcohol problem, and absences from work due to hangovers and other alcohol-related complaints account for an estimated 8 million days lost a year, three times the number lost through industrial action. In terms of lost production, this is costing the British economy around £1,700 million a year.*
>
> *The less quantifiable costs associated with alcohol misuse in terms of accidents at work are likely to inflate the figure significantly. Employees with alcohol problems also pay heavily in terms of their own health and, in extreme cases, their jobs.*
>
> IRS Employment Trends 517

The survey found that reasons given for the introduction of an alcohol policy include:

(a) the introduction of a wider programme of health promotion and awareness;

(b) health and safety concerns; and

(c) concerns about inefficiency caused by alcohol misuse.

Most alcohol policies embrace the following areas.

(a) *Positive aims and objectives* - including statistics on alcohol-related harm.

(b) *Restrictions on alcohol possession or consumption.* These may be:

   (i) a total ban on alcohol consumption on company premises; and/or

   (ii) a total ban on alcohol consumption on and off the premises during working hours. (In theory, this does not restrict off-duty drinking, but some policies add warnings about legal drink-driving limits to cover this situation as well);

   (iii) restriction of alcohol consumption to certain areas of the premises (say, visitors' dining rooms or a licensed canteen) and/or hours (usually special occasions, such as the Christmas party or celebrations with specific permission, but may also apply to designated breaks);

   (iv) selective restrictions on certain employees - usually for health and safety reasons. The policy is likely to be heavily resented if the selection is perceived to be based on the organisation hierarchy: 'operational staff' are banned, while the managers are out entertaining;

   (v) specific provisions for workplace social events.

Activity 8

What categories of employees would you think it advisable to ban from drinking at or before work?

Procedures for monitoring and enforcing these restrictions - from supervision and peer pressure to searches and tests (in safety-sensitive sectors) should be implemented.

(c) *The links between the policy and disciplinary procedure.* This is a sensitive area. Violent or illegal behaviour under the influence of alcohol would clearly trigger disciplinary action. Instances of random drunkenness and bad behaviour are usually treated under the heading of 'gross misconduct'. Deterioration in work performance or behaviour may, however, be better handled under the terms of the counselling and referral provisions of the alcohol policy - unless counselling and treatment are refused or ineffective. These fine lines will need to be clearly set out.

(d) *The roles of line and other managers in identifying and helping individuals with alcohol problems.* There should be detailed provisions on dealing with the problem drinker at work, from the initial identification of deteriorating work performance, through interviews with employees to explore whether this might be due to an alcohol problem, to assessing appropriate treatments and how to deal with the return to work.

Alcohol policies usually stress that line managers are not expected to diagnose or treat employees with alcohol problems, but to be alert and to use the laid-down procedure to identify and refer those individuals to the HR or occupational health department.

(e) *Internal and external counselling services available.* Counselling is one of the central objectives of most alcohol policies, moving the issue out of the disciplinary machinery and into the health and safety area. The policy must strive to make employees feel comfortable enough to come forward with their anxiety and their problem. It should specify provisions for time off for counselling, the right of the individual to return to his job, any 'rehabilitation' requirements and a period of monitoring.

Much of the impetus for an alcohol policy will come from the human resource department, which will also have responsibility for communication, consultation with trade unions or other employee representatives, training and education of managers and employees, disciplinary measures and job protection, and arranging (or even carrying out) counselling.

Activity 9

Having mentioned 'counselling' in connection with occupational health and welfare: what do you consider to be the difference between *counselling* and *advising*?

5 COUNSELLING

Definition

'*Counselling* can be defined as a purposeful relationship in which one person helps another to help himself. It is a way of relating and responding to another person so that that person is helped to explore his thoughts, feelings and behaviour with the aim of reaching a clearer understanding. The clearer understanding may be of himself or of a problem, or of the one in relation to the other.' (Rees)

The need for workplace counselling can arise in many different situations. The following are some frequent examples - but not an exhaustive list.

(a) During appraisal.

(b) In grievance or disciplinary situations.

(c) Following change, such as promotion or relocation.

(d) On redundancy or dismissal.

(e) As a result of domestic or personal difficulties.

(f) In cases of sexual harassment or violence at work.

Most of what follows is derived from the IPD's 1994 *Statement on Counselling in the Workplace*.

5.1 The role of counselling in organisations

The IPD statement makes it clear that effective counselling is not merely a matter of 'pastoral care' for individuals, but is very much in the organisation's interests.

(a) Appropriate use of counselling tools can prevent under-performance, reduce labour turnover and absenteeism and increase commitment from employees.

207

Unhappy employees are far more likely to seek employment elsewhere.

(b) Effective counselling demonstrates an organisation's commitment to and concern for its employees and so is liable to improve loyalty and enthusiasm among the workforce.

(c) The development of employees is of value to the organisation, and counselling can give employees the confidence and encouragement necessary to take responsibility for self and career development.

(d) Workplace counselling recognises that the organisation may be contributing to the employees' problems and therefore it provides an opportunity to reassess organisational policy and practice.

5.2 The counselling process

The counselling process has three elements.

(a) *Recognition and understanding*. Often it is the employee who takes the initiative, but managers should be aware that the problem raised initially may be just the tip of the iceberg. (*Personnel Management Plus*, February 1993, cites a case where an employee came forward with a problem about pension contributions, and mentioned, as he was about to leave 'By the way - my wife wants a divorce'.)

(b) *Empowering*. This means enabling employees to recognise their own problem or situation, and encouraging them to express it.

(c) *Resourcing*. The problem must then be managed, and this includes the decision as to who is best able to act as counsellor. A HR specialist or outside person may be better than the employee's manager.

The counselling *interview* might proceed as follows.

(a) *Factual exchange*

The interview will commence by establishing why the need for it has arisen - 'it has been noticed that you are frequently abrasive and aggressive to your colleagues', 'So and so has complained that you are ...'. Often this part of the discussion will focus on a particular incident - a highly public argument with a particular person or group of people for example.

(b) *Opinion interchange*

Once the basic facts have been established the interview should attempt to view them from the perspective of the organisation on the one hand and the individual on the other. The interviewer could explain, for example, why frequent lateness, leaving early and long absences are viewed as unacceptable by the organisation. The interviewee, in an ideal situation, will respond by explaining the personal justification for his or her behaviour. Typical causes in this scenario would be external pressures of running a home or family, avoidance of some unpleasantness at work, or dissatisfaction with some aspect of work.

(c) *Joint problem-solving*

At this stage, the interviewer and interviewee discuss various means of resolving the problem. The aim is for the interviewee to come to terms with the problem himself: the role of the interviewer is to help the interviewee to identify the options available to him. In the case of an employee who has suddenly become withdrawn, say because of some slight from colleagues (whether real or imagined), the options might be to continue with this behaviour, to confront the offenders or simply to carry on as before and brush the problem aside. The discussion will consider the consequences of taking each of these options (preserving the individual's pride but interfering with work performance; losing face and appearing weak and so on).

(d) *Decision-making*

The choice of options has to be made by the interviewee rather than the counsellor. As Rees says,

This can involve a person taking a decision that is not necessarily in the interests of the organisation - for example leave (or in some cases not to leave!). There is little point, however, in the counsellor seeking to impose the decision that is in the organisation's interests as the person would undoubtedly ignore it.

5.3 Counselling skills

Remember that the aim of counselling is empowerment: to help the employee to help himself. It is *not* to give advice or instruction. Counsellors need to be observant enough to note behaviour which may be symptomatic of a problem, be sensitive to beliefs and values which may be different from their own (for example religious beliefs), be empathetic (to the extent that they appreciate that the problem may seem overwhelming to the individual), and yet remain impartial and refrain from giving advice. Counsellors must have the belief that individuals have the resources to solve their *own* problems, albeit with passive or active help.

Interviewing skills are particularly relevant. Open questioning, listening actively (probing, evaluating, interpreting, supporting and feeding back), seeing the problem from the individual's point of view, and above all being genuinely and sincerely interested are skills identified in the IPD Statement.

Counselling checklist

Preparation

- Choose a place to talk which is quiet, free from interruption and not open to view.
- Research as much as you can before the meeting and have any necessary papers readily available.
- Make sure you know whether the need for counselling has been properly identified or whether you will have to carefully probe to establish if a problem exists.
- Allow sufficient time for the session. (If you know you must end at a particular time, inform the individual of this).
- Decide if it is necessary for the individual's department head to be aware of the counselling and its purpose.
- Give the individual the option of being accompanied by a supportive colleague.
- If you are approaching the individual following information received from a colleague, decide in advance the extent to which you can reveal your source
- Consider how you are going to introduce and discuss your perceptions of the situation.
- Be prepared for the individual to have different expectations of the discussion, eg the individual may expect you to solve the problem - rather than come to terms with it himself/herself.
- Understand that the individual's view of the facts of the situation will be more important than the facts themselves and that their behaviour may not reflect their true feelings.

> ### Counselling checklist - continued
>
> *Format of discussion*
>
> - Welcome the individual and clarify the general purpose of the meeting.
> - Assure the individual that matters of confidentiality will be treated as such.
> - The individual may be reticent through fear of being considered somewhat of a risk in future and you will need to give appropriate reassurances in this regard.
> - Be ready to prompt or encourage the individual to move into areas he/she might be hesitant about.
> - Encourage the individual to look more deeply into statements.
> - Ask the individual to clarify statements you do not quite understand.
> - Try to take the initiative in probing important areas which may be embarrassing/emotional to the individual and which you both might prefer to avoid.
> - Recognise that some issues may be so important to the individual that they will have to be discussed over and over again, even though this may seem repetitious to you.
> - If you sense that the individual is becoming defensive, try to identify the reason and relax the pressure by changing your approach.
> - Occasionally summarise the conversation as it goes along, reflecting back in your own words (not parrot phrasing [sic]) what you understand the individual to say.
> - Sometimes emotions may be more important than the words being spoken, so it may be necessary to reflect back what you see the individual feeling.
> - At the close of the meeting, clarify any decisions reached and agree what follow-up support would be helpful.
>
> *Overcoming dangers*
>
> - If you take notes at an inappropriate moment, you may set up a barrier between yourself and the individual.
> - Realise you may not like the individual and be on guard against this.
> - Recognise that repeating problems does not solve them.
> - Be careful to avoid taking sides.
> - Overcome internal and external distractions. Concentrate on the individual and try to understand the situation with him/her.
> - The greater the perceived level of listening, the more likely the individual will be to accept comments and contributions from you.
> - Resist the temptation to talk about your own problems, even though these may seem similar to those of the individual.
>
> *Source*: IPD Statement on Counselling in the Workplace

5.4 Confidentiality

There will be situations when an employee cannot be completely open unless he is sure that all comments will be treated confidentially. However, certain information, once obtained by the organisation (about fraud or sexual harassment for example) calls for action. In spite of the drawbacks, therefore, the IPD statement is clear that employees must be made aware when their comments will be passed on to the relevant authority, and when they will be treated completely confidentially.

Activity 10

Javed is a member of the section which you lead. His work is normally well above average and he knows it. You find him mildly arrogant and have difficulty in liking him, although he seems to have a great deal of respect for you. Frankly, you think he is a bit of a crawler.

Of late you have noticed that Javed's work is slipping and he seems to keep himself to himself more than usual. One day he comes to you with a problem that he would normally deal with himself, and he is obviously distressed when you send him away to solve the problem on his own. On your guard, now, you observe that none of the other team members are co-operating with Javed and one or two rather catty remarks are being made behind his back.

You decide to have a counselling session with Javed. How do you conduct the session?

5.5 Employee assistance programmes (EAPs)

Recognising the difficulty of providing an effective counselling service in-house and also the special skills involved, a notable modern trend is to use outsiders for employee support.

Companies such as EAR, Focus, and ICAS provide Employee Assistance Programmes (EAPs), offering a 24-hour telephone line with instant access to a trained counsellor. Meetings can be face-to-face if the employee wants, and their immediate families are also covered by the scheme. The providers offer thorough briefing on the scheme for all employees and management information and consultancy for the employers.

About 80% of the top 500 US companies use such schemes, and around 150 UK companies are estimated to have taken them up since the late 1980s. The cost on average is between £15 and £30 per employee, and companies such as Mobil Oil, Whitbread, and Glaxo report considerable benefits.
   (*Personnel Management Plus*, February 1993; *Financial Times*, June 1993)

6 TIME OFF WORK

Apart from sickness and maternity (discussed in Chapter 9), there are other situations in which employees are entitled to time off work.

(a) Time off work (at the normal rate of pay) for the purpose of *trade union duties* (Trade Union and Labour Relations [Consolidation] Act 1992.) This applies to *officials* of a recognised trade union who are engaged in official duties concerned with industrial relations in the organisation, or relevant training. This is the statutory basis for the existence of the full- or part-time shop steward. 'Reasonable' time is allowed - as defined by the ACAS Code of Practice.

(b) *Trade union activities*. A *member* of a recognised independent trade union may have time off work (without statutory rights to pay) for trade union activities, such as attending branch meetings: TULR(C)A, 1992.

(c) *Public duties*. Reasonable time off (without statutory right to pay) is allowed for public duties performed by employees who are:
   (i) Justices of the Peace; or

(ii) members of local authorities, regional health authorities, statutory tribunals, or governing bodies of educational institutions maintained by local education authorities.

In addition, time must be made available for jury service if an employee is called up.

(d) *Notice period for redundancy*. Employees who have received notice of redundancy are entitled to reasonable time off to look for new work or arrange for training, provided they have completed at least two year's continuous employment with the organisation. They are entitled to a maximum of two-fifths of a week's paid absence.

(e) *Duties under the Health and Safety at Work Act*. Employees who are union-appointed safety representatives are allowed time off with pay for their duties, committee work, training and so on.

Chapter roundup

- Legislation is not designed to represent 'best practice' but offers a 'floor' below which standards of conduct cannot drop, for the protection of employees.
- Health and safety legislation requires that the systems, environment, equipment and conduct of organisations be such as to minimise the risk to the health and safety of employees and visitors alike.
- Employees share responsibility for health and safety with employers, although the latter take responsibility for the environment, systems, equipment and training.

Diagram: 8cm (diagram not found)??

Systematic approach to health and safety

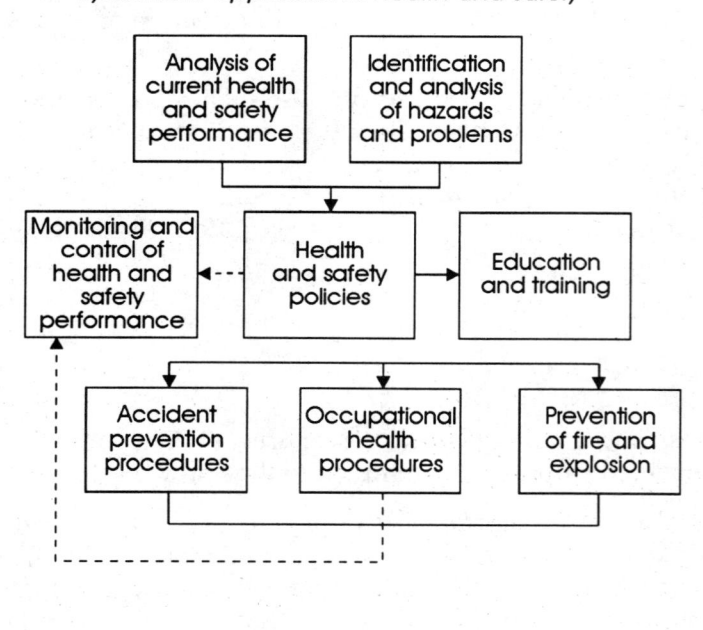

Quick quiz

1 Give four examples of circumstances in which welfare services might be provided by employers.

Chapter 10: Welfare, health and safety

2 'Health and safety problems are:
   (a) only relevant to factories,
   (b) a thing of the past.'
   How far do you agree?
3 Why is health and safety important?
4 What areas of health and safety are covered by EU directives?
5 What three categories of female employees have special protection under new Health and Safety at Work regulations?
6 Outline some of the preventative measures that can be taken against
   (a) accidents; and
   (b) fire at work.
7 List some of the symptoms of stress.
8 List the elements of an alcohol policy at work.
9 List the stages in a counselling session.
10 In what seven circumstances are employees legally entitled to take time off work?

Solutions to activities

1 Common ones are HIV and Aids, alcohol, drugs, pregnancy and financial problems.
2 You may have thought of the Bhopal chemical plant explosion, Chernobyl reactor explosion, Kings Cross station fire, Piper Alpha oil rig disaster, various bombings by terrorist groups, and so on. The main costs are reconstruction, compensation for death and injury, lost production, and loss of reputation.
5 This was a real case: *Davidson v Handy Page* 1945. It was held that the employee's injury had occurred in the course of her work, and that the employer had failed in his duty to take reasonable care to provide safe premises.
6 You may have spotted the following hazards (if not others as well...)
   (a) Heavy object on high (secure?) shelf
   (b) Standing on swivel chair
   (c) Lifting heavy object incorrectly
   (d) Open drawers blocking passage
   (e) Trailing wires
   (f) Electric bar fire
   (g) Unattended lit cigarette
   (h) Overfull waste bin
   (i) Overloaded electric socket
   (j) Overloaded tray of hot liquids
   (k) Dangerous 'spike'
8 The two most common categories are those involving driving and operating heavy or dangerous machinery.
9 Advising is proposing a solution to a problem.
   Counselling is helping someone to talk about, recognise and suggest solutions to his or her own problem

Further question practice

Now try the following questions at the end of this text
Multiple choice questions   63 to 71
Exam style question   10

Chapter 11

INDUSTRIAL RELATIONS

Introduction
Arising largely from its turbulent history and tainted with political colours, industrial relations is an emotive subject requiring careful and rational handling in essays and exams. Do not let your personal convictions carry you to extremes!

Traditionally, industrial relations are the dealings and co-operation (or lack of it) between management and workers, usually via employee representatives in a trade union or staff association. Negotiations and consultations may be carried out on behalf of the workforce:

(a) at local level, on the shopfloor and in the factory, by shop stewards. (Negotiations at this level are called *domestic bargaining*);

(b) at organisational level, by appointed representatives (for example on management-union joint consultative committees);

(c) at an area/regional and national level, by officials of the national trade union.

Not all organisations are unionised and a high proportion of employees in the UK do not belong to unions. Industrial relations (or employee relations) still exist in these organisations, even though employees might have less collective strength to pursue their interests. Issues such as communication and consultation, even participation by employees in corporate decision-making, are part of employee relations in the wider sense.

Your objectives
After completing this chapter, you should:

(a) be able to identify the role of the parties in industrial relations;

(b) understand the ideological and legal frameworks of industrial relations;

(c) appreciate the role of HRM in industrial relations;

(d) be able to outline the processes of collective bargaining and negotiation;

(e) understand the concept of industrial democracy or participation;

(f) understand HRM's role in communication and change management.

1 THE PARTIES IN INDUSTRIAL RELATIONS

The areas usually embraced by industrial relations negotiations or 'collective bargaining' are:

(a) pay;
(b) working conditions;
(c) working procedures and rules;
(d) redundancy plans or expansion and recruitment plans;
(e) fair treatment of members (with regard to non-discrimination, discipline and grievance procedures and many other matters);
(f) welfare of members (pensions and other benefits and services);
(g) new technology agreements;
(h) participation in decision-making, quality initiatives and so on;
(i) health and safety matters.

You may notice that many of these issues are already being voluntarily addressed by employers keen to be (or to be perceived as) socially responsible and people-oriented. You may also have your own opinions about whether this respect for workers' rights makes formal industrial relations machinery redundant, or whether worker representation and organisation are just as necessary to combat the new 'enlightened' methods of exploitation! We discuss trade union power, and the need for it, later, but you should be aware of the extent to which, in the UK, collective bargaining has been side-lined as a major issue for the HRM.

1.1 Trade unions and staff associations

Definition

A *trade union* is an organised association of workers for the protection of their common interests. A single trade union might include members from different organisations in the same industry and a single organisation might employ workers who belong to a number of different trade unions.

Unions are often distinguished as *white collar* unions (employees in office work or desk jobs), *craft* unions (workers skilled at a particular craft) and *blue collar* unions (workers in a particular industry such as the National Union of Mineworkers or the National Union of Seamen). Some unions represent workers from a variety of different jobs and industries (for example, the Transport and General Workers Union).

Initially, a trade union must be *recognised* by its members' employer as an organisation with which the employer is prepared to negotiate. The employer must concede that the union is a true representative of a sufficient number of its employees before it will allow the union to negotiate on their behalf.

Some of the functions carried out by a trade union are directly related to its objectives of improving pay, conditions and job security for its members: representation of employees in formal discussions with management (say, as part of disciplinary procedures), negotiation and consultation.

Activity 1

What other functions might a union have which are not directly connected to the achievement of its goals, but which might indirectly be effective?

1.2 Trade union officers

Trade union officers may be:

(a) full-time paid officials, employed by the union to carry out its policies under the direction of its executive committee;

(b) part-time voluntary officials, elected to be branch officers of the union in a particular area; or

(c) workplace representatives (shop stewards or staff representatives) who are employed by the organisation, but act on behalf of their fellow employees as their recognised representative. (Some very large firms with sensitive industrial relations may retain one or two employees on full pay to act in their union capacity full time.) Shop Stewards are the link between the work group, the union officials and management: they require extensive knowledge of the union's services, employment law, ACAS and tribunal machinery, the policies and practices of the organisation, the roles of managers and so on.

1.3 Management

What used to be a simplified 'us and them' situation has become more complicated with the development of white collar unions for management staff. A line manager may have to handle employee relations with staff from the management side, while taking on the role of representative for a union in dealings with senior management.

Line managers are in direct contact with the shopfloor and its office equivalent and so are at the sharp end of employee relations. Their involvement may include:

(a) *exchanging information* with office representatives - say, to discuss changes in work procedures, or newly introduced rules;

(b) *disciplinary measures*. In many organisations, a union representative is invited to attend disciplinary meetings between a line manager and the offender, in serious cases of breach of discipline;

(c) union representatives are likely to represent members in grievance procedures. The manager will be involved in these, as the person to whom a grievance against a colleague is brought, or perhaps as the source of the grievance;

(d) implementing any *agreements* on working procedures or working conditions that are reached between management and unions;

(e) in situations *where industrial relations are poor* and unions unco-operative with management, trying to ensure that:

   (i) difficult situations are eased and potential 'flashpoints' are defused; and that

   (ii) their authority is preserved against any show of collective power.

Management at a more senior level becomes involved in industrial relations in matters relating to:

(a) pay negotiations;

(b) negotiations on work procedures and working conditions. There might be a management-union committee set up to discuss and agree these matters;

(c) negotiations on redundancies or the introduction of new technology;

(d) appeals against disciplinary action, under grievance procedures; and

(e) resolving industrial disputes that cannot be settled by a lower level manager.

1.4 The human resource function and industrial relations

In an article in *The Administrator* (September 1992), Laurie Mullins considers where the responsibility for employee relations lies: with line managers or with the HR function?

It is sometimes suggested that in many organisations the responsibility for industrial relations still lies with line managers who are often sceptical or even hostile towards personnel ideas and techniques, and who frequently reject the concept of an industrial relations policy because it hampers their work and limits their flexibility. For example, Clegg argues that: "If line managers are left to handle industrial relations issues for themselves, the pressures of production are likely to lead to ad hoc and contradictory decisions ... If a personnel policy is introduced to promote consistent decisions on industrial relations issues, its effectiveness may depend on granting authority to the personnel department to override the natural priorities of the line managers."

The Administrator, September 1992

There *has* been a trend towards transferring key functions in employee relations to the HR function: communications, for example, and change management, as well as wage negotiations and health and safety discussions. Mullins suggests the need for a concerted organisational approach, led and supported by senior management, with a shared role for HRM and line managers, within the framework of sound personnel policies and procedures. Arguably, however, the HR function's key role will be to devise and implement policies that will make 'industrial relations', in its traditional sense of conflict resolution, negotiation and bargaining, unnecessary.

1.5 Third parties

Third parties, such as Government ministers, arbitrators, judges etc have an important bearing on industrial relations, because they set a framework for what employers and employees can and cannot do.

The government has established agencies such as the Manpower Services Commission, the Advisory, Conciliation and Arbitration Service (ACAS) and industrial tribunals, to assist or act as go-between in employment and industrial relations matters.

Activity 2

Before you read on, what is *your* idea of what ACAS does, from its exposure in the news media?

According to the Employment Protection Act 1975, ACAS has a positive role to play in 'promoting the improvement of industrial relations'. As an independent body, it can be required under the Act to settle trade union issues, by holding publishing recommendations. It may also be involved in individual conciliation cases, prior to hearing by tribunal: it is frequently called in, for example, over unfair dismissal complaints.

ACAS may thus intervene with:

(a) conciliation (getting conflicting parties together);

(b) arbitration (assisting in the appointment of arbitrators); or

(c) mediation (offering middle ground for settlement).

In *Personnel Management Plus* (September 1994) it was noted that although recorded disputes have fallen to very low levels - giving the impression that conflict at work has largely disappeared - there is still a high demand for ACAS' services on a personal level, in matters of unfair dismissal, equal pay and sex and race discrimination. In 1993, 47% of ACAS' completed *collective* conciliation cases related to pay and employment conditions disputes, 20% to redundancy and only 9% to union recognition. ACAS hit the headlines in 1994 owing to its successful intervention in the Railtrack dispute with rail union RMT.

Industrial Tribunals deal with most cases brought under employment law. They are informal (consisting of a legally qualified Chairman and two representative members, from the employer and the union) but their decisions are legally binding. Evidence is given on oath, witnesses are called and legal representation is permitted as in a court of law. Appeals on points of law only are allowed, to the Employment Appeal Tribunal (EAT).

2 THE IDEOLOGICAL FRAMEWORK: CONFLICT AND CO-OPERATION

Alan Fox (*Industrial Relations and a Wider Society: Aspects of Interaction*, 1975) identifies three broad ideologies which are involved in industrial relations.

(a) *Unitary ideology*. All members of the organisation, despite their different roles, have common objectives and values which unite their efforts. Workers are loyal, and the prerogative of management is accepted as paternal, and in everyone's best interests. Unions are a useful channel of communication, but are no longer necessary, and can offer unhelpful encouragement to disruptive elements.

> *Any business must mould a true team and weld individual efforts into a common effort. Each member of the enterprise contributes something different, but they must all contribute towards a common goal. Their efforts must all pull in the same direction, without friction, without unnecessary duplication of effort.*
>
> **Drucker**

(b) *Radical ideology*. This primarily Marxist ideology argues that there is an inequality of power between the controllers of economic resources (shareholders and managers) and those who depend on access to those resources (wage earners). Those in power exploit the others by indoctrinating them to accept the legitimacy of their rights to power, and thus perpetuate the system. Conflict between these strata of society - the proletariat and the bourgeoisie - does not aim for mutual survival, but revolutionary change.

> *The history of all hitherto society is the history of class struggles. Freeman and slave, patrician and plebeian, lord and serf, guildmaster and journeyman, in a word, oppressor and oppressed, stood in constant opposition to one another, carried on an uninterrupted, now hidden, now open fight ... .*
>
> **Marx and Engels** *The Communist Manifesto*, 1888

(c) *Pluralist ideology*. Organisations are political coalitions of individuals and groups which have their own interests. Management has to create a workable structure for collaboration, taking into account the objectives of all the various interest groups or stakeholders in the organisation. A mutual survival strategy, involving the control of conflict through compromise, can be made acceptable in varying degrees to all concerned.

Activity 3

Which view do you subscribe to? Why?

Charles Handy redefined the term conflict to offer a useful way of thinking about destructive and constructive conflict and how it might be managed. He recognised that organisations are political systems within which there is competition for scarce resources and unequal influence. He wrote that *differences* between people are natural and inevitable and emerge in three ways:

(a) argument;

(b) competition; and

(c) conflict - which alone, in this definition, is considered wholly harmful.

Argument and competition are potentially beneficial and fruitful; both may degenerate into conflict if badly managed.

2.1 Managerial response to conflict

Hunt identifies five different management responses to the handling of conflict - not all of which are effective.

(a) *Denial/withdrawal*: 'sweeping it under the carpet'. If the conflict is very trivial, it may indeed blow over without an issue being made of it, but if the causes are not identified, the conflict may grow to unmanageable proportions.

(b) *Suppression*: 'smoothing over', to preserve working relationships despite minor conflicts. As Hunt remarks, however: 'Some cracks cannot be papered over'.

(c) *Dominance:* the application of power or influence to settle the conflict. The disadvantage of this is that it creates all the lingering resentment and hostility of win-lose situations.

(d) *Compromise:* bargaining, negotiating, conciliating. To some extent, this will be inevitable in any organisation made up of different individuals. However, individuals tend to exaggerate their positions to allow for compromise, and compromise itself is seen to weaken the value of the decision, perhaps reducing commitment.

(e) *Integration/collaboration*. Emphasis must be put on the task, individuals must accept the need to modify their views for its sake, and group effort must be seen to be superior to individual effort. Not easy.

Handy suggests two types of strategy which may be used to turn conflict into competition or argument, or to manage it in some other acceptable way.

(a) *Environmental ('ecological') strategies*. These involve creating conditions in which individuals may be better able to interact co-operatively with each other: they are wide-ranging, time-consuming, and unpredictable, because of the sheer range of human differences.

Activity 4

Suggest five measures which might create a framework and 'climate' in which co-operation is the norm.

(b) *Regulation strategies*. These are directed to control conflict - although in fact they make it so much a part of the formal structure of the organisation that they tend to legitimise and even perpetuate it. Possible methods include:

   (i) the provision of arbitration to settle disputes;

   (ii) the establishment of detailed rules and procedures for conduct by employees;

   (iii) appointing a person to manage the area of conflict - usually a liaison/co-ordination officer;

   (iv) using confrontation, or inter-group meetings, to hammer out differences, especially where territorial conflicts occur;

   (v) separating the conflicting individuals; and

   (vi) ignoring the problem, if it is genuinely likely to go away, and there is no point in opening fresh wounds.

2.2 Potential for conflict between unions and employers

Definition

Trade Unions are organisations whose purpose it is to promote their members' interests, and, in the view of many trade unionists, to bring about social change for the betterment of society as a whole. Situations occur where trade union negotiators set targets for achievement of these goals which appear to be at odds with the targets set by management for the organisation (and its employees).

Disputes between management and unions may therefore be seen in the context of inter-organisational conflict, and individual members of both organisations may then feel a tug of loyalties in opposing directions. However, the officials of both organisations might succeed in reconciling their apparently conflicting goals.

Remember that trade unions have a vested interest in the success of the organisation to which their members belong because unless this organisation prospers, the security and rewards of their members will be restricted. For this reason, trade unions might be active in co-operative efforts with management to achieve growth through greater efficiency. They also share the responsibility for good industrial relations with management.

It is important to be aware that trade unions are organisations in their own right, and we must not assume too hastily or too readily that the goals of a trade union organisation are the same as those of its members or full-time officials. The potential divergence between individual goals and organisational goals exists for a union as well as for a company. This view was given a political edge by the government's Industrial Relations Code of Practice, which states that it should be the responsibility of a union to ensure that:

(a) its members understand the organisation, policy and rules of the union;

(b) its members understand the powers and duties of the members themselves and those of their union representatives;

(c) its officials are adequately trained to look after their members' interests in an efficient and responsible way.

In fact, the MSF, the general technical union, applied (*Personnel Management Plus*, August 1992) for accreditation under the British Standards Institution's BS 5750 (now BS EN ISO 9000) quality assurance scheme, as part of a programme to make the union 'user-friendly'. Members are to be given guarantees on servicing, representation and voting rights, backed by a clear set of service standards.

'Them and us' attitudes have traditionally been deeply ingrained in British industry, partly because of class and class-consciousness. You should be aware that they are to an extent inevitable, given the tendency of people to draw boundaries round any group they are in: 'them and us' can refer to white- and blue-collar workers, or line and staff (including personnel) management, as well as management and workers in general.

The root of these attitudes frequently lies in fact. Some of the distinctions between white- and blue-collar workers, for example, are unfair: flexibility, time off, holiday entitlements and so on frequently discriminate against even long-serving, skilled shop floor staff. We have already discussed ways in which less divisive systems (such as single status agreements and annual salaries down to manual grades) could be designed, in the interests of flexibility and improved employee relations.

2.3 Co-operation

The opposite of conflict is co-operation.

(a) Co-operation is a common cultural belief, and one that is basic to any economic system. In work organisations it is universally believed that co-operation is a Good Thing, and achieves greater productivity than lack of co-operation. For most tasks, this is proven by experience, although an element of competition is also healthy and team-building.

(b) Co-operation has a rational appeal. It is demonstrable that a suitable number of people co-operating on a task will achieve a better result than one person doing the same task. Synergy may enable 2+2 to equal 5.

(c) Co-operation has an emotional appeal. It incorporates values about unity, teamwork, comradeship and insiders (versus outsiders). As such, it is a useful cornerstone to the communication of corporate culture.

(d) Some cultures encourage this value-cluster more than others. In the UK, individualism is a major aspect of the national culture - despite stated views on the virtues of co-operation. Hofstede's studies of West German, Japanese and Swedish cultures, however, demonstrate an emphasis on co-operation and inter-dependence, rather than individuality.

3 THE POWER OF THE UNIONS

The power of the union representative in bargaining will depend on the following factors.

(a) The degree of support for union actions from its members, and its ability to attract and maintain membership. This in turn depends on a number of factors.

   (i) The conditions pertaining in the industry or organisation, the aspirations of members and hence the perceived advantages of trade union membership.

   (ii) Employment issues such as economic recession, or computerisation, which enhance the perceived importance of representation.

   (iii) The social acceptability of unionism within the occupational group. In particular, membership has become more acceptable to white-collar staff.

   (iv) The existence of closed shop practices or peer pressure to support the union. The 'closed shop' whereby an employee had to be a member of a relevant union in order to undertake work, was stripped of all legal protection under the Employment Act 1988. On the other hand, further legislation has protected the freedom of individuals to join the union of their choice. Section 14 of the Trade Union Reform and Employment Rights Act, 1993 provides that membership or non-membership must not be taken into account during employee selection. No action short of *dismissal* or selection for *redundancy* may be taken to compel people to be members of a union, nor to *deter* union membership: people may not be selected for redundancy or dismissal on the grounds of union membership. Nor can employees be prevented from participation in union activities at an appropriate time, and if the union is both independent and recognised by the employer, there is a further right to time off (without pay) for union activities. These protections do not require any continuity of employment.

   (v) Competition for members between unions, or between a union and staff association (for example, the split in representation for miners in the UK, after the 1984 miners' strike). *People Management* (9 February 1995) noted a trend of union mergers with other unions and staff associations, in a bid for what it calls 'safety in numbers'. It notes the merger of the Inland Revenue Staff Federation (IRSF) with the civil service union NUCPS, and the merger between the National Communications Union (NCU) and the Union of Communication Workers (UCW) to form the new Communication Workers Union (CWU).

(vi) The observed success or failure of the union in obtaining beneficial agreements for its members.

(b) The bargaining environment, including:

   (i) the organisation's wage policy. If the system is felt fair and the level of pay good, in comparison to market rates, there will be little impetus for bargaining; and

   (ii) the local labour market. If there is a local shortage of the skill groups represented by the union, the union will have greater bargaining power, but the reverse is also true: in times of high unemployment, the union movement is weakened.

(c) The culture of the union, and in particular its willingness to use industrial muscle. This will partly be a function of whether the union has a unified culture: geographical dispersion or internal variety or dissent may weaken the united voice of the union. 'Industrial muscle' resides primarily in the threat of withdrawal of labour, known as 'strike' action: this is discussed below.

Size has deliberately been left out of the above account, as a variable insignificant in itself. Size as a *proportion* of potential membership may be a more significant factor in determining the credibility of the union. The threat of industrial action even by a large union would be hollow if its membership represented a very small proportion of workers in the relevant sector. A union which is small in terms of membership numbers, may have a very strong negotiating position if its members are of an occupational category which is significant to the organisation or national life, and/or if the union has a record of successful results and a reputation for a willingness to carry out its threats of action.

The *results* of union action and negotiation form the link between the ability of the union to attract members and its ability to negotiate effectively. They create a vicious circle, whereby failures depress membership, thus further weakening the union, and increasing the likelihood of further failures, with a corresponding upturn in the confidence and aggressive stance of the employers.

Activity 5

Is it your impression, from your awareness of current events, that the unions' power is weaker or stronger than it has been in the past? What gives you this impression?

3.1 Union power: on the wane?

The power of trade unions has been affected by a number of factors, which form a continuing trend.

(a) The vicious circle described above may operate to weaken some unions in the near future.

(b) Conditions of employment and levels of pay have in general terms been improving. Self-interest, if nothing else, may urge organisations to improve them still further in future, as the falling birthrate begins to impact on labour supply, and as social responsibility continues to grow as an important element in customer choice.

(c) The unions' power was weakened by the abolition of the closed shop (Employment Act 1988), whereby dismissal for non-membership of a union was deemed unfair, and industrial action to create or maintain closed shop practices lost its legal immunity.

(d) More moderate elements came to the fore with the provisions of the Trade Union Act 1984. Part I of the Act required the election of all voting members of a union's governing body by a secret ballot of members, at least every five years.

Part II requires that a union organising industrial action must hold a secret ballot of all those due to take part; otherwise it loses its legal immunity. The Employment Act 1988 took this a step further, providing for:

(i) the right of trade union members not to be called out on strike without a properly held secret ballot;

(ii) the right not to be disciplined by a union for refusing to strike or for crossing a picket line; and

(iii) the right to a postal vote in elections for all members of union governing bodies and for key national leaders, and in ballots on the use of union funds for political purposes, with the assurance that such elections and ballots will be subject to proper standards of independent scrutiny.

(e) The observable trend towards individual rather than collective pay determination and goal-setting may reduce what has been traditionally regarded as the principle role of unions. Trends towards labour mobility and employee flexibility may also weaken the organisation of occupational groups.

Recognising these serious issues the TUC embarked on a recruitment drive in 1996 to attract new workers in insecure industries; in an attempt to halt the continuing decline in membership, which stood at just 6.75 million members in June 1996 (a fall of 150,000 from the start of the same year).

Activity 6

Suggest two major factors that might *strengthen* union power in coming years.

3.2 Strike action

Definition

Strike action is action by a workforce (or part of it) to withhold its labour because of a dispute with management, usually over pay, job protection or working conditions. Strikes might be official or unofficial. Official strike action is supported by the trade union representatives of the employees in dispute, whereas unofficial strike action is taken by a part of the workforce without recognition and support from their union officials.

Various forms of strike action (official or unofficial) may be listed as follows.

(a) An indefinite strike by the entire union membership in the workforce, either at a national level, company level or plant level (such as the miners' strike of 1984).

(b) A one or two day token strike by the entire union membership, as a protest against management's unwillingness to make further concessions. One or two day strikes might be repeated over a period of time, in order to provide a recurring disruption to the organisation's operations without a complete loss of pay. (For example, the 1996 London Underground dispute.)

(c) A ban on overtime and weekend working.

(d) A work-to-rule or go-slow. This is a form of strike action in which employees follow official work procedures to the letter, thereby slowing down the rate of output and reducing productivity as much as possible, without doing anything to justify disciplinary action by management.

(e) Secondary strike action, in which action is taken against employers who trade with firms in dispute, but who are not directly involved in the dispute themselves.

Business Basics: Human Resource Management

Legislation affecting industrial disputes includes:

(a) the power to dismiss strikers. Under the Trade Union and Labour Relations (Consolidation) Act 1992 employees dismissed while taking unofficial strike or other industrial action are excluded from the statutory 'unfair dismissal' code;

(b) the requirement for secret ballots before industrial action can be called, under the Employment Act 1988;

(c) the right not to be disciplined by a union for refusing to strike, or for crossing a picket line, under the Employment Act 1988; and

(d) the curbing of secondary picketing. *(Primary* action is that which is aimed at one's own employer, including picketing and black-listing: *secondary* or further action is against any party not directly involved in the dispute.) The Employment Act 1982 protected unions and their members against most civil and criminal actions 'in contemplation or furtherance of a trade dispute'. There is no legal protection, however, for those who organise or take part in secondary picketing. There will only be protection if a person pickets at or near his place of work, with a purpose that is 'peacefully to obtain or communicate information, or peacefully to persuade a person to work or not to work'.

According to the 1982 Act, a 'lawful trade dispute' is one between workers and their own employers, wholly or mainly about work related matters, and *not:*

(a) demarcation and other inter-union disputes;

(b) disputes between workers and other employers than their own;

(c) disputes other than those mainly connected with pay and conditions; and

(d) disputes overseas.

Activity 7

Do you think any categories of workers should not have the right to strike? If so, which?

3.3 Why might an employer want a non- or de-unionised workforce?

The benefits expected to accrue from having a non-union workforce will vary from organisation to organisation, depending on the nature of the task, environment and workforce. In a changing environment, the organisation may only survive through employee flexibility, and the creation of a culture where changes, innovation and even risk are welcomed. Organised resistance to corporate plans are obviously undesirable from management's point of view. It is notable that the most innovative companies as far as progressive personnel policies are concerned, according to a study by Deloitte Haskins & Sells, are also among the leaders in their markets, with above average financial performance: IBM is in the top ten, with Mars, Sainsbury's and Marks and Spencer, among others.

3.4 HRM and anti-unionism

HRM policies aimed at reducing the power of trade unions in collective bargaining have in the main attempted to make union membership irrelevant. Such policies are backed-up by trends in recent years towards social responsibility (voluntarily providing conditions which unions have traditionally had to negotiate for their members), abolition of the closed shop, and individualism in pay structures.

Such policies will partly be designed to fulfil some of the traditional roles of the trade union. They may take the form of:

(a) communication and consultation on all issues, plans and changes which will affect employees. Trade unions recognised for the purpose of collective bargaining are entitled to certain information (not injurious to the undertaking, protected by statute or given in confidence). If an organisation can operate a conspicuous policy of worker involvement, it can replace the union in this capacity (once trust has been built up);

(b) discipline and grievance procedures which are perceived to be fair and consistent, and the rules of which are clearly communicated to all employees; and/or

(c) pay structures, recruitment and selection procedures etc which are perceived to be fair, non-discriminatory and equitable; health and safety policies conspicuously aimed at preventing accidents and ill-health; programmes aimed at improving the work environment and so on. Another disincentive to collective bargaining may be offered in the form of flexibility of the remuneration package. If allowance is made for individual needs and priorities a greater individualism may be welcomed in reward negotiation.

Case study 1: IBM

In August 1986 the *Financial Times* carried a series of extracts from *Strike Free: New Industrial Relations in Britain* by Philip Bassett. In one of them, Bassett referred to the successful computer company, IBM.

Company management attribute the good employee relations to IBM's belief in respect for the individual. One aspect of this philosophy is that IBM does not recognise trade unions for collective bargaining purposes. To do so, they believe, would imply that without trade unions employees' interests would be neglected. Management are convinced that the company's record disproves such a belief.

IBM does not discourage its employees from becoming members of trade unions, but very few of them do so. Even of those who do, a significant minority are against collective bargaining. Pay in IBM is not a collective matter for employees; instead, the company conducts its own confidential survey of comparable companies and determines salary ranges centrally. There is scope for line managers to recommend increases for specific individuals based on merit.

The other traditional function of trade unions at plant level is to assist their members over the hurdles of the employer's grievance system. IBM believe that their own internal complaints procedures, which allow an individual to take a grievance to the very highest levels of management, remove the need for any union involvement.

Other companies, looking at IBM's industrially harmonious, strike-free, non-union record, have asked how they could emulate it. The answer given by a former personnel director of the company is simple: 'You start 30 years ago.'

Business Basics: Human Resource Management

> **Case study 2: Sheerness Steel**
>
> Canadian-owned Sheerness Steel, Kent, is the first company in its industry to have derecognised unions, led by the Iron and Steel Trades Confederation (ISTC), as part of a change to a single status company. According to the personnel director: 'We have become a single status company with personal contracts, salaries, performance-related pay and no defined jobs - people do whatever they are trained to do. We realised that we no longer had anything to debate or discuss with the unions and that they were no longer necessary.'
>
> However, according to the ISTC, the workforce is not happy. Local conditions of high unemployment 'had made it difficult for members to withstand company pressure to take personal contracts'. The change to salaried work means that employees have lost overtime payments which, according to the ISTC, has severely affected their earnings. On the other hand, many of the old disciplinary problems such as being late, are no longer a problem; just as well, perhaps, since the unions are no longer even allowed to represent individual members in disciplinary cases ... .
>
> *Personnel Management Plus,* September 1992

The TUC's HRM taskforce reported, at the 1994 TUC conference, that it found no direct relationship between HRM techniques and anti-unionism. In fact, HRM was most prevalent in unionised workplaces. Taskforce chair Bernadette Hillan said:

If an employer is really trying to improve business performance, is committed to involving workers in the running of the organisation and is seeking to develop a real partnership with recognised trade unions, then HRM and collective bargaining can work in harmony.

But she admitted that some employers were using at least the 'language' of HRM as an excuse to derecognise unions.

Activity 8

Do you feel that unions are necessary, or even helpful, even where 'enlightened' HRM policies are in use? Why?

4 COLLECTIVE BARGAINING AND NEGOTIATION

4.1 What matters are settled by collective bargaining?

Definition

When employers and employees negotiate agreements on working conditions through their respective representatives, this is called *collective bargaining*.

Collective bargaining is concerned with reaching an agreement about two types of rules.

(a) *Substantive rules.* These are rules which determine the terms and conditions of employment. (For example, for grade 1 staff, the pay scales will be such-and-

226

such, or the annual holiday entitlement will be x days, or the basic working week will be y hours.) Demarcation rules - 'what work is done by what grades of staff - are also substantive rules.

(b) *Procedural rules*. These are rules about the methods and procedures for:

  (i) arriving at substantive rules. (What negotiating machinery should be set up? Should a particular issue be discussed at national level, company level or local plant/branch level - or not at all?); and

  (ii) settling any disagreements or disputes which cannot be resolved by normal negotiation. There might be arrangements to refer disputes at plant level to regional or national level, and there might be arrangements to refer some issues to arbitration. Procedural rules would determine what the arbitration arrangements should be: for example, there might be a rule which states that disputes should be referred to ACAS (the Advisory, Conciliation and Arbitration Service).

Collective bargaining takes place at different levels.

(a) Some issues are discussed at national level between representatives of employers for the industry and national trade union officials. For example, a national basic wage or salaries agreement might be made every year.

(b) Other issues will be settled at company level. The management side will be represented by senior managers of the company and the staff side by union or staff association representatives in the company, perhaps assisted by full-time national union officials. Ford, for example, have their own company-wide pay agreements and do not join in national negotiations with an employers' federation.

(c) Other issues will be settled at more local level, by domestic bargaining. In manufacturing industries, this would be plant by plant. The management side will be represented by the plant or factory management, perhaps assisted by a personnel manager, and the staff side by local shop stewards. Phillips Electronics in the UK, for example, has abandoned its national bargaining structure in favour of plant by plant negotiations.

Domestic bargaining has increased in recent decades, because:

(a) companies wanting to make better use of their human resource did not want to be tied down by a national agreement, and were prepared to negotiate a better deal at factory or plant level for the benefit of both the company and its employees;

(b) technological developments have brought about the need for flexibility in negotiations. When a company wants to introduce new technology into work procedures, it must win acceptance from its own staff. One way of winning their acceptance is to negotiate a special deal at company or plant level which means that the company does not want to be bound by a national agreement.

(c) There has been a change in the attitudes of people at work. Increasingly, they want greater direct influence over matters that affect them, and this can be achieved by bringing negotiations down from a national to a domestic level.

4.2 Changing attitudes to collective bargaining

Chamberlain and Kuhn (*Industrial Democracy* 1965) suggested that there has been a historical development in attitudes towards collective bargaining.

(a) At first, there was a *marketing theory*, in which collective bargaining was seen as pay bargaining for the supply of labour. Rates of pay would be settled on the basis of supply and demand.

(b) Later, *governmental theory* developed. Collective bargaining was seen as a way of making rules of conduct and enforcing those rules in addition to pay bargaining.

(c) Finally, Chamberlain and Kuhn argued for the emergence of *managerial theory* which sees collective bargaining as a form of management. Decisions about matters in which both management and employees have a vital interest should be discussed and decided by collective negotiations.

More matters are being brought within the sphere of collective bargaining arrangements. Negotiations might now cover not only pay and conditions of employment such as holidays and hours of work, but also promotion, training, discipline, manning agreements or job demarcation.

Collective bargaining has also been extended to more groups of employees, particularly white-collar workers, as:

(a) white-collar workers saw the pay differentials between their salaries and the wages of blue-collar (manual) workers being eroded. They attributed much of this erosion to the union organisation of manual workers;

(b) membership of a trade union has become more socially acceptable to white-collar staff, especially since there has been a shift from manual work to desk or knowledge work;

(c) new technology and economic recession are seen as a threat to jobs, and collective power is required to defend job security;

(d) organisational change has accelerated, and requires discussion and negotiation with staff: this would be impossible on an individual basis.

On the other hand, there is a growing awareness that collective bargaining in a sense fudges the issue, and lets management off treating employees as individuals. At the Industrial Participation Association annual conference in 1988, it was argued that 'individual appraisal and employment contracts may not be appropriate in all types of business, though they will be increasingly so in the skills-based, high pay, increasingly non-unionised companies of tomorrow'.

Thus the framework of collective bargaining is influenced by:

(a) the balance of power between employers and unions. There has been a decline of union power in recent years, with a corresponding decline in the perceived importance of collective bargaining;

(b) the rise of individualism, with new emphasis on personal skill packages, work flexibility and career mobility. This trend is likely to continue, particularly as the forecast demographic downturn begins to bite and the skill shortage worsens; and

(c) the trend towards domestic bargaining or decentralised industrial relations, mentioned above.

4.3 Negotiation

There are two basic approaches to negotiation, the way in which the power of the parties involved in collective bargaining are expressed.

(a) *Distributive bargaining*, where negotiation is about the distribution of finite resources. One party's gain is another's loss: it is an 'I win - you lose' or zero sum equation. If a pay increase of, say, 10% is gained, where the management budget was 5%, the extra has to be funded from elsewhere - profits, investments, other groups (such as shareholders), or increased productivity or prices.

(b) *Integrative bargaining*, based on joint problem-solving, where negotiations aim to find a mutually satisfying solution to problems.

Activity 9

Should negotiation be distributive or integrative?

4.4 Preparation for negotiations

Formal negotiations, as opposed to constant informal 'arrangements', should follow broad guidelines.

(a) *Set objectives*, which are achievable and consistent with industrial relations policy. These are likely to be couched in optimum, most likely, and fall-back terms (see (d) below).

(b) *Research the background of issues* over which negotiations are to be conducted - trends in union response, market pay rates where available and so on.

(c) *Establish their bargaining power*. This may be approached by noting the costs and benefits to each negotiating party of a range of potential outcomes.

Chamberlain's model:

Bargaining power of A = $\dfrac{\text{Costs to B of disagreement with A's terms}}{\text{Costs to A of disagreement with B's terms}}$

and vice versa

If the cost of disagreeing is greater than that of agreeing, the bargaining power of the other side is greater.

(d) *Determine strategy*. Given a fair idea of what the other side's position and bargaining power are likely to be, the party in question should be able to predict any demands the other side will make, or what kind of offer is likely to be accepted. Each side should look for potential counter-arguments to its own case.

Atkinson has identified three possible outcomes from management's point of view.

(i) If management achieves all its objectives, what would be the *ideal* settlement?

(ii) If management makes progress, but union power is realistically assessed, what is a *realistic* settlement?

(iii) If management concedes, what is its *fall-back* position?

A position for each side should be estimated for each of the above situations, and areas of agreement concentrated on, as potential middle ground.

(e) *Determine the agenda*. The agenda for negotiation should be acceptable in advance by both sides. The order of items may have tactical significance: imposing time pressures, for example, or gaining momentum on related issues.

(f) *Issue prior information*. Information may be used:

(i) as pre-conditioning: for example, advance publicity of poor trading results and intense competition as a prelude to negotiation of pay rises or redundancies; or

(ii) as a matter of legal obligation. Information relevant to collective bargaining must be disclosed to trade union representatives (see below).

(g) *Choose the participants*. Representatives of management must be articulate, persuasive, acceptable to the other side on personal terms and authoritative enough to implement agreed decisions. Face-to-face negotiations may require particular skills in persuasion, personal rapport, reading of verbal and non-verbal signals and so on.

4.5 Disclosure of information

Trade unions recognised for the purpose of collective bargaining are entitled to certain information. An employer must provide information in response to a written request by a union representative, as long as:

(a) it relates to his (or an associated employer's) undertaking;
(b) it is in his possession;
(c) it is in accordance with good practice (as laid down in the ACAS code of practice); and
(d) lack of the information would materially impede the representative in collective bargaining.

There is *no* obligation to give information relating to:

(a) information given in confidence;
(b) information relating to particular individuals;
(c) information which - in any context other than collective bargaining - would cause injury to the undertaking; or
(d) information protected by statute (say, in the interests of national security) or subject to legal proceedings.

4.6 Conduct of negotiations

During the conduct of the negotiations themselves, participants should consider:

(a) *their opening statement*: a broad statement of the position, leaving room for negotiation. This will be a clue to strategy - and may also be an opportunity for broad general agreement;
(b) *their roles* within the negotiating team. Negotiations can be highly ritualistic, and appropriate roles will have to be adopted: the 'hard man/soft man' approach, for example, requires one conciliatory and one tough negotiator to disguise the team's true strategy, and expose any weaknesses in the other side; and
(c) *their argument and persuasive style.*

Activity 10

From your study or awareness of communication and persuasion, suggest some techniques which you would use in negotiation.

Concessions, on one or both sides, are likely to be necessary in negotiation. Tactical considerations again enter into the granting and acceptance of concessions. Early concessions may be taken for granted, or as a symptom of weakness; tough concessions, attached to requirements for reciprocal concessions on the other side, and related to the main point of difference, may be more effective.

Settlements, the ultimate objective of negotiations, will have to be communicated to the workforce and other parties represented by negotiations. It will have to be decided:

(a) how long agreements are to run;
(b) how they are to be communicated; and
(c) how to deal with disagreements once the negotiated settlement is implemented.

5 PARTICIPATION AND CONSULTATION

Definition

The British Institute of Management (*Employee Participation - the Way Ahead*, 1977) described *participation* as:

> 'the practice in which employees take part in management decisions ... based on the assumption of a community of interest between employer and employee in furthering the long-term prospects of the enterprise and those working in it.'

There are, however, different degrees and methods of involvement, reflecting the extent to which organisations wish to involve employees in decision-making. Participation may be desirable or necessary because of the following factors.

(a) *Commitment*: the perceived need to obtain a higher level of identification with organisational goals. Communication to employees, a consultative management style, the use of teams and so on, may be used at all levels.

(b) *Legislation*. Most of the legislative proposals on participation have been put forward by the EU, including the draft of the Fifth Directive, which requires limited companies to adopt:

   (i) collective bargaining on decisions; or
   (ii) a two-tier board structure, with elected worker representatives on the senior or 'supervisory' board to which the management or 'executive' board is responsible; or
   (iii) a unitary board structure with worker representatives as non-executive directors; or
   (iv) a sub-board level company council, with worker representation (on the model of a German 'works council', which is an employee-only body with legal rights to information, consultation and co-determination on personnel issues).

So far, the UK has not agreed to these proposals, having opted out of the Maastricht Social Chapter.

Board-level representation

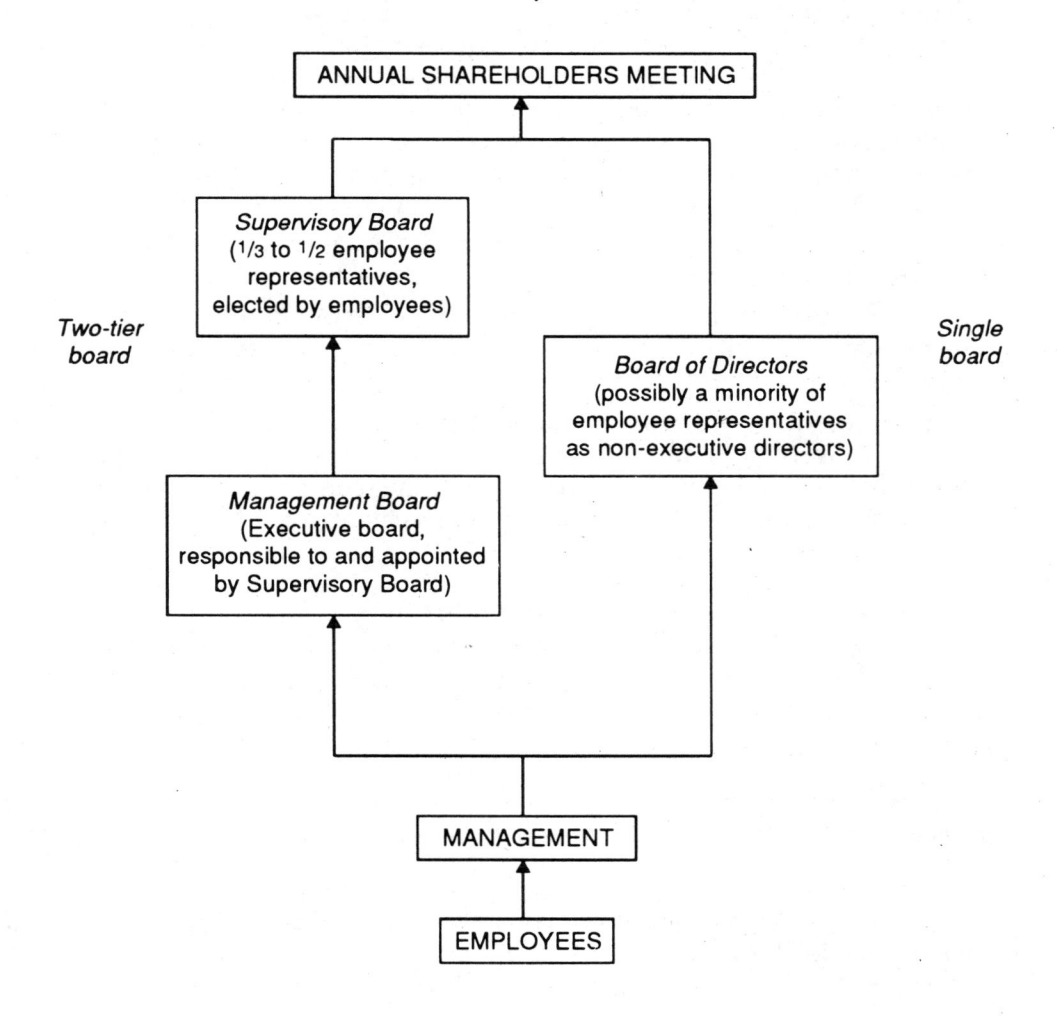

```
                    ANNUAL SHAREHOLDERS MEETING
                              ↑
          ┌───────────────────┴───────────────────┐
          │                                       │
   Supervisory Board                              │
   (1/3 to 1/2 employee                           │
   representatives,                               │
   elected by employees)                          │
Two-tier      ↑                          Board of Directors      Single
board         │                          (possibly a minority of  board
              │                          employee representatives
   Management Board                      as non-executive directors)
   (Executive board,                             ↑
   responsible to and appointed                  │
   by Supervisory Board)                         │
              ↑                                  │
              └───────────────┬──────────────────┘
                              │
                         MANAGEMENT
                              ↑
                         EMPLOYEES
```

231

(c) *Trade union pressure*. The main progress has been towards extending collective bargaining into areas traditionally considered as management concerns: manning levels, training and so on. *Joint consultation* is another prevalent form of worker involvement, where management discuss matters of concern regularly with union representatives, on Joint Consultative Committees (JCCs) or in non-negotiatory staff meetings.

5.1 Consultation

An article in *Personnel Management* (October 1994) challenges HR managers: 'Anyone who believes we have escaped and will continue to escape, legal requirements to inform, consult and involve the workforce as a result of the UK's opt-out from the Maastricht Social Chapter has overlooked the extent to which UK employers are already required to do all three.' The article summarised the requirements as follows.

(a) Employees must be provided with a written statement of the terms and conditions of employment as discussed in Chapter 4. (TURERA 1993)

(b) Employees must be informed of health and safety risks and policies (as discussed in Chapter 10).

(c) Recognised unions must be consulted (Social Security Act 1975) before contributory or voluntary contracted-out pension schemes are offered as part of the terms of employment, and before any scheme is contracted in or out of SERPS (as discussed in Chapter 10).

(d) Recognised union representatives must be consulted in the event of redundancies. The duty to consult has been extended to include dismissals made to achieve a change in contract terms. (Trade Union and Labour Relations Act 1992, TURERA 1993.) TURERA 1993 also strengthened the nature of consultation, stipulating that this must be 'with a view to reaching agreement'. It also added to the penalty for failure to consult; claims against the employer can no longer be set off against wages, or wages in lieu, paid for the period during which proper consultation was avoided.

(e) Recognised union representatives must similarly be consulted before any transfer of undertakings, with a view to reaching agreement (TURERA).

(f) Although there is no legal requirement to negotiate with unions, where negotiation does take place, recognised unions are entitled to information, as mentioned in Section 4: Trade Union and Labour Relations Act 1992.

(g) Companies with more than 250 employees must publicise in their annual report the steps taken in the financial year to inform, consult and involve employees (including encouraging involvement in the company's performance, for example, through share ownership): Employment Act 1982, Companies Act 1985.

The company continues to promote equality of opportunity in all aspects of employment. Flexible working measures, including childcare vouchers, part-time working and job sharing, help provide an environment in which staff can balance their work and domestic commitments whilst continuing to develop their careers.

The company promotes both corporate and business unit communications and other initiatives to seek staff commitment to the values of working together and working better.

Formal arrangements for consultation with staff exist through a local and company-wide framework and staff are frequently involved in direct discussions with their managers.

Regular staff consultations cover a range of topics affecting the workforce, including such matters as unit and corporate performance and business plans.

The company operates three Inland Revenue approved employee share schemes, the PowerGen Profit Sharing Scheme, the PowerGen Sharesave Scheme and the PowerGen Executive Share Option Scheme. These cover respectively shares acquired by employees at flotation under the Free and Matching Offers, options available to employees generally and options available to executives.'

PowerGen plc Directors Report, 1994

(h) A 1994 decision in the European Court of Justice (*Commission of the European Communities v UK*) found that the UK had failed to comply with EU directives by restricting information and consultation to 'representatives of recognised trade unions' rather than 'representatives of the workforce'. The UK will now need to provide for consultation of representatives even where there is no recognised trade union.

Other 'information/consultation' draft directives 'on the table' include the fifth directive on company law (mentioned earlier) and procedures for consulting and informing employees (Vredling). These draft directives propose more extensive involvement and consultation than is required in UK law. Watch the news media and HRM journals.

Activity 11

Think of your own life at home and college. What issues - whether or not they have a major direct impact on you - would you want to be informed and consulted about? What are the parallel issues in the workplace?

6 HRM AS A CHANGE AGENT

Change - in work practices, technology and so on - is an important element in employee relations. You will note that most of the requirements for consultation, discussed above, relate to changes. Change in organisations is a highly political process; it alters the balance of power and resources. It is also highly unsettling for the people involved: it can affect employees physically (for example, altered shift patterns), socially (if relationships are disrupted, or status altered) and psychologically (creating disorientation and insecurity). People tend to resist organisational changes, even positive ones, to preserve the status quo: the method of communicating and introducing change is crucial in gaining acceptance or even co-operation.

6.1 Change

The HR manager is ideally placed to be an agent of change, (that is, the catalyst or implementor of change) in several ways.

(a) The HR manager may be involved in the strategic planning processes which identify the *need* for change in the organisation, often arising from changes in its external environment.

(b) The HR manager may have the best grasp of the nature and effects of organisational values, culture, management 'style', power sources, politics, psychological flexibility or rigidity, motivation and other behavioural factors, which can be used to:

  (i) anticipate, circumvent and/or overcome resistance to change; and

(ii) create positive support for and ownership of change.

(c) The HR manager has a central role in many of the organisational processes and mechanisms which can be used to encourage and implement change in organisations. We discuss these in more detail below, but they include organisation culture, recruitment, training and development, appraisal and reward, and (crucially) communication with the workforce, including formal and informal machinery for participation and involvement.

The highly political relationship between HR and line management, and the perceived role of HRM in the organisation, will influence the extent to which the HR manager is in fact given a role in 'driving' change. The HR function's power to initiate and implement change will depend on the following factors.

(a) The extent of its *formal authority* to contribute to organisational strategy, and to change management in particular. An HR director whose objectives (and the reward and recognition based on them) are specifically related to successful implementation of change, will have greater perceived legitimacy in the role of change agent. (Unfortunately, this direct responsibility/accountability often extends only to changes such as retraining, redeployment and downsizing.)

(b) Its *credibility* in the eyes of senior and line managers, including:

   (i) its *perceived expertise in the area to be affected by change*. (In the case of new technology, for example, personnel may be considered irrelevant to the early stages of the change process, because of a perception that personnel specialists lack detailed understanding of what the technology entails);

   (ii) *its perceived expertise in the legal and administrative apparatus of the change.* (To continue our example, personnel would need to demonstrate familiarity with legislation and regulation in regard to new technology, its implications for data protection, health and safety, discrimination, union agreements, staffing levels, training etc);

   (iii) *its perceived expertise in the 'people' aspects of change per se, and of the particular planned change.* (Line managers may feel that personnel cannot in practice overcome resistance to change by its 'enlightened' techniques and behavioural theories any more effectively than a line manager simply 'laying down the law');

   (iv) *its perceived willingness and ability to handle change and innovation.* (Personnel will have small claim to be change agent in the organisation-wide introduction of new production technologies if it has refused for years to get its record system computerised).

(c) Its *influence* in the organisation. This may partly derive from formal authority ('legal power') and informal credibility ('knowledge power'), but will probably need to be augmented by political influence - usually in the form of:

   (i) *resource power*. The personnel function controls, to an extent, the flow of human resources into and within the organisation and also promotion and financial reward;

   (ii) *bureaucratic influence*. By imposing rules and procedures, paperwork and 'machinery', the HR function can strengthen its position and involvement. This is not just a political move. By setting rules and procedures, it forms or influences organisational norms and standards, which become part of the culture. (It may, however, degenerate into 'negative power': the ability to obstruct line managers can be used as a kind of 'blackmail'.)

(d) The extent to which senior and line managers believe (and are supported by organisational culture in believing) that:

   (i) people are the crucial element in change;

   (ii) change will not be successful in the long-term unless people can be committed to it;

(iii) understanding of human behaviour can be useful in practice in approaching the psychological and social aspects of change; and

(iv) the personnel function are best placed to undertake the required processes of listening, understanding, communication and persuasion to achieve that aim.

Politics is obviously highly relevant to change, change threatens the status quo, the established order, security - and particularly the security of those who have power and resources. Change is most likely to be resisted by those who have something to lose, arousing instincts of self-interest and self-preservation (if 'survival' is threatened - say, by job losses). This is why middle managers are the principal source of resistance to change in most organisations. Their position, in the face of widespread delaying of management structures, is most precarious, and they are perceived to have more to lose than either low level or high level employees.

Chapter roundup

- Employee relations is not only an element in an organisation's strategy for recruiting and retaining human resource. It also represents the interface between the organisation and other organisations in its environment: including those, such as trade unions and staff associations, of which its own employees are members. Control of the potential conflict of interests arising from the situation, and if possible harnessing the positive contributions available in employee involvement, are key tasks of human resource management.
- Collective bargaining involves reaching agreement about:
  - substantive rules concerned with pay, and terms and conditions of employment;
  - procedural rules concerned with the mechanism for arriving at substantive rules and other negotiations.
- Negotiations as part of the collective bargaining process can broadly be classified as:
  - distributive (I win - you lose); or
  - integrative (joint problem-solving).
- The trend of recent UK legislation and EU draft directives is to increase the level of consultation and employee involvement.

Quick quiz

1 At what level is a line manager likely to be engaged in industrial relations?
2 What is the role of ACAS?
3 What affects the power of a union to attract members and bargain effectively?
4 Can an organisation cost effectively 'squeeze out' the unions? If so, how?
5 Outline the 'pluralist' view of organisations.
6 What is domestic bargaining?
7 What preparations should be made for industrial relations negotiations?
8 Why might organisations strive towards greater worker participation or industrial democracy?
9 What is the effect of TURERA 1993 on: (a) trade union membership; and (b) the duty to consult?
10 How might change affect employees?

Business Basics: Human Resource Management

Solutions to activities

1. (a) *Lobbying* politicians to obtain legislation to improve conditions of work (say, a statutory minimum wage and hours of work).

   (b) Developing *political affiliations* with other trade unions, to create a power base for achieving political influence.

   (c) Providing finance for a *sympathetic political party*.

   (d) Attempting *to become involved in management's planning functions and executive decisions*. This might be achieved by means of joint consultative committees.

   (e) *Help for individual members* who need support. This help may arise from a particular incident or dispute at work, but on a more general level, a union might wish to provide financial support for members or their dependants in distress.

4. (a) agreement of common objectives;

   (b) reinforcing the group or team nature of organisational life, via culture;

   (c) providing feedback information on progress;

   (d) providing adequate co-ordination and communication mechanisms;

   (e) sorting out territorial/role conflicts in the organisational structure.

6. (a) In some categories of labour, shortages may be felt in coming years, which would weaken the power of management to resist or ignore threats of withdrawal of co-operation or labour.

   (b) A backlash of popular feeling against extensive redundancies and continuing high unemployment may revitalise support for the unions.

7. A fairly common argument is that emergency services should not have the right to strike. In fact, doctors, nurses, fire services and ambulance drivers are notoriously reluctant to strike. You may have felt strongly about teachers, if you suffered the disruption of classroom action.

8. The Sheerness Steel case study points up the issue you may have considered. Even if HRM is *perceived* as a subtle form of manipulation, there may be a problem.

9. A trick question. Not all bargaining *need* be adversarial and prone to conflict, but neither is integrative bargaining universally the best solution: an initially adversarial position may be the basis on which relative strengths are established, and integrative bargaining is worked out. The side which has a very strong position may also find adversarial bargaining desirable as a route to gains, at least in the short-term.

10. (a) Gain agreements or commitments from the other side that can be used as a stepping stone for your own logic.

    (b) Sell the benefits of your point of view to the other side: allow them to agree with you, without loss of face, wherever possible.

    (c) Preserve a tone of commitment, belief, even emotion: making your cause 'human'.

    (d) Put aside blockages and stalemates until later.

    (e) Release information with a tactical awareness of its affects on negotiating power.

    (f) Use rewards and sanctions (in effect, promises and threats) as appropriate.

    (g) Use all the inter-personal and communication skills at your command - listening, apparent sympathy and consideration, tact and diplomacy, language appropriate to the hearer, non-verbal behaviour (confident body language and expression and so on).

Further question practice

Now try the following practice questions at the end of this text

Multiple choice questions	72 to 76
Exam style question	11

Chapter 12

DISCIPLINE AND GRIEVANCE HANDLING

Introduction

The word discipline is used and understood in several different ways. The word discipline brings to mind the use of authority or force. To many, it primarily carries the disagreeable meaning of punishment. However, there is another way of thinking about discipline, a way which is far more in keeping with what has been said about good supervision. Discipline can be considered as: 'a condition in an enterprise in which there is orderliness in which the members of the enterprise behave sensibly and conduct themselves according to the standards of acceptable behaviour as related to the goals of the organisation'.

Grievance procedures are not at all the same as disciplinary procedures, although the two terms are often confused. A grievance occurs when an individual thinks that he is being wrongly treated by his colleagues or supervisor; perhaps he is being picked on, unfairly appraised in his annual report, unfairly blocked for promotion or discriminated against on grounds of race or sex.

When an individual has a grievance he should be able to pursue it and ask to have the problem resolved. Some grievances should be capable of solution informally by the individual's manager. However, if an informal solution is not possible, there should be a formal grievance procedure.

Your objectives
After completing this chapter you should:
(a) understand the nature of discipline;
(b) be able to outline a formal disciplinary procedure;
(c) be able to outline a formal grievance procedure;
(d) appreciate the human relations problems of discipline and grievance.

1 DISCIPLINE

The concept of 'positive' and 'negative' discipline makes the distinction between methods of maintaining sensible conduct and orderliness which are technically co-operative, and those based on warnings, threats and punishments.

Definitions

Positive (or constructive) discipline relates to procedures, systems and equipment in the work place which have been designed specifically so that the employee has no option but to act in the desired manner to complete a task safely and successfully. A machine may, for example, shut off automatically if its safety guard is not in place. A system may be designed to include checks and controls at each stage so that no task can be forgotten, or ill-performed, in a way that would impact on further tasks.

Negative discipline is then the promise of sanctions designed to make employees *choose* to behave in a desirable way, although this again need not be a wholly negative matter. Disciplinary action may be *punitive* (punishing an offence), *deterrent* (warning people not to behave in that way) or *reformative* (calling attention to the nature of the offence, so that it will not happen again).

The best discipline is *self-discipline*. Even before they start to work, most mature people accept the idea that following instructions and fair rules of conduct are normal responsibilities that are part of any job. Most employees can therefore be counted on to exercise self-discipline. They believe in performing their work properly, in coming to work on time, in following the supervisor's instructions, and in refraining from fighting, drinking at work, or stealing. It is a normal human tendency to subordinate one's personal interests and personal idiosyncrasies to the needs of the organisation.

Once employees know what is expected of them and feel that the rules are reasonable, self-disciplined behaviour becomes a part of group norms - the way in which employees behave as a work group, and their collective attitudes.

1.1 Types of disciplinary situation

There are many types of disciplinary situation which require attention by the manager. The most frequently occurring are:

(a) excessive absenteeism;

(b) excessive lateness in arriving at work;

(c) defective and/or inadequate work performance; and

(d) poor attitudes which influence the work of others or which reflect on the public image of the firm.

Activity 1

Suggest five more types of disciplinary situation.

In addition to these types of job situation managers might be confronted with disciplinary problems stemming from employee behaviour *off* the job. These may be an excessive drinking problem, the use of drugs or some form of narcotics, or involvement in some form of law-breaking activity. In such circumstances, whenever an employee's off-the-job conduct has an impact upon performance on-the-job, the manager must be prepared to deal with such a problem within the scope of the disciplinary process.

1.2 Disciplinary action

Any disciplinary action must be undertaken with sensitivity and sound judgement on the manager's part. The purpose of discipline is not punishment or retribution. Disciplinary action must have as its goal the improvement of the future behaviour of the employee and other members of the organisation. The purpose obviously is the avoidance of similar occurrences in the future.

Following ACAS' guidelines for disciplinary action which emphasise no dismissal on first offence except for gross misconduct, many enterprises have accepted the idea of *progressive discipline*, which provides for an increase of the severity of the penalty with each offence. The following is a list of suggested steps of progressive disciplinary action and many companies have found these steps to be workable.

(a) *The informal talk*

   If the infraction is of a relatively minor nature and if the employee's record has no previous marks of disciplinary action, an informal, friendly talk will clear up the situation in many cases. Here the manager discusses with the employee his or her behaviour in relation to standards which prevail within the enterprise.

(b) *Oral warning or reprimand*

   In this type of interview between employee and manager, the latter emphasises the undesirability of the subordinate's repeated violation, and that ultimately it could lead to serious disciplinary action.

(c) *Written or official warning*

   These are part of the ACAS code of practice. A written warning is of a formal nature insofar as it becomes a permanent part of the employee's record. Written warnings, not surprisingly, are particularly necessary in unionised situations, so that the document can serve as evidence in case of grievance procedures.

(d) *Disciplinary layoffs, or suspension*

   This course of action would be next in order if the employee has committed repeated offences and previous steps were of no avail. Disciplinary lay-offs usually extend over several days or weeks. Some employees may not be very impressed with oral or written warnings, but they will find a disciplinary lay-off without pay a rude awakening.

(e) *Demotion*

   This course of action is likely to bring about dissatisfaction and discouragement, since losing pay and status over an extended period of time is a form of constant punishment. This dissatisfaction of the demoted employee may easily spread to co-workers, so most enterprises avoid downgrading as a disciplinary measure.

(f) *Discharge*

   Discharge is a drastic form of disciplinary action, and should be reserved for the most serious offences. For the organisation, it involves waste of a labour resource, the expense of training a new employee, and disruption caused by changing the make-up of the work team. There also may be damage to the morale of the group.

Activity 2

How (a) accessible and (b) clear are the rules and policies of your college: do people really know what they are and are not supposed to do? Have a look at the student regulations. How easy is it to see them - or did you get referred elsewhere? Are they well-indexed and cross-referenced, and in language that all students will understand?

How (a) accessible and (b) clear are the disciplinary procedures? Who is responsible for discipline?

1.3 Relationship management in disciplinary situations

Even if the manager uses sensitivity and judgement, imposing disciplinary action tends to generate resentment because it is an unpleasant experience. The challenge is to apply the necessary disciplinary action so that it will be least resented. Following these basic rules will help the manager reduce the resentment inherent in all disciplinary actions.

(a) *Immediacy*

Immediacy means that after noticing the offence, the manager proceeds to take disciplinary action as speedily as possible, while at the same time avoiding haste and on-the-spot emotions which might lead to unwarranted actions. (The ACAS code of practice requires investigation to be made where possible, before action is taken.)

(b) *Advance warning*

In order to maintain proper discipline and to have employees accept disciplinary action as fair, it is essential that all employees know in advance what is expected of them and what the rules and regulations are. Employees must be informed clearly that certain acts will lead to disciplinary action. Many organisations find it useful to have a disciplinary section in an employee handbook, and each new employee should also be informed orally of what is expected. Some policy provisions are included in recruitment literature and employment contracts as well.

(c) *Consistency*

Consistency of discipline means that each time an infraction occurs appropriate disciplinary action is taken. Inconsistency in the application of discipline lowers the morale of employees and diminishes their respect for the manager. Inconsistency also leads to employee insecurity and anxiety, and creates doubts in their minds as to what they can and cannot do.

(Consistency does not mean imposing the same standard penalty every time for a particular offence: there may be mitigating circumstances.)

(d) *Impersonality*

It is only natural for an employee to feel some resentment towards a manager who has taken disciplinary action against him. Yet the manager can reduce the amount of resentment by making disciplinary action as impersonal as possible (by applying the 'hot stove rule': it burns anyone, high or low). This is the kind of thinking and reasoning which can help remove the personal element from disciplinary action. Penalties should be connected with the act and not based upon the personality involved, and once disciplinary action has been taken, no grudges should be borne.

(e) *Privacy*

As a general rule (unless the manager's authority is challenged directly and in public) disciplinary action should be taken in private, to avoid the spread of conflict and the humiliation or martyrdom of the employee concerned.

1.4 Disciplinary interviews

Preparation for the disciplinary interview will include:

(a) gathering facts about the alleged infringement;

(b) determination of the organisation's position: how valuable is the employee, potentially? How serious are his offences/lack of progress? How far is the organisation prepared to go to help him improve or discipline him further? and

(c) identification of the aims of the interview: punishment? Deterrent to others? Improvement? Specific standards of future behaviour/performance required need to be determined.

In addition, preparation will involve the organisation's disciplinary procedures, which should ensure that:

(a) informal oral warnings (at least) have been given;

(b) the employee has been given adequate notice of the interview for his own preparation; and

(c) the employee has been informed of the complaint against him, his right to be accompanied by a colleague or representative and so on.

The *content* of the interview will be as follows.

(a) The manager will explain the purpose of the interview.

(b) The charges against the employee will be delivered, clearly, unambiguously and without personal emotion.

(c) The manager will explain the organisation's position with regard to the issues involved: disappointment, concern, need for improvement, impact on others. This can be done frankly - but tactfully, with as positive an emphasis as possible on the employee's capacity and responsibility to improve.

(d) The organisation's expectations with regard to future behaviour/performance should be made clear.

(e) The employee should be given the opportunity to comment, explain, justify or deny. If he is to approach the following stage of the interview in a positive way, he must not be made to feel 'hounded' or hard done by.

(f) The organisation's expectations should be reiterated, or new standards of behaviour set for the employee. It will help him if:

  (i) they are specific and quantifiable, performance related and realistic. Increased output, improved timekeeping or whatever will be readily measurable;

  (ii) they are related to a practical but reasonably short time period. A date should be set to review his progress;

  (iii) the manager agrees on measures to help the employee should that be necessary. It would demonstrate a positive approach if, for example, a mentor were appointed from his work group to help him check his work. If his poor performance is genuinely the result of some difficulty or distress outside work, other help (temporary leave, counselling or financial aid) may be appropriate.

(g) The manager should explain the reasons behind any penalties imposed on the employee, including the entry in his personnel record of the formal warning. He should also explain how the warning can be removed from the record, and what standards must be achieved within a specified time scale. There should be a clear warning of the consequences of failure to meet improvement targets.

(h) The manager should explain the organisation's appeals procedures: if the employee feels he has been unfairly treated, there should be a right of appeal to a higher manager.

(i) Once it has been established that the employee understands all the above, the manager should summarise the proceedings briefly.

Records of the interview will be kept for the employee's personnel file, and for the formal follow-up review and any further action necessary.

Activity 3

How would a formal disciplinary procedure operate in a case of

(a) persistent absenteeism; and

(b) theft of envelopes from the organisation's offices?

> **ACAS Code of Practice**
>
> Disciplinary and grievance procedures should:
>
> - be in written form*
> - specify to whom they apply (all, or only some of the employees?)
> - be capable of dealing speedily with disciplinary matters
> - indicate the forms of disciplinary action which may be taken (such as dismissal, suspension or warning)
> - specify the appropriate levels of authority for the exercise of disciplinary actions
> - provide for individuals to be informed of the nature of their alleged misconduct
> - allow individuals to state their case, and to be accompanied by a fellow employee (or union representative)
> - ensure that every case is properly investigated before any disciplinary action is taken
> - ensure that employees are informed of the reasons for any penalty they receive
> - state that no employee will be dismissed for a first offence, except in cases of gross misconduct
> - provide for a right of appeal against any disciplinary action, and specify the appeals procedure.
>
> * The ACAS code of practice does not extend to informal 'first warnings', but these are an important part of the organisation's policy: don't forget them!

2 GRIEVANCE PROCEDURES

Formal grievance procedures, like disciplinary procedures, should be set out in writing and made available to all staff. These procedures should accomplish the following.

(a) State the *rights* of the employee for each type of grievance. For example, an employee who is not invited to attend a promotion/selection panel might claim that he has been unfairly passed over. The grievance procedure must state what the individual would be entitled to claim. In our example, the employee who is overlooked for promotion might be entitled to a review of his annual appraisal report, or to attend a special appeals promotion/selection board if he has been in his current grade for at least a certain number of years.

(b) State what the *procedures* for pursuing a grievance should be. A typical grievance procedure might be as follows.

   (i) The individual should discuss the grievance with a staff/union representative (or a colleague). If his case seems a good one, he should take the grievance to his immediate boss.

   (ii) The first interview will be between the immediate boss (unless he is the subject of the complaint, in which case it will be the next level up) and the employee, who has the right to be accompanied by a colleague or representative.

   (iii) If the immediate boss cannot resolve the matter, or the employee is otherwise dissatisfied with the first interview, the case should be referred to his superior (and if necessary in some cases, to an even higher authority).

(iv) Cases referred to a higher manager should also be reported to the personnel department. Line management might decide at some stage to ask for the assistance/advice of a personnel manager in resolving the problem.

(c) Distinguish between *individual* grievances and *collective* grievances. Collective grievances might occur when a work group as a whole considers that it is being badly treated.

(d) Allow for the involvement of an individual's or group's trade union or staff association *representative*. Indeed, many individuals and groups might prefer to initiate some grievance procedures through their union or association rather than through official grievance procedures. Involvement of a union representative from the beginning should mean that management and union will have a common view of what procedures should be taken to resolve the matter.

(e) State *time limits* for initiating certain grievance procedures and subsequent stages of them. For example, a person who is passed over for promotion should be required to make his appeal within a certain time period of his review, and his appeal to higher authority (if any) within a given period after the first grievance interview. There should also be time scales for management to determine and communicate the outcome of the complaint to the employee.

(f) Require *written records* of all meetings concerned with the case to be made and distributed to all the participants.

2.1 Grievance interviews

The dynamics of a grievance interview are broadly similar to a disciplinary interview, except that it is the *subordinate* who primarily wants a positive result from it.

Prior to the interview, the manager should have some idea of the complaint and its possible source. The meeting itself can then proceed through the following stages.

(a) *Exploration*. What is the problem: the background, the facts, the causes (manifest and hidden)? At this stage, the manager should simply try to gather as much information as possible, without attempting to suggest solutions or interpretations: the situation must be seen to be open.

(b) *Consideration*. The manager should:

  (i) check the facts;

  (ii) analyse the causes - the problem of which the complaint may be only a symptom;

  (iii) evaluate options for responding to the complaint, and the implication of any response made.

It may be that information can be given to clear up a misunderstanding, or the employee will - having 'got it off his chest' - withdraw his complaint. However, the meeting may have to be *adjourned* (say, for 48 hours) while the manager gets extra information and considers extra options.

(c) *Reply*. The manager, having reached and reviewed his conclusions, reconvenes the meeting to convey (and justify, if required) his decision, hear counter-arguments and appeals. The outcome (agreed or disagreed) should be recorded in writing.

Grievance procedures should be seen as an employee's right. To this end, managers should be given formal training in the grievance procedures of their organisation, and the reasons for having them. Management should be persuaded that the grievance procedures are beneficial for the organisation and are not a threat to themselves (since many grievances arise out of disputes between subordinates and their bosses).

Activity 4

Think of a complaint or grievance you have (or have had) at school or college. Have you done anything about it? If so on your own, or through some kind of grievance procedure? If so, what happened: were you satisfied with the process and outcome? If not, why not?

Chapter roundup

- *Discipline* has the same end as motivation - ie to secure a range of desired behaviour from members of the organisation. Motivation may even be called a kind of self-discipline - because motivated individuals exercise choice to behave in the way that the organisation wishes. Discipline however, is more often related to negative motivation, an appeal to the individual's need to avoid punishment, sanctions or unpleasantness.
- *Grievance* procedures embody the employee's right to appeal against unfair or otherwise prejudicial conduct or conditions that affect him and his work.

Quick quiz

1. What is progressive discipline?
2. What factors should a manager bear in mind in trying to control the disciplinary situation?
3. Outline the content of a disciplinary interview.
4. Outline typical grievance procedures.

Solutions to activities

1. (a) Breaking rules regarding rest periods and other time schedules such as leaving work to go home early.

    (b) Improper personal appearance.

    (c) Breaking safety rules.

    (d) Other violations of rules, regulations and procedures.

    (e) Open insubordination such as the refusal of an employee to carry out a legitimate work assignment.

3. Apart from the outline of the steps involved - which can be drawn from the chapter, this question raises an interesting point about the nature of different offences, and the flexibility required in the handling of complex disciplinary matters.

    (a) There is clearly a difference in kind and scale between

    (i) unsatisfactory conduct (eg absenteeism)

    (ii) misconduct (eg insulting behaviour, *persistent absenteeism,* insubordination) and

    (iii) 'gross misconduct' (eg *theft* or assault).

    (b) The attitude of the organisation towards the *purpose* of disciplinary action will to a large extent dictate the severity of the punishment.

    (i) If it is *punitive* it will 'fit the crime'.

(ii) If it is *reformative,* it may be a warning only, and less severe than the offence warrants.

(iii) If it is *deterrent,* it may be more severe than is warranted (ie to 'make an example').

(c) The absenteeism question assumes that counselling etc. has failed, and that some sanction *has* to be applied, to preserve credibility. The theft technically deserves summary dismissal (as gross misconduct), but it depends on the scale and value of the theft, the attitude of the organisation to use of stationery for personal purposes (ie is it theft?) etc.

Further question practice

Now try the following practice questions at the end of this text

Multiple choice questions	**77 to 81**
Exam style question	**12**

Chapter 13

TERMINATION OF EMPLOYMENT

Introduction

Remember that a contract of employment is not necessarily a written document: all that is required to establish a contract is agreement of the essential terms by both parties.

Circumstances in which a contract of employment may come to an end include the following.

(a) *By performance:* for example, the expiry of the fixed term for which the person was employed.

(b) *By mutual agreement:* retirement, or possibly 'constructive dismissal', where the employee is forced to resign because of irreconcilable differences with the employer.

(c) *By notice.* For example:
   (i) resignation;
   (ii) dismissal; or
   (iii) redundancy.

(d) *By breach of contract,* entitling the employer to dismiss the employee without notice. Examples may include:
   (i) wilful disobedience of a reasonable order, representing total disregard for the terms of the contract;
   (ii) misconduct in employment, such as dishonesty or violence;
   (iii) misconduct outside employment which interferes with work performance, such as persistent drunkenness;
   (iv) serious negligence or incompetence.

(e) *By frustration,* through the death, illness or imprisonment of the employee or employer.

Organisations would like to be able to control the outward 'flow' of people, as part of the human resource planning process. But clearly, that is not always going to be possible!

Your objectives

After completing this chapter you should:

(a) be able to outline procedures in the event of employee retirement and redundancy;
(b) be able to distinguish between wrongful, unfair and justified dismissal;
(c) be able to define redundancy and outline procedures in the event of redundancies;
(d) be aware of the legal framework on employment protection;
(e) appreciate some of the human aspects of terminating employment.

Chapter 13: Termination of employment

1 RETIREMENT AND RESIGNATION

1.1 Retirement

The average age of the working population has been steadily increasing, with higher standards of living and health care. The problems of older workers and retirement are therefore commanding more attention. The time at which difficulties occur in obtaining or retaining jobs because of age will obviously vary according to the individual, his lifestyle and occupation, and the attitudes of his society and employers.

In later middle age, many workers try to move away from jobs which make demands on their agility, energy or muscular strength. However, they are still capable of less strenuous work, and particularly in the office setting may be very valuable in jobs requiring mature judgement, conscientiousness, attention to detail or experience. They may make a great contribution to the training and coaching of more junior staff.

From the organisation's point of view, however, there are various arguments for enforcing retirement.

(a) There is resistance to late retirement from younger workers, because it is felt that promotion opportunities are being blocked. The Job Release Scheme even encourages individuals to retire a year or two *earlier* than usual, so as to create job vacancies for the pool of unemployed workers.

(b) Younger employees with family responsibilities need to have their jobs secured, and in a redundancy situation, it is common for pensioners and those nearing retirement to be discharged first.

(c) The age structure of an organisation may become unbalanced for future work requirements: there may have to be an injection of 'younger blood' through the compulsory retirement of older workers.

(d) Engaging staff above middle age can be costly for the organisation: the cost of providing pensions rises according to the age at which the employee joins the superannuation scheme. Many pension funds exclude the entry of men and women above a specified age.

(e) Individual mental and/or physical shortcomings may render an older individual unfit to carry out his duties efficiently. However, statistics show that older workers have less sickness absence than younger employees.

The HR and/or line manager will have to consider how far any of the above factors apply in a given situation. It will depend to a large extent on the individual concerned, the type of work involved and the state of the local labour market. Retirement policies, and age limits on particular posts will have to be clearly communicated, and decisions regarding particular cases discussed confidentially and tactfully with the individual concerned. Written confirmation of the decision to retire an employee should likewise be tactful, with expressions of regret and appreciation as appropriate.

Not only can employers give financial assistance to retiring employees, but also practical help and advice.

(a) The burden of work in later years can be eased by shortening hours or a transfer to lighter duties.

(b) The final stage of employee training and development may take the form of courses, commonly run by local technical colleges, intended to prepare employees for the transition to retirement and non-work.

(c) The organisation may have, or may be able to put employees in touch with, social/leisure clubs and other facilities for easing the shock of retirement.

It should be noted that the Sex Discrimination Act, 1986, introduced the concept of equal retirement age for men and women. *Employers* setting a compulsory retirement age must apply it to men and women alike: women made to retire earlier than male colleagues can claim both discrimination and unfair dismissal. The *State* retirement age is still 65 for men and 60 for women at present, but will be equalised at 65 over a ten year period starting in 2010.

Activity 1

What would be the major benefit of equalising state pension age at 65? What disadvantage might offset this?

1.2 Resignation

Definition

> *Resignation* is a termination of contract by notice. The contract itself should specify notice periods, but whatever the contract says, the statutory minimum is one week, if the employee has been employed for at least one month. Notice may be waived, or payment offered in lieu of notice. During the notice period, an employee is entitled to pay at a rate not less than the average of his or her earnings over the previous twelve weeks.

Employees may resign for any number of reasons, personal or occupational. Some or all of these reasons may well be a reflection on the structure, management style, culture or personnel policies of the organisation itself. When an employee announces his intention to leave, verbally and/or by letter, it is important for management to find the real reasons why he is leaving, in an *exit interview*. This may lead to a review of the existing policies on pay, training, promotion, the work environment, the quality and style of supervision and so on.

The principal aspect of any policy formulated to deal with resignations must be the length to which the organisation will go to try and dissuade a person from leaving. In some cases, the organisation may decide simply to let the person go, but when an employee has been trained at considerable cost to the firm, or is particularly well qualified and experienced (no employee is irreplaceable - but some are more replaceable than others), or has knowledge of information or methods that should not fall into the hands of competitors, the organisation may try to keep him.

Particular problems the employee has been experiencing may be solvable, though not always in the short-term. It may be that the organisation will try to match or improve on a salary offer made to the individual by a new prospective employer. In that case, however, there may well be a problem of pay differentials and the individual's colleagues, doing the same work, may have to be given similar increases: can so large a cost be justified?

Various arrangements will have to be made when an employee decides to leave. There will have to be co-operation and full exchange of information between the HR function and the leaver's superior so that procedures can be commenced upon notification of an intended departure.

(a) If attempts to make the employee stay have been unsuccessful, the exit interview will have to be arranged.

(b) The period of notice required for the employee to leave should be set out in the contract of employment, but some leeway may be negotiated on this. The need for the recruitment and induction of a replacement, may dictate that the leaving employee work out his full period of notice, and perhaps even longer if he is willing. On the other hand, if it is felt that he can be easily replaced, and that his continuing presence may be destructive of morale (or possibly of advantage to competitors, as he continues to glean information), it may be possible to persuade him to accept pay in lieu of notice and leave immediately.

(c) Details of the departure will have to be notified to the wages clerk, pension fund officer, social secretary, security officer and so on, so that the appropriate paperwork and other procedures can be completed by his date of leaving.

(d) The departmental head and/or supervisor should complete a leaving report form: an overall assessment of the employee's performance in the organisation. This can then be used to provide references to his or her future employer(s).

Activity 2

What value would you be inclined to place on information obtained in an exit interview?

2 DISMISSAL

Dismissal includes not only the termination of an employee's contract by his employer, but also:

(a) the ending of a fixed term contract without renewal on the same terms; and

(b) termination by the employee himself where the employer's conduct forces him to do so (*constructive dismissal*). Constructive dismissal is determined as being by reason of: 'Conduct which is a significant breach of the contract of employment or which shows that the employer no longer intends to be bound by one or more of the essential terms of the contract ... The conduct must be sufficiently serious to entitle him to leave at once' (*Western Excavating v Sharp 1978*). The employee is deemed to have been dismissed, and may be able to claim compensation for unfair dismissal or redundancy. Examples include reduction in pay or removal of job interest.

If an employer terminates the contract of employment by giving notice the minimum period of notice to be given is determined by the employee's length of continuous service in the employer's service.

Employee's length of service	*Minimum notice to be given by the employer*
1 month to 2 years	1 week
2 to 12 years	1 week for each year of service
12 years and over	12 weeks

This is the statutory minimum: longer periods may be written into the contract, at the employer's discretion, and by agreement. Either party may waive his right to notice, or accept payment in lieu of notice. An employee who has been continuously employed for at least six months (or two years, if the employment began on or after 26 February 1990) is entitled to a written statement of the reasons for his dismissal within 14 days of requesting it.

2.1 Summary dismissal

Definition

Summary dismissal occurs where the employer dismisses the employee without notice. This is only justified if the employee has committed a serious breach of contract.

2.2 Wrongful dismissal

A claim for wrongful dismissal is open to an employee at *common law*, if he can show he was dismissed without a reasonable cause or without the appropriate notice being given.

An employee will have to show that his dismissal was 'without just cause or excuse', that circumstances did not justify dismissal (say, in the case of a minor breach of rules), that notice periods were ignored (other than by his or her agreement) and that he or she suffered loss as a result. The employer is not justified in dismissing an employee unless there is some serious fault. The courts have held the following to be justifiable.

(a) Wilful disobedience of a lawful order.

(b) Misconduct, such as disclosure of confidential information, bribery, assault on a fellow employee.

(c) Dishonesty by an employee in a position of trust.

(d) Incompetence or neglect in areas in which the employee professes to have skill.

(e) Gross negligence, depending on the nature of the job.

If wrongful dismissal can be proved, the employee may be able to claim damages for loss of earnings payable during the period of notice, or the balance of wages due under a fixed term contract. No compensation is available for loss of reputation, limitation or loss of discretionary bonuses. In practice, such claims are less common, now that *unfair* dismissal provisions offer wider remedies, but the common law remedy is still useful for those excluded (notably by a qualifying period of employment) from claiming unfair dismissal.

2.3 Unfair dismissal

An employee may bring a claim before the Industrial Tribunal if he considers that he has been *unfairly* dismissed, under the Employment Protection (Consolidation) Act 1978. The employee first has to prove that he has been dismissed. The onus is then on the *employer* to prove that the dismissal was *fair*.

Under the 1978 Act, dismissal is *fair and justified* if the reason for it was:

(a) redundancy (provided that the selection for redundancy was fair) - discussed below;

(b) legal impediment - the employee could not continue to work in his present position without breaking a legal duty or restriction. (This is fair only if the employee was offered suitable alternative employment);

(c) non-capability to do the job (provided adequate training and warnings had been given);

(d) misconduct (provided warnings suitable to the offence have been given - so the disciplinary procedures of the organisation are vitally important); or

(e) some other 'substantial' reason: for example, the employee is married to a competitor, or refuses to accept a reorganisation made in the interests of the business and with the agreement of other employees.

Situations in which *unfair* dismissal can automatically be claimed include:

(a) dismissal because of membership (actual or proposed) and involvement in the activities of an independent trade union, *or* non-membership and involvement: Trade Union and Labour Relations (Consolidation) Act 1992;

(b) dismissal because of a spent conviction, under the Rehabilitation of Offenders Act 1974;

(c) dismissal because of pregnancy (having been employed for two years) unless by reason of it the employee becomes incapable of doing her work adequately, and no reasonable alternative work is available.

In order to qualify for compensation or other remedies for unfair dismissal the employee must:

(a) be *under the normal retiring age* applicable to his job or grade, as determined by the employer's practice;

(b) have been *continuously employed* for the required period - one year, in the case of employees whose service began on or after 1 June 1985, or two years. There is no qualifying period required in cases of dismissal because of trade union membership;

(c) have been *dismissed*; and/or

(d) have been *unfairly* dismissed, as explained above.

The Conciliation Officer or Industrial Tribunal to whom a complaint of unfair dismissal is made may order various remedies including:

(a) *re-instatement* - giving the employee his old job back;

(b) *re-engagement* - giving him a job comparable to his old one; and

(c) *compensation*. This may consist of:

   (i) a *basic award* calculated on the same scale as redundancy pay. Over the age of 41, the entitlement is for 1½ weeks' pay (up to a maximum limit) for each year of service (up to a maximum of 20 years). In the age group 22-40 the entitlement is one weeks' pay, and under 22, half a week's pay. If the employee is also entitled to redundancy pay, the lesser is set off against the greater amount;

   (ii) a *compensatory award* (taking account of the basic award) for any additional loss (earnings, expenses, benefits) on common law principles of damages for breach of contract; and/or

   (iii) a *punitive additional award* if the employer does not comply with an order for re-instatement or re-engagement and does not show that it was impracticable to do so. This award may be between 13 and 26 weeks' pay.

In deciding whether to exercise its powers to order re-instatement or re-engagement the tribunal must take into account whether the complainant wishes to be reinstated, whether it is practicable for the employer to comply with such an order and, if the complainant contributed to any extent to his dismissal, whether it would be just, to make such an order. Such orders are very infrequent.

2.4 Dismissing incompetent workers

In an article in *The Administrator* (June 1985) John Muir wrote of the difficulties of 'firing' incompetent employees.

> *It is a fairly common experience to hear managers at all levels say of a subordinate, 'I wish I could get rid of him. He's really not up to the job and costs us money. But he's been here years and I really don't see how I can do it.' Behind such a statement there are usually two themes. One is about the personal difficulty and the unpleasantness involved in going to the individual and starting the process leading to dismissal; the other is the fear of being taken to an industrial tribunal and being found to have acted unfairly.*

Activity 3

How can the HR function design procedures for dismissal which would protect both the employees and the organisation (from unfair dismissal claims)?

Muir also notes the particular difficulty of identifying the principal reason for dismissal (as required by EP(C)A 1978). *Capability* - or, in practical terms, incapability or incompetence - is one such reason, but must be clearly identified. Incompetence means that the employee has not reached the standard required, although he has done what he considers his best, leaving aside extraneous factors like non-availability of information or materials. If the employee has deliberately not done his best, however, this is *misconduct,* which is a dismissable offence.

> *Suppose the task is to set a machine which will then turn out work automatically. The more work that is turned out the bigger the bonus but the job should be stopped every ten minutes so as to check the settings. While the machine is stopped there is no production so no bonus accrues. In fact the machine is not stopped at all. The original setting was wrong and the entire output has to be scrapped. There is the element of misconduct in that the requirement to check the machine every ten minutes was not adhered to and there is a major element of incompetence in not setting the machine correctly in the first place. On the other hand, was the incorrect setting the result of a deliberate 'couldn't care less' attitude? If so that, too, is misconduct.*
>
> Administrator June 1985

3 REDUNDANCY

Redundancy is defined by the 1978 Act as dismissal where:

(a) the employer has ceased to carry on the business;

(b) the employer has ceased to carry on the business in the place where the employee was employed;

(c) the requirements of the business for employees to carry out work of a particular kind have ceased or diminished or are expected to.

Activity 4

If A's job is abolished, and A is moved into B's job, and B is dismissed, is this a case of redundancy?

Redundant employees are entitled to compensation:

(a) for loss of security; and

(b) to encourage employees to accept redundancy without damage to industrial relations.

The employee is *not* entitled to compensation if:

(a) the employer has made a suitable offer of alternative employment and the employee has unreasonably rejected it. The 'suitability' of the offer must be examined in each case;

(b) the employee is of pension age or over, or has less than two years' continuous employment;

(c) the employee's conduct entitles the employer to dismiss him without notice;

(d) the employee resigns voluntarily.

3.1 Procedure for handling redundancies

From a purely humane point of view, it is obviously desirable to consult with employees or their representatives, and to give warning of impending redundancies.

The Employment Protection Act 1975 imposes this as a duty. Protective awards (an order of a tribunal that an employer shall continue to pay remuneration of employees) may be made against an employer who in a redundancy situation fails to consult trade unions at the earliest opportunity, or to give notice of impending redundancies to the Department of Employment.

The employer's duty is to consult with any trade union which is independent and recognised (in collective bargaining) by him as representative of employees. The consultation must begin 'at the earliest opportunity', defined as:

(a) a minimum of 90 days before the first dismissal, if 100 or more employees are to be dismissed at any one establishment;

(b) a minimum of 30 days before the first dismissal of 10 - 99 employees;

(c) at the earliest opportunity before even one (but not more than 9) employees are to be dismissed for redundancy.

These rules are applied to the total number involved and cannot be evaded by making essential dismissals in small instalments. The employer must, within the same periods, notify the Secretary of State in writing of proposed redundancies, with details of consultations with the trade union: a copy of this notice is given to the union representative.

In giving notice to the trade union the employer must give certain details in writing, including the reasons for the dismissals, the numbers employed and the number to be dismissed, the method of selecting employees for dismissal and the period over which the dismissals will take place. Information should be accurate, clear, realistic and positive as far as possible. Ideas for retraining and redeployment, benefits and potential for voluntary redundancies or retirements should be far enough advanced that *some* good news can be mixed with the bad. The employer should allow the trade union time in which to consider what he has disclosed and to make representations or counter proposals.

3.2 Redundancy pay

Within six months from the expiry of the dismissal notice, the employee must:

(a) obtain payment; or

(b) make a written claim for payment to the employer; or

(c) take any disputed claim to an Industrial Tribunal; or

(d) make a complaint of unfair dismissal to a tribunal.

Redundancy pay is calculated on the same scale as that specified for unfair dismissal compensations.

3.3 Selection for redundancy

There are various approaches to selection for redundancy. If demand for a particular type of work has disappeared completely, the situation is relatively clear-cut: all those previously contracted to perform that work can be dismissed. Where management have to choose between individuals doing the same work, they may take the following approaches.

(a) Enforced or early retirement.

(b) Seeking volunteers, who would be willing to take their chances elsewhere on good redundancy terms.

(c) Value to the organisation, or retention by merit - keeping those who perform well and dismissing less effective workers (although this may be harder to justify to individuals and their representatives).

(d) 'Last in, first out' (LIFO). Newcomers are dismissed before long-serving employees. This may sound fair (especially in a seniority culture such as characterises Japanese big business), but may not meet the organisation's need for 'young blood' or for particular skills or merit in the individual.

3.4 Softening the blow

According to McIlwee *(Personnel Management in Context)*, there are different types of unemployment, which will impact in different ways on individuals and job markets.

(a) *Voluntary unemployment* is where people leave an organisation because they believe their prospects are better elsewhere, or that their present employer does not put a sufficiently high value on their skills and experience.

(b) *Involuntary unemployment* is where people cannot find work for what they consider a suitable level of pay.

(c) *Unemployment caused by low levels of demand for labour* includes:

   (i) *seasonal unemployment,* the periodic job-shedding which is common in industries such as construction and tourism;

   (ii) *cyclical unemployment;* and

   (iii) *growth gap unemployment,* where there is a long recession, and little prospect of an upturn in economic activity.

(d) *Unemployment caused by changes in skill requirements* includes:

   (i) *hard-core unemployment,* that small proportion of any society that are unlikely to gain any employment because of social, physical, mental or other deficiencies;

   (ii) *frictional unemployment,* where there is a time lag between a new skill requirement in the labour market and individual adjustment to it - either by acquiring or polishing skills, or by adjusting wage expectations;

   (iii) *structural unemployment,* which is caused by long-term changes in the industrial environment. The demand for labour in a given sector (for example, a declining industry such as shipbuilding) may fall more quickly than supply readjusts itself through natural wastage, redeployment and so on.

Unemployment can represent not only an economic threat to lifestyle, but a source of insecurity, loss of self-esteem, extreme stress and hopelessness. The HRM function should therefore be concerned to *prevent* enforced redundancies where possible.

Activity 5

What alternatives might there be to compulsory redundancies?

Where compulsory redundancies are unavoidable, HRM should *alleviate* its effects by:

(a) careful human resource planning, so that foreseen seasonal or other contractions in demand for labour can be taken into account, and the organisation is not over-supplied with labour for its needs;

(b) planning redundancy terms and measures early, to safeguard the interests of those who may be made redundant;

(c) retraining and redeployment programmes. This may be a solution where alternative jobs are available, employees have some of the skills (or at least aptitudes) required and retraining facilities are available;

(d) liaison with other employers in the same industry or area, with a view to redeployment within the linked group of organisations;

(e) provision of unemployment services, (or time, during the notice period, to seek them) such as:

Chapter 13: Termination of employment

(i) counselling, to aid readjustment to the situation in which the newly unemployed individual finds himself, to encourage a positive outlook;

(ii) training in job-search skills: how to locate employment opportunities; how to carry out self-appraisal and communicate it attractively on a CV; how to use application forms, letters and phone calls to advantage; how to handle interviews;

(iii) information on job opportunities and self-employment opportunities and funding. Individuals should be made aware of the role and accessibility of the Department of Employment's facilities and private sector services for careers counselling, recruitment and CV preparation.

Ultimately, most of these measures are palliatives rather than solutions. In the face of hard-core growth-gap or structural unemployment, the personnel function is likely to be powerless to prevent the shedding of jobs. Nevertheless, efforts to cushion the impact of unemployment, and particularly the encouragement of training and retraining, should be considered by socially responsible employers.

The survivor syndrome

According to Doherty and Horsted (*People Management*, January 1995), organisations should pay attention to the needs of those who survive redundancy and other downsizing programmes and remain in the job. These people might be suffering from the 'survivor syndrome', which is characterised by:

(a) decreased levels of:
  (i) motivation
  (ii) loyalty to the organisation
  (iii) morale
  (iv) career security
  (v) confidence in their own future
  (vi) confidence in the organisation's future

(b) increased levels of:
  (i) anxiety
  (ii) loyalty to colleagues
  (iii) interest in employability.

Thus, survivors will shift their allegiance from the corporation to the team. Organisations must provide full and frank information on their plans and how individuals fit into them. Yet very few actually do. According to Doherty and Horsted, although more than two-thirds of the organisations in their survey group had significantly downsized, less than half of them offered any kind of structured help to the employees who remained.

Activity 6

'Personnel Management will become increasingly involved in getting rid of people instead of recruiting them.' For what reasons might such a prediction be made? To what extent is it correct, in your judgement?

Business Basics: Human Resource Management

> **Chapter roundup**
> - *Exit* from employment takes several forms, voluntary and involuntary, but is likely to be traumatic in some degree to the leaving individual whatever the circumstances, because of the centrality of work and job security in most people's lives.
> - The organisation should consider the sensitivity of the situation - not least because it may itself be traumatised by the exit of key individuals.
> - Full account should be taken of the implications of and reasons for people's leaving, the legal obligations with regard to employment protection and so on.

Quick quiz

1. What procedures should be carried out when an employee resigns from the organisation?
2. In what circumstances is an employee 'dismissed' in the sense used in employment protection law?
3. What reasons may an employer rely on in seeking to show that a dismissal was fair?
4. What is meant by redundancy?
5. What positive steps could a personnel department take to reduce the impact of redundancy on employees?

Solutions to activities

1. The money saved on five years' pensions for women is estimated at £3 billion a year, which could be used to improve the pensions and benefits of the lower paid (especially women). However, when this was first proposed, the IPD pointed out that in reality, very few men over the age of 63 are in employment, so if they have to wait until 65 for a pension, they will be eligible for unemployment benefit for several years.

2. There is clearly a strong possibility that employees who are leaving will not bother, or will still be too intimidated, to give the full reasons for their resignation. Others may simply be vindictive. When several people leave and all give similar reasons, however, there is a problem in the organisation to be addressed.

3. (a) Ensuring that *standards* of performance and conduct are set, clearly defined and communicated to all employees.

   (b) *Warning* employees where a gap is perceived between standard and performance.

   (c) Giving a clearly defined and reasonable *period for improvement* - with help and advice where necessary, and clear improvement targets.

   (d) Ensuring that disciplinary procedures and the ultimate consequences of continued failure are made clear.

4. Yes. The overall position is one of redundancy.

5. (a) Retirement of staff over the normal retirement age.

   (b) Offering early retirement to staff approaching normal retirement age.

   (c) Restrictions or even a complete ban on recruitment, so as to reduce the workforce over time by natural wastage.

   (d) Dismissal of part-time or short-term contract staff, once contracts come to sensible break-off points or conclusions.

   (e) Offering retraining and/or redeployment within the organisation.

(f) Seeking voluntary redundancies.

6 (a) John Hunt *The shifting focus of the personnel function*: 'In sharp contrast to the search for talent is the dramatic shift in the personnel function from people resourcing to people exiting.'

(b) Pressures on intensive use of human resource, contraction of workforce (plus expansion in unemployment in UK), due to the following:

(i) competition

(ii) new technology

(iii) recession and decline in world trade.

(c) But this is not necessarily a trend which will continue in future. Technology does not always 'replace' human operation and lead to human resource savings.

(d) There are alternatives to redundancy: job-sharing, use of human resource agencies, part-time or temporary assignments, networking.

Further question practice

Now try the following practice questions at the end of this text

Multiple choice questions   **82 to 86**
Exam style question   **13**

Chapter 14

PERSONNEL RECORDS

Introduction

The main purposes of a record/information system for HRM are as follows.

(a) The personal details of employees and their employment history must be stored for reference.

(b) Data must be provided in returns to government and other agencies.

(c) Information must be gathered and processed for decision-making in all areas of HRM, as we have already seen, including:

  (i) human resource forecasting and planning;

  (ii) recruitment and selection;

  (iii) employment: transfer, promotion, discipline, termination;

  (iv) training and development;

  (v) the design and administration of remuneration systems; and

  (vi) health, safety and welfare.

Betty Ream *(Personnel Administration)* suggests: 'The importance of adequate personnel records, once seen as a peripheral, tedious and undemanding part of the personnel function, is becoming increasingly recognised and it is no longer possible or prudent to give them scant attention.' This increasing importance grows out of the perception of personnel as a planning (not just organising) function: HRM is having to concern itself with environmental and internal trends and forecasts. Paradoxically, the gathering, storing and updating of statistical information can still be 'tedious and undemanding', however, and can reinforce the perception of the personnel function as pen-pushers and filing clerks.

Your objectives

After completing this chapter you should:

(a) be aware of the information requirements of HRM;

(b) understand the issues involved in designing an information system;

(c) appreciate the role of computers in HRM;

(d) be aware of the requirement for confidentiality of personnel records.

Chapter 14: Personnel records

1 INFORMATION REQUIREMENTS

Information systems are often studied from the point of view of design. (You don't have one: how do you go about designing and implementing one?) In practice, however, there is usually a system in operation in organisations which has simply evolved in days before the theory of information systems (and the technology to back it up) were widely understood. Barbara Dwyer suggests that existing systems:

Will rarely have been consciously spelled out by any one person or group but will usually have emerged over a period as a result of individual perceptions of gaps or shortcomings in the system.

In order to re-evaluate the effectiveness and efficiency of such a current system - or indeed to design a new one - the HR manager will have to:

(a) define (or redefine) the purpose and objectives of the personnel record system, and its subsystems (individual records, returns, human resource planning statistics and so on);

(b) specify the type and range of records necessary to achieve these objectives; and

(c) assess the procedures, tasks and costs involved in establishing and maintaining these records by various alternative methods.

1.1 Employee records

Employee records are those kept by an organisation about each of its employees. They are built up and added to as the employee's career with the organisation progresses.

The information kept in an employee's record will be:

(a) his or her original application form, interview record and letters of reference;

(b) his or her contract of employment, giving details such as period of notice, conditions and terms of work;

(c) *standing* details about the employee, such as:

   (i) age;

   (ii) home address;

   (iii) current position/grade in the organisation;

   (iv) details of pay;

   (v) details of holiday entitlement;

   (vi) date of birth;

   (vii) date of commencement of employment;

(d) *accumulated* details of the employee's work history.

Activity 1

Suggest some of the details that might be accumulated throughout an employee's career with an organisation.

This data will have to be kept continuously flowing in from the department in which an employee works.

Business Basics: Human Resource Management

NOTES

EMPLOYEE RECORD CARD — **NAME:**

Date of birth _____ Nationality _____ Sex ☐ M ☐ F

National insurance No. _____ No. of dependants _____

☐ Single ☐ Engaged ☐ Married ☐ Separated ☐ Divorced ☐ Widowed

Job related physical disabilities _____

Registration No. _____

Education _____

Higher education _____

Qualifications _____

Company training _____

Other skills (eg languages) _____

Pension scheme _____ Date eligible _____ Driving licence _____ Date joined _____

IN EMERGENCY INFORM

Address _____ Postcode _____ Name _____ Address _____ Tel (work) _____ (home) _____

1st CHANGE
Address _____ Postcode _____
Telephone _____

2nd CHANGE
Address _____ Postcode _____
Telephone _____

Name _____ Address _____ Tel (work) _____ (home) _____

EMPLOYMENT HISTORY

Dates From	To	Position	Pay £	Reason for change or termination

TRAINING HISTORY

Dates From	To	Courses attended

Form ERC/1

260

Chapter 14: Personnel records

> **ACAS: EMPLOYEE RECORD**
>
> ACAS (1981) recommended that records should also show the following.
>
> - The numbers and occupations of employees required for efficient production, including future production plans.
> - How well the age balance of the work force is being maintained.
> - The rate of labour turnover and retention of key workers.

There will also be *collective* employee records, such as:

(a) age and length of service distributions;
(b) total wage/salary bill; wage rates and salary levels;
(c) overtime statistics;
(d) absenteeism, labour turnover statistics;
(e) accident rates and costs;
(f) grievances, disciplinary action, disputes;
(g) training records.

1.2 Personnel returns and statutory records

Personnel returns may be required in the UK by:

(a) the Health and Safety Executive - health and safety statistics;
(b) Department of Employment or employers' associations - human resource and earnings statistics;
(c) industrial training boards - training statistics;
(d) the DSS and Inland Revenue - human resource, earnings, pension and other benefit statistics.

Records required by *statute* include the following.

(a) *Hours of work:* hours, breaks and overtime of young employees (16-18) on outside duties; hours of work of women and young persons employed in factories; hours of work of drivers.
(b) *Disabled employees:* names of registered disabled persons.
(c) *PAYE records* (see below).
(d) *Safety:* notifiable accidents (Form F2508); records and dates of first aiders' qualifications and training; records of first aid treatment given.

1.3 PAYE records

The legal apparatus surrounding PAYE is quite strict. If the Inland Revenue suspects an employer of any irregularities or deficiencies in processing, then Inland Revenue inspectors can institute a PAYE Audit, which is a detailed examination of an employer's payroll records. Fines can be severe.

The employer's duties are:

(a) to operate the PAYE system for all covered by it;
(b) to maintain the necessary records;
(c) to pay the Income Tax and National Insurance collected from employees to the Inland Revenue every month (in most cases);

(d) to let the Inland Revenue, or staff from the Department of Social Security, inspect the records;

(e) to submit end of year returns;

(f) to give employees payslips detailing Income Tax and NI deducted and to give them an annual statement (P60); and

(g) to maintain for three years, at the minimum, after the end of each tax year, the records relating to that year.

The main pay details that must be kept for individual employees can (but do not have to be) recorded on an A3 sized form issued by the Inland Revenue known as the P11. This contains details of gross pay (week by week or month by month and cumulatively, from 6 April to the next 5 April), free pay, taxable pay, tax due, tax deducted, National Insurance contributions (employees' and employers'), statutory sick pay and maternity pay.

P11s are to be filled in manually, but employers of any size are likely to operate a computerised system. This will calculate and record all of the above details, though not necessarily in the same format as the P11.

1.4 The uses of statistics in HRM

Decision-making in a range of HRM activities will require statistical information, or data about individuals.

Activity 2

Before reading on, think back over the topics covered in this book. What areas can you immediately identify where records and statistics would aid decision-making and planning?

(a) *Human resource planning*. Forecasting the future demand for labour will require ratio-trend analysis, environmental information about the market and competitor action and so on. Forecasting the future supply of labour will require information about the labour market, as well as, for each category of labour within the organisation, turnover, age distribution, promotions etc.

(b) *Planning recruitment and selection*. Job and person specifications will be the basis of both activities. Study of past recruitment campaigns, the cost/success rate of advertising media and offered incentives will help in the design of new recruitment campaigns. Data on the success of interview and testing techniques in selection (Did the high-scorers also do well in performance assessment on the job?) may likewise lead to improvements.

(c) *Planning training programmes*. Analyses of future human resource and job requirements and training specifications will determine needs for subjects to be covered, types of courses, numbers to be trained and so on.

(d) *Planning and reviewing remuneration systems*. Statistics of wage drift, attrition, earnings fluctuations, average as opposed to target salaries in grades, cost per unit of output, rates of pay in competitor organisations and the market in general and so forth, will help in reviewing pay systems, structure and levels of pay. Merit awards will be controlled by analysing amounts and distribution in comparison to budget.

(e) *Improving employee satisfaction and relations*. Work methods, supervision or disciplinary procedures may be improved by analysis of disciplinary cases, causes of disputes, statistics on labour turnover, absenteeism or grievances.

(f) *Improving health, safety and fire precautions*, by analysing statistics on sickness, accidents and incidents in the organisation, and reports and returns on industrial disease, health hazards, inspection and audit methods and so on.

Purpose	Ratio	
Labour turnover:	$\dfrac{\text{Number of employees terminated}}{\text{Average number employed}}$	× 100
Labour stability:	$\dfrac{\text{Employees with more than 1 year's service}}{\text{Number of employees employed 1 year ago}}$	× 100
Time-keeping/ attendance:	$\dfrac{\text{Number of man-hours lost}}{\text{Total possible man-hours worked}}$	× 100
Compa-ratio: (level of salaries in a grade compared with target)	$\dfrac{\text{Average of all salaries in the grade}}{\text{Mid-point of the salary range}}$	× 100

2 DESIGN OF THE INFORMATION SYSTEM

The type and complexity of the record system will depend on the size and information needs of the company, the time, staff and money available. Most small companies are content to rely on a manual system, but larger undertakings are likely to require more comprehensive information on a larger scale, and with more flexibility, and computerisation is increasingly an option.

A record system for HRM (like any other) should be:

(a) *simple to operate and easy to maintain.* Forms should be designed so as to be logical and easily read, understood, completed, and identified for retrieval. Relevant items should be immediately isolated and retrieved, without having to wade through complicated indexing systems or irrelevant data;

(b) *accurate and up-to-date.* Records should be clearly identified. The purpose and definition of entries should not be left ambiguous. Data on the record must be checked for accuracy, updatedness, within tolerance levels dictated by the purpose and time/cost budget of the system. (If approximations are sufficient, it is not cost-effective to record data to a minute degree of accuracy - although correctness will always be essential);

(c) *comprehensive but not overloaded.* Information should be regularly reviewed for completeness (no gaps where information is required) but also, crucially, relevance (no information that is redundant or unnecessary to the system's purpose). This consideration may prohibit the setting up of a system in the first place: a one-off request for information should not inspire a permanent record or data collection system unless the information is likely to be a recurring need, and of significant benefit to the organisation (so as to justify the costs of maintaining the record).

A *manual* system might consist of:

(a) files, registers and ledgers, usually supported by summaries, abstracts, and signalling of key records to assist in the extraction of required data and the compilation of statistics;

(b) card indexes, summarising essential details of individual employees. There are various space-saving storage devices, such as boxes, rotary wheels and visible card systems (which overlap to reveal only a strip which identifies the record); and/or

(c) standard forms for recording information.

Computers are getting smaller, cheaper and more versatile, so even relatively small firms should now consider computerisation, which can help not only in information storage and retrieval, but in data processing for decision-making as well.

Activity 3

What are the advantages of computers for record-keeping?

Procedures should be formulated for the collection, analysis, transmission and updating of information.

(a) Data may be *event triggered,* or recorded when pre-specified events, which are usually key events for management control, occur or fail to occur. Triggers might include accidents (report required), resignations, bonuses, or disciplinary or grievance cases.

(b) Some data will instead be *time triggered;* recorded at pre-specified intervals of time, for example for salary review, monthly/yearly surveys of turnover, absenteeism or whatever.

Either way, procedures should be established so that record generation is triggered, so that the updatedness and completeness of records can be controlled, and not left to chance. Updating procedures should also include periodical review of the continuing accuracy and relevance of data, and efficient systems for feeding through and recording new data quickly and accurately.

2.1 The organisation of personnel records

The *centralisation* of the records system (in a file registry, or in the files of the HR department rather than individual line departments) offers the following advantages.

(a) Procedures are uniform and consistent, and staff are trained to carry them out.

(b) The number and identity of people who have access to files can be strictly controlled.

(c) The condition and updatedness of all files can be controlled.

(d) Equipment, space and staff time can be used more cost-effectively.

(e) Data needed by more than one user can still be kept in one place as a complete record. This reduces the need for duplicate documents in a number of individual departmental files.

(f) In a large organisation, many people might want to use the same file at one time or another. Unless the files are kept under the control of a central records office, individual files may go astray.

(g) Computer systems have made centralised records easier and more convenient. Centralised databases can give access to many users - but with security controls on access to and alteration of data.

Activity 4

Can you see any drawbacks to centralised file-holding?

3 COMPUTERS IN HRM

The main uses for computers in HRM are as follows.

(a) *Keeping records*: accessible, space-economical storage of all the records discussed above, on training, pay, employee history and so on. This facility may be used as a pure historical filing cabinet, or as a database for accessible information in constantly updated areas such as the administration of Statutory Sick and Maternity Pay, accident, disciplinary, absenteeism and turnover analysis.

(b) *Preparation of management information*. Computer programs can be used to provide statistics, lists (selecting and sorting data entries according to defined criteria of age, sex or grade), analyses, ratios, trends, forecasts and models. This will enable raw data in records to be interpreted and organised for manpower, succession and development planning. 'What if...?' questions can be asked in the evaluation of options with regard to salary increases, say, or reduction in manning levels. In particular, it allows routine administrative information, such as payroll records, to be made into decision-support or management information - for example, to analyse the payroll costs of a range of human resource plans.

(c) *Analysis and comparison of different records for recruitment*, selection, job evaluation, employee appraisal, planning of workflow on the basis of workload distribution. Comparison of relevant details for different jobs, applicants and employees can be made accurately and almost instantaneously.

(d) *Calculation* - for example, of payroll costs and ratios, the effect of alterations to the structure or payments on the overall pay system and levels, budgets (and performance against them), or weightings of job evaluation factors. Computers are fast and accurate (given accurate inputs) in calculation.

(e) *Routine paperwork*, such as standard letters of acknowledgement or refusal in selection, notification and confirmation of job gradings or salary reviews, preparation of contracts or statements of employment. Word processing facilities can be used to merge new text and name/address files with standard skeleton documents. Time spent on typing and editing tasks (notices, advertising material, even in-house bulletins and journals, as well as correspondence) will be reduced, and output quality enhanced.

(f) *Graphics facilities*, used in the design of forms and documents where these still have to be used.

A survey carried out in the UK by Richards-Carpenter found that the main reasons given for needing a computerised system are:

- Routine personnel reports   90%
- Human resource planning   80%
- Salary administration   72%
- Ad hoc reports   38%
- Industrial relations negotiations 38%

Once the personnel function is freed from routine burdens, personnel specialists can be used more effectively. The introduction of an electronic machine into the personnel system will not necessarily make that unit any more effective or automatically benefit the organisation. There is no guarantee. Information needs to be properly utilised. The organisation should look for, and expect, a better service and greater personal attention. High quality information can improve the fair operation of promotion, transfer, training, welfare procedures, and help spot problem areas. The database can be interrogated quickly, but outputs from the system need to be in the format which can answer the questions asked by management within a desired time scale. A computerise system presents the organisation with tremendous opportunity to change its method of working. Tedious chores can disappear for ever. It may also be possible to simplify 'reporting' functions in so far as certain statistical returns will not only be printed by the system, but with all the necessary calculations already done. Decisions and actions can become proactive rather than delayed and reactive.

Livy, *Corporate Personnel Management*

One result of computerisation may be that personnel specialists are freed from routine administrative reporting tasks to concentrate on proactive human resource management, aided by sophisticated database management and modelling techniques. However, it should be noted that part of this devolution of administrative responsibility will be to line managers. A CPIS (Computerised Personnel Information System) would allow line managers, for example, to input and access absence information or human resource planning models for themselves. A double-edged sword?

3.1 Selection of a computer system

Your studies in information technology may have indicated the kind of criteria to be examined when selecting any computer system: the extent and nature of envisaged use, flexibility and compatibility, ease of use, costs and benefits. Particular questions may include the following.

(a) Is the system going to be required for routine text production and storage/retrieval tasks only (in which case a PC may be sufficient) or is more complex management information required? If immediate access (on-line) facilities are required, for example, for swift interrogation of the data base, or modelling and forecasting facilities, or advanced graphics, a mini or mainframe computer may be necessary, with a powerful CPU and possibly special software for particular applications.

(b) Is an integrated system possible and desirable: for example, for operating payroll and personnel systems together? This avoids duplication of effort and inconsistency in the updatedness of different databases. However, the time scale for using information may be different for different users, and authority for entries and access will have to be clearly defined (and prescribed by the system itself if possible) to avoid confusion. The equivalent consideration in manual systems might be the use of multi-purpose forms or documents sets.

(c) What are the costs and benefits? Costs include direct costs (hardware, software, peripherals, supplies, maintenance) and also development, accommodation, labour and training costs. Benefits will not be so readily quantifiable. Wille and Hammond pose the following four questions as a test of whether computerisation is economical:

1   How many people are required to run a manual system?
2   How many would be needed to maintain the desirable extra records a computer system would easily include?
3   How many people would be needed if a computer system were adopted?
4   What are the additional costs involved in using a computer system?

If the cost of 1 + 2 is greater than 3 + 4, the organisation should computerise.

(d) Should the organisation use its own hardware (with internally developed, or 'off-the-shelf' software) or use a computer bureau? Bureaux relieve the pressure on client's system development and hardware resources, but the available package may not be entirely relevant to the company's needs. In the same way, commercial software packages are cheaper but not as tailor-made as in-house software.

> **Case study: IBM (UK)**
>
> IBM (UK) currently use a centralised main-line system for the personnel function. Sensitive information, such as references, confidential test results or welfare provisions, are kept in ordinary paper files, but most employment and salary data is computerised.
>
> - On recruitment (and termination), starter (and termination) 'vouchers' containing basic details are completed by the manager responsible: duplicates are sent to the central personnel unit for entry into the computer. Other personal and career information is input straight from the application form, and added as the employee's career progresses. Every two years, a copy of the 'Personnel Information Survey' is sent to each employee for checking, to ensure that personal details are complete, up-to-date, accurate and relevant.
> - Payroll is also computerised at Central Office. The system is updated every other day. The computer produces the payslip and organises credit transfers for payment. Vouchers ('employee profile - current information') are again used for changes to the record of individual salaries: the authorising manager forwards details on the voucher to the Central Payroll Group for input. Once the file has been amended, a copy of the new record is returned to the manager for confirmation, as an 'employee profile - history' voucher for the line manager's records.
> - Salary planning is aided by modelling the cost effects of any given set of pay rises.
> - Access to computer terminals is strictly limited, and areas of information in storage are also protected by passwords.

4 CONFIDENTIALITY

The Institute of Personnel and Development has produced a 'Code of Professional Practice in Personnel Management' which deals with confidentiality of information. It states that a personnel manager should:

(a) 'respect the employer's requirements for confidentiality of information entrusted to him during the performance of his duties, including the safeguarding of information about individual employees'; and

(b) 'ensure the privacy and confidentiality of personnel information to which he has access or for which he is responsible, subject to any legal requirements and the best interests of the employee'.

Especially with the advent of computer records systems, fears have arisen with regard to:

(a) access to personal information by unauthorised parties;

(b) the likelihood that an individual could be harmed by the existence of computerised data about him which was inaccurate or misleading and which could be transferred to unauthorised third parties at high speed and little cost; and

(c) the possibility that personal information could be used for purposes other than those for which it was requested and disclosed.

The Data Protection Act 1984 was passed to address these concerns.

4.1 Data Protection Act 1984

The Act is an attempt to afford some measure of protection to the individual. The terms of the Act cover data about individuals - not corporate bodies - and data which is processed mechanically (which includes any 'equipment operated automatically in response to the instructions given for that purpose', not just computers).

Personal data is information about a living individual, including expressions of opinion about him or her. Data about other organisations is not personal data, unless it contains data about their members. Personal data includes facts or opinions about the individual, but not about the data user's intentions towards the individual. Also the individual must be identifiable from the data, whether by name, or by code number (say, an employment number) from which the user can identify the individual.

Data users are organisations or individuals who control the contents of files of personal data and the use of personal data which is processed (or intended to be processed) automatically.

Clearly, these two definitions put personnel administrators within the scope of the Act, unless a purely manual system of records is kept.

The Act provides that data users and computer bureaux have to register with the Data Protection Registrar. Data users must limit the use of personal data to the uses which are registered, and must abide by Data Protection Principles (discussed below).

The Act establishes the following rights for data subjects.

(a) A data subject may seek compensation through the courts for damage and any associated distress caused by:
  (i) the loss, destruction or unauthorised disclosure of data about himself; or by
  (ii) inaccurate data about himself.
(b) A data subject may apply to the courts or to the Registrar for inaccurate data to be put right or even wiped off the file.
(c) A data subject may obtain access to personal data of which he is the subject.

The *Data Protection Principles* which must be complied with are listed in Schedule 1 as follows.

Personal data held by data users

(1) The information to be contained in personal data shall be obtained, and personal data shall be processed, fairly and lawfully. Processing means amending, adding to, deleting or rearranging the data, or extracting the information that forms the data (eg printing out).

(2) Personal data shall be held only for one or more specified (registered) and lawful purposes.

(3) Personal data held for purpose or purposes shall not be used or disclosed in any manner incompatible with that purpose or those purposes.

(4) Personal data held for any purpose or purposes shall be adequate, relevant and not excessive in relation to that purpose or those purposes.

(5) Personal data shall be accurate and, where necessary, kept up-to-date. 'Accurate' means correct and not misleading as to any matter of *fact*. An *opinion* cannot be challenged on the grounds of inaccuracy and breach of the fifth DP Principle.

(6) Personal data held for any purpose or purposes shall not be kept for longer than is necessary for that purpose or those purposes. Data users should therefore review their personal data regularly, and delete any data which no longer serves a purpose.

(7) An individual shall be entitled:
- (a) at reasonable intervals, and without undue delay or expense:
   - (i) to be informed by any data user whether he holds personal data of which that individual is the subject; and
   - (ii) to access to any such data held by a data user; and
- (b) where appropriate, to have such data corrected or erased.

Personal data held by data users or in respect of which services are provided by persons carrying on computer bureaux

(8) Appropriate security measures shall be taken against unauthorised access to, or alteration, disclosure or destruction of, personal data and against accidental loss or destruction of personal data. The prime responsibility for creating and putting into practice a security policy rests with the data user.

(The Principles are quoted from the Act, with permission of the office of the Data Protection Registrar.)

Important exemptions from the Act include:

(a) *unconditional exemptions:* personal data which is essential to national security, required to be made public by law, or concerned only with the data user's personal, family or household affairs;

(b) *conditional exemptions*, including:
   - (i) personal data held for payroll and pensions;
   - (ii) data held by unincorporated members' clubs, relating only to club members; and
   - (iii) data held only for distribution of articles or information to the data subjects (say, for mailshot advertising) and consisting only of their names and addresses or other particulars necessary for the distribution;

(c) *exemptions from the 'subject access' provisions only*, including: data held for the prevention or detection of crime, assessment or collection of tax; data to which legal professional privilege could be claimed (for example, that held by a solicitor); data held solely for statistical or research purposes; and

(d) *a special exemption for word-processing operations* performed only for the purpose of preparing the text of documents. If a manager writes reports on his employees for disclosure to third parties using his computer as a wordprocessor, he will not as a result become a data user. If he stores the text of his report on disk in order to be able to make further copies, he will still not necessarily become a data user. If, however, he intends to use the stored data as a source of information about the individual and can extract the information automatically, he must register as a data user.

The Criminal Justice and Public Order Act 1994 created new offences in the field of data protection by amending s 5 of the Data Protection Act 1984. The new offences are procuring the disclosure of computer-held information; selling computer-held information; and offering to sell computer-held information, which are all punishable by a fine. This is relevant to HR because personnel information could be quite valuable to other organisations for marketing purposes.

The organisation will need to appoint a Data Protection Co-ordinator to arrange registration and set up systems to monitor compliance with the Principles, meet subject access requirements and alert him to any changes in the organisation which may require amendment in the registered entry. The entry should be amended whenever there is a change in the nature or purpose of data being held and used. The organisation's staff should be informed of the Act's implications and their rights as data subjects, as well as their duties as data users (if they work with computers).

Activity 5

Do you know what details about you are held on file? Consider who might keep a file on you. Is there anything that you know of that might be on file that might be detrimental to you?

4.2 Security measures

Confidentiality of paper records is reasonably easy to ensure, since withdrawal of files requires the physical presence of an individual. The file storage area should be restricted to authorised personnel only, and named individuals only should be allowed to consult or remove personnel files. Third party enquiries, for employee addresses or salary, say, should not be given without reference back to the employee.

Security measures in relation to *computerised* files include the following.

(a) Access to computer terminals should be strictly limited.

(b) Areas of information in storage should be protected with passwords, so that files cannot be called up by an unauthorised user of the VDU.

(c) Printouts of records, if done by a central computer department, should be made under the supervision of a member of staff responsible for records management. If such printouts are sent through internal mail to employees for checking, they should be properly sealed and marked 'Private and confidential'.

(d) Any disks used as back-up storage of personal data should also be protected with passwords and stored safely in a lockable container.

(e) Since data must be kept safe from loss or destruction as well as unauthorised access, there should be procedures for the backing-up of stored records (keeping copies), fire-proof storage for disks and so on.

Chapter roundup

- The main purpose of a personnel record/information system are:
  - storage of personal details and employment history;
  - the provision of data in returns to other agencies;
  - the provision of information for decision-making in all areas of personnel and strategic management.
- System designs vary with the needs of organisations, but computerised systems are becoming more available, with benefits for:
  - secure and economical information storage;
  - flexibility of processing functions for the preparation of management information;
  - speed and accuracy of data manipulation;
  - versatility for text editing and production, information storage, calculation etc;
  - document design and production.

Chapter 14: Personnel records

Quick quiz

1. What information will be contained in:
    (a) an employee's personnel record?
    (b) collective records of the organisation's workforce?
2. Why would an organisation want to centralise its record system in a file registry or similar department?
3. List five uses of a computer in personnel administration.
4. How can the security of computer files be ensured?
5. What contribution can information technology make to the effectiveness of the personnel function?

Solutions to activities

1. (a) Training
    (b) Professional qualifications acquired
    (c) Holidays taken
    (d) Positions held previously in the organisation: transfers and promotions
    (e) History of accidents, sick leave and absence
    (f) Appraisal forms
    (g) Results of proficiency tests
    (h) Disciplinary measures taken against him

3. The advantages of computers are that they are fast and accurate at storing, retrieving, transmitting, formatting and manipulating data. They can generate tailor-made management information in a wide variety of formats, and can store huge amounts of information in a very small space (on magnetic tape or disk) and with easy accessibility (since records can be updated or amended without the inconvenience of rearranging or defacing a paper record).

4. (a) Retrieval requests from other departments may take time to process and carry out.
    (b) Only records staff may understand the system and procedures, and have access to data, so there may be problems and costs associated with covering staff absence.
    (c) Documents will have to be duplicated and decentralised in any case, if they are constantly referred to in the course of operations. This sort of compromise is common in divisionalised organisations, where divisional personnel records are kept, but standardised returns covering basic and globally relevant data (such as earnings or human resource trends) are made to the central personnel information unit.

Further question practice

Now try the following practice questions at the end of this text.

Multiple choice questions	**87 to 90**
Exam style questions	**14**

GLOSSARY

Assertiveness Clear, honest and direct communication. It is not to be confused with 'bossiness' or aggression. Aggressive behaviour is competitive and directed at 'beating' someone else: assertion is based on equality and co-operation. Assertion is a simple affirmation that every individual has certain rights and can stand by them in the face of pressures from other people; that there is middle ground between being powerful and powerless, between the role of 'top dog' and 'door mat'.

Assessment centres These started with the War Office Selection Board methods during the Second World War. The purpose of the method is to assess potential and identify development needs, through various *group* techniques. It is particularly useful in the identification of executive or supervisory potential, since it uses simulated but realistic management problems, to give participants opportunities to show potential in the kind of situations to which they would be promoted, but of which they currently have no experience.

Collective bargaining When employers and employees negotiate agreements on working conditions through their respective representatives.

Constructive discipline - see **Positive discipline**

Constructive dismissal Termination by the employee himself, where the employer's conduct forces him to do so.

Content theories These assume that human beings have an innate package of 'motives' which they pursue; in other words, that they have a set of needs or desired outcomes and will act in such a way as to fulfil them.

Counselling '... A purposeful relationship in which one person helps another to help himself. It is a way of relating and responding to another person so that that person is helped to explore his thoughts, feelings and behaviour with the aim of reaching a clearer understanding. The clearer understanding may be of himself or of a problem, or of the one in relation to the other.' (Rees)

Culture The shared value system of an organisation: its customs, unwritten rules, special vocabulary, mottoes and legends; its 'style'; the things it believes in, as a body; in short, 'the way we do things round here'.

Entrepreneurship The 'shifting of economic resources out of the area of lower and into an area of higher productivity and greater yield.' (JB Say)

Ergonomics The scientific study of the relationship between man and his working environment. This sphere of scientific research explores the demands that can arise from a working environment and the capabilities of people to meet these demands.

Flexitime When predetermined fixed times of arrival and departure at work are replaced by a working day split into two different time zones.
  (a) The main part of the day is called 'core time' and is the only period when employees must be at their job (this is commonly from 10.00-16.00 hrs).
  (b) The flexible time is at the beginning and the end of each day and during this time it is up to the individual to choose when he arrives and leaves. Arrival and departure times would be recorded by some form of 'clocking in' system. The total working week or month for each employee must add up to the prescribed number of hours, though he may go into 'debit' or 'credit' for hours from day to day, in some systems.

Business Basics: Human Resource Management

Functional authority Where specialist staff managers exercise authority over all levels of managers.

Human resource planning A form of supply and demand management, aiming to minimise the risk of either surplus (and therefore inefficiency) or shortage (and therefore ineffectiveness) of relevant kinds of labour.

Job analysis 'The determination of the essential characteristics of a job', the process of examining a job to identify its component parts and the circumstances in which it is performed. Analysis may be carried out by observation for routine or repetitive jobs. Irregular jobs with a lot of invisible work (planning, man management, creative thinking and so on) will require interviews and discussions with superiors and with the people concerned.

Job description A broad description of a job or position at a given time (since jobs are dynamic, subject to change and variation). 'It is a written statement of those facts which are important regarding the duties, responsibilities, and their organisational and operational interrelationships.' (Livy, *Corporate Personnel Management*)

Job design The way in which tasks are fragmented or grouped to form a given job, and what decisions are made about specialisation, discretion, autonomy, variety and other job elements.

Job enlargement The process of increasing the number of operations in which a worker is engaged and so moving away from narrow specialisation of work. It is frequently confused with job enrichment, though it should be clearly defined as a separate technique. Job enlargement, as the name suggests, is the attempt to widen jobs by increasing the number of operations in which a job-holder is involved. This has the effect of lengthening the time cycle of repeated operations. By reducing the number of repetitions of the same work, the dullness of the job should also be reduced. Job enlargement is therefore a 'horizontal' extension of an individual's work.

Job enrichment The planned, deliberate action to build greater responsibility, breadth and challenge of work into a job.

Job evaluation A systematic method of arriving at a wage or salary structure, so that the rate of pay for a job is felt to be *fair* in comparison with other jobs in the organisation.

Job rotation The planned operation of a system whereby staff members exchange positions with the intention of breaking monotony in their work and providing fresh job challenges.

Labour flexibility The development of *versatility* or 'multi-skilling' in the labour resource, and the management of that versatility through the complex human relations problems which commonly surround the application of flexibility in many of its forms.

Line management This term represents both managers involved in achieving the objectives of the organisation, *and* any manager within a hierarchy.

Negative discipline The promise of sanctions designed to make employees *choose* to behave in a desirable way, although this again need not be a wholly negative matter. Disciplinary action may be *punitive* (punishing an offence), *deterrent* (warning people not to behave in that way) or *reformative* (calling attention to the nature of the offence, so that it will not happen again).

Neuro-linguistic programming (NLP) A technique which emerged in the USA in the 1970s. It is based on:

(a) identifying and breaking down the behaviour patterns found in 'excellent' performers; and

(b) communicating these patterns to people who wish to emulate their performance; in a way that

(c) overcomes the restricted thinking processes and limiting self-beliefs that typically hold those people back.

Participation The British Institute of Management (*Employee Participation - the Way Ahead*, 1977) described participation as: 'the practice in which employees take part in management decisions ... based on the assumption of a community of interest between employer and employee in furthering the long-term prospects of the enterprise and those working in it.'

Performance related pay The pay (or part of it) that is related to output (in terms of the number of items produced, or time taken to produce a unit of work), or results achieved (performance to defined standards in key tasks, according to plan).

Personnel management function Dr Dale Yoder of the Graduate School of Business, Stamford University, defines this as follows.

(a) Setting general and specific management policy for employment relationships and establishing and maintaining a suitable organisation for leadership and co-operation.

(b) Collective bargaining (negotiations between employer and employee representatives to reach agreement on terms and conditions of work).

(c) Staffing and organisation: finding, getting and holding prescribed types and numbers of workers.

(d) Aiding the self-development of employees at all levels, providing opportunities for personal development and growth as well as requisite skills and experience.

(e) 'Incentivating': developing and maintaining motivation in work.

(f) Reviewing and auditing human resource and management in the organisation.

(g) Industrial relations research, carrying out studies designed to explain employment behaviour, and thereby improve human resource management.

Personnel manager Nick Georgiades says this person does the following jobs.

(a) 'The administrative handmaiden' - writing job descriptions, visiting the sick, and so on.

(b) 'The policeman' - ensuring that both management and staff obey the rules and do not abuse the job evaluation scheme, and keeping a watchful eye on absenteeism, sickness and punctuality.

(c) 'The toilet flusher' - administering 'downsizing' policies (cutting staff numbers).

(e) 'The sanitary engineer' - ensuring that there is an awareness of the unsanitary psychological conditions under which many people work.

Personnel specification Identifies the type of person the organisation should be trying to recruit: their character, aptitudes, educational or other qualifications, aspirations in their career and other attributes.

Positive discipline This (sometimes called *constructive discipline*) relates to procedures, systems and equipment in the workplace which have been designed specifically so that the employee has no option but to act in the desired manner to complete a task safely and successfully. A machine may, for example, shut off automatically if its safety guard is not in place. A system may be designed to include checks and controls at each stage so that no task can be forgotten, or ill-performed, in a way that would impact on further tasks.

Process theory This explores the process through which outcomes become desirable and are pursued by individuals. This approach assumes that people are able to select their goals and choose the paths towards them, by a conscious or unconscious process of calculation.

Quality circle Consists of a voluntary group of employees, perhaps about eight in number, which meets regularly to discuss problems of quality and quality control in their area of work, and perhaps to suggest ways of improving quality. The quality circle has a leader or supervisor who directs discussions and possibly also helps to train other members of the circle.

Recruitment The part of the human resourcing process concerned with finding the applicants: it is a positive action by management, going into the labour market (internal and/or external), communicating opportunities and information, and hopefully generating interest.

Resignation A termination of contract by notice. The contract itself should specify notice periods, but whatever the contract says, the statutory minimum is one week, if the employee has been employed for at least one month. Notice may be waived, or payment offered in lieu of notice. During the notice period, an employee is entitled to pay at a rate not less than the average of his or her earnings over the previous twelve weeks.

Selection The part of the process which involves choosing between applicants for jobs: it is largely a negative process, weeding out people who are unsuitable for the job or the organisation (and for whom the job or organisation might be unsuitable).

Sexual harassment Any unwanted conduct with sexual connotations, physical or verbal. It is currently a matter of concern to the European Commission, the British courts and employing organisations. The IPD issued a statement on the matter in 1992.

Staff management This term represents both managers other than line managers, *and* those with special skills.

Stress A term which is often loosely used to describe feelings of tension or exhaustion - usually associated with too much, or overly demanding, work. In fact, stress is the product of demands made on an individual's physical *and mental* energies: monotony and feelings of failure or insecurity are sources of stress, as much as the conventionally considered factors of pressure, overwork and so on.

Strike action The action by a workforce (or part of it) to withhold its labour because of a dispute with management, usually over pay, job protection or working conditions. Strikes might be official or unofficial. Official strike action is supported by the trade union representatives of the employees in dispute, whereas unofficial strike action is taken by a part of the workforce without recognition and support from their union officials.

Summary dismissal This occurs where the employer dismisses the employee without notice. It is only justified if the employee has committed a serious breach of contract.

Telecommuting According to *The Administrator,* August 1992, this 'describes the process of working from home, or from a satellite office close to home, with the aid of computers, facsimile machines, modems or other forms of telecommunication equipment'.

Trade union An organised association of workers for the protection of their common interests. A single trade union might include members from different organisations in the same industry and a single organisation might employ workers who belong to a number of different trade unions. They are

Glossary

organisations whose purpose it is to promote their members' interests, and, in the view of many trade unionists, to bring about social change for the betterment of society as a whole. Situations occur where trade union negotiators set targets for achievement of these goals which appear to be at odds with the targets set by management for the organisation (and its employees).

Training According to the Department of Employment, training is 'the systematic development of the attitude/knowledge/skill/behaviour pattern required by an individual in order to perform adequately a given task or job'.

Training needs The gap between the requirements of the job and the actual current performance of the jobholders. In other words:

Required level of competence minus present level of competence = training need.

Wrongful dismissal A claim for wrongful dismissal is open to an employee at *common law,* if he or she can show the dismissal was without a reasonable cause or without the appropriate notice being given.

MULTIPLE CHOICE QUESTIONS

Chapter 1

1. The lead body representing personnel managers is called:
   A   The Institute of Management
   B   The Institute of Personnel Management
   C   The Institute of Personnel and Development
   D   The Institute of Training and Development

   A   B   C   D

2. Who said personnel management is 'a collection of incidental techniques without much internal cohesion'?
   A   Drucker
   B   Armstrong
   C   Yoder
   D   Georgiades

   A   B   C   D

3. What was Georgiades referring to when he described the personnel function's role as 'the toilet flusher'?
   A   Cleaning up the mess others leave behind
   B   Cutting staff numbers
   C   Dealing with the unsanitary psychological conditions of work
   D   Getting rid of antiquated policies and procedures

   A   B   C   D

4. What is an internal customer?
   A   Someone who comes to you
   B   Someone who knows inside your business
   C   Someone who works for the same organisation as you
   D   Someone who you subcontract within the organisation

   A   B   C   D

5. Which of the following has not contributed to the need for a specialised personnel function?
   A   The need to comply with increasing legislation
   B   High staffing costs
   C   Pressure for social responsibility towards employees
   D   Pressure towards more complex organisations

   A   B   C   D

6. Which of the following is *not* a concern of organisational politics?
   A   Differing ideologies
   B   Competition for scarce resources
   C   Conflict and rivalry between groups
   D   Power relationships

   A   B   C   D

7 What did Handy mean when he referred to personnel specialists as 'auditors'?
   A They keep control of finances
   B They check the effectiveness of procedures
   C They listen carefully
   D They set and approve budgets

A B C D

Chapter 2

8 Which of the following aspects of the personnel management function should come within the human resource management plan?

Aspects
1 Reduction of avoidable labour wastage
2 Policies for selection and declaration of redundancies
3 Programmes for reducing HRM costs
4 Identification of training needs

   A Aspect 1 only
   B Aspects 1 and 2 only
   C Aspect 1, 2 and 4 only
   D Aspects 1, 2, 3 and 4

A B C D

9 Human resource planning can be seen in terms of supply and demand forecasting. Which of the following is a factor in the anticipated demand for (rather than supply of) labour?
   A Age structure of the workforce
   B Proposed organisational expansion
   C Skill profile of the workforce
   D Trends in the labour market

A B C D

10 Stan Duppenby-Counthead (& Sons) has 1,000 staff in clerical grade 1, the lowest grade in the company, with the following age structure.

Under 20	600
20-30	300
Over 30	100

Based on last year's figures and this year's performance appraisals, wastage rates and promotion prospects in the next two years are expected to be:

	Wastage	Promotion
Under 20	30%	10%
20-30	10%	40%
Over 30	5%	20%

281

Business Basics: Human Resource Management

The demand forecast shows that with expansion at Head Office, given constant productivity levels, 1,200 clerical grade 1 staff will be required in two years' time.

The estimated number of recruits required in two years' time is:

A   215
B   415
C   585
D   615

A   B   C   D

11   Which of the following will help rather than hinder the human resource planning process?

A   Consumer fashion
B   The importance of leadership in employee morale
C   Improvements in information technology
D   Unionisation

A   B   C   D

12   In which of the following cases will the labour stability index

$\left(\dfrac{\text{Number of employees with more than 1 year's service}}{\text{Number of employees one year ago}} \times 100\right)$

be of more interest to the human resource planner than a simple wastage rate?

Cases

1   The organisation is undergoing a period of rapid expansion
2   The organisation is worried that it is losing experienced employees in significant numbers
3   A long-term forecast of promotion prospects is required

A   Case 2 only
B   Cases 2 and 3 only
C   Cases 1 and 2 only
D   Cases 1, 2 and 3

A   B   C   D

13   Unless the organisation is *planning* to contract its workforce, the main disadvantage of 'natural' labour turnover is its:

A   cost in financial terms
B   effect on career prospects
C   effect on the age structure of the workforce
D   effect on morale

A   B   C   D

14 A 'promotion programme' includes all of the following, *except*:
   A   job analysis
   B   human resource planning
   C   planning for training
   D   establishment of criteria for potential review

   A   B   C   D

15 Carrie R Planning Ltd has a job vacancy in one of its departments. Sonya Bykemate, the personnel manager, knows that there are people in the company who could do the job if they were promoted to it. There is also a reasonable pool of suitably skilled individuals available in the local area, who are easily reached through the employment agency used by the firm. Sonya might choose to recruit from outside rather than promote from within, on consideration of:
   A   reduction of risk
   B   motivation of the exiting workforce
   C   socialisation of the new jobholder
   D   innovation and adaptability

   A   B   C   D

Chapter 3

16 Which of the following would be defined as a 'recruitment' rather than a 'selection' activity?
   A   Preparation of a job description
   B   Measurement of applicant against job description
   C   Interview
   D   Taking up references

   A   B   C   D

17 The Personnel Manager of Pullham Inn is recruiting a Head Chef. He has prepared a detailed statement of the physical and mental activities involved in the job, plus some notes to the effect that the handling of sous-chefs and pastry-chefs is a very delicate affair, and that the job requires a high tolerance of heat and pressure. This statement is expressed in behavioural terms, ie the actions, knowledge, judgement etc involved in the Head Chef's job. This statement is a:
   A   job analysis
   B   job description
   C   job specification
   D   personnel specification

   A   B   C   D

283

18 Job descriptions have advantages for all the following, except:

   A job evaluation
   B training needs analysis
   C job specification
   D personnel specification

   A B C D

19 The following items appear on the job description of the Personnel Manager of Watt C Dew Ltd.

   Items

   1 *Regular relationships*
     Departmental managers
     Works Convenor
     Shop Stewards
     Local Job Centre officials etc

   2 *Principal responsibilities*
     Ensure the efficient recruitment of suitable and sufficient staff
     Implement the company's payment policy
     Provide adequate training programmes for staff induction and development etc

   3 *Attributes/qualifications required*
     Experience in personnel or line management in a relevant environment
     Professional qualifications including membership of the IPD etc

   4 *Assessment*
     Leadership: Capable within own departmental responsibilities, but shows some reluctance in the use of functional authority
     Decision-making: has consistently made sound decisions
     Technical knowledge: shows good awareness of legislation, behavioural techniques etc

   What *shouldn't* be on the job description?

   A Item 1
   B Item 2
   C Item 3
   D Item 4

   A B C D

20 Mann & Glevilles Ltd has a job vacancy for a minor clerk/office helper at one of its offices. Of the following, the most suitable medium for their job advertisement would be:

   A the journal of an accountancy body
   B national newspapers
   C local newspapers
   D television

   A B C D

Chapter 4

21 The use of selection boards, or large panel interviews, has some advantages for selection process, mainly in its:
   A administrative aspects
   B formality
   C testing of human relations skills
   D variety and randomness of questions asked

   A B C D

22 A selection test designed to measure abilities or skills already possessed by a candidate in a job-related area is called:
   A an intelligence test
   B an aptitude test
   C a proficiency test
   D a personality test

   A B C D

23 'Ability', as diagnosed by interview and testing, is an indicator of:
   A future performance
   B current potential
   C current motivation
   D future success

   A B C D

24 Which of the following is *not* a viable category when preselecting candidates.
   A Possible
   B Probable
   C Unsuitable
   D Marginal

   A B C D

25 According to Fletcher, how many candidates admit to lying at selection interviews?
   A 20%
   B 30%
   C 10%
   D 40%

   A B C D

26 What is face validity?
   A The need to meet the organisation face to face
   B The candidates' faces at interviews will always show if they are lying
   C Selection methods seen to make sense 'on the face of things'
   D Facial characteristics are good predictors of job performance

   A B C D

Business Basics: Human Resource Management

27 Which of the following would *not* appear on a contract of employment

    A Notice periods
    B Promotion plans
    C Job title
    D Pay

A   B   C   D

Chapter 5

28 What is the main objective of the CRE's initiative 'Racial Equality Means Business'?

    A To show businesses that racial equality makes good business sense
    B To ensure all businesses employ at least one ethnic minority worker
    C To show employers that the CRE intends to get tough on discrimination
    D To highlight racial inequality in the City of London

A   B   C   D

29 Is it against the law to discriminate against job applicants because of their age?

    A Yes, in all cases
    B Yes, but only for women
    C No
    D No, except for people over the age of 50

A   B   C   D

30 Which of the following is *not* a genuine occupational qualification for women?

    A Reasons of decency
    B Provision of personal services
    C Where law or custom says a woman can't perform the job
    D Physical strength

A   B   C   D

31 Under the Disability Discrimination Act, which of the following is *not* considered to have an adverse effect on ability to work?

    A Limited ability to manage stress
    B Limited mobility
    C Limited ability to concentrate
    D Limited sight

A   B   C   D

Multiple choice questions

32 What is the cut off point for employers below which regulations of the Disability Discrimination Act do not apply?

   A Less than 10 employees
   B Less than 200 employees
   C Less than 50 employees
   D Less than 20 employees

   A B C D

33 Is it lawful to ask women candidates at interview about their plans to have a family?

   A No
   B Yes, as long as you ask this of all candidates
   C Yes
   D Yes, as long as you ask this of all female candidates

   A B C D

Chapter 6

34 If you were drawing up a checklist for the 'induction' process, for the use of departmental supervisors and managers, which of the following activities should you include?

   Activities

   1 Introducing the recruit to the people in the work place
   2 Explaining the nature of the job, procedures, rules and responsibilities
   3 Drawing up a list of learning priorities and objectives
   4 Monitoring the progress of recruits coaching/training/performance

   A Activity 1 only
   B Activities 1 and 2 only
   C Activities 2 and 3 only
   D Activities 1, 2, 3 and 4

   A B C D

35 Formal learning activities which may *not* lead to qualifications, and which may be received at any time in a working career are:

   A education
   B training
   C development
   D induction

   A B C D

36 Phil E Stein & Sons is having problems with its training programme. Staff never seem to have learnt the 'right' things, ie things that are relevant to their jobs. Some of the staff don't seem to have learnt anything at all: they don't take to the

methods used. The company hasn't been too worried so far, but the new personnel manager is passionate about training and has been horrified by some of the comments he has heard flying around the senior management offices. Which of the following comments is likely to be his own view of the matter?

A 'Training is a matter for the personnel department'
B 'The important thing is *have* a training programme'
C 'Training is both a cause and an effect of change'
D 'Training is all cost and no benefit'

A B C D

37 Three of the following pieces of information are required for the identification of training needs. Which isn't?

A Job requirements
B Entry behaviour
C Cost of training
D Learning gap

A B C D

38 You are required to draw up a training plan for the famous circus animal act, T Chanoldo Gnu Tricks. Which is the most effective of the following ways of expressing its training objectives?

A The course should improve key skills needed in the act
B At the end of the course, team members should be able to apply those skills in the ring
C At the end of the course, team members should have a better appreciation of animal characteristics
D At the end of the course, team members should be able to distinguish between a gnu and hartebeest

A B C D

39 Buttsworth Everypenny is the personnel officer of his firm. He has to justify the costs of his training programme to the company accountant. 'Quantifiable benefits, man,' says the latter, impatiently. 'Where are the quantifiable benefits?'

Which of the following benefits of his programme might Buttsworth hesitate to put forward?

A Increased speed of working
B Increased accuracy of working
C Increased satisfaction of employees
D Decreased accident rate

A B C D

40 In the process of the 'validation' of training, the question asked is:

A Did we do the right thing?
B Did we do it right?
C Was it worth doing?
D Did it achieve its objectives?

A B C D

288

41 Which of the following activities would be identified as 'development'?

Activities

1 Career planning for individual managers
2 Deputising while the boss is absent
3 Counselling and appraisal
4 Education and training

A Activity 1 only
B Activities 1 and 3 only
C Activities 2, 3 and 4 only
D Activities 1, 2, 3 and 4

A B C D

Chapter 7

42 Which of the following is *not* an application of performance assessment?

A merit rating
B identification of training needs
C potential review
D job evaluation

A B C D

43 Howie Dewing is assessing the performance of his subordinates. According to the assessment system of the organisation, he has been given a list of characteristics and performance elements, with notes on how terms such as 'application' and 'integrity' are to be interpreted in the work context. He is required to comment on how the appraisee 'measures up' in terms of each factor.

The appraisal technique is called:

A overall assessment
B guided assessment
C grading
D behavioural incident analysis

A B C D

44 *Features*

1 Behavioural incident methods
2 Overall assessment
3 Results-oriented approach
4 Grading

Appraisal techniques

(i) Also known as rating scales

(ii) For example Management by Objectives

(iii) Not based on trait analysis but observation of 'real-life' actions and reactions

(iv) Subject to managers' ability to express judgements clearly in writing

Business Basics: Human Resource Management

Which of the following matches the appraisal techniques (1-4) correctly with a feature of each (i)-(iv)

A	* 1 (ii)	* 2 (iii)	* 3 (i)	* 4 (iv)
B	* 1 (iv)	* 2 (ii)	* 3 (iii)	* 4 (i)
C	* 1 (iii)	* 2 (iv)	* 3 (ii)	* 4 (i)
D	* 1 (iii)	* 2 (iv)	* 3 (i)	* 4 (ii)

A B C D

45 Changing from 'trait' appraisal to the use of results-oriented criteria for assessment of individuals and their work - ie specific targets and standards of performance agreed in advance by manager and subordinate - will have an effect on

Aspects

1 the subordinate's role in appraisal
2 the assessor's role in appraisal
3 the subordinate's motivation
4 the effectiveness of the appraisal scheme

A Aspect 4 only
B Aspects 3 and 4 only
C Aspects 1, 2 and 3 only
D Aspects 1, 2, 3 and 4

A B C D

46 Tel Mistrate is conducting his appraisal interviews. His philosophy is simple. He tells the subordinate in question how he has been assessed - good and bad - and then gives him or her a chance to put questions, suggest improvement targets, explain shortcomings and identify problems. This approach is known as the:

A 'tell and sell' method
B 'tell and listen' method
C 'problem-solving' approach
D peer-rating method

A B C D

47 Appraisal is a complex human relations and political exercise. Appraiser and appraisee alike need all the help they can get. Which of the following is *not* necessarily a helpful factor in an appraisal scheme?

A The purpose of the system is positive, and clearly expressed
B There is reasonable standardisation throughout the organisation
C Time is allowed for appraisee preparation, appraiser training etc
D There is an implied link between assessment and reward

A B C D

48 Peter Prince-Hipple is conducting potential reviews of all his staff, so that he can work out what training they need, and whether they're 'ripe' for promotion. The *least* relevant information he will need to gather for this purpose will be:

A performance in the job currently held
B strengths and weaknesses in existing skills and qualities
C goals, aspirations and attitudes of the appraisee
D opportunities available in the organisation

A   B   C   D

Chapter 8

49 Of the following criticisms levelled at Maslow's hierarchy of needs theory, which is *not* a valid objection?

A Progression up the hierarchy does not always work in practice
B A need once satisfied doesn't always become less powerful
C Needs can be satisfied by aspects of a person's life outside work
D The hierarchy is only relevant to Western English-speaking cultures

A   B   C   D

50 Keepham (Hungary) Ltd offers its employees:

1 sensible company policies
2 good salaries and bonuses
3 considerate supervision
4 training programmes

Employees will, according to Herzberg, derive satisfaction from and be motivated to superior effort by:

A 1 only
B 4 only
C 2 and 4 only
D 3 and 4 only

A   B   C   D

51 Willy Dewitt-Ornott is an employee in Sales who is 'up for promotion' to team leader. There is always a competition in the firm in January to try and boost post-Christmas sales. Everybody knows that the winner has for the last three years been made a team leader. Willy's quite certain that if he spends December planning a campaign, sends Christmas cards to all his 'leads' etc, he will be able to win: all his mates think so too. Willy knows that as team leader he will have more responsibility - which he would like. But he would also have to work much longer hours, and he has just started a family. In

fact, he had promised his wife he would take two weeks holiday to help her organise Christmas: it is very important to both of them, since Willy 'lives' for the times he can spend at home. If an expectancy equation were used to assess Willy's motivation to work hard at January sales, based on the information given:

A valence would be high, expectancy high, motivation high
B valence would be high, expectancy low, motivation high
C valence would be around 0, expectancy high, motivation low
D valence would be around 0, expectancy high, motivation high

A B C D

52 Application of an expectancy approach to motivation in practice involves all but one of the following. Which is the exception?

A Clarifying intended results
B Giving feedback on actual results
C Immediacy of reward following results
D Consistency of reward for results

A B C D

53 The management of Ascham Nyce-Leigh Ltd has been studying the behaviour of a group of workers (wirers and solderers) at its main plant. The group appears to have established a standard amount of production that it feels is 'fair'. Members of the group who produce above - or below - this norm are put under 'social pressure' to get back into line, and do - despite the company incentive scheme. One 'over-producing' employee is told: 'If they catch you, they'll just raise the rate and ask us to do more for the same money'.

Ascham Nyce-Leigh is entitled to assume that these workers are *not* motivated by:

A job security
B maximised earnings
C satisfactory income
D social needs

A B C D

54 The approach to job design advocated by the scientific school of management was:

A job rotation
B job enlargement
C micro-division of labour
D autonomous group working

A B C D

55 Participation will *not* be effective as a motivator if it is:
   A limited in its scope
   B limited by the organisation culture
   C limited to certain employees
   D limited to trivial issues

   A B C D

Chapter 9

56 By which of the following factors may the effectiveness of pay as incentive to superior performance be limited?

   Factors
   1 Taxation rates
   2 Equity of pay rates
   3 Regular salary review
   4 Work group norms

   A Factor 1 only
   B Factors 1 and 4 only
   C Factors 2 and 4 only
   D Factors 1, 2, 3 and 4

   A B C D

57 Job evaluation puts a relative value on the job primarily on the basis of:
   A equity
   B job content
   C negotiated pay scales
   D market rates

   A B C D

58 Which of the following is *not* an advantage of job evaluation?
   A It determines a rate for the job irrespective of the merits of the job holder
   B It gives differentials a demonstrably rational basis
   C It facilitates the setting of rates of pay
   D It involves the formulation of a job description

   A B C D

59 Furr and Squeur (a Liverpool firm) uses a method of job evaluation in which a number of factors are listed, which are thought to represent sought-after qualities, and the importance given to each factor is decided by the allocation of a maximum points value. Each job is then analysed factor by factor and given a score for each, up to the maximum. Jobs are then ranked according to their total scores.

293

This technique is called:

A points rating
B factor comparison
C ranking
D merit rating

A B C D

60 In salary scales, what is the mid-point?

A The average
B The most common salary
C The point at which half the salaries are above and half are below
D A rough estimate of the middle ground

A B C D

61 Which of the following is *not* a benefit of PRP?

A Translating appraisals into pay
B Greater supervisory responsibility
C Complements other HR initiatives
D Improves business awareness

A B C D

62 What is SSP?

A Social Security Pension
B Social Security Pay
C Self Support Pay
D Statutory Sick Pay

A B C D

Chapter 10

63 Mr and Mrs Swett run a retail chain (Swett shops). At their Head Office, staff have complained about the physical environment in which they have to work: it is not that it isn't safe, but it is very *stressful* to work in. Mr and Mrs Swett are surprised. They've had the office furniture designed specially to ensure a comfortable position. The decor is tasteful, in yellow, magnolia and green. Light is provided by bright bulb lighting. There is a continuous buzz of noise from printers and telephones and conversation, of course, but they hope to get some acoustic screens and hoods later on. What can be causing stress?

It's most likely to be the:

A furniture
B decor
C lighting
D noise

A B C D

Multiple choice questions

64 Ergonomics is a sphere of scientific research which explores:

- A the best workplace layout to facilitate work flow
- B the design of machinery and furniture, to maximise comfort
- C the relationship between man and his working environment
- D the similarity of the control mechanism in man and machine

A B C D

65 A person is less likely to suffer stress if he or she is:

- A emotionally sensitive
- B flexible and easily influenced
- C competent in interpersonal relations
- D acutely conscientious

A B C D

66 The activities of:

1. identifying substances which are actually or potentially hazardous
2. identifying the effect of methods and processes of work on the human body and mind; and
3. controlling the environment and substances, so as to minimise risk;

are all part of:

- A ergonomics
- B occupational health programmes
- C safety programmes
- D welfare services

A B C D

67 Which of the following costs of accidents would be significantly reduced if the organisation had successful accident prevention procedures?

Cost

1. Cost of providing first aid facilities and/or materials
2. Time lost by the injured employee and others
3. Insurance of employees against injury or death at work
4. Compensation payments and fines issuing from legal action by injured employees

- A Costs 2 and 4 only
- B Costs 2, 3 and 4 only
- C Costs 1, 2 and 4 only
- D Costs 1, 2, 3 and 4

A B C D

68 Grace Fuhl is going on an inspection tour of the company's branch office in Norfolk. She is dismayed at the image it presents to visitors. Everything is shabby and untidy, with frayed

295

carpets, peeling paint and files piled on the floor between desks. The staff have obviously got wind of her coming and tried to straighten things out: quite a bit of the mess has been hidden away on the back stairs, behind the fire door and someone has rather obviously been mopping the floor, which is still wet as she walks in. There's consternation as people see her in the doorway. The supervisor is standing on a swivel chair trying to dust the top shelf of her bookcase. 'Welcome to the Diss Grace Fuhl office', she says.

How many common causes of injury or potential hazard can you identify in the scenario above?

A 2
B 3
C 5
D 6

A B C D

69 Which of the following is *not* the duty of an employer, under the Health and Safety at Work Act 1974 (and regulations under the Act)?

A To allow safety representatives (appointed by a recognised trade union) access and inspection in order to check the effectiveness of safety measures
B To establish a safety committee at the written request of two safety representatives
C To comply with recommendations made by the safety representatives or safety committee not less than three months after consultation
D To prepare and keep up-to-date a written statement of policy on health and safety

A B C D

70 Under the Factories Act 1961, the occupier of a factory has an absolute duty to fence securely all prime movers (ie machines which provide power), all transmission machinery and every dangerous part of any machinery. The employer will *not* have complied with the Act if:

A he fails to fence the dangerous machine because there is no practicable way of fencing it
B he fails to keep the fence in place while the machine is not in motion
C he fences a machine securely, but not so as prevent a determined and reckless employee from reaching through
D he fails to fence a machine which would not normally be considered capable of causing injury

A B C D

71 Under UK law, an employee is entitled to time off work with pay for all the following purposes - except one, and that is:

- A ante-natal care, for pregnant women
- B duties or training in the employee's capacity as a trade union official
- C public duties performed by employees who are Justices of the Peace or members of local authority bodies
- D duties under the Health and Safety at Work Act, in the employee's capacity as a union-appointed safety representative

A B C D

Chapter 11

72 Collective bargaining is concerned with reaching an agreement about two types of 'rules': *substantive* rules, and *procedural* rules. Which of the following are substantive rules?

Rules

1. Demarcation rules
2. Rules determining pay scales
3. Rules for what disputes should be referred to ACAS
4. Rules for what negotiating machinery should be set up

- A Rules 1 and 2 only
- B Rules 1 and 3 only
- C Rules 3 and 4 only
- D Rules 1, 2 and 3 only

A B C D

73 Japanese labour relations are often considered to be superior to those prevailing in most Western countries. The following are some of the possible reasons why this might be so. Which of them, according to current thinking, is *no longer* a major contributory factor?

- A The use of quality circles
- B Guaranteed lifetime employment
- C Consultation and communication between management and workers
- D The use of first-line supervisors, who have risen through the ranks rather than been appointed by management

A B C D

Business Basics: Human Resource Management

74 According to UK law, which of the following would be considered lawful trade dispute(s)?

Disputes

1 A dispute between workers and their own employers, wholly or mainly about work-related matters
2 An inter-union dispute about demarcation
3 A dispute between workers and employers other than their own
4 A dispute overseas (eg in support of South African workers)

A Dispute 1 only
B Disputes 1 and 2 only
C Disputes 1, 2 and 4 only
D Disputes 1, 2, 3 and 4

A B C D

75 Which of the following is *not* a typical management response to conflict?

A Denial/withdrawal
B Suppression
C Head-on confrontation
D Compromise

A B C D

76 What is the newly-merged union called that formed from the NCU and the UCW?

A CWU
B NCWU
C NCUW
D UWC

A B C D

Chapter 12

77 The purpose of disciplinary action which is less severe than is warranted by the offence is likely to be:

A punitive
B informative
C deterrent
D permissive

A B C D

78 An example of what is technically termed 'constructive' or 'positive' discipline would be:

A an administrative procedure incorporating tight internal controls and checks
B an informal warning to an employee following a slight offence
C an immediate, consistent and impersonal scheme of disciplinary action
D offering incentives to employees who have a 'clean sheet' in a given period

A B C D

79 Streyton (Harrow) Ltd is having to justify itself to an Industrial Tribunal over a disciplinary action against an employee, a Mr Rock Arde, who had (allegedly) been persistently defiant and lax in his time-keeping. The supervisor failed to give an informal verbal warning when it first occurred, but issued an official written warning on a second offence. The offender was allowed to state his case; despite his protest, the supervisor insisted that the two of them discuss the matter alone, so as not to escalate the conflict. When Rock turned up to this interview he appeared to have no idea of the offence of which he was accused: the official warning had simply threatened him with 'further action should your recent conduct be repeated'.

At which of the following points did Streyton (Harrow) contravene the ACAS Code of Practice on disciplinary actions?

Stage

1 Informal warning
2 Written warning
3 Disciplinary interview

A Stage 2 only
B Stages 2 and 3 only
C Stages 1, 2 and 3
D At no stage

A B C D

80 Which is *not* amongst the most common reasons for discipline?

A Lateness
B Poor attitudes
C Moonlighting
D Poor performance

A B C D

81 Does a grievance always have to be raised with your immediate boss?

A Not if he is the source of the problem
B Not if you don't like him
C Yes, always
D Not if he hasn't taken action before

A B C D

Chapter 13

82 Which of the following circumstances for dismissal is *not* defined as redundancy under the Employment Protection (Consolidation) Act 1978?

   A   The employer has ceased to carry on the business
   B   The employer has ceased to carry on the business in the place where the employee was employed
   C   the requirements of the business for employees to carry out work of a particular kind have ceased or diminished or are expected to
   D   The employee is not or is no longer capable or competent to carry out the work for which he is employed

A   B   C   D

Data for questions 83 and 84

Jobbs (Comforters) Ltd makes sundry woollen goods. Ray Troubel has worked there full time for three years. He has just been 'sacked' by the company because - despite suitable warnings he has persisted in absenteeism and poor timekeeping. Tina Toyle has worked there six months and Jane Bubbal two years. They have both been given notice because of pregnancy - although they are both capable of carrying on their work adequately. Tom Hubble has reached the end of a fixed term contract, and the company is not renewing it on the same terms, having shut down Tom's area of the business, and selected him fairly for redundancy.

---

83 Who has been dismissed under UK law?

   A   Troubel only
   B   Troubel and Bubbal
   C   Troubel, Bubbal and Toyle only
   D   Hubble, Bubbal, Toyle and Troubel

A   B   C   D

84 Who will be entitled to compensation for unfair dismissal?

   A   Bubbal only
   B   Bubbal and Toyle only
   C   Bubbal, Toyle and Hubble only
   D   Hubble, Bubbal, Toyle and Troubel

A   B   C   D

85 If you have worked for 18 months and your employment is terminated, how much notice must you be given?

   A   1 month
   B   1 week
   C   1 week for each year of service
   D   None

A   B   C   D

86 Which of the following is *not* a fair approach to selection for redundancy?
   A Enforced early retirement
   B Last in first out
   C Keep those who perform well
   D Keep those with the right attitudes/personality

   A   B   C   D

87 Which of the following bodies does *not* have a statutory right to request statistics from an organisation?
   A The TUC
   B The HSE
   C Department of Employment
   D The DSS

   A   B   C   D

88 What is the name of the annual statement of pay, tax and national insurance given to employees?
   A P11
   B P15
   C P60
   D P45

   A   B   C   D

89 What information will the ratio

   $$\frac{\text{Employees with more than 1 year's service}}{\text{Number of employees employed 1 year ago}} \times 100$$

   give to an organisation?
   A Induction crisis
   B Compa-ratio
   C Labour turnover
   D Labour stability

   A   B   C   D

90 Which of the following pieces of information is it lawful (under the Data Protection Act 1984) to withhold from an employee?
   A Pay progression and history
   B Disciplinary Records
   C Promotion plans
   D Appraisal data

   A   B   C   D

EXAM STYLE QUESTIONS

1 EFFECTIVE HR MANAGERS

'To become an effective human resource manager, you should spend the first few years of your career in another part of the organisation altogether.'

Examine and evaluate this view.

2 HUMAN RESOURCE PLANNING

'Manpower planning is not a lifeline that can be thrown to a company in distress, though it may be helpful to liken it to the practice of navigation.' (Bramham)

To what extent, in your view, can the analogy between human resource planning and navigation be sustained?

3 JOB DESCRIPTIONS

Some organisations seek to produce comprehensively detailed job descriptions, while others come close to avoiding them altogether. What are the reasons for these differences in approach? How might job descriptions be designed so as to maximise the benefits, and offset the disadvantages?

4 CONFESSIONS OF AN INTERVIEWER

'Most of the recruiters with whom I've had contact are decent, well-intentioned people. But I've yet to meet anyone, including myself, who knows what he (or she) is doing. Many interviewers seem to have absolute faith in their omniscience, but I suspect that their 'perceptiveness' is based more upon preconceived untested assumptions than upon objectively derived data.' (R Martin, *Confessions of an Interviewer*). What is the possible justification for Martin's observation? If the selection interview really is as ineffectual as Martin claims, what can interviewers themselves do to improve its reliability and validity?

5 DISCRIMINATION AGAINST WOMEN

Outline the major reasons why women may be discriminated against at work. What policies would you suggest an organisation adopts in order to tackle such discrimination?

6 TRAINING AND DEVELOPMENT PRACTICES

A recent article makes the following criticisms of many training and development practices in organisations.

(a) Training and development are often not fully integrated into the management process.

(b) Training and development activities perpetuate 'introverted' management.

(c) The priority given to training and development depends too much on the attitudes of individual managers.

(d) Much training and development is insufficiently related to individual needs.

To what extent do you believe these criticisms to be justified? How can they be prevented or minimised?

7 EFFECTIVE APPRAISAL

What are the key requirements for an effective performance appraisal system?

Exam style questions

8 SIGNIFICANCE OF WORK

'The question "Why do people work?" is quite different from the question "Why do people work well?"' Discuss.

9 THE PERFORMANCE OF PRP

It has been claimed that performance-related pay does not work because it does not motivate people to improve their performance. It is also divisive, and because judgements about performance are always subjective, it lends itself to the exercise of managerial prejudice. How far do you agree with these views? In what circumstances can performance-related pay be worthwhile?

10 ERGONOMICS

Show how a concern for ergonomics can be financially and psychologically worthwhile in either:

(a) a factory; or

(b) an office.

Note. In assessing your answer, generous credit will be given for the citation of real life examples and research evidence.

11 MIDDLE MANAGERS AND CHANGE

Several writers have suggested that middle managers are the principal opponents of the kinds of organisational changes typical of the 1990s. Why should this be the case? What sensible and practical steps can organisations take to ensure that middle managers are more receptive to change?

12 DUNTOILING NURSING HOMES

You are the personnel officer for Duntoiling Nursing and Retirement Homes PLC, a chain of residential complexes for senior citizens in the West Midlands region. Recently, Gareth Cheeseman, the bullish, entrepreneurial director, sent a brief memorandum to all staff informing them that all premises now constitute 'No smoking' areas for patients, visitors and staff alike. Notices to this effect have gone up all round the homes. Duntoiling is also declaring its 'No smoking' policy in recruitment advertisement.

The abruptness with which Cheeseman introduced this policy is now causing problems. It seems that some staff are continuing to smoke 'behind closed doors', and visitors and patients are flouting the ban in corridors and toilets. Staff rebuking them have been subject to verbal abuse. Some staff also complain of suffering from stress because they cannot give up the craving.

The crunch came last week, when one supervisor issued a formal oral warning to a member of his staff caught 'red handed' smoking in her office, and stated that if she repeated the offence she would be dismissed. The employee in question resigned in a fit of pique and is now claiming constructive dismissal, with union support.

Cheeseman has asked you to brief him on what action needs to be taken:

(a) to deal with the disciplinary case; and

(b) to ensure that the policy is complied with in the future.

What advice will you give? Present your answer in the form of a memorandum to Gareth Cheeseman.

13 REDUNDANCIES

You have been asked by your superior to prepare a paper on ways to avoid compulsory redundancies in your organisation. What proposals would you consider and how would you justify them?

14 NOVALUX PLC

You have recently been appointed as personnel officer for Novalux PLC, a large engineering firm just outside Bristol. One of your key responsibilities is to produce regular management reports to all members of senior management. These reports should be interesting, succinct and valuable, and should present personnel information in a clear and digestible form. One of your other key tasks is to recruit and select new employees.

You are astonished at how many people seem to come and go from Novalux, suggesting you have some kind of retention problem. Therefore, you have decided to combine both issues and produce a management report on staff turnover. You have created the following table.

LENGTH OF SERVICE

Entry age	0-4 weeks *number of staff*	5-26 weeks *number of staff*	27-52 weeks *number of staff*	53+ weeks *number of staff*
16-24	25	14	13	10
25-34	10	16	25	15
35-49	6	20	18	9
50-64	8	16	13	11

Your task is to analyse these figures to see if age has an impact on length of service. What additional information would you require in order to draw other useful conclusions on the pattern of leavers from Novalux?

ANSWERS TO MULTIPLE CHOICE QUESTIONS

Business Basics: Human Resource Management

1	C	31	A	61	A
2	A	32	D	62	D
3	B	33	B	63	C
4	C	34	D	64	C
5	D	35	B	65	C
6	A	36	C	66	B
7	B	37	C	67	A
8	D	38	D	68	D
9	B	39	C	69	C
10	D	40	A	70	A
11	C	41	D	71	C
12	D	42	D	72	A
13	A	43	B	73	B
14	B	44	C	74	A
15	D	45	C	75	C
16	A	46	B	76	A
17	C	47	D	77	B
18	D	48	A	78	A
19	D	49	C	79	B
20	C	50	B	80	C
21	A	51	C	81	A
22	C	52	C	82	D
23	B	53	B	83	D
24	B	54	C	84	A
25	A	55	D	85	B
26	C	56	D	86	D
27	B	57	B	87	A
28	A	58	C	88	C
29	C	59	A	89	D
30	D	60	C	90	C

ANSWERS TO EXAM STYLE QUESTIONS

1 EFFECTIVE HR MANAGERS

In an organisation where 'human resource management' is simply a trendy name for what is traditionally called personnel management - hiring and firing, training, industrial relations and manpower planning - it could be argued that what the manager most needs is the specialist skills and knowledge relating to this task.

However, personnel management has been changing in various ways in recent years. Many of its activities have become more complex and sophisticated, and particularly with the accelerating pace of change in the business environment, less narrowly concerned with traditional personnel areas.

The function has become more concerned with issues of broader relevance to business and its objectives, such as change management, the introduction of technology, and the implications of falling birth-rates and skill shortages for the resourcing of the business. Hence the recognition that people are a resource to be managed, and hence the name 'human resource management'.

Managers in this role therefore need to be concerned to integrate their work with the strategic objectives of the business: the objectives of the personnel function should be directly related to achieving the organisation's goals for growth, competitive gain and improvement of bottom line performance.

The question asserts that effective HR managers need to spend the first few years of their career in a non-HR role. Given the above profile of HR this is clearly desirable. Somebody whose only experience in organisations is in a staff role such as personnel cannot expect to have a sufficiently wide perspective of the business to enable them to contribute fully to the organisation's strategic initiatives.

A production manager, for example will learn what it is like to have to meet deadlines imposed by senior management while coping with too few staff or inadequately trained staff. He will also learn about the co-ordination of the organisation as a whole - the demands placed upon production resources by the marketing department, or the need to liaise with the distribution function on matters such as packaging, or the value of effective administration of, say, payroll for production costing purposes.

Moreover, someone who gains experience in functional management can acquire quite considerable experience of 'people' issues. Mullins, for example, sees personnel management as a shared responsibility: line managers should deal with all the day to day operational aspects of personnel management such as:

(a) the organisation and allocation of work;
(b) minor disciplinary matters and staff grievances;
(c) standards of performance;
(d) on-the-job training and induction;
(e) communication;
(f) health and safety.

A line manager with such experience under his belt understands the use of people as a resource. Without this sort of experience there is strong potential for conflict between personnel managers and both functional managers and the senior management of the business.

(a) If he lacks the credibility earned from experience elsewhere in the organisation, there may be a tendency to regard the personnel manager as a mere overhead who adds nothing to the bottom line but has considerable nuisance power in imposing rules and policies.

(b) The personnel manager may believe that his job is to protect the interests of employees, whereas functional managers will feel that they should be responsible to the senior management of the business, as they are.

(c) The personnel department may offer advice that is totally impractical from the point of view of line managers.

(d) Actions might be taken that are contrary to the long-term strategic aims of the organisation, for example implementing a redundancy policy that takes no account of the future skills needs of the business.

2 HUMAN RESOURCE PLANNING

The process of human resource planning can be outlined as follows.

(a) *Forecast future human resource demand.* This forecast can be made by reference to detailed corporate plans, if they exist. Managers may otherwise make estimates or use statistical techniques and models to assess the effects of environmental trends on demand for the organisation's products and demand for particular skill groups.

(b) *Investigation of human resource utilisation.* The ways in which human resources are utilised in the organisation affects the quality and types of employees needed. Changes in human resource utilisation may come about as a result of legislation, productivity agreements or job redesign, for example. Analysis of human resource and skill availability within the organisation, can be analysed in terms of numbers of people in each occupation and occupational group, by age and by division of the company for instance.

(c) *Internal human resource supply forecast.* This is an attempt to predict future internal human resources, perhaps using trends from the past to predict what may happen in the future taking into account transfers, labour wastage and turnover, and other causes of human resource movements, promotion potential and training facilities.

(d) *External human resource supply forecast.* Where internal supply looks insufficient to meet future demand for skills and labour, the external labour market, locally and more widely, must be assessed, with future trends in training and education, relocation, cost of recruitment and so on.

(e) Supply and demand are then compared. Discrepancies between them in the numbers required/available, their grade, skills or location can be handled through the application of an integrated human resource strategy covering policies for pay and conditions of employment, promotion, recruitment, training and industrial relations.

In summary, human resource planning can be defined as 'having the right people in the right place at the right time'. Certainly there are a number of strong parallels with navigation.

(a) The navigator is given a destination to reach by a given date. This could be compared to the corporate plan.

(b) The navigator uses scientific methods to establish how he is to get from his present position to his intended destination in the time available, given the type of vessel at his command. This is akin to the human resource planner's statistical forecasts and his assessment of the resources available to him and their capabilities.

(c) Further data is used by the navigator in order to take account of factors outside his control: the weather, the current, tides, other shipping. This may be compared to the need for reliance on external labour supply, the impact of demographic factors and so on.

(d) Finally the navigator sets out on his journey and in the course of it he is likely to have to reassess his strategy and make new plans to account for changes in the factors that are outside his control. Likewise the human resource planning expert has to deal with unforeseen changes such as changing economic conditions, action by competitors, a glut of leavers, strikes and so on.

An excellent example of the need to 'change course' in human resource planning was provided by the short-sighted actions of the major accounting firms. Most of the 'Big Eight' as they were then called took an over-optimistic view of their capacity for growth in the second half of the 1980s and recruited far more graduate trainees than they could sustain in the long-term. The recession of the late 1980s and early 1990s together with a spate of 'mega-mergers' led to serious over-manning problems. Redundancies inevitably followed in 1991, and these were costly both in financial terms and in terms of public image. In 1994 the 'Big Six', as they had become, were beginning to find that they had a shortage of newly qualified accountants at their disposal.

3 JOB DESCRIPTIONS

Tutorial note. Read the question carefully. It would be all too easy to write down everything you know about job descriptions without addressing the specific question asked.

A job description is a broad description of a job or position at a given time (since jobs are dynamic, subject to change and variation). 'It is a written statement of those facts which are important regarding the duties, responsibilities, and their organisational and operational interrelationships.'

Livy, *Corporate Personnel Management*

It is true, however, that many organisations do not produce job descriptions at all, except insofar as the jobs have names. To determine the reasons for this it will be helpful to consider what purposes job descriptions serve where they are in use.

In recruitment, job descriptions are used:

(a) to decide what skills (technical, human, conceptual, design or whatever) and qualifications are required of the jobholder. When formulating recruitment advertisements, and interviewing an applicant for the job, the interviewer can use the resulting job specification to match the candidate against the job;

(b) to ensure that the job:

(i) will be a full-time job for the holder and will not under-utilise his capacity by not giving him enough to do;

(ii) provides a sufficient challenge to the jobholder - job content may be a factor in the motivation of individuals;

(c) to determine a rate of pay which is fair for the job, if this has not already been decided by some other means.

In other words the preparation of a job description helps the organisation to understand its own requirements and what it has to market when it places its job advertisement.

Job descriptions can also be used in other areas of personnel management.

(a) For job evaluation (used in establishing wage rates).

(i) A standard format for analysing jobs makes it easier for evaluators to compare jobs.

(ii) Job descriptions focus attention on the job, not the jobholder, which is important in the job evaluation process.

(iii) Job descriptions offer opportunities for the jobholder and his manager to discuss any differences of opinion about what the job involves, allowing fairer and more accurate evaluation.

(b) In induction and training, to help new employees to understand the scope and functions of their jobs and to help managers to identify training needs of jobholders on an ongoing basis.

(c) To pinpoint weaknesses in the organisation structure (such as overlapping areas of authority, where two or more managers are responsible for the same area of work; areas of work where no manager appears to accept responsibility; areas of work where authority appears to be too centralised or decentralised).

(d) To provide information for work study (or Organisation and Methods).

Where job descriptions are not prepared there may be a variety of reasons.

(a) Small organisations may not have the resources, in terms of time and staff with suitable expertise, to prepare comprehensively detailed job descriptions and may consider that if it cannot be done well it is better not to do it at all. This is not necessarily a valid argument, but it does reflect reality.

(b) Certain jobs may be considered to describe themselves by their title or little more. 'Newly qualified chartered accountant with Big 6 firm' is a complete description of a job, both, as far as the employers of such a person are concerned and as far as suitable potential recruits are involved. This is because the training and experience that must be obtained in order to qualify as a chartered accountant are closely controlled by the Institute of Chartered Accountants. (The same is true of Chartered Secretaries to some extent, although individual job experience may be far more diverse.)

(c) Townsend *(Up the Organisation)* suggested that job descriptions are only suited for jobs where the work is largely repetitive and therefore performed by low-grade employees: once the elements of judgement and initiative come into a job, a description becomes a straitjacket. Management jobs are likely to be constantly changing as external influences impact upon them, so a job description is constantly out-of-date.

(d) Many of the difficulties with job descriptions arise because they encourage demarcation disputes, where people adhere strictly to the contents of the job description, rather than responding flexibly to task or organisational requirements. As more and more organisations find that they require flexibility above all in their workers, job descriptions are likely to become progressively less detailed. Otherwise they would have to be changed too frequently.

In 1976 the Institute of Administrative Management summarised the essential information to be included in a job description as 'details of the department and section in which the job is found; a job code number if jobs are classified; the person to whom the jobholder is responsible; the job title; the names of the jobholder, analyst or manager responsible for preparing the description; the date of preparation; and possibly the grading subsequently allocated to the job ... a brief general description of the purpose of the job, usually consisting of one or two sentences, and possibly a small organisation chart showing how the job relates to other jobs immediately above, below, and around it in the departmental structure ... a concise summary of all the main duties of the job'.

The problems with this have already been identified: where jobs involve discretion or flexibility it is counterproductive to straitjacket them by specifying their 'duties'. On the other hand, if the summary is too vague there is little point in including it.

Perhaps the best way to enjoy all the potential benefits of job descriptions is to call them something else, depending on their purpose. The description of the job used for recruitment purposes would contain sufficiently detailed information to enable recruiters and potential recruits to understand the current content of the job; one used for induction may need to be more detailed in relevant aspects; a different type of description again would be needed for job evaluation; comprehensive and detailed descriptions might only need to be prepared if the intention was to redesign the job at a particular point in time.

4 CONFESSIONS OF AN INTERVIEWER

Robertson and Makin conducted research to determine how reliable various selection techniques are and found that on a scale of 1 (meaning a method predicts how well a person will do every time) to 0 (meaning a method is no better than a random choice) interviews were found to score only 0.2 - little better than tossing a coin.

Possible reasons for the ineffectuality of interviews include the following.

(a) Errors of judgement by interviewers. These might be:
  (i) the *halo effect* - a tendency for people to make an initial general judgement about a person based on a single obvious attribute, such as being neatly dressed, or well-spoken, or having a public school education. This single attribute will colour later perceptions, and might make an interviewer mark the person up or down on every other factor in their assessment;
  (ii) *contagious bias* - a process whereby an interviewer changes the behaviour of the applicant by suggestion. The applicant might be led by the wording of questions or non-verbal cues from the interviewer, and change what he is doing or saying in response;
  (iii) a possible inclination by interviewers to *stereotype* candidates on the basis of insufficient evidence. Stereotyping groups together people who are assumed to share certain characteristics, then attributes certain traits to the group as a whole, and then (illogically) assumes that each individual member of the supposed group will possess that trait: all women are weak, or whatever;
  (iv) *incorrect assessment* of qualitative factors such as motivation, honesty or integrity. Abstract qualities are very difficult to assess in an interview;
  (v) *logical error*. For example, an interviewer might decide that a young candidate who has held two or three jobs in the past for only a short time will be unlikely to last long in any job.

(b) Lack of skill and experience in interviewers. The problems with inexperienced interviewers are not only bias, but:
  (i) inability to evaluate information about a candidate properly;
  (ii) inability to compare a candidate against the requirements for a job or a personnel specification;
  (iii) bad planning of the interview;
  (iv) inability to take control of the direction and length of the interview;
  (v) a tendency to talk too much in interviews, and to ask questions which call for a short answer;
  (vi) a tendency to jump to conclusions on insufficient evidence, or to place too much emphasis on isolated strengths or weaknesses;
  (vii) a tendency to act as an inquisitor and make candidates feel uneasy; and
  (viii) a reluctance to probe into facts and challenge statements where necessary.

There is much that can be done to improve the selection interview's reliability and validity. As mentioned above, proper preparation is vital. The interviewer must have a clear idea of what the interview is setting out to achieve, and must be in sufficient control of the interview to make sure that every candidate is asked questions which cover the same ground and obtain all the information required. The agenda and questions will be based on:

(a) the job description, and what abilities are required of the jobholder;
(b) the personnel specification. The interviewer must be able to judge whether the applicant matches up to the personal qualities required from the jobholder; and
(c) the application form.

Answers to exam style questions

The interview process should be efficiently run to make a favourable impression on the candidates: they should be clearly informed when and where to come, whom to ask for, what to bring with them etc and should be expected by the receptionist or other receiving staff. Arrangements should have been made to welcome and escort candidates: they should not be placed under the extra stress of being left stranded, getting lost, or being ignored. Accommodation for the interview should be private and free from distractions/interruption.

The layout of the room should be planned. Most interviewers wish to put candidates at their ease, and so it would be inadvisable to put the candidate in a 'hot-seat' across a desk (a psychological barrier) from them.

During the interview itself, the manner of the interviewers, the tone of their voice, and the way their early questions are phrased can all be significant in establishing the tone of the interview, and the ease with which the candidate can talk freely.

Questions should be paced and put carefully. The interviewer should not try to confuse the interviewee, plunging immediately into demanding questions or picking on isolated points; nor should he allow the interviewee to digress or gloss over important points, although the candidate should be given the opportunity to ask questions. The interviewer must retain control over the information-gathering process.

A variety of questions may be used, to different effects.

(a) *Open questions* or open-ended questions ('Who...? What...? Where...? When...? Why...?') make interviewees put together their own responses in complete sentences. This encourages the interviewee to talk, keeps the interview flowing, and is most revealing ('Why do you want to be a Chartered Secretary?')

(b) *Probing questions* are similar to open questions in their phrasing but aim to discover the deeper significance of the candidate's experience or achievements. ('What was it about HRM that particularly appealed to you?')

(c) *Closed questions* are the opposite, inviting only 'yes' or 'no' answers: ('Did you...?', 'Have you...?'). A closed question elicits answers only to the question asked by the interviewer. This may be useful where there are small points to be established ('Did you pass your exam?'). However, there may be other questions and issues that he has not anticipated but will emerge if the interviewee is given the chance to express himself ('How did you think your studies went?').

(d) *Multiple questions* are just that: two or more questions are asked at once. ('Tell me about your last job? How did your knowledge of HRM help you there, and do you think you are up-to-date or will you need to spend time studying?') This type of question can be used to encourage the candidate to talk at some length, but not to stray too far from the point. It might also test the candidate's ability to listen and handle large amounts of information, but should be used judiciously in this case.

(e) *Problem solving questions* present the candidate with a situation and ask him to explain how he would deal with it. ('How would you motivate your staff to do a task that they did not want to do?'). Such questions are used to establish whether the candidate will be able to deal with the sort of problems that are likely to arise in the job, or whether he has sufficient technical knowledge (in which case a line manager rather than the personnel manager might be the best person to ask the questions and judge the responses).

(f) *Leading questions* lead the interviewee to give a certain reply and should normally be avoided. ('We are looking for somebody who likes detailed figure work. How much do you enjoy dealing with numbers?' or 'Don't you agree that...?'. 'Surely...?') The danger with this type of question is that the interviewee will give the answer that he thinks the interviewer wants to hear, but it might legitimately be used to deal with a highly reticent or nervous candidate, simply to encourage him to talk.

The interviewer *must* listen to and evaluate the responses, to judge what the interviewee:

(a) wants to say;

(b) is trying *not* to say;

(c) is saying - but doesn't mean, or is lying about;

(d) is having difficulty saying.

In addition, the interviewer will have to be aware when he:

(a) is hearing something he needs to know;

(b) is hearing something he *doesn't* need to know;

(c) is hearing only what he expects to hear;

(d) is not hearing clearly - when his own attitudes, perhaps prejudices, are getting in the way of his response to the interviewee and his views.

5 DISCRIMINATION AGAINST WOMEN

Reasons for discrimination against women at work include the following.

(a) Social pressures on the woman to bear and rear children, and on the man to make a lifelong commitment to paid work as the 'breadwinner'. Employers assumed - and sometimes still assume - that women's paid work would be short term or interrupted, and that training and development was therefore hardly worthwhile.

(b) The nature of earlier industrial work, which was physically heavy: legal restrictions were placed on women's employment in areas such as mines, night work in factories etc.

(c) Lack of organisation of women at work and influence in trade unions (except in industries like textiles), up until the 1980s.

(d) The reinforcing of segregation at home and at school: for example, lack of encouragement to girls to study mathematical and scientific subjects.

(e) Career ladders which fail to fast-track women. Apprenticeships, for example, are rarely held by girls. A woman graduate starting as a secretary is less likely to advance than a male graduate who starts as a management trainee. In addition, organisations like banks, which have traditionally developed staff on the assumption of a lifetime career with the one employer, have tended to assume that women are unlikely to want a lifetime career. Commitments to geographical mobility are similarly assumed to be undesirable for women.

(f) Child-bearing and family responsibilities. Part-time work has enabled many women to continue in paid employment, but tends to apply to jobs which carry little prospect for promotion.

Steps to tackle such discrimination include the implementation of a policy and code of practice; the monitoring of the numbers of women; and positive action such as career breaks or return-to-work schemes for women, and the provision of workplace nurseries for working mothers.

6 TRAINING AND DEVELOPMENT PRACTICES

The integration of training and development into the management process

Training and development are most likely to be systematic in large organisations which can employ specialist staff. However, the very creation of a specialist training department can lead to training becoming detached from the management process. Because trainers do not directly produce revenue they are not easy to fit into the normal line management structure.

The use of training and development resources can also fail to be integrated into the management process, even when there is no specialist training department.

Answers to exam style questions

Managers may, for example, just decide that each member of staff should go on one external course a year, and send people on courses without thinking of their relevance to the individuals' careers.

One remedy is to encourage managers to be more aware of their labour resources, not just as so many people but as so many people with particular skills. Training and development should be linked as directly as possible to production and revenue. Thus if it is anticipated that a new branch will be needed two years hence, management should recognise that it will need staff with a range of skills, and should plan to select and train staff in exactly the same way as they would plan to obtain premises and equipment.

Introverted management

Training and development tend to be planned by departmental managers for their own staff. Inevitably, such managers will concentrate on what they believe their own departments appear to need. Staff too will also be keen to relate their training and development to their own jobs, without perhaps thinking enough about the organisation as a whole. Thus there is certainly scope for training and development to perpetuate introverted management.

A possible remedy is for top management to prescribe training and development requirements, which must then be implemented within departments. In some cases, where comparatively non-specialist skills are being taught, it may be possible to mix staff from different departments on the same course. External training courses may also be better than internal courses in this respect, both because the course might include people from other organisations and because external trainers can offer alternative perspectives.

The attitudes of individual managers

Some managers believe strongly in training and development, and may even devote excessive resources to them. Others see training and development, and particularly external training courses, as excuses for virtual holidays at the organisation's expense. It is therefore perfectly possible for the level of training to vary widely across departments of an organisation.

The obvious remedy is for top management to insist on a certain amount of time being spent on each employee's training and development. Ideally, the budget for this should be kept completely separate from the normal line managers' budgets, so that there is no temptation to cut down on training to meet profit targets.

Individual needs

Training is intended to give employees specific knowledge or skills. Inevitably, some of it will be misdirected in that some employees will already have the knowledge or skills being offered. On the other hand, individual tuition would in most cases be uneconomic.

Development is wider than training, covering each employee's career plan and using training courses as one resource among many. Here it is less likely that individual needs will be ignored, although it is of course still possible to impose standard career plans on individual employees.

One remedy is to have detailed decisions on training made by managers as close as possible to the employees concerned. This may not be incompatible with the intervention by top management encouraged above, because top management could still prescribe broad areas of training and the number of hours per employee per year. Another remedy is to use a wide range of external courses, sending perhaps only two or three employees on each one, so that training at all levels is available.

7 EFFECTIVE APPRAISAL

> *Tutorial note.* It is important that you read the question and understand the meaning of common HRM terms like 'job description', 'appraisal', 'counselling' and so. Do not write about job evaluation instead of performance appraisal, or take the term 'performance' in the phrase 'performance appraisal' to mean that the appraiser should dwell at length on such 'performance' measures as time-keeping, lateness, work absences, and so forth, rather than substantive 'output' criteria like productivity, flexibility and 'added value'.

'The conventional approach to performance appraisal places the manager in the untenable position of judging the personal worth of his subordinates and of acting upon those judgements'. (Douglas McGregor 'An uneasy look at performance appraisals' 1957').

Appraising people's activities is a skill which is not easy to learn. It can be both subjective and personal. Prejudice and bias can never be completely removed, and in the absence of training may completely distort an individual's judgement. MR Williams (*Performance Appraisal in Management,* 1972) wrote: 'Despite the many apparent advantages of what should be an intrinsic and critical part of management control, there is much evidence both in the UK and abroad to suggest that many appraisals are largely a waste of time.'

However, most commentators agree that appraisal and counselling are key managerial activities which, effectively carried out, can reinforce strengths, identify weaknesses and improve future performance. Appraisal is seen as a process involving key decisions and having important consequences.

Changing ideas in appraisal

Much of the criticism levelled at appraisal stems from the use of inappropriate techniques. There has been a failure on the part of many companies to use the most appropriate, realistic and valid schemes and to train managers to operate them.

In the early days of appraisal much play was made of personality traits such as loyalty, dependability, co-operation, initiative and self-confidence which placed much strain on the appraiser owing to potential ambiguity and subjectivity. Inadequately defined personal qualities combined with numerical rating scales which have an all too convenient 'average score', provide managers with little more than a superficial and often inappropriate basis for judgement. There is also a dangerous and spurious air of authenticity about many rating scales. Numerical ratings, particularly, often imply both an accuracy and validity they do not possess.

It is not surprising, therefore, that the moves in appraisal are away from trait or behaviour appraisal and towards, in the words of Livy 'the use of results-based appraisals (such as Management by Objectives) and the development of job related performance criteria'. It is now generally considered that personality is only relevant where there is reason to suspect that it is a factor in poor performance.

New methods

In most new methods appraisal techniques use verifiable preselected goals on which to base judgement. Personnel are assessed not on what they do, but on what they produce; not on how they spend their time, but on what they contribute. All the best methods emphasise that there should be a contribution from the person being appraised. One company might, for example, ask individuals well in advance of the interview to complete a form containing headings such as:

'What have been your best achievements'

'What problems have you had in meeting goals'

'What went badly during the year'

and so on.

Among new methods the following stand out.

(a) *Grading*. Managers are asked to select one of a number of levels or degrees to which the individual displays the given characteristics. These are also known as rating scales and their effectiveness depends to a large extent on the relevance of the factors chosen for assessment and the definition of the agreed standards.

(b) *Behaviour incident methods or critical incident system,* as described by Flanagan and Burns. This technique requires the appraisers to record any specific examples of outstandingly good or bad performance to the exclusion of the day to day average (which is usually the real measure of a person's effectiveness). Generally, the analysis is carried out by key tasks which are identified as critical to success in the job and for which specific standards of performance must be reached.

(c) *Results orientated schemes.* A wholly results-based approach (such as Management by Objectives) sets out to review performance against specific targets and standards agreed in advance by manager and subordinate together. In this scheme, the subordinate is more involved and capable of self-appraisal since he already knows what is expected of him. The manager is therefore relieved, to an extent, of his role of critic, and becomes a counsellor with a problem-solving approach being adopted.

(d) *Two-way schemes*. The majority of techniques are sensitive to the part played by the subordinate in the interview. Some schemes, however, go further than that and Mary Williams ('Little brother is watching you') in *Personnel Today* 1993, suggests a system of upward appraisal where, as the title suggests, managers are appraised by the people who work under them. Daunting as this may be for managers, successful examples have been noted in Cathay Pacific, Post Office Counters and the Foreign and Commonwealth Office.

(e) *360-degree feedback.* Taking upward appraisal a stage further, Gerard Dugdill ('Wide Angle View') *Personnel Today* September 1994, focuses on a technique which involves appraisal by those above, below and to the side of an individual employee. There are many well-known organisations exploring its potential including Northumbrian Water, Mercury One 2 One and BT. The main advantage is that results are aggregated by a facilitator making it virtually impossible for individual comments to be identified.

The final comment should be reserved for Professor Clive Fletcher ('Appraisal - an idea whose time has gone', *Personnel Management,* September 1993). Writing about the demise of the traditional, monolithic approach, he says 'Doubtless the idea of a universally applied, personnel-driven, standard procedure that stays rigidly in place (perhaps kept there by the weight of its own paperwork) within the organisation for years on end will lumber on in some quarters for a while yet, but its days are certainly numbered. In its place is evolving a number of separate but linked processes, applied in different ways according to the needs of local circumstances and staff levels. The various elements in this may go by a variety of names, and perhaps the term appraisal itself has outlived its usefulness'.

8 SIGNIFICANCE OF WORK

Two different questions

The basic distinction suggested by the question is that between different 'types' or 'levels' of motivation. People are 'motivated' (in the sense of the mental process of choosing a desired outcome) to work by a number of needs or wants, primarily to do with physical survival and security, social acceptance and psychological health. They are motivated to work 'well' by something more or different: the satisfaction of 'higher order needs', perhaps.

This kind of idea underpins several of the major theories of motivation.

(a) Maslow's *hierarchy of needs* suggests that people's innate needs can be categorised in a hierarchy of 'relative pre-potency' so that, generally speaking, he must satisfy the more basic needs before progressing to 'higher' needs. Maslow did not intend his views to be applied to the specific context of behaviour at work (and there are other problems of validity associated with the theory) but as a broad framework for human action, one may apply the theory to the equally hierarchical idea of 'working' (or 'merely' working) and 'working well'. 'Working' per se may be said to satisfy basic physiological and safety needs, providing livelihood, order, predictability and, in many cultures, a sense of social value and 'worth'. Simply working may *not* of itself, however, satisfy higher order needs for esteem - competence, achievement, independence, recognition, respect, appreciation - or self-actualisation, the fulfilment of personal potential. In order to satisfy these needs, the individual may try to 'work well'.

(b) Herzberg's two-factor theory of motivation draws more clearly the distinction between 'maintenance' conditions which are taken for granted as the basis of continuing to 'work', and things which *motivate* the individual to a higher level of performance.

In this framework, there is no explanation of what makes people choose to work, but it is suggested that maintenance of conditions under which people will continue to perform at an acceptable level is a constant task. Factors such as support systems, supervision, work relationships and even pay are considered to have a purely 'hygienic' role: they prevent 'ill-health' (alienation, incapacity, starvation), but cannot give 'good health' (a positive motivation to a sustained high level of performance - working 'well').

Herzberg suggested that in order to get people to work 'well', 'motivator' factors had to be brought into play, satisfying the need for personal growth and satisfaction. These factors were said to be involved in the job itself and to offer 'job satisfaction', and included challenge and interest in the work, achievement, 'growth' in the job, responsibility and so on.

The question 'why do people work?' thus addresses issues of basic needs: financial security; the calculation (suggested by the Affluent Worker research of Goldthorpe et al) of how much income is 'enough' to outweigh the deprivations associated with work; the socio-political, cultural and psychological pressures on individuals to work in order to be acceptable, meaningful and capable members of society.

The question 'Why do people work well?' addresses issues of motivation and incentives, and of what more people need to be offered in order to consider an extra input of effort, energy and emotion, worthwhile. It addresses performance in the job, and differences in individual performance.

Complicating factors

The question is not quite so simple as the above summary suggests, however.

(a) Vocational choice seems to indicate that for some individuals, job satisfaction and the fulfilment of 'higher order' needs are part of the decision to work - without reference to levels of performance once in the job, or 'working well'. In other words, factors such as social belonging, achievement and self-esteem, recognition and fulfilment are part of the basic calculation of whether to work and at what.

(b) Conversely, the role of pay is ambiguous: for many individuals it is *not* simply a reason to work, but an incentive to work well or better. (Herzberg himself recognised that pay is the most important hygiene factor.) Incentive schemes are based on this assumption - and it would be naive to suppose that, even in comparatively affluent sectors, money has lost its power to motivate, in favour of 'job enrichment' and other such satisfaction-oriented rewards.

(c) Job satisfaction has still not been proved to cause higher level performance. Scientifically speaking, the reasons why people work in the first place are just as likely to motivate them to work *well* as the supposed 'motivator' or 'higher order' factors.

(d) The expression 'work well' begs a number of questions related to other areas of organisational behaviour (which would in themselves fill whole exam answers). The level of performance of any given individual depends not just on *inclination* or *motivation* (as, arguably, does his decision to 'work'): to 'work well', an individual must also have the capacity to do so. This will involve the individual's own skills, aptitudes and abilities, education and training, experience, physical health and attributes, and maturity - *and* the organisational context of his work: management and supervision, fellow workers, task and technology, organisational structure and systems, and work environment. The question 'Why do people work well?' can therefore be answered not only with reasons why they would *want* to, but with ways in which they are *enabled* to do so.

9 THE PERFORMANCE OF PRP

PRP does not motivate

There can be no doubt that pay acts as a motivator in a basic sense: if people were not paid they would not work. However, pay is one of Herzberg's *hygiene* factors rather than a *motivator* factor - it gets taken for granted and so is more usually a source of dissatisfaction than satisfaction.

The question is whether paying people *more* in return for better performance naturally leads people to perform better. It certainly *may* do so. Pay is the most *important* of the hygiene factors, according to Herzberg. It is valuable not only in its power to be converted into a wide range of other satisfactions (perhaps the only way in which organisations can - at least indirectly - cater for individual employee's needs and wants through a common reward system) but also as a consistent measure of worth or value, allowing employees to compare themselves and be compared with other individuals or occupational groups inside and outside the organisation.

However, people must be *able* to perform better. They must be given whatever resources they need to be able to turn in an improved performance, and they should not be penalised for factors beyond their control. More fundamentally, people need to understand and accept the organisation's definition of good and bad performance. Frequently neither of these conditions apply.

PRP is divisive

PRP can be divisive if some employees are paid by results and others are not. This may occur because one manager is able to negotiate better terms for his staff than another (which is quite unfair for the employees) or because the work of one set of employees is felt to be more easily measurable than that of another set (for example sales reps as compared with administrative staff).

Judgements about performance are subjective

Again, this is true: even when quantitative criteria are used (number of widgets produced per hour, say) the selection of the criteria is subjective and the distinction between a 'good' performance level and a less good level is subjective. If judgements are made on the basis of performance appraisal by a manager, subjectivity cannot be avoided.

On the other hand, attempts may be made to mitigate subjectivity. Depending on the job it may be possible to obtain performance evaluations from customers. Arguably all employees have customers, either external to the organisation or internal to it, although many employees would find it difficult to accept a system that entailed their pay being determined by their colleagues. An alternative might be to appoint as evaluators or arbitrators persons within the organisation who were accepted by all parties as being objective.

Can PRP be worthwhile?

The preceding paragraphs indicate that PRP can be worthwhile as long as a number of conditions hold true.

(a) If pay is valued by staff.

(b) If individuals have sufficient control over their own performance.

(c) If 'good' performance can be clearly defined.
(d) If *all* staff are included.
(e) If awards are perceived as being made fairly.

10 ERGONOMICS

Ergonomics

Ergonomics was initially a branch of Taylor's scientific management and could be described as the scientific study of the relationship between man and his working environment. This sphere of scientific research explores the demands that can arise from a working environment and the capabilities of people to meet these demands.

Through this research, data is made available to establish machines and working conditions which, apart from functioning well, are best suited to the capacities and health requirements of the human body. Thus computer consoles and controls, factory layout and so on, can be designed so that the individual expends minimal energy and experiences minimal physical strain in any given task.

For example, the comfort of a machine operator in a factory will depend on many factors connected with the particular job, but there are certain general considerations which ensure a comfortable position.

(a) The operator should be allowed to sit where possible.
(b) The chair should permit alternate sitting and standing.
(c) In either case the elbows should be 2-3 inches above the working surface. This often calls for benches to be higher than those normally found.
(d) There should be room for the operator to put both legs under the bench.
(e) Work, tools and equipment should be within easy reach.
(f) Movements should be natural, rhythmical, and symmetrical.

Regarding the environment, there are statutory requirements that all workplaces must adhere to for certain factors, such as lighting and temperature.

Psychological factors

More recently ergonomics has developed into a field that embraces the whole range of psychological factors that affect people at work. The Health and Safety Executive estimate that 30-40% of all sickness absence from work is attributable to some form of mental or emotional disturbance.

Thus, besides equipment and workplace layout, ergonomics is about the fit between people and their work activities and systems.

"The way work is organised - its systems, procedures, allocation and scheduling - can have a significant impact on how well people work, and also on their psychological and physical well-being. ... It is as important for work systems to be "people-shaped" in terms of mental and behavioural demands as it is for chairs and desks to fit people's physical dimensions."

(Alan Fowler, *People Management*, September 1995)

In a factory, for example, an assembly line may be set to run at a constant speed that is slightly too slow for some workers. They will be frustrated by this and perhaps become inattentive and bored, and either make mistakes or injure themselves. Again, a work system that penalises mistakes or breakages too harshly will mean that many workers are in a constant state of anxiety about getting things right first time.

Fowler cites the example of noise as a source of stress rather than as a health risk: 'levels below 80 decibels are unlikely to damage hearing, but extreme annoyance and distraction can be caused at well below this level'.

Financial considerations

From a financial point of view, a concern for ergonomics may have noticeable benefits.

Answers to exam style questions

(a) It will often be possible to perform the ergonomically designed task more quickly and efficiently, so productivity will rise.

(b) Less time will be wasted on sick leave.

(c) Accidents often result in a production line being closed down temporarily while the cause is investigated and any problems corrected. This means that all workers on that line, not just the one who has been injured, are prevented from getting on with their jobs.

11 MIDDLE MANAGERS AND CHANGE

Opposition to change

When security is threatened opposition to change is at its height. Security for middle managers, however, is a thing of the past. In the processes of downsizing, right sizing, delayering, flatter management structures, whatever the preferred routes may be to 'slimming' organisations, controlling costs and responding to the changing demands of the market place, it is the middle managers who suffer the most. The introduction of new technology, the recession and a growing trend to restructuring and re-engineering organisations has taken a serious toll on middle management.

A situation like this means that everything comes under scrutiny, including management. Paternalistic attitudes, with cushy bureaucracies offering cradle to grave employment are becoming a thing of the past. In the 1990s employers can no longer afford to make the sort of traditional pact of 'do your job reasonably well and we'll promote you every two or three years'. New technology has played a central role. Not only was it seen by middle managers as a threat to their traditional decision-making role, but many were reluctant to use it. The middle managers of the 1980s, born in the 1940s and 1950s, lacked technological background. Unlike the children of the 1980s and 1990s who are computer literate and accept the technology as a fact of life, to middle management, the computer was a new-fangled gadget which was at best grudgingly accepted and at worst positively rejected.

Unfortunately, during the late 1980s, organisations were, at the same time as introducing new technologies, ill-advisedly carrying out cost cutting exercises on their training programmes. Many enterprises expected their managers to do homework, read technical manuals and experiment with the machinery. Few were so motivated. This lead inevitably to their downfall.

At the same time the threatened takeover of middle management decision-making was, indeed, taking place. Computer networks and the like meant that decision-makers at the top could stay in touch with and control people closer to the operational base without going through the middle layer. Bruce Reed of the Grubb Institute commented in 1990 that 'middle management is often used as a punctuation mark, a control between top and bottom. That is reduced with information technology. People are managing and controlling themselves'.

The recession exacerbated the problem. Many of the middle managers could well have lost their jobs much earlier. The recession provided an excellent excuse. As the new generation of computer literate executives ascends, whole swathes of the older generation middle management have gone and will continue to go.

Job losses are not the only factor. Equally important is the change in role for those people left behind. New organisational structures mean new career paths. Yet once again middle management views this as a threat. A recent career audit carried out by Sundridge Park for National Westminster Bank concludes 'attitudes have not changed. Our people don't see themselves as career changers. They look for further progression within the bank. I think it will take a long time for any change to get through'.

As Robert Heller 'The Managers Dilemma' *Management Today,* January 1994, writes: 'plainly the doomed resistance, both to the computer and to the new management modes, has deep roots. Most managers have not yet come to terms with fundamental changes in their worlds. The horizontal principle is displacing the vertical in everything, from organisation structure to the markets themselves.'

Acceptance of change

As Heller says, the new manager will 'advance in prestige and pay by moving from one successful assignment to the next, not by exchanging one title for another'. In these days of cross-functional, synergistic and inter-departmental and task-specific teams, organisations will seek to tap peoples' own motivation by involvement, by liberating their energies and rewarding their initiatives.

In 'Management careers facing the new realities', *Professional Manager,* July 1993, Kerr Inkson states: 'if the future world of work means that the corporate career is over, we need to develop a new orientation, a new psychology of aspiration that fits better with the harsher, more competitive conditions. Rather than assuming each new job is ours until we choose to leave it, we should assume it is temporary until it proves permanent'.

The constant threat emerging through the literature counsels the middle manager to assume nothing, to remain flexible and to develop skills and abilities in relation to the future rather than remaining embedded in the past. As Kerr Inkson says: 'focusing our career in our own terms, seeing it as a means of personal fulfilment and divesting it of the trappings and expectations of public definitions of success or failure, may also enable us to adapt to changed conditions.'

Whilst much of this new focus must come from individuals themselves, the organisation can pave the way by offering development seminars during which new attitudes are fostered. Many management consultants run sessions on this new orientation and within house it is possible to set up 'discovery teams' and 'transition management teams' which perform 'reality checks' on the need for change, to arrange meetings open to anyone and everyone, to stimulate conversation and communication across functions and specifically include people who are opposed and have power to obstruct change.

Change is made easier if people are allowed, encouraged and rewarded for taking risks, being innovative and looking for new, better solutions. If the company culture is consultative and participative and individuals are urged to express their views, change becomes accepted. Finally, if redundancies are inevitable and the company is seen to be fair and generous in its severance terms, its staff will be more relaxed in their attitude to the 'slimming' process.

12 DUNTOILING NURSING HOMES

To deal with this difficult situation effectively you need to do the following:

(a) introduce a disciplinary procedure if none currently exists;

(b) consider the Health and Safety at Work legislation, particularly the employer's obligations of duty and care towards staff.

(c) define constructive dismissal (this means where an organisation has changed terms and conditions of employment to such an extent that the employees feel they have no other option but to resign);

(d) consider the wisdom of unilateral changes in terms and conditions without notice (ie Cheeseman imposing these changes without any consultation);

(e) consider reinstating the employee with possible concessions (eg counselling to give up smoking);

(f) prepare your ideal and 'fall-back' positions when negotiating;

(g) question why the policy was introduced in the first place;

(h) ask why there was no involvement from the personnel function in implementing the smoking policy; and

(i) develop the 'best practice' model, showing how to introduce a smoking policy,

Answers to exam style questions

and do it again (remember the employer's duty to protect employees from the effects of passive smoking). The model should include:

(i) a consultation period (say three months);

(ii) establishing a consultative committee;

(iii) conducting a staff attitude survey;

(iv) making provision for special cases;

(v) make formal changes to terms and conditions;

(vi) retrain line managers in disciplinary matters; and

(vii) review and monitor the policy.

Remember that the question asks for your answer to be in the form of a brief to Mr Cheeseman.

13 REDUNDANCIES

Before making practical suggestions it is worth briefly reviewing the law on redundancy.

Redundancy is defined by the Employment Protection (Consolidation) Act 1978 as dismissal where:

(a) the employer has ceased to carry on the business;

(b) the employer has ceased to carry on the business in the place where the employee was employed; and/or

(c) the requirements of the business for employees to carry out work of a particular kind have ceased or diminished or are expected to.

Redundant employees are entitled to compensation:

(a) for loss of security; and

(b) to encourage employees to accept redundancy without damage to industrial relations.

The employee is *not* entitled to compensation if:

(a) the employer has made a suitable offer of alternative employment and the employee has unreasonably rejected it. The 'suitability' of the offer will have to be examined in each case;

(b) the employee is of pension age or over, or has less than two years' continuous employment; and/or

(c) the employee's conduct entitles the employer to dismiss him without notice.

An employer should seek to avoid compulsory redundancies where possible for several reasons.

(a) To reduce the financial cost of redundancies.

(b) Because alternatives are more humane and more socially responsible.

(c) To reduce the cost in terms of adverse publicity.

(d) Because it is damaging for the morale of workers, even if they are not made redundant.

(e) Because it may lead to talented individuals becoming available for competitors to employ (depending upon selection policy).

There are a number of ways of avoiding, or at least reducing the number of forced redundancies that have to be made. Some of the more dubious ways that unscrupulous employers have used - such as drastically worsening working conditions - do not fulfil all of the criteria above. In any case, they would probably be treated by the courts as constructive dismissal, so these are not considered further here.

Realistic possibilities are as follows.

(a) Use manpower planning. This means determining the future manpower needs of the organisation and forecasting the amount by which the labour force will be reduced through labour turnover. In other words the workforce will reduce over time through natural wastage. This process may be speeded up by an early announcement of likely future redundancies: some employees in threatened groups may seek new employment immediately.

This measure is justifiable under each of the criteria listed above except (e) - talented individuals will easily find other employment and the cost of losing their services may be considerable.

(b) Stop all overtime working, if there is any, or put employees on short-time working (a three day week, say) or lay them off temporarily. In law employees are entitled to claim redundancy pay if this is done (so long as they also give in their notice), but it is probable that an agreement could be reached with trade unions that employees would not do this.

This type of measure would be justified when the need for redundancies arose because of factors beyond the organisation's short-term control, but where it was anticipated that normal working would be resumed in future. It is damaging to morale and wasteful of resources.

(c) Enforcing the retirement of staff over the normal retirement age. This is allowed in law, but is difficult to justify if the individuals in question are employed because of exceptional talent or desperate need. If the individual has exceptional talent he or she should be retrained. If he or she is desperately needy, it would be easier to justify the redundancy of someone younger, with better alternative employment prospects.

(d) Dismissing part-time or short-term contract staff, once contracts come to convenient break-off points or conclusions. This measure is justifiable under all of the criteria listed earlier.

(e) Offering retraining and/or redeployment within the organisation, assuming such opportunities are available. This is by far the most constructive use of existing human resources, and the cost of taking this route should be carefully weighed up against the cost of the redundancies and the cost of recruiting for the new positions from other sources.

(f) Offering early retirement to staff approaching normal retirement age. This, again, is justified under all of the criteria listed earlier.

(g) Job-sharing. This is becoming increasingly common, especially as women who do not want to give up their family responsibilities become a more significant part of the labour force. It is fully justified so long as the job itself is suited to sharing and there is an advantage in cost terms. Some redesigning of the job may be required.

(h) Seeking voluntary redundancies. This has the advantage of being more humane than an enforced redundancy, but there is little else to recommend it. It is very much the last resort before enforced redundancies, once other avenues have been exhausted.

14 NOVALUX PLC

The figures here have been designed not to provide a simple answer, and some statistical application is required. To test whether the differences between age groups, in terms of staff turnover, are significant or not, you would actually have to use a statistical test that is beyond the scope of this module.

However, the broader issue here is what else you can draw out from the figures provided, and what further information you might need in order to make other, more meaningful, conclusions. For example, you might consider finding out further information on the following.

(a) The distribution of grades amongst leavers.
(b) What types of jobs they had.

(c) Which departments they come from.
(d) Whether any gender or ethnicity pattern emerges.
(e) Have reasons for leaving been given via exit interviews?
(f) Do new employees go through an induction programme?
(g) Are new employees trained properly?
(h) What is the age profile of the organisation? For example, if it's a very young population, the turnover figures by age might not be as alarming as they first appear.

INDEX

16PF test, 72
60-degree feedback, 125, 132
360-degree feedback,
    pros and cons, 127

-A-
Abbey Life, 154
Abrahamsen, 66, 73
Absenteeism, 179, 201, 238
ACAS, 216-217, 239, 258
ACAS Code of Practice, 242
Accidents, 97
    cost of, 197
    investigating, 199
    preventing, 198
Accountability, 164
Activists, 103
Admiral Insurance, 177
Advertising, 89
Alcoholism, 205
Alfred Marks, 92
Annual hours contract, 37
Application forms, 89
Appraisal
    bases, 123
    follow-ups, 123
    interview, 123
    objectives, 122
    procedures, 122
    report, 123
    problems, 130
Aptitude tests, 71
Armstrong, M, 4, 12, 13, 168, 171
Assertiveness training, 109
Assessment centres, 133, 135
Association of Accounting
    Technicians (AAT), 101
Atkinson, 34
Atlas Copco, 149
Attendance rate, 263
Awareness training, 90
Awareness-oriented training, 108

-B-
Barclays Bank, 190
Bargaining, 222
    disclosure, 229
Barnard, 142
Barrell, J, 195
Bartholomew, 20

Bassett, P, 225
BBC, 91
Beattie, D, 5
Behavioural incident methods, 124
Behaviourist psychology, 102
Benchmarking, 60
Benefits, 177
BIM index, 26
Body Shop, 190
Bonus schemes, 175
Bowey, 172
BP, 129
Braddick, W A G, 114
Brent Council, 205
Brewster, 13
British Aerospace, 153
British Airways, 90, 129
British Institute of Management,
    160, 176
British Telecom, 153
Brown, W, 164
BS EN ISO 9000, 99, 174, 220
Buchanan, 144, 150

-C-
Calor Gas, 35, 40, 4, 86, 111
Cambridgeshire County Council,
174
Candidates' questions, 68
Capability, 252
Career
    breaks, 90
    development, 116
    prospects, 29
Cars, 181
Case studies, 74
Catering services, 181
Cattell, 72
Chamberlain, 227
    bargaining model, 229
Change, 19
    management, 4
    HRM and, 233
Changes in behaviour, 111
Chase Manhattan Bank, 205
Classification method, 162
Clayton, T, 92
Closed questions, 67
Co-operation, 220
Coaching, 107

329

Code of Professional Practice in Personnel Management, 267
Codes of Practice, 88
Cognitive approach, 102
Cole, G A, 33, 45
Collective bargaining, 215, 226
Collective implied terms, 78
Commission for Racial Equality CRE, 84, 87-88
Communication Workers Union (CWU), 221
Companies Act 1985, 232
Compensation for redundancy, 252
Competence analysis, 100
Competence based training, 100
Competency framework, 132
Computerisation, 264-265
Computerised personal information system (CPIS), 266
Concessions, 230
Confidentiality, 211, 267
Conflict, handling of, 219
Connock, Stephen, 38, 59, 101, 132
Constable, 114-115
Constructive discipline, 238
Constructive dismissal, 249
Consultation, 232
Contagious bias, 70
Content theories, 142
Continental (3-2-2) system, 36
Contingency planning, 19
Contract of employment, 77
Control of Substances Hazardous to Health (COSHH) Regulations, 204
Core group, 34
Core job dimensions, 149
Cost-effectiveness of recruitment, 59
Costs of labour turnover, 27
Counselling, 207
    checklist, 209
    interview, 127
    process, 208
Criminal Justice and Public Order Act 1994, 269
Criteria for appraisal, 123
Crude labour turnover rate, 26
Cultural flexibility, 33
Culture, 153
Cuming, M W, 9, 24, 28, 38
Curriculum vitae (CV), 64
Customer care, 6
Customer needs, identifying, 7
Customers
    external, 7
    internal, 7
Cynics, 113

-D-

Data collection, 264
Data Protection Act 1984, 267, 269
Data Protection Co-ordinator, 269
Data protection principles, 268
Data Protection Registrar, 268
Data users, 268
De-unionising, 224
Deficiency of labour, 22
Democratic leadership, 151
Demographic trends, 22
Demotion, 239
Department of Employment, 261
Derby County Council, 205
Development, 114
Direct discrimination, 86
Disability Discrimination Act 1995, 87
Discharge, 239
Disciplinary action, 239
Disciplinary situations, 238
Discipline, 238
Discrimination, 82
    policy, 89
    age, 85
    disabilities, 87
    ex-criminals, 85
    exceptions, 86
    married people, 87
    recruitment, 89
    racial, 84
    religion, 88
    sexual, 83
    the disabled, 85
Dismissal, 249
Distributive bargaining, 228
Doherty, 255
Domestic support, 191
Double-day system, 36
Drucker, P, 3, 9, 113
DSS, 179, 261
Dwyer, B, 259

-E-

EAR, 211
Earnings drift, 171
EC Directive 92/85, 180
Ecological strategies, 219
Economic climate, 28
Education 114
Elements of competence, 101
Employee Assistance Programmes (EAPs), 211
Employee development programmes (EDPs), 117

Employee records, 259, 261
   collective data, 261
   standing data, 259
Employee shareholders, 175
Employment Act 1982, 232
Employment Act 1988, 221, 223-224
Employment agencies, 57
Employment Protection Act 1975, 217, 253
Employment Protection (Consolidation) Act 1978, 183, 250
Empowerment, 150, 208
Engels, F, 218
Enthusiasts, 113
Entrepreneurship, 5
Environmental strategies, 219
Equal Opportunities Commission, 87-88
Equal opportunities employers, 89
Equal Pay (Amendment) Regulations 1984, 85
Equal Pay Act 1970, 85
Equity, 154, 164
Ergonomics, 200
Ethnic minorities, 84
Evaluation of recruitment, 59
Evaluation of training, 111
Exit interviews, 28
Expectancy equation, 147
Expectancy theory, 146
Experiential learning, 114

-F-
F values, 147
Factor comparison, 162
Factories Act 1961, 181, 199
Fair Employment Act 1989, 88
Fast tracking, 90
Feedback, 102, 130
Fell, A, 5
Fire, 199
Fire Protection Association, 200
Fitt, 165
Five point pattern of personality, 53
Fletcher, C, 73, 132
Flexibility of man hours, 32
Flexible working hours, 36
Flexible working methods, 33
Flexitime systems, 37
Focus, 211
Folkard, 37
Follow-up, 129
Ford, 117
Forecasting
   labour demand, 21
   labour supply, 21
Formal training, 105
Fox, A, 218

Fraser, M, 53
Fringe benefits, 177
Functional authority, 10
Furnham, A, 129

-G-
Gatekeeping, 180
Georgiades, N, 3
Gillespie, M, 136
Glaxo, 211
Goldthorpe, Lockwood et al, 155
Graded salaries, 168
Grading, 124
Green, J, 89
Grievance interviews, 243
Grievance procedures, 242
Group incentive schemes, 175
Group selection methods, 74
Guided assessment, 124
Guides and role models, 116

-H-
Halifax Building Society, 129
Halo effect, 70
Handy, C, 13, 113, 141, 149, 151, 218-219
Harr, 111
Harvester restaurants, 151
HAY-MSL method, 163
Health and Safety at Work Act 1974, 192, 194
Health and Safety Executive, 261
Helicopter ability, 134
Henley Centre, 39
Herzberg, 142, 145, 149-150, 155
Hillan, B, 226
Holidays, 181
Honey, P, 103
Hopwood, 152
Horsted, 255
Housing assistance, 181
HRM and change, 233
HRM and the EU, 14
Huczynski, 144, 150
Human relations school, 141
Human resource audit, 25
Human resource management, 2
Human resource planning, 20, 23, 46
   definition, 19
Human resource utilisation, 25
Human resources, 18
Hunt, 219
Hygiene factors, 145, 155

-I-
IBM, 91, 224-225, 267
ICAS, 211

ICI, 94, 153, 175
Ideologies, 218
Immigration, 84
Implied terms, 78
Incentive schemes, 173, 175
Incentives, 141, 153
Incompetence, 251
Indirect discrimination, 86
Induction training, 107
Industrial fatigue, 148
Industrial Participation Association, 228
Industrial relations, 215
Industrial Relations Code of Practice, 220
Industrial training boards, 261
Industrial tribunals, 183, 218, 250, 253
Information processing, 102
Information systems, 259
Inland Revenue, 261
Inland Revenue Staff Federation (IRSF), 221
Input factors, 165
Institute of Administrative Management, 160, 163
Institute of Personnel and Development, 2, 85, 161, 267
Integrative bargaining, 228
Intelligence tests, 71
Interviewers, 71
Interviews, 66, 89, 208
 limitations, 70
 preparation, 66
 process, 66
Investors in People, 174
Iron and Steel Trades Confederation (ISTC), 226
Itinerants, 40

-J-
Job advertisement, 55
 content, 56
Job analysis, 46, 49, 100
Job application forms, 64
Job appraisal, 49
Job content, 51
Job demarcation, 32
Job description, 46, 50, 66
 contents, 51
Job design, 148
Job dimensions, 149
Job enlargement, 146, 149
Job enrichment, 146, 149
Job evaluation, 160
Job requisition, 46
Job rotation, 107, 146
Job satisfaction, 142

Job sharing, 34
Job specification, 46, 49
Job summary, 51
Job title, 51
Joint Consultative Committees (JCCs), 232

-K-
Kolb, D, 104
Kuhn L, 227

-L-
Labour, 18
Labour flexibility, 32
Labour market, 25, 45
Labour sources, 46
Labour stability, 26, 263
Labour turnover, 26
 causes, 28
 pros and cons, 27
 ratio, 263
Last in, first out (LIFO), 253
Lateness, 238
Law is a floor, 192
Lawler, 155
Layoffs, 239
Leadership exercises, 134
Leading questions, 68
Learning
 cycle, 104
 objectives, 102
 reinforcement, 103
 standards, 102
 styles, 103
 theory, 102
Legge, K, 14
Legislation affecting disputes, 224
Leicester City Council, 94
Level of competence, 100
Line management, 9
Littlewoods, 84
Livy, B, 4, 20, 45, 50, 97, 123, 167, 266
Logical errors, 70
London Borough of Lewisham, 174
Luncheon Vouchers, 181
Lupton, 172

-M-
Maier, 127
Maintenance factors, 145
Management, 216
 by objectives, 125
 development, 112
 education, 114
 succession, 29
Management of Health and Safety at Work (Amendment) Regulations,

1994, 196
Management of Health and Safety at Work Regulations 1992, 192
Managerial estimates, 24
Managing disciplinary actions, 240
Manpower, 18
Manual handling regulations, 195
Market intelligence, 46
Market rates, 165, 172
Marks and Spencer, 224
Mars, 167, 224
Martin, 189
Marx, K, 218
Maslow, A, 143, 150
Maternity Allowance and Statutory Maternity Pay Regulations 1994, 180
Maternity pay, statutory, 180
Maxwell, R, 178
McClelland, D, 143
McCormick, 114-115
McGregor, 150
McIlwee, 254
Measures of potential, 134
Medical benefits, 181
Mentors, 116
Midland Bank, 84, 154
Misconduct, 252
Mobil Oil, 211
Monitoring the workforce, 59
Monk, 37
Morale, 201
Motivation, 102, 141
    effect of appraisal on, 130
    theories, 142
Motivator factors, 145
MSF, 220
Muir, J, 251
Mullins, L, 11, 216
Multi-skilling, 46
Mumford, A, 103
Murlis, 165

-N-

Naive proponents, 113
National Aids Trust, 190
National Commission on Education, 117
National Communications Union (NCU), 221
National Vocational Qualifications (NVQs), 101
Need theories, 143
Needs hierarchy, 144
Negative discipline, 238
Negotiated pay scales, 164
Negotiation, 228
    conduct, 230
    preparation, 229
Nervous tension, 201
Neuro-linguistic programming (NLP), 110
Newham Council, 205
Notice, 212, 248
NUCPS, 221

-O-

Occupational health, 200
Occupational Pensions Regulatory Authority, 178
Offer, provisional, 75
Offices, Shops and Railway Premises Act 1963, 194
On-the-job training, 106
Open questions, 67
Organisation of data, 264
Organisational climate, 28
Organisational politics, 11
Output factors, 165
Outworkers, 40
Overall assessment, 124
Overtime, 36

-P-

P11, 262
P60, 262
Panel interviews, 69
Part-time working, 38
Participation, 151, 230
Passive smoking, 204
Pay, 28, 141
    as motivator, 154
PAYE, 261
    Audit, 261
Payment-by-results (PBR) scheme, 172
Payroll, 182
    administration, 167
Pension schemes, 177
Perceived fairness, 171
Perceptions of HRM authority, 13
Performance appraisal, 121
Performance indicators, 59
Performance related pay (PRP), 173
Peripheral group, 34
Personal development plans (PDPs), 116
Personal records, security, 270
Personality, 53
    tests, 71, 134
Personnel as staff function, 11
Personnel function, 2
    clients, 6
    needs for, 9
    tasks, 3
Personnel records, 259

Personnel specification, 46, 53-54, 66
Peter principle, 133
Peter, L J, 133, 153
Peters, T, 47
Picketing, 224
Piecework, 172
Plumbley, 70
Pluralist ideology, 218
Points rating, 163
Points scheme, 173
Positive discipline, 238
Positive discrimination, 87
Potential, 121, 133
    indicators, 133
PowerGen, 232
Pragmatists, 103
Pregnancy and maternity, 196
Presentations, 134
Problem solving, 163, 208
    approach, 125, 128
    questions, 68
Process factors, 165
Process theories, 142
Productivity plan, 23
Proficiency tests, 71
Profit-sharing schemes, 175
Promotion, 29
    policy, 30
    programme, 31
Psychometric tests, 73, 133
Public duties, 211

-Q-
Quality, 99
Quality circles, 152

-R-
Race Relations Act 1976, 86
Racial discrimination, 84
Radical ideology, 218
Range statement, 101
Rank Xerox, 40
Ranking, 162
Rate for age system, 169
Ream, 177
Record system, 263
Records, 90
Recreational facilities, 181
Recruitment, 30, 44, 46
    code, 47
    consultants, 58
    plan, 23
    planning, 262
    policy, 47
    procedures, 48
Redevelopment plan, 23
Redundancy, 191, 212, 252
    alleviating, 254
    plan, 23
    procedures, 252
    selection for, 253
Rees, 207, 209
Reflectors, 103
Regulation strategies, 219
Rehabilitation of Offenders Act 1974, 88
Remuneration planning, 262
Repetitive Strain Injury or RSI, 195
Resignation, 248
Results-orientated schemes, 125
Retention plan, 23
Retirement, 191, 247
    age, 248
    assistance before, 247
Reviews, 171
Reward review, 121
Rewards, 141
Richards-Carpenter, 265
Richbell, 13
Risk assessment, 196
Risk management approach, 19
Roberton, I, 141
Rodger, Prof A, 53
Role play, 134
    exercises, 74
Rover, 117, 136
Rowe, Kay, 124, 130, 136, 151
Royal Commission on Safety and Health at Work, 1972, 191

-S-
Saab-Scania, 149
Safety committee, 193
Safety Representative Regulations 1978, 193
Sainsbury's, 167, 224
Salary
    administration, 167
    attrition, 171
    distortion, 171
    limits, 172
    progression curve, 170
    reviews, 171
    structure, 168
Save as You Earn, 176
Saville and Holdsworth, 128
Sceptics, 113
Schein, E, 154
Scientific management (job design), 148
Scudamore, 83
Secret ballots, 224
Seear, Baroness, 83
Selection, 44, 63
    approach, 47

Index

boards, 69
procedures, 64
process, 64
testing, 71, 90
Self discipline, 238
Self-appraisal, 132
Self-selection, 57
SERPS, 178, 232
Seven point plan, 53
Sex Discrimination Act 1975, 86
Sex Discrimination Act, 1986, 248
Sexual discrimination, 83
Sexual harassment, 92
Sheerness Steel, 226
Shift working, 36, 201
Sick building syndrome (SBS), 204
Sick pay, 179
Sickness benefits, 190
Simulation, 133
Single status, 172
SmithKline Beecham, 35
Smoking, 204
Social Chapter, 231
Social Security Act 1989, 180
Social Security and Housing Benefit Act 1982, 179
Squeezing differentials, 171
Staff associations, 215
Staff management, 9
Standards of competence, 100
Statistical information, 262
Statistical methods, 24
Statutory implied terms, 78
Statutory records, 261
Stereotyping candidates, 70
Stockport County Council, 205
Strain, 201
Strategic planning, 5
Stress, 148, 201
management, 203
Strikes, 223
Subjective probability, 147
Suggestion schemes, 174
Summary dismissal, 249
Sun Alliance, 154
Surplus of labour, 23
Survival rate analysis, 27
Survivor syndrome, 255
Suspension, 239
Systematic approach to training, 98

-T-
T groups, 109
Tact, 23
Targets, 130
for employers, 87
Tarmac Professional Services, 136
Task fragmentation, 148

Taylor Walker, 154
Taylor, F, 148
Telecommuting, 39
Telephone references, 76
Teleworking, 39
Tell and listen method, 128
Tell and sell method, 128
Temporary promotion, 107
Tests of interests, 71
The London Borough of Brent, 174
The Police Act 1997, 88
Theorists, 103
Thomason, G, 122, 165
Three-shift system, 36
Townsend, 50
Trade Union Act 1984, 222
Trade Union and Labour Relations (Consolidation) Act 1992, 224, 232, 250
Trade union Trade Union Reform and Employment Rights Act (TURERA) 1993, 180, 184, 196, 221
Trade unions, 211, 215, 220, 253
mergers, 221
power of, 221-222
Training, 87, 97
definition of, 114
for quality, 99
methods, 105
needs, 99
needs analysis, 100
objectives, 99, 101
plan, 23
programme, 97
system, 98
Transport assistance, 181
Trends in tests, 73
Truck Acts (1831-1940), 183
Trusthouse Forte, 154
TUC, 204, 223
Two-factor theory, 145
Types of interview, 69
Tyson, S, 5

-U-
Unemployment, types of, 254
Unfair dismissal, 250
compensation for, 251
Union of Communication Workers (UCW), 221
Unipart, 117
Unitary ideology, 218
Units of competence, 100
Upward appraisal, 129, 132

-V-
Validation of training, 111
Value added schemes, 175
VDUs, 196
Volvo, 149
Vroom, Victor, 147

-W-
Wage systems, 172
Wages Act 1986, 184
Wages councils, 184
War Office Selection Board, 135
Ward, P, 125, 127
Warnings, 239, 241
Waterman, 153
Welfare benefits, 189
Welfare, who provides?, 191
WH Smith, 84
Whitbread, 211
Withdrawal, 201
Women in the workforce, 83
Work permits, 76
Work study methods, 24
Workforce age structure, 28
Working conditions, 28
Workplace directive, 194
Workplace nurseries, 90
Written particulars, 77
Wrongful dismissal, 250

-Y-
Yoder, Dr D, 2

ORDER FORM

To order your BUSINESS BASICS books, ring our credit card hotline on 0181-740 2211. Alternatively, send this page to our Freepost address or fax it to us on 0181-740 1184.

To: BPP Publishing Ltd, FREEPOST, London W12 8BR   **Tel: 0181-740 2211**
                                                       Fax: 0181-740 1184

Forenames (Mr / Ms): _____

Surname: _____

Address: _____

Post code: _____   Date of exam (month/year): _____

Please send me the following books:

	Price	Quantity	Total
Accounting	£13.95	....	....
Human Resource Management	£13.95	....	....
Law	£13.95	....	....
Organisational Behaviour	£13.95	....	....
Economics	£13.95	....	....
Information Technology	£13.95	....	....
Marketing	£13.95	....	....
Quantitative Methods	£13.95	....	....

Please include postage:

UK: £3.00 for first plus £2.00 for each extra   ....
Europe (inc ROI): £5.00 for first plus £4.00 for each extra   ....
Rest of the World: £8.00 for first plus £6.00 for each extra   ....

Total

I enclose a cheque for £ _____ or charge to Access/Visa/Switch

Card number ☐☐☐☐☐☐☐☐☐☐☐☐☐☐☐☐

Start date (Switch only) _____   Expiry date _____

Issue number (Switch only) _____

Signature _____

REVIEW FORM

Name:

College:

We would be grateful to receive any comments you may have on this book. You may like to use the headings below as guidelines. Tear out this page and send it to our Freepost address: **BPP Publishing Ltd, FREEPOST, London W12 8BR.**

Topic coverage

Objectives, activities with solutions, chapter roundups and quizzes

Glossary

Multiple choice and exam style questions

Student-friendliness

Errors (please specify and refer to a page number)

Other